I invite you to take this book up and read it with a soft and gentle attention, an attention so soft that it is like a bird's feather floating down to settle upon the surface of some water – floating down so lightly that it doesn't even break the surface of the water. Such is the gentleness of the attention we need if we are to hear and recognise the deep beauty of the street-woman or street-man.

Look at the cover picture of this book: Touch connects when words cannot. The hands listen. They hear the vibration of soul-energy with-in them. When our hands are relaxed, this life-energy flows through them. Then, we become aware of our own powerful energy of love with-in the hand and only then can we reach out and touch another in love.

**Catherine Fenton, P.B.V.M**

*This book is dedicated to my parents,*
*Mary and Ignatius Fenton,*
*and*
*Kate, Danny and Mary,*
*my beloved nieces and nephew,*
*who are now enjoying total bliss.*

# CONTENTS

Acknowledgements     vi

Foreword     vii

Introduction     1

1996     7

1997     10

1998     41

1999     91

2000     132

2001     155

2002     178

2003     209

2004     230

2005     244

2006     259

2007     275

2008     288

2009     304

Epilogue     312

# ACKNOWLEDGEMENTS

I owe an immense debt to the following people, who supported me in so many different ways as I was writing this book.

Each person will recognise his / her own name here, I trust: Patrick, Sheila, Joan, Danny, Aileen, Teresa, Helen, James, Patti, Kathleen, Mary, Joetta, Mairín, Colleen, John, Dan, Mai, Regina, Eve, Catherine, Steve, Angela, Jack, Goretti and Julia. I will always treasure their nurturing presence.

Deep gratitude to the Cork Simon Community, Directors, Staff and, of course, street-friends, without whom this book could not have been written.

I wish to thank my family for always being there for me.

I'm grateful to: the Presentation Congregation for allowing me the sacred space I need for writing; the Provincial team for their support, especially Sr. Anne Coffey for giving of her precious time to read the book before publication; the Provincial Bursar, Sr. Noreen, and Joyce, her assistant; the Ballygriffin team for their graciousness always; and many, many Presentation Sisters at home and abroad.

My appreciation reaches out to: Anne, Jim, Sharon, Eithne, Angela, Séamus and Michelle for the typing of the script over a very long period of time – their great patience was inspiring and their respect for the content was unique; Patrick Buckley, solicitor, for his reviews, affirmation and wise comments; Brian O'Kane, editor, who very painstakingly edited and reviewed this manuscript at great personal sacrifice; Rita and Anne for their attentiveness and warm welcome always – Rita's kind remark, "You put great love into this book", was very affirming and encouraging for me; and all the people, nameless companions on the journey, from whom I received the gift of friendship or who have influenced this work in any way.

Last, but not least, I wish to say a very big *"Go raibh maith agaibh"* to those who loved me when I was at my worst!

# FOREWORD

I felt honoured and humbled when Sr Catherine asked me to write the foreword of her book, **For You Are Beauty-full – A long loving look at the essence of the homeless person**. It is a collection in diary form of her time among men and women who are homeless in Cork since 1997. The book is groundbreaking in many respects.

The book captures very honestly and starkly the lives, loves and losses of people who have found themselves homeless. These lives are often forgotten or described in negative or detached clinical terms: the tramp, the beggar, the addict, the mentally ill, the alcoholic. Sr Catherine reflects on each person, goes behind the label and, in these pages, brings to life often difficult and heart-breaking lives. She shares each person's unique story with us. Sr Catherine is privileged to be thus confided in and she appreciates this privilege. People's willingness to share their lives and stories with her marks the esteem in which Sr Catherine is held by people whose life experiences have taught them not to trust and not to tell.

But this book goes beyond being a thought-provoking and sometimes harrowing account of lives that have been broken but not bowed. Sr Catherine relentlessly challenges herself and, by extension, all of us, especially those of us in the 'caring professions', to take a long look at ourselves through the lens of 'street-people' as she describes them. This is the most powerful aspect of the book.

Sr Catherine puts her own faith and spirituality to the test in her daily encounters with people who have lost everything except their own humanity. The humility and honesty of Sr Catherine's words and deeds reminds us all to see in others, irrespective of outward appearances, the 'light of love and wisdom' and to recognise 'their gifts and their beauty in the midst of their brokenness'. Anyone who is lucky enough to know Sr Catherine knows that she 'walks the walk'.

Were Sr Catherine's words to be truly acted upon, just think of the kinder world we would live in ... her words, and the challenge they imply, can illuminate our journey to a better place, for us all.


**Colette Kelleher**
**Director**
**Cork Simon Community**
**November 2009**

# INTRODUCTION

## I: THE ORIGIN OF THIS BOOK

Since 1994, I've been accompanying and being accompanied by numerous street-people – people who are homeless and live pretty much on the edge of society, as we know it today. As I was privileged to accompany them and be accompanied by them on a daily, weekly, monthly and yearly basis, writing down the conversations we had shared together came as a natural consequence of these special times of sacredness we had together. Since 1996, I had so many stories, which I felt ought to be shared with the world at large. The most important person in that world, at this precise moment is you, who are about to read this book.

The book has been written mainly in an environment of silence. It is a book about presence, it was written from presence and is about the sacredness of the presence of the vulnerable human being and perhaps in some way, it may help awaken the reader to her or his own beautiful presence deep within. Words are used here as my faltering means or gateways to a reality far out and beyond the limited form of the word. It would greatly aid the reader to be in a state of presence and stillness as you read, so that the inner core of the person / persons may become more real for you then. It would also, I feel, perhaps be of assistance to be in a non-resistant, non-judgmental state as one listens to the sacredness of the conversations.

"I am not just my behaviour" and "I'm more than my behaviour", one of my spiritual teachers, Fr. Pat Murray, often reminded us. This is the thread running through these conversations. I have met some of the deepest and most truly contemplative people I've ever met on the streets. I believe that every person carries the seeds of enlightenment in them and, if given the material and human environment they need, they can bloom where there are planted.

Every word of this book was originally hand-written. The book is written in journal form. You will notice it is written in years, i.e., 1995 is one chapter, 1996 forms another chapter, 1997, another chapter, etc. You will notice a symbol of a heart at the end of each year / chapter thus.

This could be a reminder to us, if we have allowed our ego or false self (critical self) take over, to return to

which is my symbol for feeling presence / becoming still. You may wish to stop reading and perhaps feel and experience the good in the person / persons about whom you have read. If you read with the mind only, you may miss the beauty, your own beauty as a reader and the other's essence, too. It can also be an opportunity to experience communion with people mainly on life's margins. How does the most vulnerable person on the street touch you? Do you find it difficult to look at them with love? If so, why? Just like our street-friends, we all have some times of despair and desperation. What can make some people happy often passes us by, e.g., a smile or a kind word costs nothing. When we really listen to the faltering voice of the street-man or woman, can we hear our own vulnerability in it? Is that why we attempt to avoid them or look the other way, because we can't cope with being naked in front of the vulnerable? Perhaps, like them, we can remember when we were rejected, unwanted by others in our lives. What does it feel like when someone passes me without noticing me? This book is about how the openness and realness of these beautiful street-people can change lives. I found that they were my special teachers.

This is a book of true stories. At times, I have told the story the way the story was told to me. At other times, I have joined together some stories. All the stories are about things that happened in people's lives. You have to go *inside yourself* to hear most, if not all of these stories. You may find your own truth in these stories, or you may not. Your neighbour may recognise his / her truth here in one way and you may experience something totally different, as you read the story from the inside. You can see for yourself which story resonates with you. In order to do this, you have got to know the story, hear it deeply and feel it. In time, you may find that what you feel about these stories / conversations is more important and transformational than what you think about them. Take time to savour and taste the experiences of these great people. They are special.

All names mentioned throughout the book are fictitious to preserve anonymity.

# II: CAREER BREAK

In 1994, I was happy to take a career break from school. I loved being in the school and found the staff, parents, and pupils a wonderful group of people to be with in South Presentation Primary School. I am grateful to the then Provincial team, who enabled me to take time to creatively explore this way of accompanying the many people on the edge of life today. Uppermost in my mind was the idea to go to work with people who slept rough on the streets. Why, I wondered, was it with these people I wished to be? I had no answer, except that I sensed a compelling call to work with these people and I had no idea how I was to even set about the task.

# III: EXPERIENCE OF THE STREET

In September 1994, I went out alone to the streets and met some people. I said, "Hello", to one lady who was waiting to be 'picked up' later. She said, "Can you help me?". She was too intoxicated with drink to even hear my answer, if I had one. I did not have an answer for her. I invited her to call to see me another day, and told her where I lived. She did not turn up. I felt she would not even have remembered that I had met her, the next day! It was my poor attempt at 'trying to help'. It was an experience of rejection. I was devastated.

Another lady stood in the South Mall and asked for money. I gave her a voucher to buy food. She thanked me and I felt I really had done something worthwhile this time! I felt good.

Another time, I met some 'punks' and I said, "This is it. I'm meant to be here with these"! I already knew a lady who would have called herself a 'punk'. It happened that the lady that night on the street was her friend. I was very pleased until such time as the man with her, who had a dog, walked away. I was disgusted that he would not stay and talk to me, who was there 'to help' them. I found myself trying to make conversation with the lady who was sitting there, but I 'got nowhere' with her. Where, I wondered, did I really want to get anyway? It was about 10.00 p.m. at this stage and I walked back by Abbeycourt House and said, "I will meet the real street-people here getting the soup". There was nobody there. I went home and felt a disaster, but I could not admit I had failed.

I later realised that I ought not be surprised at rejection by broken people. They have suffered a great deal at the hands of the knowledgeable, the powerful, police, social workers and others at times. They have suffered so much from broken promises. Rejected people are sick and tired of 'good' and 'generous' people; people who claim to be Christians; people, like myself, who came to them on a pedestal of pride and power, to do them good. No wonder their hearts are closed to new people. What they need is someone who sees in them the light of love and wisdom, who recognises their gifts and their beauty in the midst of their brokenness. I was being called on by the poor and the broken I met to touch my own poverty and brokenness and leave my throne of 'power, knowledge and security to become little and humble'. The cry and anguish of many more people in these and similar circumstances triggered off my own cry and anguish and touched my point of pain and helplessness at times. The most painful part of it eventually was that I realised that I was the poorest person on the streets. The fuller implication is only gradually and painfully coming to my awareness as days go by. I can even see the opposition and rejection now as a great gift. I kept asking myself, "Am I meant to do this work at all?".

In 1997, Rosetta O'Leary, a Bon Secours Sister, accompanied me on this awesome journey. She has been a most devoted friend to the street-people, too. They hold her in great esteem as a person of great integrity and wisdom, who is very practical and has great common sense. Due to Rosetta's deep and very profound spiritual life, she can both reverence and respect the street-person's rare hidden value as a child of the universe.

# IV: IDEAL V REALITY

I felt great unease in me as I set out to do this work. Could it be an ego trip? A project from my head? I believe it was partly that. I was very gifted to have lived that experience before I could really appreciate and treasure the depths to which I have been led now. I needed to be lost before I could be found. Looking back, I see that I depended almost totally on my own very limited resources and that only led me more deeply into frustration. I believed I was at the centre, operating everything. I needed to shift from the illusion of self-centredness to the reality of other- / God-centeredness. I had huge expectations of myself. What tools had I to do this work? None really! I then realised that there was something missing in my life, as a Sister called to minister in the world of the 20th century. My ideal was to work with the people on the street, but the reality was far from that.

That deep contemplative dimension of my life had got lost somewhere along the way, I believe. I had done a week in Athy at one stage and felt a few more weeks would do me no harm. I could go back to the streets then and get on with it. I started in Athy in late September and said I would stay until Halloween, maybe. I resisted this having to 'unlearn' all or most of what I had learned in the past 25 years or so! Through the encouragement, patience and total dedication of Fr. Pat Murray, Director of the Athy course, I persevered there and the few weeks became two years! I'm still on that sacred journey. I call it my 'second Novitiate'.

I respect today where people are at, but I feel a deep need to enter on a new phase of religious life where this contemplative aspect of life is of paramount importance – gets priority and all flows from it, not the other way around. Work had become my life, instead of becoming an expression of my life. As I see it today, I lived an 'automatic' way of life and because of this I was not in touch with what was real. I had been reading books on the Desert Fathers' spirituality and listened to eloquent talks on various types of spirituality, but I did not even hear it, not to say experience the reality behind this. How could I, when I did not hear my own reality? Today at a much deeper level, I hear that life in me, as it were, flowing like a stream. The mystery into which this prayer and meditation leads me is a *PERSONAL MYSTERY*, the mystery of my own personhood, which finds completion in the person of the Christus. In this state of selfless attention, which is prayer, I experience my own goodness, reverence, respect, wonder, awe. I have now, over time, discovered that these are with-in me, in my own essence. I discover my own am-ness. It could only be heard in the silence.

# V: BALLYGRIFFIN / CORK

During my 'second Novitiate', I continued in Athy and then came to Cork, each month for one or two weeks, having spent two or three weeks in Athy. During the weeks in Cork, I would spend one or more part of it in Ballygriffin, in silence and solitude, living out what I had learned in theory. I was then privileged to take some people from the street-scene (which I again returned to), to spend some time in Ballygriffin. A special word of thanks to Catherine, Eileen and Josephine, who have been the essence of kindness and hospitality whenever I took a group to Ballygriffin.

I was in awe at some of the street-people's ability to reverence everything they were invited to be part of. Being in the present moment enabled me to be with them where they were, as they were then. They surely were my gift. Their simplicity touched me. Only in the depths can I hear that simplicity. One of the biggest obstacles I find in being with these wonderful people is that I can complicate things – no wonder I was so removed from them! I know now all I need do is listen and when I speak lovingly to these people, in time they may come to the awareness that their unique role is to be 'at home within their own home'. Even if they do not understand the words I say, it may be by the way I am gently present to them, by the way I reverence them, that they may be touched. In their misery often, they have no voice, but their bodies are the temple of the Spirit of life and love.

Today, as I am privileged to continue to be with the people on the street, I find it a wonderful experience. I feel I have moved from indoctrination to conviction, to freedom and even true liberation. I could sit now in awe in the Simon Community at one lady's reverence as she spent one hour eating two slices of brown bread and drinking a cup of tea. I felt a communion with her. Out of my own deep reverence, I could hear her gentleness. She was in no hurry. It was a Eucharistic experience. My own inner journey was wonderful, because when it came to 'compassion' and being compassionate, I learned that it would be out of my need I would be compassionate if I did not experience first of all, my own deep compassion. These are a few of the many wonderful experiences I've had with the street-people. In this book, I hope to share this awesome journey more fully with you.

The support of the North and South Presentation Communities has been an invaluable source of energy and inspiration for me. I never cease to be filled with awe at their infinite capacity to open their home and hearts to countless marginalised people, who are privileged to avail of their undying hospitality, over many, many years. Many friends, too, have affirmed me and encouraged me along the way. Ann, Annette and Geraldine have in a wonderful way enabled me to continue with this journey, too. Their love and care of the homeless has been another great life-awakening experience for me. I appreciate the hard work done by the Ministry Group to provide me with funding to continue on this road. It is a journey. Last, but not least, I owe a great debt to my family, who have been a constant source of love and care. I especially wish to mention Kate, Danny and Mary, who are now enjoying the bliss of that fullness of life. I get a tiny glimpse of this fullness, too, at times. Kate had a deep love for people on the margin of life whom she could not see deprived even of a coat, or a cigarette. If they looked miserable, she could see more than the dirt, too. She, too, is with me as I go on my rounds.

# 1996

*Thursday, 27 June*

**Beginning at Simon Cork:** I wrote this on 27 June, 1996: 'Simon were not gushing to have me. I felt unsure, fearful, unwanted, poor. There is a lot of uncertainty in this work'. I felt inferior. It is new for me to experience being in a place where I did not know whether I was unwanted or not needed. I felt my own poverty. It was a scary place in me, and around me, then. I met volunteers and residents. I feared rejection by the Simon people. I felt terrified and I wished I could run away.

### Friday, 28 June

I gave Declan Calbaras my brief *re* what I hoped to do there, i.e., enable people to come to a sense of their own dignity through: (1) meditation; (2) listening to them; and (3) spending day /days at the Presentation Retreat Centre in Ballygriffin.

### Thursday, 15 August

At Declan's request, I was invited to speak to residents at Thursday's meeting, 15 August 1996. During my time there, one lady verbally abused me – two walked out! One person asked *re* his inner life – he was interested in how to find it. One lady came to Ballygriffin Retreat Centre in August, for three days. She continued meditation afterwards with me.

### Tuesday, 26 November

Five months from the time I first visited Simon, Declan Calbaras invited me to meet him at 11.00 a.m. Declan was very sceptical of me. He invited me to do meditation with the residents for three months after Christmas: February to May. I still continued doing meditation, outside Simon, with the lady who came to Ballygriffin.

A French poet wrote:

#### IGNORANCE

*The older I grow, the more ignorant I become,*
*The longer I live, the less I possess or control,*
*All I have is a little space, snow dark or glittering – never inhabited,*
*Where is the giver? The guide? The guardian?*
*I sit in my room and am silent.*
*Silence arrives like a servant to tidy things up,*
*While I wait for the lies to disperse.*
*And what remains to this dying woman that so well prevents her from dying?*
*What does she find to say to the four walls?*
*I hear her talking still and her words come in with the dawn,*
*Fire, imperfectly understood.*
*Love, like fire, can only reveal its brightness on the failure and the beauty of burnt wood.*

This was how I felt, when I was not very well accepted by the authorities in Simon, in the early years. Later, I saw that it was one of the greatest gifts of my life. I admired the person, who had such regard for the street-people, as he was, it seems, protecting them from someone coming in, *trying* to help them. He loved these people too much to see them in anyway not respected for who they were. This man was one of my greatest teachers of the preciousness of the human being. I was 'doing' good to 'feel' good, but he could see through me. How humiliating this was, in time, when I really woke up. I felt called back into nothingness and emptiness. It was a bleak spot to be, then. The uncertainty was paralysing. The darkness became even darker. Some voice said to me, "Catherine, stay with it, all is well". It took deep searching to hear this was where I was exactly meant to be. The street-person became an icon of mystery and wonder for me. When I met myself in them, life took on a very new diversion for me. I felt touched by the sacred.

# 1997

I start this year with Eckhart Tolle's story from his book, *The Power of Now*.

> *An old man had been sitting by the side of the road for over 30 years. One day, a young stranger walked by. "Spare some change?", asked the old man, mechanically holding out his old baseball cap.*
>
> *"I have nothing to give you", said the young stranger. Then he asked, "What is that you are sitting on?".*
>
> *"Nothing", replied the old man, "Just an old box. I have been sitting on it for as long as I can remember".*
>
> *"Ever looked inside?", asked the stranger.*
>
> *"No", said the old man. "What's the point? There's nothing in there".*
>
> *"Have a look inside", insisted the young stranger.*
>
> *The old man managed to pry open the lid. With astonishment, disbelief and elation, he saw that the box was filled with gold.*

Eckhart continues, 'I am that stranger who has nothing *to give* you and who is asking you to look inside. Not inside any box, as in the parable, but somewhere even closer, inside yourself. "But I'm not a poor old man", I can hear you say. Those who have not found their true wealth, which is the radiant joy of Being and the deep, unshakable peace that comes with it, are poor indeed, even if they have great material wealth. They are looking outside for scraps of pleasure or fulfilment, for validation, security, or love, while they have a treasure within, that not only includes all these things, but is infinitely greater than anything the world can offer'.

Our experiences, in some ways, we have in common with most people, but each one's journey is unique to him or her. Each now is a new beginning. I am always travelling with the L-plate on my back. When I know nothing, I'm at my best. The journey is into this emptiness, the space where nothing is happening it seems, but where more real life is found than one can ever imagine.

When I look at the broken body of the homeless person, I see how their inner life and intimacy of essence / soul / core within longs to find an outer means to express this mystery. The body is that form through which this essence can be seen, felt and touched. The body is their form for the expression of their intimate world within. This journey of the soul can meet with many obstacles on the way through the vulnerable, fragile and very weak human frame. The ability of these street-friends to get up and begin again never ceases to amaze me. It is this soul, the deep hidden secret world within them, which is far more precious than gold, which enables them to begin to live again. May they continue to inspire each of us, who falter along the way, to always be aware, that we can make a new and fresh start after every fall. Peace.

## Wednesday, 12 February

To Simon, 11.00 a.m. to 12 noon. The first time I did meditation there, four people meditated with me. One was interested in going to the Retreat Centre. This gave me hope!

## Wednesday, 19 February

Two people came to meditate in Simon with me. The girl, who had been in Ballygriffin with me, rang after leaving, to say she was still mediating. This gave me great hope.

## Wednesday, 19 March

It was the first day I was able go in with no expectations! I could now, maybe for the first time, gaze on the Maker's creation in a resident, whereas before I could see only his behaviour. He may never see his own goodness himself.

## Friday, 4 to Monday, 7 April – Ballygriffin

One man came to Ballygriffin. The staff were amazed he would sit into a car and stay off drink for four days. Isaac Mak, a 22-year old man, said to me, "The essence of a person is not (often) heard / seen by people". He said he sits for four hours at night, now, to clear his head. He said he meditates. Before meditation, his head is full of the day's noises. It eases after the meditation. He loves the word 'infinite', he said.

## Monday, 5 May

Rosetta, a Bons Secours Sister, joined me. We invited two street-people to Ballygriffin. One man said, "I'm not ready for meditation". One lady had been in Ballygriffin several times already. It took this lady one and a half years to *see* a tree and say, "The tree is beautiful".

## Tuesday, 20 May

I went to Simon with Rosetta. At the start, I felt scared. I wondered which table would I sit at. Would anyone talk to me? As the months went on, I began to feel more confident. Rosetta joined me full-time in September 1997. This was a wonderful true gift.

The contemplative dimension of our lives is of primary importance, as it is from this that our ministry flows. Rosetta and I meditate four or five times for half-hour periods every day, journal on how we are living and share this on a weekly basis. We also spend time in silence, and communing with nature. We meet people mostly in the dining-room and we've drank many cups of tea there over the years. We are given a room upstairs, where some residents join us for meditation. The Simon Community is a facility to enable us to build up relationships with street-people / homeless people in a safe place. We have meditation in the workers' quarters later in the day to facilitate the staff.

### Friday, 23 May

I went in to Simon today, without any expectations. I met Kieran Fahy and he said he used to be on drugs, but was off them. He hated his mother. His dog was his only friend when he was young. He is sleeping out since he was 15. He drank at 13, went on drugs at 14 and went from home at 15. He could go to Germany on a lorry, he said, at no charge! He'd just phone his girlfriend to say he was going! He was sad, as he lost his son (3) in a car crash in France. He lost his girlfriend, too. He looked after his father, when he was dying of cancer. His family are in College. His teeth were very neglected-looking and not clean. He's a fine looking lad at 34. I could gaze on the Maker's creation in him. He may never know what this is, his own beauty and goodness with-in.

I met Jamie Caar. He looked well. He was sober. Jamie resented having to do things out of *obligation*, e.g., as an altar boy, if he was not there at the church when it was his turn to be there, he was beaten by his mother and his teacher. He hated having to go to Mass. When I said about Ballygriffin, he said, "Would there be *Rosaries*, Masses, etc.?". I said, "No". He said he would be interested then. His mother goes to prayer meetings, says *Rosaries*, goes to Mass, too. "What good is it?", he said. She beats him so hard afterwards.

### Tuesday, 10 June

I met Joachim Randon. He watched T.V. , so when I said what I was doing, he said, "I will go to the meditation". He came up. We meditated and chatted. Joachim said he read, "The measure of our anxiety is the measure of our distance away from God!". He goes to A.A. meetings. A man called to take him while he was with me, but he said he would not go today. I could see him trying to please, by saying, "I would not like to put him out by not going when he came in". Later, he made a conscious choice not to go.

### Wednesday, 18 June

Laura Sage was amazed when she heard Noelly Lavi came with us to Ballygriffin. She said she never remembered him off drink for that many days. Laura said, "Did Noelly really go with ye in a car?". I said, "Yes". She said he had a squat to shelter, not a flat as such! They seemed very surprised that he came and stayed off drink for so many days. He had a bath in Simon before he went to Ballygriffin – his first bath in 40 years!

Jonah McAlvey called. I went to meet him. He said he stole the carpet out of a prayer room in Cork. He needed it to sleep on and keep him warm, he said, but later did not use it, as he would destroy it. It is now in someone's house. He said, "Because you were so good to me, I feel ashamed of what I did. I want to give it back. Next week, I will return it. I will get a taxi to bring it back". I said, "Jonah, it took a lot more courage to *say* you stole the carpet, than it did to take it. Now you want to give it back". He cried and said, "I don't know what is wrong with me". He got T.B. "I'm sick and need to get in somewhere. I could *BE*". All he needs sometimes is five minutes to talk to someone. He was like a two year old wanting instant attention. His brain is affected by drug abuse. Behind all this is a person of supreme value. He is of infinite worth.

## Tuesday, 24 June

Declan Londes is 68. His body is doubled over. Declan's hands were an expression of his great gentleness. They were not a bit rough, considering he worked with pikes and shovels always. He worked for farmers. He always tried hard to please, I would say. This is the result – literally bent over 'forwards', not backwards, in this case, to please. His great dignity shines through his hands. His face began to light up a bit and smile, as the day went on, and he looked at me in the face. Up to that, his head was down and he faced the ground. He had a very strong, dirty smell from him. He was very frightened-looking. He did not want to say about family much. He said, "I felt at peace in Ballygriffin. I would like to stay there and have a bungalow for the winter there".

## Wednesday, 25 June

Samantha Caden said she was street-wise now at 26 years of age. She looks 16. She was a year in Wales and slept on the street with 12 pups and 2 dogs chained near her, so that no one could touch her. I invited her to meditate and she came for 40 minutes. Her beauty was so real. She may never see it.

I met Laura Sage and spoke about Kyle Bakala, who died with a bottle in his hand. He spent the night in Simon, had a good meal, went out and then died of a heart attack. He had gone to Ballygriffin on two occasions, attended the Eucharist and received Holy Communion on 4 April at 10.00 a.m. in Ballygriffin oratory, with the three women.

The poet Rabindranath Tagore wrote:

*The night kissed the fading day with a whisper*
*I am death, your mother*
*From me you will get new birth.*


### Saturday, 5 July

We met Seán Curdy in the T.V. room and I asked him if he would like to meditate. He said he would. We then went up with Seán Curdy, who meditated with us in the recreation room. His silence at meditation was awesome. He said he was used to the silence. We had a long chat with him and we were very much in awe of his wisdom. He was 20 years of age and did not drink or take drugs. He spent some time in and out of institutions. He loved to walk and sit in Fitzgerald's Park, go to museums and art galleries. One picture, he said, always seemed to draw him to it. He was not yet sure what it was saying to him. He had a beautiful presence. He could walk for two to three hours each day. He said his feet, and his hands, were over-worked – what keen awareness! He trained as a chef and worked in a Cork hotel. He loved to cook. He is taking time out for himself. He suffers from epilepsy and was a bit tired. He felt he would take it a bit easy for the week-end. He had such respect for himself. I could hear his reverence for Seán. We were privileged to be with Seán for about one hour.

Bernadette Lee called over from another table and said, "Do ye come here all the time?". I said, "Yes". She was a dark-haired lady, whose teeth were nearly burned away from cigarettes. She had a very beautiful smile and seemed to be very appreciative of what was being done for her, by the volunteers in Simon. She said, "I was married, had six children, my husband died and the children were split up and put into care". She went on to say, "We had nothing, we did the best we could. I understand people in need". She was, at this stage, looking at Seán and some helpers getting ready the plates for the soup-run. She said to me, "Are ye helping people here?". I said, "No, they are helping us".

I had a deep sense of Rosetta's support in the Simon Community today. I sensed that it was all meant to be this way.


### Tuesday, 8 July

I met John Gabie. John was cooking lunch for the group – sometimes, maybe 13. He has a presence. I can see it so clearly. He invited me to lunch any day I wish. His day consists of getting up at 7.30 a.m. and working at preparing the meals, etc. until about 1.30 p.m. He then takes his bottle of whiskey and goes on the street to drink it! He may have one bottle or two and part of another some days! He earns about €100 per week in the Simon. I remember his daughter, Joan, in school, whom he hasn't seen, he said, for about two years or more. John Gabie comes in about 8.00 p.m. with what is left of his second or third bottle! He'd feel confident with drink, he said, and gets a buzz. It seemed to me as if the whiskey is his 'way to the light'. He may need to drink himself to death. John Gabie is 46 and drank since he was 12½.

## Wednesday, 16 July

I met Courtney Hamet in the £1 shop. She looked well. She said she would be having some tests in the South Infirmary and asked if I would remember her in prayer. I invited her for a cup of tea, anytime she would like to call. She went to Fountainstown on the bus during the week with her four children. She has a daughter married, who has two children. Courtney has a beautiful smile. She is / was in the business of prostitution to make money for her family. She did not share her story to date with me. Her boyfriend, Stephen, and brother are drinking. She has not seen her brother for three weeks. I could see Courtney's beauty shining through her smile.

Chelsea Calcott called at 5.25 p.m. and stayed until 7.55 p.m. Chelsea looked very well. She was beautifully dressed, had her nails painted and carried a nice hand-bag. She said it made her feel like a woman. She had a cup of tea and I had a cup. She got some nice clothes from the press and said she would now like to go away and dress up in her high heels and her long new dress. She is well. She met Joachim Randon and gave him some clothes last week, but had a sense he was unwell. She has her children (two) every week now – Monday, Tuesday, Thursday and Friday – and the three other children on some Saturdays. She said her circumstances were not good but she could wait and someplace better would turn up for her, in which to live. It is about waiting. There is so much gentleness in these people.

## Friday, 18 July

I met a red-haired man with a very red, sore-looking face. The red-haired man said he saw me at the Simon Community. I told them we do days in Ballygriffin and the red-haired man said, "What good is that when we have nowhere to sleep? Did you ever sleep on the streets, Sister?".

## Sunday, 20 July

I met Fergus Park, Dave Doos from the Scottish Border and Gloria Reed from England also. They came for tea and a sandwich at about 12.45 p.m. I asked them if they could wait. They sat on the ground without a word. I was touched by their great patience and reverence. They slept – the three of them – under a bush in town last night. Fergus had only on a short-sleeved shirt. He said it was cold out at night. He asked for a blanket. Sister Rosario gave him a blanket. The three of them said they would like to come to Ballygriffin. Dave plays a guitar and banjo in town and Gloria plays the flute. Fergus is here six weeks now. He was here before. Gloria is around 10 years. None of them, I felt, had washed! Gloria's hands were very dirty. She had a gentle face. Fergus and Dave were gentlemen. They could wait. I had a sense of them 'being in the *now*'. There was a sacredness about them.

## Tuesday, 22 July

Chelsea Calcott called at about 12.30 p.m. She was very upset. I gave her tea and sandwiches. I could prepare them out of my in-depth love. She was to have her little daughter, Paula, today for the day. The social worker arrived in to her this morning to say she (Paula) did not wish to see Chelsea, her mother. Paula is about 1½ to 2 years old! Chelsea was deeply hurt and said she would have to drink. I invited her to meet me in Evergreen Street. She came along with me to the sea, but was very low. She did not speak on the way down. I asked her if she would like some music. She said she would. She smoked some cigarettes. I bought her a can of *7-Up* and an ice-cream. On the way home, she let off a lot of steam, which was good. She still felt she may drink. I said, "Chelsea, maybe you do need to take a bottle and drink it". She said, "Maybe I need to go out and find a man and have sex with him". I said, "Chelsea, maybe you do". I felt I was in my own gentleness as I expressed my view on this. I am to meet her and take her to Ballygriffin tomorrow morning. I have no expectations. I spent four hours with her. It was a sacred time to be with a very fragile human being. It was my privilege that Chelsea so openly shared her sacred story with me. In meditation, I was conscious of my positive energy being directed towards her. She appeared totally helpless. If her pain could surface more fully, she would feel better eventually, when she could 1) express it; 2) feel it; 3) grieve it. There appears to be a mountain of hurt there, which is slowly surfacing. It is enough to kill someone. Her positive self is emerging well at times – sometimes Chelsea has enough joy to balance her affliction.

## Wednesday, 23 July

I went to Simon to collect the people for Ballygriffin. When I went in, Chelsea was in a very bad way. Her top was half-down over one shoulder and she was very intoxicated by drink. I brought her a packet of cigarettes and invited her to go to Ballygriffin, if she wished. She needed care. She sat into the car and then decided she would not go. I felt, too, she needed to go to bed and rest. I gave her some sandwiches and bars to eat. There was a social worker there, when I called in, and also the landlord, who was very concerned about Chelsea. He later came up to the convent to meet me.

I was in Ballygriffin. I could be in my own gentleness in Ballygriffin and believe Chelsea would be fine. I went to nature and the field by the river drew me to it. I stayed there and the withered grass found me. What I heard was that the green shoots were coming up through it so beautifully, in spite of it nearly being all withered. I was reminded of Chelsea who, though withered and destroyed externally, still has a beautiful soul that lies hidden beneath the ravages of loneliness, which she was earlier experiencing so painfully. Later, I saw some cut withered grass found me and I heard the *Gospel* line, 'Without me, you can do nothing'. I put in 'without the awareness of me, my inner soul / being (inside), anything I do is futile. If I don't live from my soul, I have to live from either my body, feelings or intellect'. I may not see much done after me in terms of worldly success, but the inner journey from my inner self is one of total awe, whose outpouring can only touch in a positive way whatever or whoever it reaches. It is my privilege to accompany these sacred people. I'm deeply enriched by having met them. It enables me to go deeper and deeper into the reality of this beautiful life flowing in me. Because I have been gifted to recognise it in myself, I can hear it clearly and more clearly as time goes on in these people, no matter what their behaviour is like.

## Tuesday, 5 August

I had hoped to go to the Simon Community at 3.00 p.m. but Isaac Mak arrived and wished that I would meet his girlfriend, Susan Max. She was a beautiful girl. Susan and Isaac are together for six years. They have travelled extensively on the continent, sleeping in a tent. Susan was a beautiful, gentle girl, who remembered getting a cup of tea once at the back door. She spoke of her inner being and also being 'at one'. It was as if all her beauty shone through her smiling eyes. Isaac smoked home-made cigarettes. He spoke of his love for nature and admired the plants as he passed by them. He could hear 'have no expectations'. He loved Susan, he said, and I sensed they are fairly happy. He could speak of inner truth and say outer truth is different. He spoke of understanding *v* knowledge. He said one could never know another. 'Know thyself' is a life-time's work. He did not read *The Bible*, he said, but felt he needed the experience first and then he may be able to read it. He is reading his own book first. They went away at 4.45 p.m. They gave me their address and invited me to visit them.

## Thursday, 7 August

I went to Simon and met Declan Calbaras with Ursula Walk and Mel Lahive. Mel's face was so beaten that I could not see one of his eyes at all. I could just *be* in the presence of such pain, and beauty. The beauty of Ursula's soul shone through her eyes. Her intense suffering, caused by drink, robbed her of seeing this beauty in herself. She was totally almost pulled out of her soul. Mel would beat her and she would beat him, but when Declan said, "But you love him", she said nothing. I sensed the gentleness with which Declan could let her go, in such a dignified way. Sometimes, people like this lady need to be allowed go the way they choose.

I invited anyone who would wish to do meditation to come along. No one was interested.

## Tuesday, 19 August

I went down and met Eugene Papkov, Simon Tannes and Edmund Walket, who chatted with me and said they slept in a ruin of a church, in a graveyard last night. They were peeling potatoes. I said peeling the potato could be a very sacred experience, if we are attentive. I notice *how* they peeled them. They could enjoy themselves doing this simple act. I said it could be the most important thing they would do that day. I said, "What counts is not *what* we do, but *how* we do it" I said I hoped to partake of a meal someday, to be privileged to eat a meal in the evening.

John Gabie quoted a Chinese writer, 'A good traveller does not need know where he is going and a perfect traveller does not need to know where he came from'. I said I would need to hear the second part again, when John said out loud, "It is about being in the *NOW*". Such wisdom, he had. He said if you can do the small things *well*, you can then do the big things. I said they inspired me and they were my teachers. I said I always felt better, when I left the Simon, as I had been so enriched upon meeting people like them.

I met Cyril Paller then, who said from another table who he was! He was anxious and told me he had a girlfriend called Emma Jarvis. He would love a physical relationship with her. He came from abroad and, when his mother died, he fell apart and lost his health. I could gaze on the Maker's creation in him. He had lovely eyes and a very beautiful face, behind the torn skin, from the constant pulling it apart, out of his intense anxiety. Eventually, he meditated with me, when I invited him. His presence was beautiful, his silence was awesome. His face began to light up and he said that he felt better. I could see the change in his face when I affirmed him. I said I was enriched by his presence. I went out feeling the better for the visit.

## Saturday, 6 September

I went to Simon. I met Alex Dart. He told me that one day he walked from Dublin to Cashel – 72 miles – all day and all night! I said, "Why would you do this?". He said, "It is a hobby". He has 'some' children and a wife living in Dublin. He sees these sometimes.

## Sunday, 7 September

John Cadec rang and called at 4.45 p.m. and stayed until 6.10 p.m. He showed me what he wrote about his experience with nature – how the tree, river and rose spoke to him. He keeps plants in his room. He has a sexuality difficulty, not being sure about his gender, or perhaps it could be that maybe he is getting more in touch with the feminine side of his life. He wears perfume and earrings. He senses great freedom in all this. He spoke about having to keep rules in the past and said how oppressive it was. He was at Mass recently for the first time in four months. It meant more to him now. He spoke about food and how he respected it and, because of it coming from the same source of life as ourselves, it must be reverenced and not abused, he said. He is pained when he sees so much food was wasted in a hotel. He spoke of the *life-awakening* properties of water.

## Friday, 12 September

Chloe McAlinden called. I could be with her. I feel she needs very gentle attention. She does not seem to be ready yet to take on this personal work on a regular basis, e.g., her journey on her own interior road, because she seems too vulnerable. She can take it in small amounts only. One needs great gentleness here. It is a gift.

## Friday, 19 September

Ezekiel Mahy sat near me. He is a full-time worker. He told me about the man, Jarlath Raissa, 62 years old, who is sleeping out under the bridge in Cork. The group doing the soup-run were called out to help him during the week. He came from England. When the volunteers asked him if he needed some blankets, he said if they took his three dirty ones to wash them, then he could take three clean ones from them. He did not need a dinner one night, as he had one already, he said. People near him give him some food.

We went to meditate with Scott Bacon. He shared his story. It was a painful one. He had not seen his daughter for 14 years. Scott Bacon walked, one evening, with a friend of his, to *Jury's Inn* and could not admit he was homeless and in the Simon. He could not say to other people either that he had a difficulty with drink, he said. O.K.

## Monday, 22 September

I left with Rosetta to go to Simon, on John Gabie's invitation. We had to wait in John Gabie's kitchen when we went into the Simon, until some people had finished lunch, as they did not have enough chairs to seat us all! We walked around the workshop and admired the candles, shelves and cribs which the people had made. We went to sit down when there was a chair for us after 1.00 p.m. and shared stories with Daniel Baginski, David Gabbay, Peter Hall and Christopher Cassidy. Later, Jerry Laar came in. John Gabie served a big plate of turnip, bacon and potato for the four people. Brandon Dawes came for a bit of lunch then. Christopher Cassidy made a pot of tea. We were offered a meal, but left the food for those who needed it.

Jerry Laar, who had been many times with us in Ballygriffin, came in and chatted. He said how much he liked the meditation and his time with us in Ballygriffin. He is a very gentle man, who is only 29 but looks like a person of 49!

## Tuesday, 23 September

Chelsea Calcott called at 10.40 a.m. Chelsea talked about the years when she had lots of men and said how much she missed sex. Once, she contracted a disease and gave it up after that for a long time, out of fear.

*Wednesday, 24 September*

I went into Simon today and met John Gabie in the hall, who said he loved to drink whiskey. He said, "It is a big devil! I drink mostly whiskey". He slept with three more men outside a church last night. He said he loves to be out in the air and he's O.K., because, "I have God with me". He had a lovely smile and beautiful bright eyes. He had a great sense of humour. He said he would like to meditate with us. We said we would meditate in a while and he'd be welcome.

I could sit with Mohammed Day. He is 26 years old and is hurt by life's experiences, especially so when he is kind to people, as he said, and they do not appreciate it. He was baptised a Catholic, but was baptised later, in a swimming pool by 'the Christians', as he called them. He has often heard some people giving great testimonies of how they have been healed of one thing or another and he said he wished he could be healed, too. He reads *The Bible* and he said some words jump out at him. Some are in the *Book of Proverbs*. He said it mentioned wine being like a serpent, when it's not respected, but abused. He had a beautiful presence. He felt he needed time to get away and get space from society. It can be so cruel. I said I felt he was taking the first step, perhaps, in coming home to himself, to his own beauty and goodness, which I could easily see in him, but which he may not have experienced yet, himself. I said I felt he had heard more, now at 26 years, by stepping off the rat-race track, than some people would have heard at 70 years of age! I said to him that he was my teacher. He said, "I could live with insecurity and have nothing". He could be in the 'now' and go along with what came up. He hoped to meet some relations in Ireland. I told him about Ballygriffin and he said he may like to come there with us sometime. I had a sense of his 'being'. His gentleness was so real and inspiring.

Gillian Goa, who spoke to Rosetta, invited me over. She is a volunteer on placement work from a Social Studies course and said she would be very interested in meditation and, maybe later, going to Ballygriffin. She asked when we would be in again and said if she were here, she would do it with us. We felt we would meditate then, as already Alex Jack and David Gabbay said they would meditate with us, "after their bowl of soup". Alex Jack waited patiently, read his book and washed his shirts while he waited for us! David Gabbay did not come up, but Jordan Gallog, who had done Buddhist meditation, joined us. Later, a young lad in his late teens or early 20s sat on the floor in the lotus position with us to meditate. Five people in all meditated. Jordan Gallog later showed us the lotus position, in which he was used to sitting when he did Buddhist meditation. 'All shall be well', from Julian of Norwich, he said, was his mantra. We introduced him to our mantra and he asked if we would write it down for him. I wrote 'Má – Rá – Ná – Thá' reverently on an envelope. In the envelope was the lovely poem, *The Touch of the Master's Hand*, which Jordan read and asked if he could keep. Alex requested some more copies and one for Jake Fair, whom he said he saw looking at that same poem in the assembly hall wall in Ballygriffin – a few times – at different stages during the days he was there.

### THE TOUCH OF THE MASTER'S HAND

'T'was battered and scarred and the auctioneer
Thought it scarcely worth his while
To waste much time on the old violin,
But he held it up with a smile.
"What am I bidden, good folk?", he cried,
"Who'll start the bidding for me?"
"A dollar – a dollar – then two, only two –
Two dollars, and who'll make it three?
Going for three" – but no –
From the room far back, a grey-haired man
Came forward and picked up the bow.
Then, wiping the dust from the old violin,
And tightening the loosened strings,
He played a melody pure and sweet
As a carolling angel sings.
The music ceased and the auctioneer
With a voice that was quiet and low
Said, "NOW what am I bid for the old violin?"
And he held it up with the bow.
"A thousand dollars – and who'll make it two?
Two thousand – and who'll make it three?
Three thousand once – three thousand twice –
And going – and gone", cried he.
The people cheered, but some of them cried,
"We do not understand
What changed its worth?"
Quick came the reply,
"The touch of the Master's hand".
And many a person with life out of tune,
And battered and scarred without,

*Is auctioned cheap, to a thoughtless crowd,*
*Much like the old violin.*
*A 'mess of pottage'– a glass of wine,*
*A game – and the person travels on:*
*This person is going once – and going twice –*
*Is going – and almost gone!*
*But the Master comes, and the foolish crowd*
*Never can quite understand*
*The worth of a soul and the change that's wrought*
*By the touch of the Master's hand.*

Across the road, sitting on a shop window sill in Oliver Plunkett Street, we met Jamie Caar, who had a bottle of wine inside his coat and a sandwich in a blue plastic bag in his hand. He said he had slept in the crane on the docks last night! He said Mel Lahive had gone to the Garda station and he was going to get him out, but said he would probably be locked in then himself! He has a wonderful sense of humour. In his eyes, I gaze on the Maker's creation in him.

While we spoke to Jamie Caar, I was noticing the disdainful way some of the people who passed by looked at him. Some looked out of fear, doubt, anxiety, anger maybe, but the pitiful sight of a human being, reduced to the gutter by alcohol, evoked compassion, perhaps from some, as was the case on the road to Mount Calvary. His soul was so radiant in the midst of his terrible brokenness of body. I'm reminded of St. Augustine's phrase: 'That you fill us, not as water fills a vase, for even if we are broken in pieces, you will not flow out of us and away'. I saw the image of his Maker solid in Jamie Caar today, because I saw it in myself. I need to see it and experience it in myself first of all. *All is well in this Now.*

I met Adam Cafferkey in Simon today and he said he ran in a marathon for Somalia and made £89. He wrote a cheque and sent it straight so they would get it. If he put it in with the rest, it may never reach them. His first marathon was for the Third World. He said if he had money, he would feed those who had no food. He would like to *give them the food himself.* Adam Cafferkey is a homeless man, who each year runs in a marathon for charity.

## Wednesday, 1 October

We met Conor Damery and James Abernathy at Simon. We helped peel the potatoes and meditated at 2.00 p.m. Conor Damery, Alex Dart and James Abernathy came with us. Conor Damery is 18 and felt a bit giddy. Anthony felt giddy, too. We could let them laugh first and then meditate. Their silence was awesome. James Abernathy had to go after about five or 10 minutes and Alex went after about 15 minutes from the start. That was O.K.

### Thursday to Friday, 2 / 3 October

I went to Ballygriffin with Rosetta, Bernard O'Byre, and Laurence Saiche.

Bernard was very deeply hurt. He shared his pain. He had great wisdom, though. He could say going out to nature, "Stay with only one thing". It was the wisdom of John Cassian, a Desert Father, 'Will only one thing'. I was deeply moved by it. He loved the outdoor life and would be happier outside, than under a roof closed in by four walls, he said. He went out of the Simon with nothing at 1.00 a.m. the night before and came back at 3.00 a.m. He walked all up around Sunday's Well, sat occasionally and walked on again. He talked about having a tin of beans and peas on the street. Bernard said he himself had a path to follow in life. He looked forward to the future.

Laurence Saiche was honest and open, when he said he did not understand the page that was read about meditation. I knew Laurence was touched a lot by the experience of the day. He held Rosetta's hand and my hand and said he hoped he would see us soon. He said he loved the day.

The sharing was great after, as each person shared. I was not happy, when they laughed at my sharing, because I felt they did not see me or hear me. I felt hurt. It was a great day.

### Tuesday, 7 October

I went to Simon at about 10.00 a.m. I met Dylan Caball, as he is called in there, inside the door, sitting down, having a cup of tea. He chatted! His mother is alive. He looks 70. He showed me his wounded leg and I saw his badly-broken face. He oozed with gentleness. His hair was matted into his head. It could have been some time since he washed, I'm not sure. He *is* a gentleman.

### Thursday, 9 October

We went in and I went over to John Gabie and I said, "Did you sleep outside the church last night?". He said, "No, I like to change my hotels. I slept outside the bus office last night"! He had no whiskey yet to-day, he said. I said to him that he was like Francis of Assisi with the beard! He said, "St. Patrick, too!". He was very tanned.

Basil O'Brier came over to me and said he felt he knew me. I did not recognise him. It was O.K. and I could say I did not recognise him out of my truth, gently. I could hear by him that he was not in touch with his feelings, but used foul language at others. He was living at, maybe, two years of age! 'Hear me, they are all wrong, only myself'. He was in a caravan in Mayo with another man. He had no water. He got fed up and went off. He is a compulsive helper, I felt. He was always helping. He was with his father before he died. He drinks a bit, but says he's not an alcoholic. "I don't like that name. It labels a person. It is meaningless really. A person is beyond labelling", he said. His mother was a snob, he said, and his father had a very high standard for the family. Once, when he played a match and got three points, the other team won by a goal and his father said, "Why could you not get that goal?". Later, in the pub, he did not praise him for getting the three points. His best was never good enough. He laughed and joked a lot. It covered a lot. I would have been delighted with this before to cover up my shyness, but today I experience it differently. In the past, I wanted to cover up myself. Today, I can *BE* myself. I could hear the deeper pain in Basil and the defences. He is hurting. He said the only 'meditation' he does is fishing!

### Friday, 10 October

Rosetta and I went to Simon. One young man sat. His hair looked matted and uncombed for days. His head was down and he did not answer when we greeted him. I felt his abandonment very much. I could cry for him, because of my own feelings of abandonment at times.

### Tuesday 14 October

James Abernathy came out and said that he went to Declan Calbaras, to ask him to give us a quieter place to meditate this week as he, James, felt it was too noisy where we were last week. Eventually, we met Laura Sage *re* venue, as Declan Calbaras was out. We could be gentle with not knowing where we would be going. To experience 'having nowhere to go' was awesome, not frightening. I felt if we were meant to be there, we would be given a suitable place. If not, that was O.K., we had 'no fixed abode'. James Abernathy, Rosetta and myself meditated on the corridor outside the flat.

James told us of the man who gave him £170. One day, James was going along by a toyshop and saw a child looking in at a car. The child was with his mother, who had just arrived from England, with not much money. James had a word with the child's mother. He said he took the child in and gave £150 for the car and, he said, his reward was the smile on the child's face. This child's eyes were like diamonds, he said. The child threw his arms around James (Jimmy) and he kissed him. He said when he was a child, he wanted things / toys, etc., but he couldn't have them because his parents had no money. He did realise that he saw himself in this little child. Such love in his heart, coming beautifully alive. He said it gave him great joy to be kind to the little child. The experience awakened him to great joy within himself. We need to hear this story in / out of our inner being or we can miss the essence of it and judge really. It was, I believe, lived out of gentleness and can only be heard in deep gentleness. He may need to be heard / seen. That is O.K. It is not my place to judge.

We met Basil. It was his birthday. I was so happy to see a man, who had his head down last week, walking up straight today. He could look us in the eye, for the first time since we saw him. I could sense his abandonment, because I, too, had a sense of abandonment as a child and it came up, too, today.

### Wednesday, 15 October

Shaun Danaher was my teacher yesterday morning, as, when I went in, he sat there totally still. He had a cup of tea at each side of his chair and a plastic bag with some few bits in it. Eventually, when we were ready to go, Shaun was not around, not sitting on his chair in the front hall, but missing! Someone said, "Maybe he went out". Laura Sage looked for him in his sleeping quarters and he came out in his own time, so gently, all dressed up beautifully in his tweed hat and coat, on over many more layers of clothes. It was his gentleness that touched me. He said *NOTHING*. He said no word. Still, his silence spoke more than any words. How truly contemplative Shaun is. He could be still and silent before his own essence. In Ballygriffin, we meditated and went to nature – the tree was our theme for the day. Shaun sat motionless under a tree. The total stillness of the tree I felt drawn to really moved me, as I heard my own inner stillness in it. I awakened myself to my own inner stillness. Shaun Danaher did not use a stool, but sat on the ground outside, drinking tea and eating.

### Thursday, 16 October

I went to Simon. We met Charles Davio inside and he said his six weeks were up and he was going out with Laura Sage to look at a flat. He said he would keep in touch with us, let a message in the convent where his flat is. "When I get settled, I'll invite ye over to do meditation with me and it would be a blessing on the house", he said. That would be a special privilege.

I called to the recreation room and asked if anyone would like to do meditation. Michael Baily was the only one there and he said, "I would like to do it, as I often wanted to see what it was like". I said we were doing it there and then, so he said he would come up with us, which he did. We meditated. He liked it. He said Charles Davio told him about it. He asked a lot of questions about it – its origin, what 'Má – Rá – Ná – Thá' means, etc.

## Tuesday to Thursday, 21 - 23 October – Ballygriffin

We arrived at Simon around 2.00 p.m. to collect Richard Hair and Jerry Laar. They were ready. Richard had been drinking the day before, having been off it for four weeks. His wife has cancer and had her leg amputated. He separated from her after 17 years of marriage and drank for about seven of those and was sober for 10 years. He began drinking when he was 14 years old. He was very reserved. He was on *Valium*, and was getting the shakes when coming off them, as he forgot to bring them with him to Ballygriffin. He felt he might not need them anymore. He felt he would drink again on Friday night. We had mediation and his silence was awesome. He shared his story, right up to when he was about 12.

Richard and Jerry did not get up for 10.00 a.m. meditation on Wednesday. They did meditation twice on Tuesday. Jerry found it a bit more difficult to do the half-hour, but that was O.K. as he did what he could. Compared to when he first came to Ballygriffin, now he can stay still for much longer. At the start, he could only listen to the music. Later on, on the third visit, he listened to the talks and said he enjoyed them. He would never before have heard the music tape and stayed for the full half-hour.

He walked each day to Killavullen with Richard. He asked me for a 'loan' of a box of fags for him and Richard! I was happy they both co-operated with the wash-up, washing floors, laying fires, etc., too.

Richard said he attempted suicide three times. That was O.K. He was pining away after his girlfriend, Dolly Doxe, who would not have him back because he drank. They met in a help centre. I was happy to remove the T.V. No radio or T.V. Richard was polite and showed respect by going out the door to listen to the sports results on the radio. He would be sleeping rough tonight, Thursday, he said, maybe in the 'skip'. Richard's other option of being housed was to go to a friend's house. He (Richard) has a wife and five children. Richard was very grateful, so was Jerry. Jerry was not clean. He smelled of body odour. I got a bit used to it. Richard was not washed either.

## Saturday, 25 October

Chelsea Calcott called at 3.20 p.m. I finished meditating and went down to her. I knew when I saw her that she was not well. She drank Monday, when the solicitor would not give her an appointment on the spot, but asked her to call on 6 November. She paid £23. Seán, her son is back in care. She drank Tuesday, had a man in bed with her. She met a lorry driver on the quays when she went down for drink in the boats. There were no boats in. She stole two bottles of wine. The shopkeeper complained her to the Gardaí, who arrested her and took her into the cell in the Garda station. She stayed until she was sober. They withdrew the charges. She was glad, because she said if they didn't, she would not get her children back, because she stole goods. She asked for tea and some sandwiches. Chelsea stayed from 3.20 p.m. to 5.10 p.m. She needed underwear and clothes from the bag.

## Sunday, 9 November

Chelsea called at 1.45 p.m. She told me she went 'on the game', to get more money for drink. I said she needed to do that. She felt ashamed after being with one man and went with another then, "to blot out the pain", she said. She needed drink again. She had tea and sandwiches. She looked for some clothes. She had a lovely black leather jacket on, a warm wine-coloured jumper and black leggings. She looked well-ish. Her eyes were a bit strained. She spoke of Noel and how she did not want him around her. He had bought the leather jacket for her a couple of weeks ago. She brought Japanese men to her flat when she was drinking. She left at 3.40 p.m. or so. I could *be with* her, as she so openly, truthfully and humbly told her sacred story to me. Her gentleness (no judging herself) is emerging slowly. She went to two prayer meetings last week – charismatic meeting – Wednesday and Friday. She said these and meditation are for her now – not A.A.

## Thursday, 13 November

I remembered Richard and Bernard went to Nano Nagle's grave and Richard said he felt very good – an unusual feeling – after it. He did not know the grave was in Douglas Street until then.

*Tuesday, 18 November – Ballygriffin*

We left here around 10.20 a.m. and were home at 10.30 p.m. or so. I waited until 10 a.m. for Gilbert. I went to Simon. Gilbert did not turn up at all. I left a message for Gilbert, if he called, to come at 9.30 next day. Norbert was ready to go when I went down. We went off and collected Rosetta about 10.45 a.m. We did the shopping. We got what we needed. Some roads were flooded. The road near the shop was heavily flooded. We turned back and went through the town. All was well. The field in Ballygriffin was covered. It looked deep. We had our meal. The sausage rolls were not that hot. I did not like the quiche at all. I could tolerate it. I savoured the soup and roll. The yoghurt was good and the tea and milk. I savoured the potato. I was glad I could choose for me. The beans were O.K. I could have eaten them cold. We went to nature for two hours. I meditated with the flood in the river, but what came to me more and more was the interdependency of the two trees opposite the door. Each one stood on its own space – close and free – the branches were entwined but none of them wanted to make the other different to what they were in that now. They could let each other be. I sense tension in my hand now and pain as I write. My being can't be expressed through my body, when I'm so unfree here. I can be gentle with it.

Norbert looked up a couple of times and he opened his lovely blue eyes, which I had not seen fully until yesterday. He opened them up, as if he were experiencing a new world in him when I took him on the tour of the rooms, hall, chapel, etc. He talked a lot and had great wit. He was sent an E.S.B. bill once and he went in and said that he did not even own a candle! Someone used his name to pay his or her own bills. His medical card was stolen. It was used once by a man, who arrived in at Norbert's doctor and the doctor realised that the man was not Norbert, but the man used his card! The doctor got the police! He saw a friend once put his bottle of wine down near him on the seat on Merchant's Quay, saying, "I'm going for a swim" – he went in, but never came out! He told us, as we passed a brewery, that he and Jamie Carr stole a barrel of what they thought was *Guinness* but, when they opened it, it was full of wash-up liquid! What a shock. They went in to the brewery and said they did not drink wash-up liquid! They got a bottle of *Guinness* each! He spoke of going away every Wednesday to collect his money – disability – at the G.P.O. and celebrate his 'birthday' with a bottle of *Europa* wine! He said he wanted PEACE and to get away from the people in Simon. He said he prays to Nano Nagle (when I showed him her icon yesterday) for peace of mind and love. He spent time in Brixton Prison. He was glad, he said last night, that he was not sleeping in doorways or around the streets, as he used to in the past. On account of his condition now, he could not sleep rough any more. He suffers from epilepsy. If he drank with the medication, he said he would get an attack. I could gaze on the Maker's creation in Norbert. He is a great character.

## Tuesday, 25 November

I went to Simon and it was after 10.00 a.m. when I eventually got there. I went to Declan to see about Maurice Moss who was to travel with us. He was barred, Declan said, for abuse and violence, sexual and other. Declan was busy, as Dave is in the Regional in a critical condition. He was in the process of contacting relatives. He came down and asked if anyone in the T.V. room or dining-room would be interested in Ballygriffin. No-one was interested. Jerry asked if he could go to Ballygriffin. I met Mark Caher peeling potatoes in the dining-room. I invited him to Ballygriffin and he said, "No". He eventually said he would go with us. Jerry also encouraged him. He was an extremely gentle person, very, very hurt by life. He and Jerry came with us.

Mark's father died when he was 8! His aunt reared him – his mother may have been unwell – then his aunt got ill and he was put into care for five years! He loved Ballygriffin – the peace and quiet. He was a very handsome young lad, maybe in his 30s or so. He had a beautiful smile.

We meditated and went to eat and then to nature. I was drawn to a tree with a beautiful white and pink blossom on it – on 25 November! What a treat, when there was a sign of withering and dying mostly all around. My *inner being* is very much alive, I felt, even in the midst of anxiety, darkness. I then saw another tree with the similar blossom. It had a beautiful perfume. As the evening darkened, the tree's colour faded into a silhouette against the evening sky and I heard its stillness in a wonderful way – re-echoing my own stillness. In today's talk, we said that, in meditation, we are led into the silence. In this space, we hear love in us. It is the same love flowing in us and all creation from the one source of life. The mantra brings me deeper into that silence. We shared later. Mark asked if he could come down again with us to Ballygriffin.

## Thursday, 27 November

About 12.40 p.m., we went in to the Simon Community and I met Ursula Walk and Mel Lahive at the door. I was inside later when they were outside again – the barred door was between us – I felt the unease in me, as I spoke through the bars. What bars in me block me in my communication with another human being? Fear is one.

Ursula lives in Cork and sometime on the street perhaps? I asked her what her surname was and she said, "Walk". Mel then said, "Lahive"! She said, "Not yet". I asked then if they were going to get married. Ursula said, "Maybe". I said, "Don't forget to ask me to the wedding". She said they wouldn't. She said she couldn't find Mel sometimes around town. I could see how much she loved him in his filthy coat, covered with dirt from the road and his mouth full of sores, but he could smile. Ursula had a most beautiful expression. Her own inner beauty was radiated through her eyes. She had a lovely complexion. She wore a fur coat. She asked in the Simon for her boots. When it was not possible to get them, she was not angry, but could go away and said, "I'll ring later and see if ye found them". She and Mel went away 'happy' in their misery or what appeared to me to be misery! Who was the most miserable they or myself, I wondered? I have no answer, but I can be / stay with the question.

I met Fraser Cairne, who said his family business is a fruit business. He said he is not in the Simon but only stays there some nights! I spoke to him about the meditation and he said his brother goes away and does 15 minutes meditation before his tea. He said, "It does him good. It is supposed to be good". He said he would be interested in Ballygriffin sometime. I said, "It would be a place where we would spend time in solitude and silence". He said, "Oh, that would be lovely". Richard Hair was standing near the lift and said he would go up with us to meditation. We meditated then, up in the corridor near the flat. All was well.

Writing is my way of honouring the sacredness of these people. It is sacramentalising the experience in writing. I sense a communion with these special people only when I allow the experience to touch me and put me in touch with my own poverty.

## Wednesday, 3 December

I went into the Simon and met Mark Salim. He had just come in from the docks, where he had slept the night before. He held his hands tightly around the cup of hot tea to keep him warm. Mark, Abel Ardesen and Agatha Oakley were in Ballygriffin about one year and nine months ago. Agatha did not drink since! She has her children back and is doing well. Abel got beaten lately, Mark said. Mark asked if we would put down his name for Ballygriffin. I said he could come along when he was meant to. Mark had a lot of drink taken.

It struck me that what we are *called* to is to respond to the need, if possible, on the spot – be with it, no matter what a person's behaviour is like. The image of the Creator is imprinted in each unique person.

I invited Laurence Saiche and he was ready immediately. Laurence was from England. He was separated from his wife. He once owned an £80,000 to £120,000 house! He did not say how he lost it. He just said, "Things did not work out with my wife". He was very gentle and had a radiant smile. His daughter, Chelsea, is 18 and his son, Mick, is 14. He had both these names tattooed on his arm. On the other arm, he had the English flag. He said he loved leeks. Rosetta chose leek and potato soup last night without realising that leeks were his favourite vegetable! We heard that later! He lived in Italy for a year. He is an electrician by trade. He lived in Ireland for about a year. Also, he loved food. He would cook well. He would buy leeks especially and cook them! He had a brain tumour operation and has a plate inside his skin. In the very cold weather, it gets very cold. He suffers from headaches and epilepsy. He gave us a talk on the use and abuse of E.S.B. in the home as we travelled back to Cork. It was great.

He meditated twice with us and, while he found the first one long – more like an hour – the second one was great, he said. He was very relaxed. We did one in the centre and the second one in the chalet by the fire in the sitting-room. He said he would like to go down again after Christmas. The cold is not good for him. He loved the peace. He would go to his room at night around 7.00 p.m., before the people came in. We could have lit the fire earlier. The frost and ice were very severe last night. We saw some ladies of the night out near Simon, waiting in the freezing cold for their 'pick-ups'! One lady was a most glamorous, very respectable-looking lady. We returned about 9.30 p.m. Laurence said he had been exposed to the Pentecostal and Baptist Churches. His grandmother told him *Bible* stories. He would like to try the meditation, when he would get his flat. It was new for him. He had a good scriptural background, he said. Laurence had a deep sense of gratitude for food, the bed and other people's kindness.

## Friday, 5 December

Rosetta and I went to Simon. We met Edward Papize there and invited him to meditate with us. He came up with us and was later called away to meet his mother and sister, who called to see him during the meditation. That was O.K. We chatted in the place that was totally empty of anything material. It had three chairs, no pictures on the wall. I felt it is a sacred place now as we meditated there.

*Tuesday, 9 December*

Declan invited me / us to Midnight Mass in the Shelter.

Having spent about one hour in Simon, I met Jerry and asked him if he would like to go to Ballygriffin. He said, "Yes". He got ready and I mentioned it to Declan, so off we went! He was meant to go! It was 11.10 a.m. or so when I left there. We collected Rosetta and went to shop. I felt it took us ages – in my woundedness, I wanted to hurry on and get going smartly! It was after 1.00 p.m. when we were in Ballygriffin.

Jerry spent one year sleeping in a tent on his own in the Lee Fields! Jerry spoke a lot at the meal at 7.00 p.m. He told us later, before we went home and in the car, too, that the reason he would stay in bed at times was because he hears some noises in his head and they say to him that, even when he is dead, they know where he will be! He gets an injection every Friday and it helps a bit but, when the injection wears off (it is not effective for long), they come back again, he said. He used think that people in town used be out to get him, too, when they would be looking at him. Eventually, his friends persuaded him that they would not do anything to him – these people whom he felt were threatening him. He said it was a great relief when that feeling went away. He said he can't or doesn't feel like getting up some days because why would he bother, when these sounds keep coming up for him – 'the voices' as he calls them! They seem to terrify him. Three or four times, he attempted to commit suicide. The first time he took an overdose of tablets. He was knocked out in his room – the room was going round and round and he could not speak. A man got the ambulance for him. He went to hospital, was pumped out and was O.K. The second time, he jumped in over the footbridge into the river, with the intention of committing suicide. He went under the water, but then said he could not do it and decided to swim. He swam over to the steps and came out.

It has been about six or seven times now that Jerry went to Ballygriffin, either overnight or for a day, and it was only on the seventh time that he really shared his personal and family story. It was an awesome privilege to listen to him and hear his tiny bit of confidence emerging! He did say he had hardly any confidence in Jerry. I was so touched when he said yesterday that he would like to walk to the village. He went off and was out for about two hours maybe. I had not remembered that he had gone for that long before away on his own in Ballygriffin. It was Jerry's first time staying overnight on his own with Rosetta and I and I felt it was much better for him on his own than with others down there this time. He had no T.V., no radio, total silence, except at mealtime and when we were sharing. He was doing well and we noticed that, when it was almost time to come home, some of the people (like Jerry last night) were beginning to open up. He put on more slack on the fire around 7.00 p.m. and a big block! I could take out the block and move around the slack. Jerry thought we were staying again last night and I felt he would have been quite happy to stay. Rosetta and I felt privileged to accompany Jerry today. His openness inspired me.

## Thursday, 11 December

We went to Simon and met Anna Cagney. I notice more *women* in Simon lately. Why?

Bernard O'Byrne came down the stairs. He said he was not well at all. He would go home before Christmas to see his mother and sisters, but he said that, if he met his father, he would only fight with him. He remembers his father as taking drink and fighting with his older brother and he was looking on in disgust. He did not like school, so one night, he said, he went over and broke all the windows in the school and was expelled afterwards. He blames his father for the break-up with his girlfriend, to whom he was engaged and would have married two months later. He misses his son. His girlfriend now and his son have joined a sect. He said he is a Catholic and feels he will always be one and anyone leaving it for a sect is wrong! I could see his father in him! He worked in Sweden for one year and his father was all about him because he was working. He got a job in a restaurant for three days and left again, as he could not stick it. He may leave his flat now. He would like to go to a place like Ballygriffin, to fish and meditate! He asked if they would take people permanently! We mentioned a tent. He said he might get a horse! I shared about the people I met in the caravan, who said that they move on when the horses have eaten all the grass in that place! We stood for one hour talking to Bernard! We meditated then upstairs.

What touched me deeply on Wednesday was that Jerry sat down by the river on the tree trunk, which has green grass on it, and he said he found it peaceful there. He sat near water / a river that once he asked to end his life and now could help him get in touch with his peace. When I said that, this peace he experienced there was *in himself,* he said 'Oh, yes"! What he once used to end his life could now, by his just 'being with it', put him in touch with *the source of that life*. This is awesome. He's beginning to discover the true Jerry.

## *Friday, 12 December*

We went to Simon later. We met Richard who was to go away today. We meditated then, having asked the people in the T.V. room and kitchen if they were interested. No one was, so we went up ourselves.

Bernard O'Byrne sat down and chatted a lot. He was peeling turnips. He said he would miss his son mostly at Christmas. Bernard said he does try our way of meditation and combines it with his own. His son will be 4 on 27 April. His girlfriend took his son out of the country. He will wait until he is 12 and then get him back. Bernard said he has slept in snow, old cars, etc. His father put him out in the snow. He would like to come with us for a few days to Ballygriffin and bring a fishing rod! He can't stay in the flat, but feels he's meant to be out! There is a free week in the Simon at Christmas!

Bradley Eakin said it was a break for him to go to prison. He purposely broke a barring order and went in for six months from 1 May to 1 November. He had been in Ballygriffin in April for three days! Bradley's last day in Simon was supposed to be tomorrow, but still at 4.00 p.m., he was only talking about going to *Flatfinders*!

## *Saturday, 13 December*

At around 1.40 p.m., Chelsea called with a new man, Dan Mahon. When I went into Chelsea and Dan, Chelsea asked me for tea and sandwiches. I asked Dan if he would like some and he said, "Yes, cheers!". I could prepare the food attentively. Chelsea said she was in the Simon for a couple of days. She went there, she said to get a man. Dan had just come back from England. She asked him if he would like to tell me his story. He said he would share it.

He spent eight years on heroin and took it not through injection, but in 'joint', as they call it. The injection gives a flush to the head and initially there is a huge buzz, which lasts a while. This does not happen with the 'joint'. In smoking heroin, he said one gets a 12-hour buzz and then when it wears off, the person gets very sick and feels awful for three days. It hurts then to eat food. He drinks milk-shakes. The third day off is the worst. When one gets over that, they are O.K. The withdrawal is terrible. When one is on the heroin, it is like being wrapped up in cotton wool. I said that meditation could give a person that sense of harmony, too, and peace with no negative side *effects*! This is what everyone is looking for. Dan was a very gentle person. He said he came to Cork, because there was no heroin here and, if he was tempted to take it, he could not have it. Some people though, he said go to Dublin for it. He is off it for five and a half weeks now.

## Tuesday, 16 December

Jamie Carr came in. He is a real gentleman. He had a beautiful soul shining through his weather-beaten face. He looked as if he had had a lot of battering and beating in his day. His leg was cut, because he fell into a hole, when he was drinking and skinned his shin. He said he used drive a van, but his licence was taken off him because he was caught drinking and driving. He has a beautiful gentle voice. He used to fish around Rosscarbery Pier. He put on a coat and went out.

Bradley looked very sad. He was in great pain. He only goes out once a week, he said, to get his wages. I asked Bradley if he would like to meditate with us. He said he would. The corridor we meditated in smells like the new chapel in Glencairn Abbey. I love the total simplicity of it – nothing superfluous – it is very fitting that we don't have a room! We are meant to be on the corridor. I was touched by the positive energy I sensed up in the meditation area and felt today it was so tangible. Bradley could rest and be in a very loving place. We did not need to say anything – just *BE*. Being always emanates goodness. I could sit alone and be totally at one in the dining-room today, as I looked around at the people.

I then saw the Christmas tree. It was very nicely decorated. I felt that I could really experience the true Christmas spirit there today – nothingness – poverty. Each person sat there in an unique way, in the beauty of his / her own soul, which she / he may miss forever.

## Thursday, 18 December

A man called yesterday, while we were out. Simon Tannes was his name and he said he would call today at about 9.30 a.m. He was here at 9.12 a.m.! He told me he broke out in drink, took his cat out for a walk and the cat ran away! She returned later and went away again. His landlady did not like the cat in the flat, he said. He told her once she was gone but, while she was collecting rent, he had put the cat in the outhouse. He said he told her a lie two weeks ago. He was heartbroken after the cat. She used sleep on / in the bed with him! He spent all one day looking for the cat! No luck! He sounded to me like a 3 year old almost, crying after his cat! He said he hoped she would be looked after, wherever she was, but wished she would come back. A lady in Simon gave him the cat. He asked a priest to say Mass for the cat! The priest said, "We don't do that but, if you went in to the office, you could ask the lady to have Mass offered for a special intention"! His care of the cat reflected how he would like to be cared for himself, I felt. It reflected his goodness. I found it hard to keep a straight face at times.

## Friday, 19 December

I went over to where Rosetta was with Jerry Laar and she introduced me to Fraser Cairne. He was sleeping rough since he was about 14 and tried to commit suicide. He had a hard life. I put my bag down and waited, because I did not want to control the situation and say, "Will we meditate?". I could wait until Rosetta was ready. We meditated then with Jerry, who initially was not going to meditate, but when Rosetta asked Fraser if he would go up, he said, "Yes", and then Jerry said he would do it, too. Jerry had already told Fraser that it was very good. Jerry stayed for the music and talk and Fraser stayed for 25 minutes of the meditation. We moved off then.

## Tuesday, 23 December

We went to Simon. We admired the decorations on the Christmas tree; some were hand-made by an artist. She was a friend of a lady who does fundraising and is training to be a counsellor. I was moved by the gentle atmosphere there, no trace of materialism. The simplicity touched me a lot. It was the Bethlehem experience. It is a holy place. It was a Christmas experience as I gave birth to my own gentleness. Handmade ornaments on tree spoke of each person being handmade – great care was taken in making a person, too.

## Wednesday, 24 December – Christmas Eve

I greeted some of the residents and Ursula Walk gave me her ear-phones to listen to the lovely waltz music on it. She wore a trouser suit of black, with a very low-cut neck. She and myself waltzed around the foyer, as I still listened to the music with the earphones on! Mel Lahive had been drinking and sat on the floor. I returned the Walkman to Ursula. I wished Jerry Laar and a man called Bobby James a "Happy Christmas".

Father came for Midnight Mass at 12.00. James Abernathy sat behind me and snored out loud every so often. Someone shouted at him and said, "Stop that snoring"! The man who played the guitar sat on the table and sang. The group joined in as best they could. One man was a line ahead most of the time in the *Gloria*! Father gave a lovely simple introduction, saying he had attended a sick man of 43 in the hospital, before coming over, and asked the group to remember him. He spoke about calves, lambs, etc., when they are born, they can suck their mother – at least they can do something, but a human being, when it is born, is the most helpless of all. Jesus chose this form to come among us. The Mass began. In the middle, at the top of the room on two chairs, just in front of the altar, sat Ursula and Mel! They were the only two in that row! They asked Father if he would marry them! At the *Gloria*, Mel went over and gave the Christmas tree a big hug! It was lovely to see him hugging the tree! It seemed as if he were giving life a hug – life was O.K. for him just then anyhow. At the *Alleluia*, Ursula leaned over and stayed close to Mel for a few minutes. It was awesome to see – on such a special night. I could sense their in-depth love. Mel later put his arm around Ursula and I could sense the tenderness out of which he held her close to himself. At *Silent Night*, someone shouted out and put his hand on Bobby's shoulder, "What are you doing here?". I was invited to read. Ezekiel Mahy read the first reading. Another lady, Julia Yango, and some other girl read the prayers of the faithful. A man read the second reading. I read the beautiful Christmas Reading after the *Gospel* – a type of homily – to emphasise a point – the incarnation made more real! It was awesome.

### A CHRISTMAS PARABLE

*Once upon a time, there was a man who looked upon Christmas as a lot of foolishness. He wasn't a Scrooge. He was a very kind and decent person, generous to his family, upright in all his dealings with other men. But he didn't believe in all that stuff about an Incarnation, which churches celebrate at Christmas. And he was too honest to pretend that he did. "I am truly sorry to distress you", he told his wife, who was a faithful churchgoer. "But I simply cannot understand this claim that God became man. It does not make sense to me". On Christmas Eve, his wife and children went to church for the midnight service. He declined to accompany them. "I'd feel like a hypocrite", he explained. "I'd much rather stay at home. I'll wait up for you".*

*Shortly after his family drove away in the car, snow began to fall. He went to the window and watched the flurries getting heavier and heavier. "If we must have Christmas", he reflected, "It's nice to have a white one". A few minutes later, he was startled by a thudding sound. It was quickly followed by another, then another. He thought that someone must have been throwing snowballs at his living room window.*

*When he went to the front door to investigate, he found a flock of birds huddling miserable in the snow. They had been caught in the storm and in a desperate search for shelter had tried to fly through his window. "I can't let these poor creatures lie there and freeze", he thought. "But how can I help them?".*

*Then he remembered the barn where the children's pony was stabled. It would provide a warm shelter. He quickly put on his coat and galoshes and tramped through the deepening snow to the barn. He opened the doors wide and turned on the light. But the birds didn't come in. "Food will bring them in", he thought. So he hurried back to the house for breadcrumbs, which he sprinkled on the snow to make a trail to the barn. To his dismay, the birds ignored the bread and continued to flop around helplessly in the snow. He tried shooing them into the barn by walking around and waving his arms. They scattered in every direction – except into the warm-lighted barn. "They find me a strange and terrifying creature", he said to himself, "and I can't seem to think of any way to let them know they can trust me. If only I could be a bird myself for a few minutes, perhaps I could lead them to safety".*

*Just at that moment, the church bells began to ring. He stood silently for a while, listening to the bells pealing the glad tiding of Christmas. Then he sank to his knees in the snow. "Now I understand", he whispered.*

**Louis Cassels**

God became a person / woman / man so that person / man / woman could become God. At a deeper level, I get a tiny glimpse of the awesomeness, of the reality, of the Incarnation. It seemed to speak so much to me about solidarity with these special people. The fact that I was asked to read about birds was most fascinating really and touched me deeply. The stillness came to live in me again and, when it said in the parable about becoming a bird, free to be me, this is when I now really hear that, when I'm in my own stillness, I can gently be myself first and then reach out safely to others.

# 1998

## Sunday, 4 January

Chelsea Calcott and Gregory Raft called about 5.20 p.m. I was glad to see them. Chelsea has a new flat. She is not happy in it. There were people on drugs near her. Gregory offered to take her in, while she awaited a new place. I am amazed at her ongoing ability to bounce back each time. She said the prayer meetings were too high-powered for her. She said the only thing that really helped her was the meditation. Chelsea mentioned going to the Simon Community before Christmas and said, "It is not possible to go any lower!".

## Tuesday, 6 January

Rosetta and I went to Simon and met John Gabie outside the door. He came over to us and chatted. I was very cold at the start but, when I was touched by his sharing, I did not seem to mind the cold. He had a bottle of Scotch whiskey in his pocket. He asked us if we were afraid of him. He said he had been out for eight nights and slept with no blankets in a doorway for two nights. He asked us for three blankets. I said if he would like to go to South Pres., he could perhaps get some there. He did not wish to do this. He was to be allowed into the Simon at 7.00 p.m. tonight, so he would get blankets from them. I said I did not have any blankets myself.

John was my teacher today. He said, "God is very close to me". That was a profound theological statement. He said he asked God to take him last night in his sleep. "He did not", he said, "I must be meant to be around for another while". He had a lot of drink taken. He said at least six times about himself, "I am a good person". It was wonderful to hear him say this. I could gaze on the Maker's creation within him. I said his behaviour was one thing, but inside is a beautiful person. He could partly hear, I felt. I feel he is richer, because of experiencing God so near him, than many who have endless material wealth.

### THE FLAWED LIFE

*It's strange how I'm made – half mystic and half nut:*
*My eyes upon the stars, my feet deep in the mud.*
*One moment I'm lying and the next I'd die for the truth!*
*One moment I'm kind, big-hearted, understanding, loyal:*
*The next sneaky and cruel.*
*It's weird how a soul can be split up like that –*
*Part Creator, part scallywag.*
*It's inconvenient too.*
*Because you're never quite sure which part is on the job!*
*Just when you think you are all set to act the saint,*
*Something inside goes flop – and there you are – anything but a saint!*
*Yet, at other times, when you don't care how you behave,*
*Something in you leaps up like a flame,*
*All the muck in you is burned away,*
*And for a flash, you're tall and clean and strong.*
*Once it used to get me to be like that: I hated myself … I hated life.*
*I felt I'd been betrayed by my Creator who'd made me such a mess.*
*What was life worth if one was so full of flaws?*
*So strong, yet weak; philosopher and fool?*
*Yes, once, because I could not be the perfect thing I wanted to be,*
*I hated life.*
*Now, I know that flawed lives are good,*
*And serve a purpose in the Creator's kindly plan.*
*Only those who've lied can feel a liar's shame;*

*Only cowards know the bitter blame cowards must face;*
*And only those who've failed can understand the fear of defeat.*
*So, through my weaknesses, I possess the key*
*To every heart that's sad, shamed or soiled.*
*Through my blunders, I've found tolerance*
*And pity in the place of my lost pride.*
*So, my Creator, I'm glad you made me as I am –*
*Mystic and nut, philosopher and fool;*
*My eyes upon the stars, my feet deep in the mud.*
*For I've learned that flawed lives can serve you well.*
*I have found that both stars and mud are swell.*

**Author Unknown**

## Thursday, 8 January

We went to Simon today, Thursday. I came out and sat near Rosetta in the foyer, chatted with Tom from Wales, then Jordan sat down near Grace and Jack. Jerry stood.

Jack spoke of his travelling background and said how he defended his brother of 8 in the toilet from a homosexual man. He said he gets very violent when he has drink and threw a bottle at a man in a van, New Year's Eve. Jack is 22 years of age. He attacked a man another time, whom he felt was gay. He said, "God made Adam and Eve, not Adam and John, or Mary and Eve!". He said he can't abide homosexual people. Jack needed very much to be heard and seen. That was O.K. He was very intelligent. He had a mighty temper, I would say, if he broke out or if a homosexual person came in his way! He *could* kill out of his anger.

Tom showed us some photos of a home in Wales – the farm he was on, when he was coming off drugs. He showed us beautiful pictures of the sea, mountains, sheep, a pig and piglets. They were very well-taken photographs. I said it was as if they represented different aspects of his own beauty. He found it hard to hear this. He spent five years in prison and was on drugs for 14 years. He is off them four years! He said he can't read or write but he has his eyes! I found it hard at times to understand the Welsh accent. That was O.K. Tom was a lovely gentle person. The parts of Tom I saw reflected in the photographs were his rock-like solidity, the wave-like gentleness, the silence of the trees, the vibrancy of the animals, their reverence and patience. He had a lovely smile and I could gaze on the Maker's creation in him.

## Friday, 9 January

I chatted with Wayne Dee, who said he slept out last night with only a sheet. He had no blanket.

A lady, perhaps a visitor, stood in the hallway. She looked around the lobby. Could she have felt Rosetta and I were two of the residents? I would be happy to feel she would.

## Thursday, 22 January

I sensed I needed to see Norbert. We sat for a long time with Norbert and that was a lovely privilege. I was touched when he held up his head to look at the T.V. He bent his head forward mostly and looked out under his eyelids. His hands usually covered his face. When he opened his eyes fully, they were beautiful. He had a beautiful smile also. It was a very quiet room, too. There was a plant – a sign of life near the broken window. Norbert's presence touched me as he sat in total silence at times and very gently talked at other times. That was O.K.

## Tuesday, 3 February

Job Russ called about 1.20 p.m. or so. I met him at the door for about 10 minutes. He said he called yesterday and a person said I may be gone to the Simon, so he went down and asked for me. I was on the streets. I wasn't in the Simon at all. 'Leahy', he thought, was my surname! Job said he was recovering from Hepatitis B – he got it from food poisoning. He had it since 10 November. He said he had more oestrogen (female hormone) in his body than male and said that he was a woman, maybe, or meant to be one! He might have a sex change, he said! He won't go to work for another few weeks, he said. He said the Word was enfleshed in the body – 'Word made flesh', meant something to him, he said, when he realised this. He said in Tony de Mello's book, *Awareness*, he talks about touching the body – aware, aware. He said he goes deeper himself in the meditation and this world doesn't exist for him them. He is in the Legion, but does not believe in saying the *Rosary* every day. I said to Job that I had a visitor. I would love to have invited him in and heard his story and shared a cup of tea with him. It was not meant to be now. I could let him be and let go of *want*!

## Wednesday, 4 February

Tom is 35 years old, was running a business, a shop in England. He abused alcohol, ran into some difficulties with some people there and came home in October. He lost his business. He slept on the street. He was very well-dressed – collar and tie, lovely suit and shoes, waistcoat-like cardigan. He showed us the side of his pants, which was all dirty, as he slept behind Simon last night in Cork. "There was no bed in there", he said. The temperature was -5 last night, he said. He sells blocks now sometimes and gets £15 a day. His nose was broken in England, when he was attacked. He was in London for 15 years. He originally came from Cork. He was a manager in Cork also.

Joseph sat down. He was in prison for Christmas. He broke a barring order and was sent in. He wanted to go to prison, so he purposely broke the barring order, so that he would be put in but he went off drugs and drink in there. It helped him stay off them. They weren't available to him. Steve did not stay too long at meditation. That was O.K.

We had a bowl of soup. Adam sat with us and spoke of his poem on *Hope* and also told us about the card he got from Mary McAleese. He sent her a Christmas card, as he said he had no one else to send one to! He spent three weeks in hospital. He said he drank whiskey and wanted to die before he went to hospital, but someone found him. He was sorry they did!

## Thursday, 5 February

We met Adam when we went in and we sat down and chatted with him for a while. I could sense being totally in my being, as I listened to him talk about his sacred history, some of which, through no fault of his own, was spent in psychiatric hospitals. He does not like churches, nor people who go there, nor what priests say! He went to school to learn to speak properly, he said. A nun taught him as an adult. He was in a home as a child with nuns, and he said they *made* him do that and made him do this! He did not like it. He said he had a hot temper.

I was greeted by Andrew and Deirdre, who slept rough on the streets of London. Andrew had a very beautiful face and was so friendly. He spent terms in prison. Deirdre had been on drugs for seven years and was also into drink and sex. She said she was not interested in sex, because it was over in a few hours, but the good in us lasts! No one can take that from us – the good with-in. They were not interested in the institutional church. They had been Catholic, but were more interested in being Christian. Andrew said, "You turn to God in the street, when you sleep rough in doorways and don't know what will happen to you".

Pete Bradd had a *Bible* and he opened it. I thought the *Book of Wisdom* was in it, but it was only the *New Testament* and *Psalms*. I read and shared about four lines of *Psalm 22* and said, "My essence is my Shepherd. It is not a God outside us somewhere". Pete said he takes the *Bible* around with him. "It is a good book", he said.

I could gaze on the Maker's creation in these lovely people.

## Friday, 6 February

We went to Simon at 10.45 a.m. We met Mel Lahive. We had a card for Ursula's birthday. She will be 42 years old on Monday. She was in a lot of pain. We went to the table and Rosetta gave her the card at breakfast.

Later, I sat near Mark Salim, who was so dirty, I could scrape the dirt off his hands and face! His clothes were very dirty from sleeping in them. He wore a green and white hat, with Ireland written on the front of it. It was my privilege to be with him, but I don't know what the 'dirt' is saying yet. Mark Salim has a beautiful face. He said, "When are you taking me to Nano Nagle's?". I said, "When you are ready, Mark".

## Saturday, 7 February

We went to Simon at 10.00 a.m. We went in and sat in the hallway. Many people passed in and out. I felt there was '*nothing happening*' and I was so happy when I was in my soul, that I could stay with the nothingness of it all. It was meant to be that way and it was O.K.

I sat near Jer and another man. Jer told me he went home at Christmas for the first time in 13 years. He went to his child's grave (who died at four weeks old from toxaemia) and his mother's grave, too. I asked him if he could cry and he said, "Me". The tears were in his eyes as I listened to him. He said he also visited his uncle after 17 years and he had so much drink taken that he can't remember how he got back to Cork. He said the whiskey takes an awful lot out of the body. He said he went to England at 16 and missed the last Underground one night – the doors closed too fast and he was left on the platform at midnight, when an Irishman met him and invited him to stay in his house for a while. He was knocked down by a car after a week and was in hospital on traction for three and a half months, then he was brought back to Ireland and was a year on crutches. Later, he went back and was injured on a building site. He was interested in going into the pub business, but it did not work. He worked in pubs, too. He injured his spine and was in hospital again. They thought he broke his spine. The bones were on top of each other. When his marriage went and they separated, he was living with a girl in England. He got a job in a company in Dublin then and seemed to have many friends in Dublin. He said he would like to go to Dublin. He would look for work. He was very disappointed – he lost a good job – a permanent job in a hotel, through going on the drink again. He was encouraged by his doctor to go to a care centre to dry out for one week. He said it was 'tops' and one could meet doctors and social workers there. The food was good. Vitamins were given, too. He went to another centre for one week. He felt he could do the programme himself, as it was the same as going to the A.A. meetings on a regular basis, while staying in Simon. He did the programme twice already.

We then went to meditate about 2.20 p.m. or so. Con came up with us. His silence was wonderful. He chatted a lot after it. He said he had been in an orphanage since he was 1 year old. At 10 years old, they left the nuns' orphanage and went to the Brothers. He though he had a vocation, and maybe he ought to have entered the Brothers. He read about the Franciscans and saw where they were looking for new people to join. He said he may be able to do the garden or cook. I said he was not late yet. He looked in great pain. He mostly folded his arms. He had a beautiful face. He only had the shirt and pants he wore. I could hear by him that he was interested in getting well again. He said he would like a place of his own, where he could sit quietly and read the paper, go to the shop for some groceries and keep to himself. It is very understandable why he would like a place of his own – he probably never had a home – like Adam, who never had a home either, he said. Con read a book about someone who made it in life and who had been in an orphanage. This encourages him.

## Wednesday, 18 February

Des Dorl slept in a hedge last night, after having been beaten by the Gardaí and taken into the Garda barracks. He had slept in London, Victoria Station, etc. He is from Scotland. His mother died when he was 9 years old. He is a half-twin. There are four sets of twins in his family – in all, there were 11. Two brothers died. He was going to go home to his mother. He reads a lot. His twin is married and has two children. He said on his mother's doorstep, she has a mat, which has written on it, 'Oh no, not you again'! He said he would like to write a book someday. Maybe, if someone sat down with him and had a word processor, he would do it. He did a line with a girl and he said she wanted to change him. He asked her to go because he liked his dope / smoke! He showed us the special pipe yesterday for smoking hash. It was made of copper piping. Des was very intelligent.

I remembered this morning's reading on Saint James, "*Listen* and be slow to speak". Several people passed in and out. I could be there from my soul 100%. We meditated.

## Thursday, 19 February – Ballygriffin

I had a chat with Don Leese and was deeply moved by his wisdom. I returned his poem, My *God the Enemy*, to him. I said I was so moved by it that I wrote it out to keep it. I hoped he did not mind. He said it was fine. He said the poem was about his addiction to drugs. Don said, "Drugs lead you to three things – jail, frustration, pain. I take drugs to kill the pain, not to be thinking of home and how upset it is. It helps to get me out of the real world for a while". Don was Danny's age – 18 years old.

## Friday, 20 February

John Gabie and Daniel were in the hall and one had more drink taken than the other. George held my glove and also held Rosetta's hand. He said (as I had a glove on), "I have no disease!". He held my glove for a good 20 minutes, I would say. That was O.K. I could look straight at him and look into his eyes. He had such huge pain in his big blue eyes. It was awesome for me to keep looking at his eyes. I hardly took my gaze off them. He was no threat to me, as he had drink taken and maybe could not even see me all that well either! I find it much harder to look and stay looking at a person's eyes when they are in their senses. I may need to look more at my own eyes and be at home in them. I am not at home in my own eyes.

We went to Mass later. I read the names of the people who had died in the Simon Community, before the Mass, so that each one's name could be special to me during the celebration of the Eucharist. I was touched by the words of *Bind us Together*: 'Born with the right to be free'. It was each person's right, there, but how many experienced the freedom – real freedom?

## Saturday, 21 February

Chelsea Calcott called at 1.30 p.m. I heard her story regarding the new flat. She was like a child, who was looking forward to getting a new toy for Christmas. Chelsea was most excited about having a double bed in her room in the flat! It is a one-room flat for now. Later, she hopes to get a two-bedroomed flat. I asked her if she would like to meditate. She said she would. John Cadec came in and he joined us in meditation. None of us had a watch! We did not need it! Their silence was wonderful.

## Monday, 23 February

I met Aidan. His mother got a stroke, when he told her he was on drugs – she died since. He said he would love if she were alive now to let her see him 'clean', as he said. He is off drugs for nine months. He is 20 years old. He said he has it constantly in his head about committing suicide. He said, "A man cut his wrists and died in Simon on Friday night – it could have been me". He blames himself for his mother's death. He said his father comes from a very respectable family. I talked a bit about his deep goodness.

## Tuesday, 24 February

Maria Mooney and Tony Axon spent three days with us in Ballygriffin. At one stage over the days, I shared with Maria and Tony about meditation, as a means of enabling them to get in touch with their own goodness. Tony, at one stage, when he had done the meditation, felt so relaxed and said, "It is better than worrying". We went to the mountain that day and they both found it a good experience. Some people may go back and drink over and over again on the street. That is O.K. We can be gentle with that, too.

The day before, I saw a daffodil in the garden of the Bon Secours convent. It was as if it were hiding from the world, as it was under a bush and not easily seen, unless I made a point to return and look at it, which I did. It reflects for me what this ministry, in which Rosetta and I are privileged to be involved in, is saying to me today. It is hidden (the real beauty of it) from the world – the world of success, achievement, wealth and power. All I'm called to is to *be*. Like the daffodil, it is hidden and can only be seen by such people as have eyes to see and ears to hear. Rosetta shared with me the day before, too, that "we meditate so that we can live more contemplatively every day and in every situation of our lives".

A resident / volunteer did one day with us in Ballygriffin. Another volunteer asked if he could also go. It is a great privilege also to share with voluntary workers. The workload there seems heavy. They are all wonderful people. They need days to go to bed, perhaps, after work. Declan enables everyone to be 'at home' in the Simon Community. There is a lovely friendly atmosphere there.

## Thursday, 26 February

In Ballygriffin last night after tea, Sam told us about his time in an orphanage from the age of 1 to 10 years old. The nuns were marvellous to them. Adam and Joe were with him. He has great time for the Christian Brothers. He told us about his brother in Limerick. He chatted from about 10.00 p.m. to 12.00 midnight. It was hard to hear him say he was sent into the orphanage at 1 year old. He has seven brothers and four sisters. He is very intelligent. He doesn't *smoke* or *drink*. Sam talked about wanting to work in some charity shops, or do something good for others. Also, several times, he mentioned having the *key of his own door* and being able to have family and friends in to visit him. He cooked in a centre at 15 years of age and then spent four years there, then went to Dublin, to the Salvation Army and to England where he worked in the building trade for 12 years. He is very sociable. He stayed in East End, West End and Kent, etc. He did not mention when he used drink, except on his way down he said he knew what it was to be in the gutter. He seemed to have been in the old Simon, too, before. He is a very intelligent man. He loves to read a lot. He does not smile much. He is very hurting, I feel. He said his past comes up at times.

## Friday, 27 February

We went into Simon at about 11.30 a.m. and stood for a while in the hall. Later, I could hear a man say at least twice, "Hello, Sisters". We went over to Lee and chatted with him for a long time. He had been knocked down by a car and his hand was very shook up. He was knocked down by a car as he was on his way to the cemetery in Dublin where his brother (half-twin) and mother were buried. He said that, whenever he goes to the cemetery or makes an attempt to go there, something happens always. Once, he hired a taxi and it broke down. Another time, he got a loan of his brother-in-law's van and it broke down. He had a wife and family and would be in Mountjoy if he went within a two miles' radius of his own home. He is barred, but sometimes he sees his children O.K. He has spent time in the open prison, where he said he had a great time. He said you can get drink there and go out around the grounds. Lee went away in the middle of the chat for a wash and shave. He said, when he came back, that he was meeting a bird! He said, "Someone to look after me!". He's in Cork for a few years, he said.

Chelsea called at 7.15 p.m. and there was a man with her, whom she introduced as Andrew Badcon! I invited them in then and Andrew chatted almost non-stop. Chelsea talked about drinking again last week. I said, "Chelsea, you are doing all that is possible for you". Andrew could hear that, too. He said he had an addiction to drink and was off it a while. He said Chelsea did not drink the night before or that day and that was good. He appeared to be very wounded and hurt and said he had a friend, a lady, who had an accident lately. Joy-riders ran into the back of her car. She is in hospital in Dublin. He said he was going to see her. Andrew said he met me before. I did not remember at all. Andrew said he knew Chelsea years ago and she was very good to him. He said she put him in touch with the positive in himself – his inner goodness. He took her in off the street this time and gave her a bed. Chelsea went back drinking on the streets last week again, with Jack, she called him. I felt I met Jack sometime there in Simon. Chelsea was hurt because the flat she was promised was gone and Noel got Sean, even though Noel, according to Chelsea, was on drugs and drink. Her hurt sent her back to the streets. Chelsea and Andrew spoke for an hour.

### Tuesday, 3 March

George and Joseph were peeling potatoes. I asked them if they would like to go with us to Owenahincha Retreat House and they said, "Yes". It was like Peter and James mending their nets and Jesus said, "Come, follow me" and they left all and followed. Jesus here is their inner being. I asked Declan for sheets and a towel. We collected Rosetta. We shopped and it was good. Sister Regina in the convent in Rosscarbery was so welcoming, offered us tea and asked us who we had with us. She said maybe we would talk sometime to her girls about our work. We did not say "Yes" or "No".

Joseph is 26 years old on 21 March. He said his girlfriend was taking him back. He has a daughter, Shauna. She is a 1½. He did not see her for a year. He would like to be able to see her. His wife's name is Sheila. He began taking drugs at 12 and still took them when staying with a friend. He is from a rural village and it would not be acceptable there for anyone to be taking drugs. He was in a treatment centre four times. He also went on hash and speed. He was 'put on' *Valium* once, he said, and got addicted to it. He is now coming off them, he said, but took them even this week, too. He has a beautiful face and I can gaze on the Maker's creation in him. He deeply appreciates everything here.

George and Joseph meditated with us each time we meditated. Their silence is awesome. We said that we would like to ask them what time we would (have meditation) do the next exercise in the afternoon. We said, "We are all four of us in this together", and George said, "There is no boss"! Joseph asked what time we do meditation. We said we do it three times a day, but we would not like to put pressure on them to do it at any time. When I saw they were interested in doing it, I said, "Could ye say a time?". George said 2.30 p.m. That was great. Later, when asked about the dinner, Joseph left it to us. That was O.K. Joseph and George washed the ware.

## Wednesday, 4 March

Joseph said he slept like a log the first night here. That does not usually happen him either, when he's coming off drugs. Last night, he slept for a bit O.K., but could not go to sleep for a while when he went to bed. Joseph wore a woolly hat most of the time, as he said he has no hair. He said he was bald. He showed us his bald head and had only a small bit of hair in front. He had his hood over his head, too, at times. He did not take off his coat at all during the three days, only when he went to shave last night! He took off his hat for a few minutes today, but put it on again, as he said he was cold without it. His fingers were all burned from cigarettes. They were nearly as brown in spots as George Faiss' were. George Faiss is 70 plus years old. Joseph is 25 years old! Joseph's coat was like a protective layer around him and so was his hat – a sense of shame or something negative was echoing through the wearing of this clothing and not taking it off!? Even at the fire, when he was hot, he still did not take off his coat. That was O.K.

They both liked to sit near the fire on the armchairs. "It is like home", George said the first night. George spoke of how his mother wanted him to go to school to do the Leaving Cert. and he would not, but left at about 14 or so. His father was delighted that he left, as he said he could help with the farm. Joseph said he would like to do a live-in on a farm, but said, "With my scarred face, who would have me?". George's father had a small boat as well. George used go out and his mother would give out to him when he would come back. He used to keep on going out because, as he said, she kept annoying him. He knew he was not meant to go to school. His mother wanted it. His two sisters went as boarders to a secondary school. One sister does not like school at all. He does not get on with his brother, who is in college. He had his own path to follow and his mother had a different path to follow for him! The two never met. We admired him for the great courage he had in setting off on his own to find life for George.

I noticed neither of them could sit for long at the table – they had their meal and they went away for a smoke and washed the ware. They were in a hurry to get going. There had been, I'm sure, a lot of woundedness experienced around their family table. Last night, both of them shared a lot, at the fire. It was great. The environment was made for it. Even though we put no pressure at all on Joseph and George to come to the meditation, they did not miss one.

## Friday, 6 March

Today, Friday, at 3.10 p.m., we went to Simon. We greeted John. He said he drank last night, but before that, he was off it for a week and two days. He said he has steak and onions three times a week some times when he is off the drink! Molly Gaffney rang him while he was there. He said Molly drinks about two and a half flagons of cider, when she is down the Coal Quay on Friday and Saturday, then gets the bus and goes home! He said Molly speaks very loudly. She must be hard of hearing, he said! He gets on well with Molly. He does not get on with David, he said. He drinks too much. He was barred from Simon and is now out in the street. Teresa O'Fiache, his girlfriend, is five months pregnant and is in a B & B.

Jerry Laar came along and was well. On his jumper was the word 'Respect'. "Respect for Jerry first", I said, "and then for others".

I felt 200% at peace today.

Today was a day of mind-ful-ness, awareness and attentiveness.

I met Con Lang today. He needed to share on how his life's burdens are becoming heavier. He feels he is carrying a lot on his shoulders. He is 25 years old and is very deeply in touch with himself. He believes in his own inner goodness and is convinced that it *never* changes. He said he hopes he does what is good for people in his life. Love guides him, he said, and people are very sacred. He said listening is very important. He listens to people, rather than giving them advice. I felt his quality of presence is beautiful.

## Tuesday to Wednesday, 10-11 March – Ballygriffin

I went to Simon and met Teresa and David out near the corner. David had slept out the night before and his face was cut. His hat was all dirt from sleeping on the ground. His leg was sore. Teresa later told us he had been mugged in town one night. His leg needed dressing and she said she tore up old T-shirts and wrapped them around his leg. It reminded me of the *Gospel* story, i.e., Samaritan. Teresa had heard before, 'being her own good Samaritan to Teresa', and now she could be that for David. Perhaps there was a part of her response from her need, too, to cure him and that was

O.K., fix him up / take care of him. I invited the two of them to come with us to Ballygriffin for two nice quiet days. David said he would, but needed to get a shave in the bus office toilet! Teresa said she would go if David went.

David said, "Jesus ate with the poor", when he was having his dinner with us yesterday evening. David told us that he was 18 years in prison, through drink mainly. He hates doing things out of obligation, as he used to do the opposite at home, when he was made do something. David talked about committing suicide a few times. Rosetta sensed David's need for space last night.

Both David and Teresa spoke about the centre they were in. Teresa said she began drinking four years ago in 1994 when her mother, her father, aunt, her son aged 4, all died. She never drank before that, she said. She said she originally came from the country, where they had a big farm, pub, horses and the lot. They later moved to another area. Her mother drank. She was very close to her father. When she had the baby, she said that her Dad was there, holding her hand, and waiting for the whole birth to take place.

David also said he sleeps in Fitzgerald's Park, because it is a safe place. He got a spike through his leg recently, as he tried to climb over the railing and go into the park to sleep there one night. I was touched by the way Teresa cared for his leg. She dressed it and I felt she was doing it out of her love. Another night, David was afraid to climb the bars, in case he would fall into the river. All the gates are locked at night in the park. The caretakers know David and look after him, Teresa said. Teresa said she can never sleep if David is out.

David said he only wishes three things in life: 1) peace; 2) happiness; 3) love. He said he has the last two with herself beside him there now, referring to Teresa. Teresa and David went for walks to the village near Ballygriffin and across the fields. They walked hand-in-hand a lot of the time. It was lovely to see that they were 'happy' for now.

On our way home from Ballygriffin, Teresa said she slept out for six nights with David, under a bridge. She is four or five months pregnant. He did not wish her to do that, but she chose to do it. She woke up one night, she said, at 1.30 a.m. and went out of the B & B where she was staying, in order to look for David.

I saw Lydia on the South Mall later, sitting near the Imperial Hotel drinking out of a bottle. Rosetta put it well when she said, "The baby needs her bottle".

Later on in the day, I saw Chloe Duner. I said, "Hello, Chloe". She came over and talked and talked. Chloe runs a well-known brothel in Cork. She had been to Spain to see her family. She said that was not her home in Cork. Her home was in Mississippi. She was delighted with Rosetta's card and said she showed it to her son. She has it in a safe. I could hear her great reverence for the card and the sentiments on it. She asked Rosetta if she was thinking of her when she was doing it. She said, "Yes, I did it especially for you". Chloe talked a lot about street-men going over to her and asking her for money. Mark Salim came over and she gave him £5. She said they know she has money, as they see her business is thriving. She said, "I could make £400 in a night". When I asked her what time she goes out, she said 8.30 p.m. and finished at 11.30p.m. She's in bed at 12.00 midnight, she said and gets up at 11.30 a.m. During the day, she is bored, she said.

## Friday, 13 March

Today, we went to Simon at 10.05 a.m. We met Mel Lahive, as he calls himself, and Ursula, sitting on a window drinking a bottle between them. *Cream Sherry* was written on the bottle. They had every second 'slug' at it, until it was finished. Mel then began to drink a can. Ursula said she wants to give up drink. Mel drinks first and then she does. Mel is a permanent resident of the Simon. He came in last night, then went out again and slept rough for the night. Ursula bought Mel or 'James Bond' as she calls him, a mug with a picture of a man drinking a pint on it, the map of Ireland on the other side of it, and written on another part of it was 'May you never be poor in misfortune, may you have many blessings and few enemies'. I forget the rest! That is O.K. Ursula got a lovely hot mug of soup for Mel from the Simon. "He slept out last night", she said. I noticed she could wait and wait and wait and not get impatient, until Mel was ready to move. He kept talking and talking. I did not get some of his sentences, but Ursula could sit there and *be with him* and perhaps understand everything he was saying. Love has its own unique form of communication. I would hear St. Paul's words, 'Love is patient, is kind', being lived out here on the side of the street. I could, at one stage, experience such oneness with Rosetta, Ursula and Mel, that I sensed in a very real way the *presence* of their Maker. It was awesome. A *sacred experience*, of *being with*, in the *now*.

## Wednesday, 18 March

I went to Simon. Samantha Caden was waiting for me. I met Laura Sage regarding people going to Ballygriffin, as Declan had a week off. No-one else wished to go. That was O.K. Samantha came with us. She did not speak going down much. In the car, before we met Rosetta, she said she doesn't cry, because it would be too much for her. She has got hardened / tough outside, but a lovely gentle person lives in her. She meditated with us and used the meditation stool for part of the meditation. She then sat on the chair. Samantha is 27 years old. She has dark jet-black hair, with some brown streaks through it. She is very pale. She enjoyed her lunch. It was delicious.

We went to nature then until 5.00 p.m. I sat at the back of the house, where the new dining-room is. A bird sang one note. I heard *now* in his note – the nowness of what is – the newness of each note, each now. It was never there before, nor never will come again. I moved up to where the sun shone later and could be with the bird. A thorn stuck into my head at the back and I realised it was saying that my *crown of thorns* is when my intellect / ego takes over, the thorns of my mind / intellect press hard on me, when I'm not *connected* to my inner being. I saw a lovely white blossom in front of me – life is here, too – the bird brimmed over with life. The sun was life. I meditated. I sensed deep peace. I meditated with Rosetta and Samantha. We had tea.

Samantha is very vulnerable. She spoke briefly about being put into care, at a couple of weeks old. She did not wish to speak much of that. When she was two weeks old, she went into care and was there until she was 6 years old. Her father took her out, when she was 6. She said she hated her mother. How could she love her, she said. "She abandoned me. If she died, I would not need to care at all but she didn't die. She lived and disowned me". I could be with Samantha when she was sharing her sacred history at tea. Samantha spoke about her boyfriend, Donnacha. It was love at first sight, she said. They hope to get married in 11 months. She would like to save and get a nice place. She would not like to have children and be in the Simon Community. Later, when they would grow up, she said they could say their mother was homeless. She would not like that. She does not sleep well.

Samantha Caden's father beat her, she said, and one day the neighbours heard her screaming and called the Gardaí. She used to go out her bedroom window at 6 years of age and chase around the street and go back again without being found out. She went on the streets at 17 years of age and was there almost since. She loved it in England. Four of them used go around together. There was a great bond formed between them, she said.

When Rosetta asked her what name was she called at home, she said, "I had no name". She told us she had 20 dogs protecting her in Sweden: Rottweiler, Doberman, Alsatian. She had 96 rats. She bred them. Rats breed every four weeks. A man asked her once to take a rat out of his caravan. She had 97 rats then, as the rat from the caravan 'walked home' with her and was made feel very welcome by the 96 others! As she said, "He was welcome into the family". I could hear her own story in all this. She said rats are loners. They need love and care. She had great feeling for children who were beaten – she said that she had been there and knew they were screaming for help / love. Samantha had a great love for animals – there are many St. Francis walking around in the gentleness of these street-people. It was like, at times, as if she were using the animals to recreate what the ideal family ought to be like – one big happy family – something she never knew herself. Samantha seems to be very angry, but I could see the beauty of her soul shine through her lovely face.

## Thursday, 19 March

Josephine called here around 9.45 a.m. It was lovely to see Josephine, but I sensed deep frustration and anger coming up in me, because I had to go away again. Each time Josephine calls in, I am not available to have a chat with her. I was going to the Simon today when she called and also I was on my way out the last day she called. What do I do? I was disappointed today and feel now, what is it all about? I asked her to give me a ring when she would be calling again, if she could and I would contact her about when I could meet her, if the day she chose did not work out for me.

She is a lovely lady and this month, two years ago, she was in Ballygriffin with Jack and Mark. She did not drink since. She has her children back with her. She said she could go to Ballygriffin for a day, as Jack would mind the baby. Her other two children are lovely. They, or one, had been abused by an uncle and, as far as I remember, his girlfriend, too, when they were doing baby-sitting for Josephine.

Noel, who works in Simon, sat down and we chatted to him. We spoke about taking the people to Ballygriffin and that we live this contemplative way of life ourselves there and invite the people to join us for meditation, nature, etc. Noel looked tired, as he said he had been at a wedding in Donegal. He was away for five days.

Rosetta said, "Hello" to a man, Matt, who came over and chatted with her for a while. He sat later and Rosetta introduced me to him. He said that he worked and worked in a centre. He was in the kitchen and worked as a night-watch man there, too. Matt is 35 years old and said he hopes to get his act together and wished, too, that things would work out for him soon. He left the centre five weeks ago and is two weeks in Simon. He stayed for three weeks with a family in Kilkenny. He said he likes to move around. He does not know how he stayed two and a half years in the centre. He said he made great friends there and enjoyed it, too. What I heard was that it gave him a great chance to live childhood dependency and that was great, as he may be able to reach to adolescent stage more readily now. I could hear he lived that, too, partly when he lived in Manchester, Germany and Holland. He is a fine person. I could identify with him in the overwork. He said he is a loner, but finds it hard to stay with himself. I could hear his presence and felt that it awakened me to my own, too. I could hear the small child living in him, and needing to be seen and heard, when he was in the centre. I could hear myself in him, too. It brought up a lot for me.

### Friday, 20 March

We met Christy. His family keep an eye on him. He has asthma. He had come out of hospital after two weeks. He said he got a tape from one of the counsellors on meditation and he listens to it, then meditates and reads the A.A. books and said he prays a lot since. He says the serenity prayer and finds the meditation very good. He said it calms him down. He said he does not want to drink again. He made a fool of himself. He sees this in the other people when they come into the Simon Community, having taken a lot of drink. He said he would like to go to Ballygriffin, and there and then when he saw Declan he said he'd give him his name. He did.

### Saturday, 21 March

I met Louise. Louise has two children. She had three children. One died as a baby. One girl, aged 4 years old, has kidney trouble and the boy who died, aged 2, had chronic asthma. Louise does business on the street also. A man walked with her and I asked her if he were the children's Dad and she said, "No". I feel he could be the pimp. I'm not sure. She got married after her baby's death. Most of her family would have been in the business of prostitution on the street at one time or another. I'm not sure if they are still in it. I invited Louise to Ballygriffin for a day. She looks like a person that it would do good. She said she would like that. I asked her to leave a message in the Convent regarding when she could go and I'd talk to her again about it, if a day came up and she was meant to go.

## Tuesday, 24 March – Ballygriffin

I went to Simon at 10.31 a.m. Morgan was waiting for me since 9.45 a.m. I was a long time – almost 20 to 25 minutes before I could find Declan. That was O.K. I asked George if he would like to go to Ballygriffin. He said was there room! I said, "Yes". Declan said Abel would like to go, too. Augustine did not come in and Samantha was gone. The four of us left around 11.00 a.m.

Morgan has diabetes and asthma. Abel was a business man and feels the terrible effect of being labelled 'an alcoholic' – getting bank loans, etc. George feels it being in Simon, and hopes to get a job. Abel said his father died when he was 12 years old. At 17, he had huge responsibilities. His mother had angina and he often had to take her off the street, as she would have fallen in an attack. I was happy to hear how Abel and George were living the Simon experience. When they fight what is, there is tension – when they accept what is, there is peace. "I change most quickly when I accept myself without any change", I said. I was conscious the first night of George and Abel being negative about the place: 1) it is too quiet; 2) no T.V.; 3) Abel said a man coming off drink needs a flat and T.V. to keep him going; 4) "This quiet bores me"; 5) nothing to do. Today, he said one could not do it week after week. Abel said today he slept and felt the peacefulness of it all. He looked better, I felt. I was in awe at my own solidity in the midst of all this and commended them both for their truthfulness and openness last night. Their truth touched me and awakened me to my truth. If they trigger hurt in me, they are my gift, because I know I have work to do then, if I feel hurt.

## Thursday, 26 March

I felt for Abel and George last night, as they went back to Simon. I was amazed Abel was only in his 30s. I was delighted Rosetta mentioned to Abel about a further meeting with him, and that perhaps they could have a chat when she would go again to Simon. Abel needs *support* very much. He mentioned the word 'support' many times.

## Friday, 11 August – Feast of St. Clare

I went into the Simon Community yesterday and I got a deep sense of reverence – the sacredness and the awesomeness of being there was nearly too much for me. The more I hear my own deep woundedness, the more humbling an experience it is to go in there. I sensed a deep unworthiness in me to be there. I felt, at times, that it was too much. When I am open to allowing the people to accompany me, it is great – I hear it then as 'we are companions on the journey'.

I was happy to meet Jerry and to see how well he looked. Matt sat on the chair near me when Jerry went away. He said he was nearly dead from alcohol. His face was badly bruised and he had stitches on his ear and lip. He said he had an 8 year old son. He himself had great devotion to St. Clare and he said, "I did not know that it was St. Clare's feast day, but I'll go to Mass today now". I asked him if he knew where the Poor Clare Convent was and he said, "No", so I explained where it was. I told him a bit about St. Clare and how she opted for a life of poverty and founded the Poor Clares – *poor*, I hear. I was telling him about the life – they live in great poverty, have little of the material things of life, pray and depend on the people for food. They have never been short yet, I believe. It struck me that could it be possible to have a meditation community out of which energy the street-people could be accompanied. The Simon Community depend on the generosity of others, for food etc. Why could not this type of community follow that pattern, too, if they dare accompany these sacred souls? Matt said he had great devotion, too, to St. Joseph. He prays to him, too, he said.

I met a man called, I think he said his name was Steve. He said he had been a sinner, but was on the way back. He asked me if I were a nun and I said, "Yes". He said he would like to go to Calcutta to help there – to talk to the people, not wash floors or ware, though he would respect the people who did that. He said he would love to help people. He said he loved Mother Teresa. I felt he may not have realised she was dead. I let him be.

### Wednesday to Thursday, 23-24 August

James Ballard came over to peel the potatoes then and he was very quiet. I asked him if he was interested in meditation and he said, "What kind?". He noticed we use a mantra – 'Má – Rá – Ná – Thá'. He said he does his own – he does breathing exercises. He did Buddhist meditation in Holland, when he was there. He told me about the *Tibetan Book of Living & Dying* then. He said that it said in that book, 'when people meditate enough they can experience what the dead experience – total peace in this life before they die at all'.

### Thursday, 3 September

We went to Simon at 11.20 a.m. and met John Gabie inside the door. He looked very down. Inside is a beautiful human being but, outside, he looked a wreck. He seemed worn out. I could *be* there. I felt at times, he had no mind to talk. I had a word with John Gabie, who said he had a bad cold.

## Tuesday, 8 September

I noticed many street-people today huddled together, under shelters, so that they would not get wet in the heavy rain that fell today. They were drinking alcohol to help them cope and keep warm, too. One lady said one day, "I love the rain tapping on my window at night, when I'm lucky enough to have a bed. It is company. The wind, too, is my friend. It, too, keeps me company, when I hear it blowing outside". Nature, for the street-people, too, can be an unfailing fountain of inspiration. The *GOOD NEWS* that is *always* coming from *NATURE* arrives out of *SILENCE*. Many a street-person, to calm their mind, would go for a walk at dawn in the park, or watch the dew on the rose in a garden. They lie on the ground and gaze up into the sky and let their minds expand into its spaciousness. They can stand by a stream and mingle the mind with its flow, becoming one with its ceaseless sound. They can sit by a waterfall and let its healing laughter purify their spirit. One, too, can walk on a beach and take the sea wind full and sweet against one's face. I notice street-people can celebrate and use the beauty of moonlight to poise the mind. One can sit by a lake or in a garden and, breathing quietly, let the mind fall *SILENT*, as the moon comes up majestically and slowly in the cloudless sky. They are, at times, it seems, more alert for any sign of beauty or grace, than many so-called 'respectable' people in the rat-race of life. Some do become masters and mistresses of their own bliss. They move out of society to learn to 'be myself', as some so very wisely say. They can notice (and hear the energy of) a small flower growing in the crack of a cement pavement. Everything – a smile, a face in the street, a lovely dress in a shop window, the way the sun lights up a room and the raindrop on the window – can be used as an invitation to meditation. Meditation is an art. Music can be used (which helps mostly to exalt you) to open your heart and mind. All is a great gift, not to be taken ever for granted.

## Tuesday, 15 September

I went to Simon with Rosetta. We arrived there at 11.45 am. Jerry waved out to me from the kitchen. I went in to say "Hello" to him then. I asked him how he was and he said very good now lately. He said he was in staying in Simon again for the past week. I said, "What has helped you lately to feel better, Jerry?". He said, "Friends" – people have been good to him. I said he looked more relaxed.

## Wednesday, 16 September

Simon was ready to go to Ballygriffin and he said Michael Baily would like to go also. That was great. Simon was very happy to be going to Ballygriffin, he said. It was lovely to be in Ballygriffin. I'm writing this on *Friday morning*. It was lovely to meditate in Ballygriffin again. The deep silence moved me – I heard now that there are deeper and deeper levels of *silence*. I sensed it was the deepest silence I ever heard in a group there, too. It was awesome. I sensed a regenerating of good energy. Without saying a word, that was *power-full*. Rosetta mentioned during the week *"Holiness is a great power in the world"* – I could hear this in the meditation experience and later on. I felt myself in a kind of *stunned* silence, at times, too, that day there. Simon talked a lot. Am I like that, too, at times? I could hear him getting a bit of a buzz out of the meditation and that was O.K. I can't remember much of what was said. I felt drawn to a tree which was spread out like an umbrella. It began to rain and I went in under its branches. They spread out over me like an umbrella. As I sat there, straight in front of me on the branch was a leaf broken in about four places – but one place was more broken than the others – there was a big piece missing out of the leaf. Over this yellow broken leaf spread very gently a lovely green leaf gently touching the broken leaf. Under it, too, was another green leaf resting on a yellow leaf also and barely touching the broken leaf. I notice the broken part was not touched at all by the green leaves – it was allowed to be broken, but was all being *held* in reverence by the green leaves. I could hear the green leaves reflecting my Being, holding all *gently* in its own reverence. It was being with the brokenness, without smothering it but allowing it to *be*. When I'm intoxicated by my deep experience of being – I can smother myself. My positive sensibilities don't allow me space to be. I miss my Being. My Being is – is never uncomfortable, but always is in its gentleness and patience. I experienced in Ballygriffin out in nature how awesome it is to experience being able to embrace my own woundedness – it has to be embraced out of *deep* love.

We then had tea and again I was very moved by Michael's story about the awful place where they were in a hostel, beside people who were injecting themselves with needles. He said you had to snore when you were wide awake and be tough in the midst of these people. Also, he said there was a derelict house near by, where many stayed who were on drugs and who intimidated those who walked out of the hostel to such an extent that they had to give them money or whatever, or they may kill them. Michael also shared about the kind cab office attendant who made him tea and offered him a stool to lie on for the night. I sensed I could listen to him in deep reverence, as he shared his story. I do not remember all the details he shared. That is O.K. I'm not meant to remember them, only what comes to me. There is more gentleness in this way, as what I write then comes out of gentleness, not *trying*.

## Friday, 18 September

Craig Baka sat on the stairs. He remembered doing the meditation more than once upstairs in the pool room last year, in July or so – 1997. He said how much he liked it. He is Craig. I could place him then. He asked me when would we be doing it. I said, "After lunch". He said he was in Ballycotton last week. His father was drowned at sea, aged 30. He was 1 year old then. Craig is 22 years old now. His mother lives with her boyfriend. Craig said there were 13 of them in the family – four in his first family, as he called it – one of his sisters had a cot death. He does not bother getting to know the other nine. He suffers from epilepsy and is on three types of medication for it but, he said he still gets attacks even when he is on the medication. He has not taken his medication for a month, so he has got an average of one attack a week, he said. He has not any medication with him now. His mother 'threw him out' the day before, as he said when she was in one of her moods. He said he needs his prescription renewed. He does not eat well. He says he drinks coffee all day. He has a bad chest now and sore throat.

I sat near Simon Tannes. He looked more neglected than he was in Ballygriffin. I enjoyed a long chat with him for about an hour. He told me he was *abandoned* by his mother, and his grandparents looked after him until he was 7 years old. He was taken from them then and brought to England. He was in deep pain and hurt. He told me about taking a pint and said he had no guilt about it – but enjoyed it. I was delighted to hear that. He said he used to play cricket and chess and had a lovely wife, but lost it all. He began to panic when he heard he may only have a week left in Simon. He may get in somewhere else. He said he never could express his feelings, as he really had no one to talk to. He said he was a very private person. I told him I would be meditating upstairs with Craig, so he asked me if he could join us. The three of us went up.

*Tuesday, 22 September*

I left my room to go to the Simon Community at 11.07 a.m. I walked down by the City Hall and met a lady I knew called June. She was looking in at the apartments and I said, "Hello". I recognised her face, as she approached me. She had a daughter in the Presentation school years ago. In those days, she brought up her child with no father. The word 'illegitimate' was used then, and there was a huge stigma attached to it. The girl's mother was also without a Dad and both mother and daughter were born out of wedlock. I always felt great compassion for them. June said she had sores on her heels and they were very sore. It was like putting a needle into them, she said. She had the same rash on her left hand. She lives in a damp house in Cork and hopes to move to a better one in the same area, when they are done up better. Her only daughter's marriage broke up – her husband used beat her. She has three children – Sean (9), Jack (12) and a boy aged 18. I got a start, when she said Jack was 12 years old and she had her boy now 18 years old. Danny and Kate came to mind. I spoke to her for a while and moved on.

I took a different route today, as I crossed the bridge across from the City Hall and went down by Connolly Hall. On my way, as I gently walked down, I met Mark Salim, George, David and Liam, sitting on a wall, as I passed, when I crossed the main road. I stopped and had a chat with them. They were passing around a bottle of cider among them and under Mark's feet was what to me look like an empty bottle – flat bottle of whiskey – he even drank the last drain out of it. I could see nothing in it but there was a drop, maybe! I had not met Liam or David before.

Liam said, "You'd want to see me when I'm cleaned up!". He said he was from the North. His mother will be 70 years old tomorrow, his Dad is dead. His anniversary is on Friday, 25th. There are 10 children in the family and they each gave £100 towards the birthday. They will have Mass tomorrow night (which she booked last January, he said, as they were so booked out, she may not be able to get it booked if she waited any later) and afterwards, the family will take her to a meal and give her the rest of the money for her birthday. Liam said he would clean himself up, get a wash and shave in Simon and go down for the Mass and come away after it. He said he only came to Simon yesterday. He sat on the footpath.

I was in Simon at 11.55 a.m. I recognised Josephine, who came in with Mary a couple of weeks ago. Josephine is 22 years old. She did as far as fifth year in secondary school – left then – lived with a man for four years, has a son James, aged 2 years old. James is in foster-care. The man beat Josephine a lot over the four years, she said and she showed me some bruises that are still on her hands / arms. She left him six months ago, left all her stuff and came here. She is from Cork. She was in national school in Cork. She said she told her father one day that she was going to school no more and left. Her Mam and Dad separated. Her mother lives in Cork. She said she loved animals. She had 4 dogs and three goats. She had hamsters, guinea pigs and a chicken, too. The dog used sit on her lap and mind her when her boyfriend would beat her. I could sense how she loved the animals and she *felt loved* by them. One goat would lick her face and pull her hair, she said. She said her favourite animal was a cat. She would love to do riding lessons. Her boyfriend is now in Cork. I asked Josephine what keeps her going? She said talking to people and telling her story. She said she talks to the staff and people in Simon.

Kyle asked for Rosetta today. "She's my ally", he said.

## Friday, 25 September

William came over and chatted. He told us he slept for three months in a shed in a Kerry town with three greyhounds and a horse. He said the three greyhounds used to walk with him around the town some days. He said he loves to do the meditation. He said he does not listen to the music but starts 'Má – Rá' at the very start and goes out then when finished. William asked me if we did the meditation once a week. I said, "Yes, we do". I said when we're in there, we normally do it. He said it was one thing he never missed in a centre he was in. William asked me what time we meditated. I said later on, when we were ready. I said I'd let him know.

Later, Samson McAlweer came and sat down. He got a mug of coffee and told us his story about Amelia, a new lady he met, who worked in the residential house. She is Greek. He was very taken by her, I could gather. I could hear he was in 'an excited state', but could control it well. I said I would have a cup of coffee to celebrate, as this was a very special experience for him. I could hear it as a life-awakening experience for him and I could rejoice with him in it. I could hear that, as a young man, he needs to live his adolescence. He said later to me, that I said to him away back in his early days, that he may need to meet a girl. I had a deep sense in those days, I said that he needed to 'go mad' yet and have his fling! I sensed how shy Samson was by his body reaction the day at the table. Afterwards, having many chats with him, I sensed at times he could be escaping into Simon from himself. I sensed his depth from day one and that he had tremendous potential. Samson said since his Dad left, he put up the shutters and was 'locked in there' all those years. I could hear his pain. It is anyone's guess what way life will turn out for him. He is a lovely person and I will always be interested in hearing how he's doing in life, if I'm meant to. I asked him to keep in touch and he said he would send a postcard from where he'd be, God knows, he said. I did not feel the need to give him my address.

I had a chat with Conor Babalo who said he used to sleep in a shed. His mother threw him out. His brothers had no time for him.

Luke Fabers came over to the table earlier, when Rosetta and I were there, to ask if he could come to the retreat we do. He was coming off drugs and it would be a great help to him to do a retreat, he said. He was in his 20s. His brother died on Christmas Eve and another brother died of an overdose of heroin or ecstasy – not sure – not so long ago. Someone else died, too, belonging to him, he said.

I went out and, when I went through town, I met Ursula, Lydia and John sitting down on the steps outside the shop, *Gentleman's Quarters*! Lydia was sitting in the middle of the two of them, drinking a beer. John had his bottle of whiskey, half gone, and Ursula had a green bottle in a brown paper bag! John began to sing about being trapped. Ursula sang, too, about Mel. John asked what kind of songs I liked. I said, *"Days, The Wind beneath my Wings and The Hero"*. He sang one of Elvis' songs. I sang *Wooden Heart*, another one of Elvis' songs. They were hilarious.

Later, Ursula asked me if I would go to see Mel in prison. I said, "Would I be let in?". She said that I would. This morning, I rang the prison and the lady said when I asked for Mel, that he was in Block B. He was in bad shape, she said and was coming off drink and needed to be in there. The doctors were keeping an eye on him. I asked if I could see him. I mentioned Ursula. The lady who answered the phone said to wait a few days. She said to ring first. I said I would ring early next week some day. I left it at that. I now realise I can be with Mel in my meditation in a special way and hold all my Simon friends in my love there.


## Tuesday, 29 September

Lee Bago was sitting in the hallway. He fell on the steps of the Peace Park and broke his leg in four places. He had a plaster on it. He was very chatty and told us that his parents were very well off. There were 12 children in the family. He said his mother got compensation from accidents. He told us he left school at 14 years old. He stole biscuits and, when the teacher came in, the boys told on him. They pointed at him and said he took the biscuits. The teacher asked him to stand at the wall and he said he wouldn't but went home, not to return to school again! He spoke of the evil in the teacher who slapped them in school, on the back of the hand with the ruler. He said his parents got the teacher sacked.

Lee Bago himself ended up picking potatoes for a farmer. He is very intellectual and is very articulate. He is funny, too, and entertaining. I was deeply moved when he said he was really loved by his Mam and Dad. I sensed he *felt* that, too. His father had only one woman and they are together for 47 years. He loves his mother still and she loves him. He likes to sleep on the street and would sit during the day and make £200 a day on Pembroke Street. I wondered what he does with all the money. He sleeps on the Docks and has one eye open always as he said, "You never know who is going to attack you". He seemed to be 'hail fellow, well met' with most of the residents.

### Wednesday, 30 September

I went to the Simon Community today and Regina left me in. I went in and said, "Hello" to Ursula who was on her way out. She said she visited Mel yesterday and he was grand. I said I would be going up tomorrow morning and she said that was great. The workers went today. Ursula said she hoped to go again on Saturday. I asked her if she would like to come with me tomorrow and she said no, she'd go Saturday. It occurred to me that maybe Ursula's visit would be cut out, if he had more visits per week than the number allowed. I mentioned it to Declan that I was a bit concerned about this. He said Mel was doing great and it was a pity he could not stay in for a while, as it would give him a chance to pick up. I said I'd ring the prison again to ask about visiting, in case I'd deprive Ursula of her visit. The person who answered me said he'd put me on to the Chief's office. He said, "A spiritual visit is different and you have no problem going up – that would not be counted".

I sat near Amy Ladde. I said I was touched by her lovely gentle presence. She could hear that, I knew. She said often people would say to her, when they would see her sitting on her own, "Are you down and out?". She said they could not understand that she could be fine on her own. She said she signed herself out of the hospital.

Lee came in. He went to Blarney today for a while. He said he would come up with us today to meditate. I asked Amy if she would like to come up and she said she would. Simon looked for William, but could not find him. The four of us went into the room. Amy went away about three minutes before the *Our Father*. I said to them before we began, if they would like to go at any time, that was O.K. After the *Our Father*, Lee talked a lot.

Lee talked about his shame at going home to his father, who lives alone in the countryside. The neighbours would ask his father about him and he said they were only doing that to gossip. One saw Lee around. He said then, looking at Lee, "Oh yes, you are the man who has the drink problem". Lee felt annoyed and said, "Who told you that?". He said he got a shock and said no more. He said he is ashamed today, in case he'd meet people in town who used see him tapping and also who might have seen him drinking a lot. He said when he used to be 'steamed', he'd rob wine, a shirt, etc., from shops. He said if he were sleeping rough or in Simon, he would not tell his father. He'd say that he was on the way back from Dublin and dropped in. He told us he was in a bed-sit the size of the small space we're in now in Douglas Street for seven years, and had to get out of it. I could *feel* his pain of shame. He had tears in his eyes a lot, as he spoke. I could hear that he really loved his father, too. He can't go to his brother's house for the past 23 years and could not give his address for job correspondence either. He only met his brother's wife three times. His mother died two years ago. Lee said he worked with the monks in Mellifont for six months and it was one place where he found peace, he said. Of course, without realising it, it was his own peace being awakened within Lee.

### Thursday, 1 October

I went to the prison this morning. Gertrude asked me if she could come with me there and I said that was grand. She said she would be interested in seeing if there were people there who had no visitors and maybe she could visit them. We went to the wrong door first and rang the bell to find out that it was the supplies door! No one answered us, even though we rang the door-bell three times. We asked some people at the bus-stop to know how does a person get to the prison – even though I had been there some years ago, I had forgotten how to get there – to the main door. We eventually found it and were asked by the Garda at the gate to go to the waiting area for visitors. There the Garda on duty issued us with a visiting slip. I gave him both of our names. He wrote 'spiritual visit', on the form. We waited until we were called out and then the Garda beckoned to us to go out. It was moving to see the visitors waiting in the waiting room. A woman and her son waited. A big number of young men and young woman waited there, too.

When we went in, Mel was there waiting behind the long counter with the plastic strip of glass about 8" high on top of it. I noticed a notice on the wall was written in a few places – *No smoking. No physical contact. No foodstuffs*. I counted at least 11 Gardaí around. Mel looked very, very well and was delighted to see us. He chatted away. He said he was in a six-man cell. They are locked into the cells for the meals, 8.00 a.m. to 9.30 a.m., 12.30 p.m. to 2.00 p.m., 4.30 p.m. to 5.30 p.m. and at 7.00 p.m. for the night. They play cards and, during the day, they play football and walk around outside for air. You have to be there 12 months if you wish to go to school. You can't go to school when you're only in for a month. Ursula got a month, too, but only spent a day in Limerick prison, he said, as they must have been over-crowded. The food is good in Cork prison, he said, and he can eat now. In the Simon, he used not be able to eat at all. He'd get very sick every morning in the Simon, he said. He had no drink in the prison, only tea, since he went in, and he does not need it. He said Ursula came up on Tuesday and had drink taken and was shouting around the place. He said it was not fair to himself, as when someone is on it, or talks about it, he feels he wants it then. He asked me if Ursula is eating. He said, "I suppose she was out drinking with Molly yesterday?". Susan came up to visit with Ursula on Tuesday. Maud and Jessica were up yesterday. I told him Rosetta was asking for him specially.

Gertrude had a very caring and compassionate presence there. I sensed it in her face. It must not have been easy for her to stand all the time. Gertrude talked to him about reading. He said he could not read but hoped to go to the night classes, when he got out. He said Adam Cafferkey went there, as he could not read or write either, and now he can.

## Friday, 2 October

I met Chelsea Calcott and Marty Lagrue near the car park. Chelsea invited us up to her home. It would be lovely to go there and meditate, too, if that was possible. Perhaps we could go up on the number 3 bus some morning.

Andrew said he doesn't drink much now. He said he used drink a bottle of whiskey every day before. He said yesterday he had a bottle of vodka and 16 cans of *Carling Black Label* in the skip. What does he mean then by, "I don't drink much now"?. I could really hear he was dwelling in 'the shelter of the Most High', no matter what he said. He had not much of a notion of this, I felt. He talked non-stop almost. It would have been great if he could cry. I said, "You are a good man". I could see the tears coming into his eyes and later, when I said, "You need to take care of yourself, Andrew, you are precious", I could see his eyes fill us. He could talk and talk about Jesus, but have little or no experience of the life within himself. He went away.

## Tuesday, 6 October

John Gabie began to tell me about his early years with his family. I noticed I needed to sit on the street with him, while he was drinking whiskey, before he could talk about his wife and children. He was very sad about them and told me his wife had been drinking, when his children were young, the three of them under 7 years of age. He got custody of them and stayed with them nine months. He could stick no more, he said. He said what would I say the judge thought of him, to give him custody of three children. I said he saw a good man inside in him. He said he found meals, changing nappies, doing homework, all very tough. When he went to court, the children were taken from him. He left the court and the children said, "Dad, where are you going?". He meets Jill, now aged 22, Maisie, aged 23, and Bill, on the streets. They say, "Hello, Dad". He had tears in his eyes, when he was talking about them.

We told Declan about the International Presentation Association coming to see our ministry, as part of their Cork visit. He very kindly invited us to do everything there and said the recreation room would be available to meet the Sisters there, and do our presentation, and then they could go around to see the place and meet the people.

We met Adam. He was in the laundry. He talked a lot about teachers going into classes with briefcases and suits, and the children being afraid. He said the poor child would be terrified and later he'd leave school and beat someone up in anger and drop out. He'd go drinking then, too. He also talked about himself being so angry that he cannot achieve all he would like to. He is very intellectual. He talked in the third person about professional people giving tablets and doing no more for a person – instead of listening and talking to them. He used the words 'talk to them', several times. He is screaming to be seen, heard, *recognised* and *believed*. I said he could still do well and find his niche in life – in gentleness. He seems to blame himself for the way he is. He is in terrible pain, I feel. He knows he is stuck and, in drink, the torture of it comes at him. We stood for a long time at the laundry door listening to Adam. It was a great privilege, but would have been better if we had a seat! It was a great privilege to hear him share – even in the third person – 'they' is O.K. for now. It shows how the frightened rabbit is alive and well in Adam. He told us more about Adam than he may even have been aware of himself. He likes to talk to people, who are not in uniform. He does not like talking in the dining-room. As Rosetta said, "Some of our friends need to go on talking for a long time, while at the same time summing us up and later may share their pain or hurt. They test us".

## *Thursday, 8 October*

We went to Simon. We met John coming in the door and he had about nine stitches in his forehead. He had been sleeping out and was in for food, I suppose. He asked me at the door for that book – the *Bible*. Rosetta bought some 65p *Good News from Luke* and gave me one for John. I noticed later I found it on a table in the dining-room – the one near the wall, where George was sitting. John came over for it later. Then I saw it in the front hall, when we were going to meditate. I was tempted to take it away, but said, "No, I could leave it". My feelings were: "Oh, he has no *meas* on this – take it and give it to someone who will". I could let it be.

I sat near Fergus Fay, when I had the cup of tea. He said he spent 11 years in England. He used to love the meat of the cow's foot and said it was like jelly, also he loved to drink the soup. The hat he wore was speaking volumes! He had a black eye today. The hat was a real cry for attention – one did look a second time at him.

We met Fiona Fors, who is doing social studies in U.C.C. and is on her third year there, I think. She was in Simon last year, too.

Sue told us about Bruce Ard who died. She was upset that a hospital did not take him in. He was killed on the Mallow road by a lorry. Declan went to identify him. He had gone four times to the river. He used to eat the food off the floor in Simon, as he was so unwell.

## *Tuesday 13 October*

Cillian showed me his photo on the paper with a Government Minister – under it was 'homeless Cillian from the Cork Simon Community'. I don't know for sure, but I have a feeling she may have visited them. Cillian was giving out the pay, he said. He said he had a phone call from home and whoever rang said that they were all disgraced, because of what was on about him. He said his children were crying when they came in from work.

Today, it struck me as one reason why *Jesus* spent so much / most of his life with the poor, because 1) it enabled him to go beyond self-consciousness – transcend it; and 2) why he spent so much time communing with the Father – source of life – was so that, in being rooted in this source of life, he was free to leave all self-consciousness, and be assured that he and the *Father* are *one* – he could not then have any fear. Perfect love casts out all fear. He was at one with source of his own life. This also enabled him to suffer persecution – but he had to let his humanity take its course, too.

*Wednesday, 14 October*

I went to collect Chelsea and Marty. Chelsea was out at the door. It was great, as it was hard to see the door numbers. She invited me in. Marty offered me a cup of tea, so I had boiling water. Chelsea showed me around their house. It was like a bungalow, she said. It was a ground floor flat. I was amazed how big it was. I noticed they had the child's bed in the biggest of the two bedrooms. Sean, her son, had been up one day last week and he was due up again next weekend to stay. She had the room very nicely laid out with toys, etc. Nice lace curtains hung on the window, which she got from her mother, she said. She was meant to take another old pair her mother had, but took this new pair instead. She had a plaque inside the door which read: 'My home is small, no mansion of a millionaire, but there is *room* for love and *room* for friends, and that is all I care'. She also had the plaque of *Desiderata* that I gave her one year for her birthday. She got great help from the Welfare, she said, and from St. Vincent de Paul, too. She had a lovely suite of furniture she got in Nano's shop. Her cooker had only two rings working. The back patch of grass was overrun with weeds and the front garden was very overgrown. The environment outside the house was quite poor, in the sense of there being graffiti around, too, etc. It was a stark contrast to the warmth of the home inside. So with our inner being – the outside behaviour may be full of graffiti, weeds, paper thrown all over the place, but inside is beautiful.

It was about 10.50 a.m. when we set out to go to Ballygriffin. We went up to Knocknaheeny and out the same way to Blarney as usual. I went to the shop. We were in Ballygriffin at about 12.20 p.m. We meditated and had lunch. It was a most beautiful sunny day. I sat at the back of Chalet B and stayed with the song of the bird, but I could hear the crow much louder than the bird – the crow drowned out the sweet note of the bird. The ego drowns out my inner being, too, at times. I meditated. I felt myself drawn back to the bird's song again and as I stayed with it, I could hear the sweet music reflecting the *sweet music* of my own being. I remembered the page on the 'music of being'. My humanity is called on to reflect my being – that is what reflective living is about; 'recollect' – this is to collect again the parts of me that are gone everywhere – my humanity is re-collected by my being. These words 'reflect' and 'recollect' are so glibly used and we can give them lip service too often. I now realize why I felt the saying of Nano Nagle, 'The Almighty chooses the weakest *means* to bring about His / Her works', jumped out at me from all the others. It spoke of *my being*, being mediated through my humanity – the Divine revealed through the human, the

Incarnation (Christmas) – nothing could be *weaker* than my humanity. I really hear this now in my feelings and skin.

We meditated again at 6.00 p.m. I felt it was better leave Chelsea and Marty for a while in the afternoon. I did not feel Chelsea had the same need for talking as she used to have in the past. She was in good form. I saw Marty with his arm around her once, as they walked over the path. It is hard to know how he really is – I could see woundedness attracted to woundedness. They are O.K. for now and doing what they can, I feel. Marty said he would like to stay for a while in Ballygriffin – he liked it so much. They went for a rest after their walk. It was a very good day. I felt very energized after the day, as I do always when I spend time in nature. I could start a day's work, I felt so alive, when I come in.

## Thursday, 15 October

Noel Lam sat down near me and said how upset he was about Steve Renn. He grew up with him. He said Steve's father was working as a foreman in a mill. His sister was very upset. Noel told me he was sleeping out in the woods for about a year now, in a tent. He comes in every day for food. He said a fox comes up to him and he puts out food for him. He said the fox has now built up TRUST in him. I could hear how pleased he was that someone / something could TRUST him. The fox awakened him to his own trust. There are rabbits and birds there, too. He talked about his car accident when he was brain-damaged and got epilepsy. He said he has cancer and had a test lately to see if he was O.K. Noel is 45 years old, he said. He said he never gets a cold. He is afraid of the results, he said.

Craig Baitson asked me if he could talk to me. I said, "Fine". He talked before to me. He is very well-dressed. He talked about a home problem regarding who gets the house, etc. He said he wanted to go on for the priesthood, but thought he was too old. He said he had a lot of guilt, because he had so many talents, etc., and let them go. I told him that he had a lovely presence and that his presence was his greatest gift. I said I felt he was a bit hard on himself. He said someone else told him that, too. He told me about all the good things he did in life – he seemed to *do* good to *feel* good. He gave up everything for some project he was pursuing – he is off drink for 14½ years and really believes that is due to the Lord's intervention. He said that a person can't go on the road of sobriety without experiencing the spiritual in their lives. He said it very beautifully. I need to hear it again exactly as he said it. He said he used go to the church and say the *Rosary*. He has some ear trouble. It's like a constant buzz. When there is noise, it's not too bad, he said but in silence, it gets worse. I asked him about the meditation and he said he did it, but the buzz was there. He said he heard that the meditation is a great way for some people. Some found it a marvellous help, he said. I was aghast when Craig Baitson said what his favourite psalms were. One was *Psalm 90*, the one I was in awe at lately. He quoted line 1 for me: 'He who *dwells* in the shelter of the Most High, and abides in the shades of the Almighty says to the Lord, "My refuge, my creator, in whom I trust"'. I was speechless when he quoted this. He said he used read the *Bible*, but later gave away his *Bibles*. He said his being off drink was as much a miracle as the miracle at Cana!

I am in awe at the *dignity* I have seen today in the people I met. They are *made out of love*.

## Friday, 16 October

Lee sat near me and said he slept on the docks last night in torrential rain. He said he likes female company outside. They sleep near him. He said there are lots of women sleeping out at night aged between 20 and 25 years old. He said he bought food for the dog. I think the dog is Julie's. When the dog would not eat the food, he threw 20 single pound coins into the river, he was so fed up! He was out on the street looking for money at 4.00 a.m., he said. He had about £15 left in his inside pocket. He put it all out on the floor to count it. He began to sing *My Lovely Rose of Clare*.

I said, "Hello", to another man, Fabian Pards is his name. He sat opposite me first across the hall and later came over. He said he spoke to the other sister (Rosetta). He does not talk to everyone, he said. He told me then he was in a centre for six weeks, I think. He said it was O.K. when he was there and it helped him get a bit sorted out. He told me he was staying in the Simon a while ago and only comes in now for a break and space for himself. He said his girlfriend is three months pregnant. She suffers from epilepsy. He worries about her a lot, he said and also his own gambling and drink problem. He said he takes space to find out who he is. He is worried he will meet some of the crowd (maybe he owed money to, as far as I could see), as he said, "You know what they could do?". He used be with this crowd before and is afraid he will fall back into it again, as he gets the temptation, at times, too. I could hear how genuine he is in his search for his own real life. He said he could not sleep last night, as his girlfriend was sick and he said someone had to make the *Lemsip*. He said he also spoke to Laura Sage and even that time today as Laura passed by, she said, "Hello, *Fabian*, how are you?". I could hear he was happy in that caring environment – *no* judgement. Someone mentioned lately in Ballygriffin that the Simon Community was the only place where a person isn't judged. Fabian was happy he could just *be*. He said if it gets rough with the residents there, he can go outside the gate. I told him he looked relaxed and he said he writes down all the positive things and does not concentrate on the negative. He feels he has wasted 14 years since he was 16 years old – he is about 30 now. He could hear, "You need to be lost before you can be found". "You are a gentle man", I said. I could be 100% with him.

I feel so humble, when these beautiful people share their sacred history with me. I thanked him for sharing his sacred history with me. I could see he waited a long time before he opened up. It was like hearing confession – it was awesome, the energy of trust that comes alive between two human beings when one can be open, truthful, gentle and humble with another. When I sit in front of another human being in my *love*, my energy increases. I had that experience today. It was a life-awakening experience for me, too. He awakened me to my own trust.

## Tuesday, 20 October

We went into Simon. We arranged six chairs in a circle. Moss was washing the floor and David was sweeping it – he was already washing the landing when we went in. I felt Declan asked them to do a bit of a clean-up. The five Sisters had arrived through the dining-room. Sister Ann Coffey came to let us know they were there. After welcoming them, we proceeded to the recreation room. We met Declan. When we went in to the room and were seated, someone had added a chair or two to the circle since we set them out earlier! That was O.K. Rosetta very gently went through the introductory details and presented each Sister with a booklet outlining briefly our ministry. She then spoke about our contemplative stance. I spoke of the street-scene and Simon Community and what we do in these two areas. Rosetta went on to talk about Ballygriffin, Owenahincha, Declan, co-workers and that, as there was not enough time to cover everything, the Sisters may wish to read the remainder of the booklet in their own time. We both quoted from our respective foundresses. We moved towards the meditation room and sat in silence for a moment or two. It was nice to feel the sense of solidarity with these people – we are all united in the silence – our deepest form of communicating. We moved among the residents then and they were so gracious to the visitors. We introduced them, as we met them. I sensed a real bond with the residents today. It was due, as Rosetta said, to the relationship we had built up with them over time, that they were so gracious to *our* visitors. That was very moving.

The second group came around 11.15 a.m. or so. We welcomed them and proceeded upstairs. We did our presentation and tour. I felt Susan heard us. She is the second Indian Sister to hear this way of life and what it is about. She could hear the value of the contemplative dimension and said on her way down, about a priest in India who fed and clothed the hungry. He was asked by the people to tell them about his God. Susan said this is what people are looking for, the spiritual food. Later, as I shared more with her, I could hear how she valued the contemplative dimension of our ministry. I was so happy they, too, interacted so well with the residents. We meditated.

Later, Joss, a relation of David's, sat opposite me. He is in a care house and is a permanent resident. He said he is old – he will be 65 years old at Christmas – he looks 85! He said he would love to go to Ballygriffin with us sometime for a few days. He said he could listen for hours to the birds and look up at the stars. He said he loves the stars and looks out his window at night at them. He said they are the lights of heaven – they remind him of heaven, how beautiful. He said he loves 'the man above' and he prays. He keeps him going. He said he is a Catholic. He has not seen his wife for 40 years – does not know whether she is dead or alive! He has two sons, one in Barcelona and the other in India. They write and he writes to them, but he was sorry they did not come to see him this summer. They did come every other year. There are six of them in the care house. Joss reared his own sons. He was put into an industrial school at 8 years of age and left there till he was 16. He was in the band there and played the drums. He then went to Artane, where he went to another reformatory industrial school and was in that band, too. He often played with them in Croke Park. I was very moved by the way he *always* gave Jim a light of his lighter to light up his cigarette – which went out very often! Joss said, "Anytime, come over", to Jim. He had infinite patience. He said he taught music in a School of Music. His favourite music is opera. He loves the song, *Catarin*. He said it is very hard to sing it. *Because* is another one he likes. There are / were 21 in Joss's family. I knew one of his sisters. She drank an awful lot. There are 10 of his family dead and 11 alive. He does not have anything to do with them. He said his father was taken out of the river. His mother died two years ago. He wrote words of songs. He was listening to a song on the radio, while we were in the dining-room. The song was called, *I'm All Alone*. He said, "I like that song". He said he has three pints of *Beamish* every Wednesday, Thursday, Friday and Saturday. He gets £70.50 on Wednesday. He pays £15 rent. In Ringabella last year, when he went for a holiday, they had a week free rent. He knew some musicians I knew. I told him I used to play the violin. He said he is not afraid to die at all. He said Declan was a gentleman – he saved his life twice. He is 8 years in Simon.


## Thursday, 22 October

Norbert sat down and Noah, whose brother, James, is Molly's partner. They are not married, he said. He said he used drink wine on Patrick's Bridge for years and get money there. He sleeps in a garage under a canopy, and has six blankets and a quilt. He goes there at 10.00 p.m. and leaves at 6.00 a.m. He hides the blankets then before he leaves; a few times they were stolen, so he slept at his sister's. Simon people give him blankets, when they do the soup-run, if they know at 8.00 p.m. that he needs them and then they deliver them to him then. Norbert said he used to be on Patrick's Bridge, too, and they ought to have called it Norbert's Bridge, as he was so often on it! His mother passed one day and gave him money and said, "Get good clothes". He said she meant a collar and tie – he got it. He said some of his many cigarette lighters were not working. He said, "I must get a Mass said for them"! He said he got a letter from the *Reader's Digest* offering to put his name in a draw for £1 million. He said he had to find the key in the letter. He said he can't find the key of his door not to mind the key in the letter! He said if he won the million pounds, he would buy an off-licence and bar them all and lock himself in! Norbert drank the tea out of a willow-pattern jug! He said that was all he could find. Noah had a huge glass mug. He said it was the biggest he could find. I said to Noah that he was very calm and he said he could only live one day at a time.

Norbert got a new hat – purple. He said he was like a Bishop or Pope! It was waterproof. He said he was out early this morning, before the meeting at 9.30 a.m., to see if he could drain any barrels! There was nothing. He said he walks a lot. Yesterday, he wanted to get out of town and walked to Our Lady's Hospital, and then beyond *The Anglers' Rest*. He said they would get lots of free drink now when the Jazz Festival is on, as fellows would get taxis from night clubs at between 3.00 a.m. and 4.00 a.m. in the morning and leave maybe a pint after them on benches on the street. Norbert and Noah would drink these. Norbert said he is fed up of being in Simon and would like a break, so he would like to get a flat. I made him tea in the jug he liked. I noticed him again out in the hall and he opened his eyes wide several times, while we sat there. I could sense a trust building up in Norbert in himself.

Alexis Obaris, with the yellow hair, joined us and hardly drew a breath the whole time, as he was talking about his home. He is going to take them all to court to get his *rights*. He seemed very unnerved altogether. He was very upset that he had to do all the milking of cows, etc., at home and his father used to take the money and not give him anything. He had huge hurt in him, too. He reminded me of the son who left home in the *Gospel*. His Mam and Dad are dead. He owns the house but would not live on his own in it, as he said his mother's spirit would be there. His sister wants to get the house from him. He said he 'killed himself' working all the years for nothing. He spent 16 Christmases on his own. Last New Year's Day, he cried a lot on his own. He was 'the black sheep' of the family, he said. I invited him to meditate and he said, "Maybe" – I felt he was not able.

I was gone out when I heard footsteps behind me and a cough. Craig caught up with me at the lights and said was I going up along. I said yes, I was going home. He walked up with me along Oliver Plunkett Street. He stood at Princes Street and talked for about 55 minutes. I was delighted with the air, but he was like Alexis, as he hardly drew a breath. He is very articulate – but very wounded. He has been down a bit and finds his head is driving him mad because of all the business, etc. He said he has so many more problems – the emotional ones were huge and all he wants to do at times is go to bed and stay there. I said, "When I fight what is, I hurt like hell". I said to Craig he may like to come to Ballygriffin with us sometime. He said he would, but his head is so full of all this now, he can't relax. Craig said maybe his way to God or his road is one of persecution, and that might be what he is called to stay on, he said. That was a dawning for him.

## Friday, 23 October

I met Craig and asked him how he was. He said he was O.K. Later, he came over and sat beside me. Why do some people choose to sit *beside* me and others sit opposite me at a table? Why do I do this, too? He said, "I'll sit beside you there, if you don't mind". I said, "You are welcome anytime, Craig". I could *be with* him. I could be totally in awe at the inner being of another person longing for clarity. My energy always increases when I'm in this sacred journey with another, especially when I hear their deep aspiration for truth. He said he couldn't make out how a priest who received the Eucharist every day could abuse three times. I said that perhaps lots of people go to Mass out of dutiful or possessive love – to go when one is ready is different. He talked about meditation and asked if it was the way to all this. I said it was the way I found real for me, having gone through various ways in search of the real, but never discovered it or experienced it until now. I said you could experience heaven on earth!

## Wednesday, 28 October

It was lovely to meet Jerry and see how he could stay with '*doing* nothing'. There is a wonderful gentleness about Jerry.

Alexis Obaris reminded me of myself dreading his mother's anniversary. He was told his mother had died one week and one day after she had been buried. He even passed the hospital, where she had been sick every day and did not know she was inside. He said he could have brought her a bottle of lemonade. The pain of this must be huge in him. He wants to put his Mam and Dad's photo on the tombstone later. I could hear today how much I need to be in touch with my own pain to hear / be with another in their pain. A lot of what Alexis was talking about, getting back his home, etc., and making his mark in life is about 'see me, please hear the very hurt little boy in there' – the terrified little boy is living his independency well. That is good.

## Thursday, 29 October

Cameron Rolder really touched me yesterday when he said, "What are *you* looking at? Why don't *you* look at me?". I sensed I was meant to sit near him today. He told me he was going to be a teacher. He took a ruler out of his pocket. He said he was not much good at Maths, but he used play snooker instead. He learned Geometry, he said. He said, "Look and you shall see". He smiled a beautiful smile. I could hear, "Look and you shall see". When I don't look, I can't see. Maybe I don't look at another person at times, because I don't believe what I see. I'm not safe and secure enough yet in what I see in me, to really look. I could not believe it, when he said that today, "Look". I knew I was meant to sit near him, even if it was only for about 10 / 15 minutes maybe. It was fine. I mentioned about our home within us. He was taken aback and said, "Is there a home in us?". We talked about the Spirit and I said it is in everyone – not everyone sees it in another, because most people only see behaviour – no more. He really listened to this, I felt. I said, "No matter what anyone does, that inner self never changes. It is always good". He is very, very fragile.

I could sense an extraordinary energy in the room, where people who had 'gone down to the last rung in the ladder' could be so full of the spirit. I could hear this so clearly in them, but it is tragic they can't hear it themselves.

The care of Molly for the residents was beautiful. I could hear her, too, asking Rosetta if she'd like soup. She is proud of her soup. I was not seen by her today, but that is O.K. How fragile we all are. Jeanne told me later that Molly cooks all the vegetables separately first and then puts them in the soup. It is so beautiful when it is the work of her own hands. Many only see Molly drinking with her hands; few hear the love in her heart. Maybe the residents hear her goodness. There was love in warming up the bread.

John Gabie has the most beautiful blue eyes – his soul shines through them. They are dancing blue eyes. It is hard to see them with all his hair, unless one is close up to him. I was near enough to him today to see their real beauty. He asked me how long was I a nun. I said 36 years. He said he was 44 years old, but he looks 70. I said I was 53 years old. He said I looked young. He talked about *enjoying* the bottle of whiskey. He said he got free drink – people even gave him bottles at the Jazz Festival and one man gave him £15.

## Friday, 30 October

Later, a young man came in the door rather quickly and said to Rosetta, "Can I speak to you, Mam?". She said, "Yes". He sat down and began to talk to both of us. He introduced himself as Maurice Buke. He appeared to be over-anxious and said he came from England and talked about going to a hospital. He asked if there was a hospital around and Rosetta said there was the Regional. He asked how long it would take him to walk to it and Rosetta said about an hour. He had an upset in his family. He moved away shortly after that and seemed very grateful to us for listening to him.

Jasmine and Renee were there, too. Renee said that they (I presume she meant the residents) loved us coming in here. She said Declan told them about us and she asked me about what we do. I gave her a run-down on what we are about.

I sat in the chair and saw Craig Baitson and asked him how he got on. He sat down beside me again. He talked a lot about himself and his family – he has two sisters and two brothers. His mother, who had an alcohol problem, is in Kent. She was not separated from his father, he said. His sister, who lives in Yorkshire, did not let his mother home for her husband's funeral. Later, she brought her home and left her in the house on her own. She would not stay there, so she went back again to Kent. Craig said he was not great in school and, when he used come from school in the evening, he'd throw his bag on the floor and go to his room on his own. He felt so ashamed, in a small village, of his mother, running a shop and having a huge drink problem. He said he blamed her, too, for his drinking.

Craig thanked me for being there to listen and he said he felt great healing in himself through it. I said he is welcome to talk to me any time here in the Simon. I thanked him for the privilege, for his openness, truthfulness, gentleness and humility. I was in my in-depth love there with Craig and most of the day, too. It was an almost effortless day – in spite of all the trauma. I could write more pages on all we talked about, but I am almost three hours writing all this!

## Tuesday, 3 November

David said, "Sit down, Sister". I sat on the chair and later David invited me to sit on the soft chair. I did accept graciously. I could hear David needed our *full* attention, as he asked the other people to go out and bring in the groceries. Was it myself I was hearing in this?

David showed us his leg and asked us to feel the heat from it. It looked as if it was full of 'cowdung'! He said he went into the river about a week ago, when he had drink taken, and a sailor pulled him out! He showed us his hands, where he had cut them, when he wanted to commit suicide. The scars were his 'nails'. He talked about his family. David talked to me for a while. He said all people need is peace, but it is not to be found in this life, he felt. There is always something, he said to take it away from us. He does not get on with his wife – he doesn't want to be doing things all the time – when she says 'jump', you're expected to jump, etc. I sensed a common denominator in a lot of these people is that they wanted to get away from people telling them what to do – controlling them. I remember Joachim said that, too, on Friday. They probably had enough people all their lives telling them what to do – as children and maybe 'doing it to please'. It could be that their anger is not dealt with now, and they opt out.

Later, Craig came down and I said, "Hello, Craig". He asked me if I'd have a cup of tea. I said, "Yes". Later, I went in and Craig had the cup of tea made for me. I noticed he gave me a big, clean cup. I sensed very negative energy in Craig. He said he was 'up the walls' until 5.00 a.m. and it was only after that he slept. He said he had so many things in his head. It struck me that people married to these people or living with them must nearly go mad. It is not their fault. He said he only *ran* in and out to see his father, when he was alive. His father was 85 years old when he died not so long ago. No one of his family knows about his situation regarding his homosexuality. He seems to regret, and be guilty about, how he treated his

Dad. His mother is in Kent 20 years and he has never seen her. He reminds me a bit of Alexis, as he talks on, almost without taking a breath. He said, "You haven't lived at all, if you have not fallen in love"! I said, "No, you haven't". I talked to him then about not being seen in his essence as a child and that he was hurting, because he was improperly revealed to himself. He had no sense of worth in himself, did not see himself as important or of any value. A person is *always* good. Its behaviour is not. He agreed. He said he did not even go to Sunday Mass. He said he is so selfish now. He then said he does an hour a week to help A.A. people. He would give cigarettes away and have none for himself. Then he said he remembered what I said about pleasing people.

## Friday, 6 November

I felt I would like to meditate with Rosetta and others. It was lovely Jer and Sean joined us, too. It was O.K. that Sean was saying the *Hail Marys*! I saw he had his Rosary beads out. Gently, in time, he will hear there is a time, too, to say the *Rosary* – but that this half-hour upstairs is for silent meditation. He likes to call it 'prayer', as he said he does not like to call it 'meditation'. I did 20 minutes.

I was happy to celebrate Rosetta's birthday with her in Simon. She was giving birth to another aspect of her goodness. There was so much sharing and caring around that table. Sharing of food, cigarettes, smiles. Each person being so uniquely beautiful in their unique way, in expressing who each one is. It was for me a truly Eucharistic experience.

## Tuesday, 10 November

Netta came in then and sat down. I was very moved by how she could *wait*, when it was not possible to have her laundry done today. She was in touch with a lot of people, I could gather. If she had lost touch with some, she asked about them. She had a compassion for Sue and Joss and some other young people. Was she being curious about others, or did her enquiring flow from her love? When I said to Netta, "You are a beautiful lady", she graciously said, "Thanks very much, Sister".

Joss was very entertaining. He meditated later with us. Sometimes, I feel, they are meant to hear only a short input.

I remember how Julie used like the talks we did and one word touched her – 'TRUTH' – and her life changed. I wonder what is best for all. I feel that will unfold, too, without trying.

I felt great compassion for the poor dear lady. I felt at a loss to know how to help. I could put myself in her place this night. I see can I even imagine as vividly as I can, what I would be going through, if I were suffering the same pain as she is. I ask myself, "How would I feel? How would I want my friends to treat me? What would I most wish from them?". In this way, my own compassion can be released. I can also imagine Betty to be my brother or cherished friend in that same kind of painful situation. It is natural that my heart opens and compassion will come alive in me, as what more would I wish than that they would be free of their suffering. I can take the compassion released in my heart now and transfer it to Betty. My help then will be inspired more naturally. I can now direct it more easily to her, as I remember my brother or cherished friend in the same kind of painful situation. Thinking / remembering them with such love and deep compassion will help them, and can bring about the healing of whatever suffering or pain they may have gone through before, may be going through now, or may have yet to go through. Who knows? They have been instrumental in awakening my compassion, even if it is only for a second. This, in turn, will bring them benefit. They have been partly responsible for the opening of my heart and for allowing me to help Betty with my compassion. I may feel inspired, too, sometime to say it to them that they helped awaken me to my own compassion. Compassion is a powerful and miraculous energy. It blesses and heals: 1) The person who awakens compassion. Today, it is my brother; 2) The person through whom the compassion is awakened, i.e. me, today; 3) The person to whom that compassion is directed. Today, it is Betty. Evoking the power of compassion in me is not always easy. The simple ways can be the best. When we feel compassion coming up in us, it is important, if possible, not to cast it aside and attempt to get on with 'the business of living'. Apathy can set in when I don't allow myself to feel vulnerable. Could it be at times that I have my eyes closed to the terrible sufferings of those special street-friends? What is pity? Pity is built on fear. There can be condescension here, too, and even an arrogance in 'I'm better than you, anyway' and even that complacent 'I'm glad I'm not in the same boat as her'. Someone said, "When fear touches someone's suffering / pain, it becomes pity, when your love touches someone's suffering / pain, it becomes compassion".

## Friday, 13 November

We went to Simon. John Gabie was full of chat. I was amazed at their life-style, as I sat in awe at the Maker's creation in each of them. They are totally loved *as* they *are*. The more this new energy I'm experiencing is emerging to my consciousness, the more in awe of them I am. I could hold them in total reverence. I got a sense before they came, when on my own, that it must be so tough sitting in there being homeless, not having much money, etc. Then it dawned on me, that they are tremendously brave people to be able to live the emptiness this calls for. I could go on my knees before each one.

## Monday, 16 November

We went to the Simon. Martin sat down. He sounded full of anger and I felt all he could do with it was be the little 3 year old shouting at his mother. I could hear huge hurt in him and the only thing he could do was wallow in it. Everything and everyone was wrong, according to him, the system, etc. No one cared about anyone, etc. I could hear him saying through all this that he had huge self-hatred. It was a projection of his own condemnation of himself that I heard, in his condemnation of the system, etc. He was aware enough though to know he needed to look after Martin. He needs to go on wallowing for another while, I'd say. I could hear his love for his children, which was great, as that awakened him to his own at bit, I felt. His own love could not grow, I sensed, as he had it almost stifled by the negative. It was choked by the negative. I could hear his goodness was awakened by his mother, to some degree, too. She could let him be himself, I felt. He possibly could have had the same expectations of his wife and is very frustrated. His mother and father looked beautiful in the photo on their memorial cards. I was touched by Rosetta's very gentle presence with him. He was testing her out, I could hear, and when he heard the gentle presence, I felt he was encouraged to loosen up a bit. I could hear the frightened rabbit – the scared rabbit slowly emerging. It was beautiful to hear how he could express his unbeautiful truth. It touched my own unbeautiful truth at the start and I could hear now the beauty of wallowing, as this is a stage, too, of our sacred history. It was the first time I could hear wallowing as the unbeautiful truth. I was too stuck in it myself before, even to *listen* to another going through it. I hear now the wisdom of letting it live. Martin is on the road to true freedom. I could sit and say nothing, but be there in my deep love and gentle strength. He gave an odd look at me and that was O.K. He was too wounded even to receive any affirmation at all, almost. If he had asked me to go, then I felt I could go gently, otherwise it was a great privilege *to be with* Martin and Rosetta. I could gaze on the Maker's creation in him.

## Friday, 20 November

Nonie came in and she said the place was so quiet – she was not comfortable in the quiet at all. She has a lovely smile. Her son, Victor, was there, too, as he was down from Athlone for the Mass for those who died since last year. His brother, Ben, was one of those people.

I sat near three people I did not know. I asked them if it were O.K. for me to sit there and they said, "Yes". Amy Trul, Dave Deet and Joe Gralp were their names. They were from England. They came over on the boat yesterday and got the bus to Cork from Dublin. They slept in the railway station last night on pallets. Dave Deet was in the middle, they said, so he slept, as he was nice and warm! Dave is Annie's boyfriend. She got engaged to him about two months ago. I was admiring her ring, and asked her was it an engagement ring, as it had a diamond and reminded me of the traditional engagement rings. She said it was. I said, "I suppose ye'll have a big day soon", and she said, "Not for a while". Her partner died of cancer. He has a brother in Cork, she said. If she could locate him, he'd give her some money, she said. She rang, but would not like to meet his wife, she said, as she does not get on with her.

Joe Gralp's wife died of cancer also. He showed me a tiny cross he had on a chain around his neck and he said he never takes that off, even when he's in the bath. It belongs to his mother, he said. He loves fishing.

Annie said to me, "Are you a nun?". I said, "Yes, how do you know?". She said, "I know". I said could you put a word on it and she said, "Yes" but she would not tell me, then she said, "It is the way you look at me, or something like that". She said nuns in England were very good to her once. She seemed favourable towards nuns. I told them about Ballygriffin and that they would be very welcome to come with us, if they were around Ireland for a while. There was no bed in Simon for them. Dave seemed very interested in the idea of Ballygriffin; the peace, he said, he'd like. Annie said he is very quiet. They got names of other hostels from Declan. I could *be* with them.

## Tuesday, 24 November

Jessica was in swearing with Molly Gaffey and Molly said, "Stop that in front of the nun". I said, "That is O.K., Jessica. You need to express *your* feelings!". I said to Molly, "These are Jessica's *feelings* and she is more than that. She is good inside". She looked exhausted. I gave her a hug. How can they be any way civil when they seem to be *constantly* going beyond their strength? It appears to be a form of cruelty; a violence.

## Wednesday to Thursday, 25 - 26 November

Maura Pram came with us to Ballygriffin. Maura was in awe at how open she herself was to receiving that day as a gift. I could hear she was ready for it. She kept saying it was great to have this now – to have a place with others to experience the contemplative way. She said at some group she was at, it was requested that they have a contemplative group or something and she said nothing was done. I felt no one may have been called to that up to now. Also, I remember mentioning it. Nothing could be done, unless someone was called to it, I feel. Maura was full of gratitude to be invited and she said she never had a day or experience like that.

## Friday, 27 November

Jack Roshe lay his head on the table near me and I sensed deep compassion for him. Today, I remembered saying to him, "Jack, you are a good man". I put my hand, out of my love, on his shoulder. He asked me if I had any place for him to stay, as he was out for five days walking. His feet were sore. He would not get blankets until the soup-runners would go out, Mary told him. He asked me to ask for blankets for him. I asked Mary as she passed the table.

Maudie Lept came out and told me about her work then. She was a nurse, specialised in learning disabilities and later did psychiatric nursing. She was in a shelter in Wales where men over 25 could come in and drink from 10.00 a.m. to midnight. I said it was a pity that there was not a facility for that here. Maudie said she was interviewing everyone in the Shelter and she'd have two-hour sessions together with most of them. I affirmed her, and said she had a lovely presence and that her presence was her greatest gift. She said, "I must remember that!". I told her about our ministry a bit, when she told me about hers. I was very taken by her eye contact and said it to her. "I'm slowly hearing this", she said. She can put on a front at times and show another side of herself, outside, but, inside, she can repress a lot, she said. I feel she could hear a *tiny* bit about presence. I could hear how she could listen, too, so well and it must be easy for the residents to spend *two* hours with her. I could sense her empathy. I said if she'd like to do the meditation with us anytime she'd be welcome. I told her about Ballygriffin and what happens there and she said the residents do not have much space to themselves for quiet in the Shelter, so she could see the value of an experience like Ballygriffin for them. She offered the flat anytime for meditation when she wasn't there – as she did that day.

## Tuesday, 8 December

I mentioned to Declan about the Dublin Christmas card. He did not hear of it. I must show it to him. I then asked him if there were any people he knew who would get no Christmas cards. He said maybe Norbert gets none. Shaune gets some, Jack may get none, George does, Jerry Laar does – some workers send some of them cards, he said. I asked him if he'd give me a list, if he could, of those who'd get no card at Christmas. He said they'd give to some they'd know wouldn't get them and maybe would be contacts of the soup-run. He said people on the street who have no address – they would not get any, maybe. I thought of Jer, Joseph, Suzie, etc.? It has not yet come up for me to whom I will send the 20 that Mary, my niece, made for me personally. It will unfold.

## Wednesday, 9 December - Ballygriffin / Simon

Liam came along then and I invited him to go and he hopped to it. It was now 11.20 a.m. and 90 minutes since I went in. Declan left us out. Declan said to Liam to call back after Ballygriffin, to see if they could give him a bed. Liam gave a big wave out the window at Mel and Ursula near the garage. Mel made to come across the road, ignoring traffic, but we moved as the light changed. We collected Rosetta about 11.30 a.m. or so. We got our groceries. We had a lovely lunch. We meditated.

I felt Liam said a lot about himself, as he talked about others and drink and drugs, etc. He did say he took some, O.K. He is a lovely gentle person, terribly wounded by life. It was lovely he could receive the meal and ask for the boiling water. I went to nature – meditated in the rain, sitting by the river. It was *great*. I could sense the peace in the is-ness – letting the rain fall on my coat – it was / is O.K. It came to me about the people like Liam on the street sleeping out that they must be able to be a lot with what is – no wonder that there *is* so much serenity tangible in them. They don't fight the is-ness of the cold or rain. They can let it be. It's occurring to me a lot lately that is-ness is about the is-ness of everything that happens every moment of every day – not always pleasing to my feelings though. I can be with what is.

Liam slept on the way home. Liam, who was with us today, slept in a field last night. He is not 30 years of age yet. He likes to be on the move. He said he slept in 'The Vatican', travelled in France, Italy and London, too. Where will he sleep tonight? Is he out in that wind and rain I now hear?

*Thursday, 10 December*

I met Kelly. I feel he may be in the soup-run. I met him earlier in the kitchen and I said, "Hello". He asked me if I were looking forward to Christmas and I said, "When I'm in my own peace, this is Christmas for me". I said I was not interested in the material side of it at all. He said he gets caught up in the material side himself, but he then said he makes a special effort to *do* something more around Christmas. I said that is part of it alright. It is there to remind us of and get in touch with our own goodness and other people's, too, maybe. He said he was not very religious at all. I invited him to go to Ballygriffin sometime. I said when you can experience your own deep joy in giving, that is Christmas. He later peeled potatoes. I said he is a good man but he does not yet know it. He said, "I don't hurt anyone". He is a gentle man.

*Friday, 11 December*

I sensed Noel was not too happy with the people in Simon. When Mary came over to tell him it was 2.00 p.m., he was not too happy. He said he'd go in a while. She came a second time to ask him to leave. I could sense great gentleness in her, as she asked him. I said it to her later, when she sat down. She told me how badly she felt about asking him to go on such an awful day. She said, too, that when he was talking to me, she did not like disturbing him. I told Mary that it was her gentleness that touched him and he went out like a lamb. He had told me he could be very aggressive before that. Mary said she is finished her three months next week. It was the best experience she ever had, she said. I talked to her then about making the tea for Noel out of the positive energy. She could hear a lot, I felt. She could hear about expectations, frustration. She asked me again about Ballygriffin and how it can help people. I briefly told her about it. She is from Cavan.

*Monday, 14 December*

I sat in the hall and had a long chat with Kay. She showed me photos of her family 1) Her seven-month old baby had a cot death three years ago; 2) Her brother died 14 years ago. A cab knocked him down; 3) Next, her brother died one year ago. She told me about her Indian husband. He 'looked' handsome in the photos. He beat her. She said she saw the film *Not Without My Daughter*. He wanted her to go to meet his family once. He was a Muslim. She did not go.

I remembered that poor Liam called himself 'a beggar' the day we were in Ballygriffin. That moved me. In my childhood days, the term 'beggar' would be used for the lowest of the low. It was like a piece of dirt to be despised, to be cast aside. The infinite value of the person was missed.

John sat for ages talking about how much whiskey he'd drink. At times, he would mix it with brandy or vodka. There is something appealing about him. He said Linda Bere was very good to him and, while he was with her for two months, she was able to keep him off the drink. He misses her, he said. They used go to A.A. meetings and then Linda said she'd leave Simon. John began to drink then, he said, and two days later Linda broke out. He said he would like to meet her again. He said he needs to have someone to help him. He said he must get some Christmas cards to send to the children. He was paid today and said he needed to send his son a birthday card. He would put some money into it, he said. His birthday was Monday last. He said he drank Friday night and was very violent on drink and caused trouble. Declan told him, if he did that again, he would be barred for life! I feel John needs a lot of support.

He said he was very upset at the week-end. When he was thinking of the child of his who died, it made him very sad. He could not sleep, got up and kept banging his head off the wall. A worker came in and asked him if he could sit down and they could talk. He did. They told him he could be dead, if he kept doing that. He said he might be as well off. He said he is no use to anyone this way. He can't stop drinking. I said, "But John, you were able to stop for two months and maybe you could do that again sometime. Enjoy the drink while you are drinking it". He said he could enjoy two beers and it would not affect him. He said he went up the mountain in West Cork one day and drank a bottle of brandy! His wife asked him to give up the drink. His children range in age from 14 to about 8 years old, I think.

## Thursday, 24 December

We went to Simon at 12.00 midnight. We said, "Hello", to Jerry Laar and some others. Jim waxed eloquently and showed us the newsletter with comments from residents at the Conference.

Kevin Stone asked me if I was a nun. I said, "Yes". He said any woman who gives her entire life to God is something else. He said he loved Latin and Irish and asked me had I any knowledge of either. I said I knew both. I said the *Gloria* in Latin and the *Our Father*. Then we had some few words in Irish. He had a great sense of humour. He told me he had gone to visit

Mount Melleray. He liked it, listening to the monks chant and also to the English lady playing the organ.

Sean Lyre came to meditate and went again before we started!

We went to Mass and Leo was creating a stir, but he went to Mass O.K. I met Basil. His friend, Len Caffe, asked him and me to share the prayer of the faithful. Basil was to read the first half and I was to do the second three. By the time he read five, I had only one to read, when he gave me the sheet! Basil sat behind me on a table. He offered to bring my chair in to Mass for me from the hall, which I was sitting on earlier. I accepted.

Father gave a talk and Leo kept on butting in. He kept rubbing a woman's hair near him and she was annoyed, I could see. A man played the guitar and Len Caffe sang some lovely hymns. All joined in at *Silent Night* and the *Little Drummer Boy*. Jerry Laar sang *Only Your Rivers Run Free*. It was beautiful. Mary Cotes sang and then all sang together. It was great fun. They sang *Danny Boy*.

## Saturday, 26 December (St Stephen's Day)

We met John Gabie and David, his brother, in a doorway. John Gabie had a big bottle of whiskey. We chatted for a while.

We sat for a long time in the office with Mike Newar. He touched me when he said, "The homeless people have a hard time at Christmas", and he said he did not go home to Sweden to his family, as he'd like to stay in Simon instead. He would like to be a nurse and work in the Swedish Rescue Corps.

# 1999

A lady asked me how *I* got on over Christmas and I said, "It was not an easy time for me. My nephew, Danny, died during the year".

I was delighted to sit with Rosetta and Norbert, and was happy to make tea for Rosetta and Norbert. Norbert hesitated first, but when I said, "Could I have the privilege of making you a cup of tea on your birthday, Norbert?", he allowed me make it. Jonathan joined us later. I enjoyed the crack with Norbert and, when Lee brought over the three slices of Christmas cake to us, it was a lovely way of ending our little get-together with Norbert on his special day.

Lee looked well. I said it to him. I was really listening to him when he said, "You're saying *I* look good to feel good *yourself*". Perhaps this was true of me. I was unaware of it though. Thanks Lee for helping me to be more aware of what I say. I sense a huge defence here and felt he was reflecting his own pain of doing good to feel good at times. I was more aware of his reaction and could hear it, as he had told me before how very difficult it was

– almost impossible for him – to receive love. I could feel his pain in 'see me'. He is screaming to be loved. It would be nice if he could come to Ballygriffin with us. From what energy do I invite people to Ballygriffin? I need to be more aware of that.

## Monday, 18 January

Isaac Mak had said he'd show us his photos when we spoke to him later, so I felt I'd go back to see them then. They were great photos. I saw a tulip in a beer can on the mantelpiece of their squat in Galway. It reminded me of the candle in the potato, when the sisters started in North Pres. The potato was their candlestick! I was touched by the simplicity of the squat, blankets for curtains, etc. They had their own art on the wall, with their own writing, too, and anonymity being totally respected. Isaac Mak said they can't go by their real names as they need to hide these from the Gardaí. Isaac Mak is Samtex. Under his name on the wall was written 'woz ere' in this spelling. Then, there was tiny writing and he wouldn't tell me what that was! Another man drew a car – a Cadillac – this would be very classy. Six of them slept in the house or part of it. The sea was stormy, very much reflecting their inner storm, but there were lovely gentle waves, too. It is their road to freedom. Society must be an arch-enemy. I was touched by his openness. He really liked it that we admired his photos. They are such talented people. I feel they had a good sense of the 'nowness' of life, too.

Later, Fabian Pards came along and, in the middle of the conversation, Noel Lam came over to me and said I looked sad and was like 'one on the edge of the cliff'. I said, "That is what I'm like", now listening very attentively to Fabian. I said, "How ever I look outside, I feel very peaceful sitting here". Could it be that he saw a reflection of his own sadness in my face? I felt deep compassion for Fabian, and also for Noel, when he said, "No one listens to me". I could hear his deep loneliness. Rosetta invited Fabian to meditate and he came with us.

I asked a man in black clothes if I could sit near him. He said, "Grand". He had a lovely expression. The side of his head was shaved and there were some scars – he had some hair left behind his ears! He said, when I asked him what is his name, that his name was Darren Cherry. He said he was in an institution in Dublin from age 9 to 16 and learned nothing – only religion and that was no good. He learned to read and write in England later. He said he reads a lot when he's locked up, about two to three books per week – he only needs the radio and books, not T.V., and he's happy locked up! He said he was locked up from 9 to 16 years of age and he's O.K. now when he's locked up. He remembered us here last year, he said. He had to go at 2.00 p.m., as he was only in between 11.00 a.m. and 2.00 p.m. and needed to get a place to stay. He said the Welfare only pays if they get a place for €7 a night. He's on a disability allowance. He said he was in Mayo and it was very cold there, so he came here. He has to have his address changed, when he moves – he has no address now, yet to put down. I told him about Ballygriffin and he said he'd need to get himself sorted out first, *re* accommodation.

I had a great hour from 2.00 p.m. to 3.00 p.m., on my own facing the wall! 'There is nothing I shall want'. I closed my eyes and relaxed for a while during the hour. It was awesome. Today, I heard 'the deepest communication is silence'. I could be fully there in my silence. Chelsea Calcott looked in amazement. I had no need to explain anything. All was O.K. I learned that silence is the deepest form of communication with myself, and then with other people.

I remembered back in 1997 meeting Alan Cade, a street-man, who lived for eight weeks 'with myself', as he said, in the woods. These people do not need organised religion – it could kill their spirit. They can be real mystics.

## Tuesday, 19 January

I sat near Noah McAlorey and felt he was 'there' – he had an amazing presence, even though he had some drink taken. I could gaze on the Maker's creation within him. He looks a lot more shook than he did before Christmas. He said, "Jesus Christ had no home, no roof over his head, he wandered around and had disciples with him". It struck me today that, in the eyes of the world, Jesus was a total, out and out, complete failure – so many turned the opposite way, so few really heard him. It is a good sign, it struck me, when so few hear us. It is a hidden ministry – no one can see any, or very little outward signs of any such thing as results. I feel in writing this, I'm in touch with what's really real. Noah said, "Lazarus took up his bed blanket". He said that was what he had. As Rosetta said, "It was important to Noah that the man had a blanket – whatever his name was". Noah said that Jesus said, "Take up your blanket and walk". Noah McAlorey said he read *The Bible* over and over. I would like to have stayed longer with Noah.

Alexis Obaris came over and talked '90 to the dozen'! He showed me his medal and said he takes that everywhere with him. He takes Rosetta's card, too, and they stay with him and mind him. He got his poem copied upstairs and gave me his original copy, which I read and carefully put into a plastic folder in my Simon file tonight. It is sacred.

## Wednesday to Thursday, 20 - 21 January

I sat over near Norbert Taffer and I was amazed to find myself giving him my gloves. I could give them out of my deep love.

Fergus Tarrat spoke about children in boarding schools at 9 to 16 years old. He talked about himself being locked up from 9 years to 12 years. He said he was put off food a bit, when he was in the institution. They used to get some food that was like paste and he said, "You could stick up the wallpaper with it". He does not eat much, he said. I told him about Ballygriffin and he said he'd be interested sometime but needed to get himself straightened out first.

A young man came over and introduced himself as Ambrose Bassett. He lived in Dublin at one time. He said his parents did not want him anymore. He lost the use of his left arm when he was on the road, I think he said when he was thumbing. I could not hear some of what he said. He said he used write with his left hand and the teacher used slap him and make him write with his right hand and he couldn't, he said. He said they said, "It was the devil that was making you write with your left hand". When he had the accident, he had to learn to write with his right hand. He had a special gadget to do the roll-up cigarettes. He could use this with one hand. He said he could tie his shoes and do everything else O.K. He said he loves vodka and would take two bottles some or all days. He said he'd be thinking of his family and would be so sad, but the vodka eases it for the time. The ligaments in his good hand are affected more, he said, "And if that hand goes, there is another person for the river". He's in a bed-sit and came down yesterday to say thanks to Declan Calbaras for the settee.

Jack Feeny came down and sat with us. He is 21. He told us about his awful flat / girlfriend who shared it with him and about cooking on the fire. He stays in his father's house during the week and told us about the lovely meal he cooked for himself last night. His father is away during the week. He left the flat and the girl went to the North of Ireland. He spoke very well.

## Monday, 25 January

I met two secondary school pupils, Anne and Don, who were in for the day, as they were doing a project on 1) Simon Community and 2) *Big Issue* magazine. Their teacher, Susan, came later about 2.30 p.m. to collect them.

A man, Mattie Mose, was found dead in a doorway at 3.00 a.m. He was Joshua's brother, who used to be with Mary Sallower. This man was in his 30s. Molly Gaffey showed me his photo in the hall. He used not be that much in Simon, Dylan Caball said, but he used drink with him on the street, he said. He has young children, Declan Calbaras told the two students. Dylan said Joshua was on drugs and drink!

## Tuesday, 26 January ~ Ballygriffin

I did not feel too well today, so I wondered how I would get through the day. Something in me said, "There is no need to cancel it, you'll be O.K". Rory Mano was in no hurry. We collected Rosetta and went along. We ate and then meditated. Rory Mano was 'wound up'. Rory washed his clothes and some bit dried them. He was out of the Simon and in a B & B. He told us the story of the male prostitutes' quarters in Cork – he talked about boys being dropped off there from 18 years of age. Rory said he was sleeping out under some wood pallets and plastic, too. He could light a fire. Why does he choose that particular spot? He may have been on some drugs, as he seemed very tired in Ballygriffin. He talked about the positive effects of cannabis. He was in Mountjoy for three years and only came out last August. He seemed to be able to charm the governor, etc. Rory is well able to live. I was happy to see he realises how silence is an integral part of the time in Ballygriffin – even for one day. I was very happy we had the privilege of accompanying Rory during this day.

## Wednesday, 10 February

I went to Simon. I met Jeremy Malcome on the way near the City Hall Bridge. I said, "Hello" to him and asked how he was. He said he had some rum and that helped him to forget everything. Such pain being drowned. I looked at his arthritic hands. The knuckles of his left hand were like big marbles, they were so disfigured. He carried a small plastic bag, with probably most, if not all, of his worldly goods in it. I asked him if he were cold and he said he had plenty clothes on, so he did not feel it and the rum also helped. I said he had a lovely scarf, too. He wrapped this around his neck. He said he was going up to *Roches Stores*. He said he loves *Roches Stores*. He said he studied the scholars in England. I said, "You had the Gaeilge too". He said he had and I said, "Thank you for talking to me". He seemed amazed I'd thank him for that.

John Gabie said his coat was taken from his room with the medal in it and asked me if I had another for him. It came to me that children, too, can behave in this way – losing things, etc., not having much responsibility.

On reading a book, recently, I was reminded of what Noah said, "The homeless people are seen by some as invisible / untouchable".

*Thursday, 11 February*

Mary Sallower said she preferred being in the Simon to all the hostels. Joshua McAllenor was drinking a lot, she said, after his step-brother's death. One other brother was shot, one stabbed, one committed suicide (hanged himself) and this fourth now choked on his own vomit. His mother is in hospital and has not been told about Mattie who died. Mary Sallower lives in the caravan with Joshua. She is a lovely-looking girl. She looked a bit sad today, I thought. She got two rings from Joshua.

I sat near Cillian O'Carrag, who told me he was drinking for four months. He slept out a lot. He said everyone tries to help him – his daughters used give him money for flats and he'd drink it all. He said he used to send birthday cards to his wife, until she put an end to it. Sometimes, he'd ring home at 3.00 a.m. to talk to his daughters. He said he never wanted to go home and make it up. He said it would not work out. He told me he used get some person to get I.D. bank cards. He'd rob these and also rob cheque books and he'd go off – maybe to Kerry in the past, write a cheque for £300 to pay for four Aran jackets then sell them for more and make a profit on each. He said he would buy himself very posh clothes first and 'dress to kill', then go 'hoaring and touring'. He would usually only cash about seven cheques out of the cheque book, as if he kept cashing them, he may get caught! He'd then drop the cheque book into a drain or down a hole and go on to negotiate how he'd get another one! He said one day he walked through a building site with wellingtons and builder's gear on, got muck on his boots etc., went to the bank to cash a cheque for £2,000 – some building company cheque book! He then went to the bus office, changed his clothes, wellingtons, etc., and dressed in good clothes, then went to Dublin, booked into the *Gresham* for two or three nights where 'wine, women and song' followed. He said he lived it up! He then went to Galway for a few days and booked into a big hotel, lived it up and then came back to Cork with £1,000 left! He must have cashed more cheques in between! I could really hear the totally unintentional and automatic way of living he was caught up in. I felt he had no control at all over his behaviour, but there is a lovely person inside, waiting to emerge. I feel I only heard about one thousandth part of his story! I hope Cillian O'Carrag hears some day that he is much more than his behaviour. He has a soul, essence, that is always good.

Rosetta came over and Adam Cafferkey joined us. It was about a two hour session. He talked about (1) truth; (2) how he could do anything bad when he had drink taken; (3) how he'd sleep rough. He described a lady's disdainful look at him, as he was lying on the steps of a church. She was coming out from Mass with her dog. She said to the dog, "Come on, sweetie, and we'll have breakfast". She was still looking 'down at' him, he said as if he were a piece of dirt. He felt this lady, who was dressed herself in very fine clothes and even had a fine coat on the dog, may have gone to Mass to be seen, etc., but he questioned her Christianity. She seemed to have no respect for Adam. He is very aware, I felt, and highly sensitive to all energies both negative and positive in him and around him. I felt deep empathy with and compassion for Adam Cafferkey. He is doing great to be able to share all that today. He questioned was it worth going through such pain. When we face and deal with it, it can bring us to the truth of who we really are in our essence. "Jesus", he said, "died on the cross for truth. The Spirit was sent to us and doesn't judge us. We may need to wait for our spirit to be one with God's spirit, before we're fully free, when we die". He said he was not afraid to die. His sins are (1) cutting his arm and (2) drinking too much. Again, as in Cillian today, I could hear the totally unintentional and automatic way both live, as they can only live like that for now. What I heard both had in common was that they would love to be different but can't yet. They sense (especially Adam) that there are better ways to live. Adam Cafferkey has a deep aspiration for the truth. His inner being is coming alive for him, slowly but surely. I felt deeply moved a few times at his story and found it hard not to cry. It was a wonderful privilege to listen to Adam. His sharing was like confession. The more fragile and more vulnerable he allowed himself be, the more awesome it was to listen to him. He was healing slowly.

## Friday, 12 February

Rosetta came in. Jonah McAlvey came over and shook hands with us. He said, "Could I go to a room to have a chat?". I said, "Would you like to sit here instead, Jonah?". He said he would. I was afraid he'd burn my skirt with his cigarette roll-up, as when he lit it, it was hard for him to hold it in his hand! He seemed to have no power in his hand. The lighter fell, too, quite often, on the floor. He said he had migraine, so he kept his hands a lot over his eyes. I encouraged him to rest and sleep on the chair if he could. He said he needed to confess to me that he took drugs, had a slip yesterday, and took prescription drugs, too. He was quite well cleaned up. His hair was shining. Later, I felt food might be important to him, if he could eat it. It was a huge struggle for him to eat. He told me he needed to ring his girlfriend, as he is madly in love with her, he said. He said it is platonic and sex can ruin this type of relationship. He said he hates the word 'sex'. He broke up with his wife. His son will be 15 in April, he said. He said he felt sad on talking to his mother, because of how old she got. I said he might like to do something for her on Valentine's Day, Sunday. He is very sensitive.

Jack Feeny came over in the hall and thanked Jonah McAlvey for giving him some help during the week.

Cillian told me he stole a ring belonging to a woman once. He did not know she was a nun! He found it in a bathroom and was going to pawn it, as it was valuable and he'd have got a lot of money from it for drink, but he put it back, he said when he found out it belonged to a nun!

## Tuesday, 16 February

Clement O'Carren was like a small child giving out, because 'Mammy would not give me my bottle' (Laura).

Jonah McAlvey is very well up. He seemed to want to go to prison, as he found it would keep him off drugs, whereas on the streets, he would be back into them. He said he came out of prison on Wednesday and he seemed to be back on them again on Thursday. He would even have broken a window in town, he said, to get locked up. He talked about his girlfriend being so loyal to him and she'd feed him, when he was not capable of feeding himself. He'd walk her to work in the morning and home in the afternoon, he said. He has a lovely, sensitive nature and has no control over the addiction at the moment, it seems. I could see the Maker's creation in him, a beautiful person. He used the word 'shell' in relation to himself. He only saw himself as a 'shell' and nothing else.

I felt tired today. These days are maybe best, because I can leave 'me' out of it (expecting success) and be with the sacredness of the person. There is no expectation in being.

What does it mean to be aware of one's inner being, i.e., the self beyond the rational mind? It means to go beyond the ego. The ego is the external / false self, which works through the senses and reason. As long as I remain on the level of sense and reason, I remain under the control of the ego. It is only when I go beyond sense and reason that I become aware of my deeper self, that I contact the reality, the real person in me. At the same time, I begin to make contact with the reality of the people around me and the world. As long as I live on the surface of life, I see only the surface of the world around me. Only when I enter my own centre do I find the centre of the world around me. To go beyond the ego is therefore to find myself not in isolation, but in communion. It is to realise my intimate relationship with everyone and everything. From my experience in the past, I have seen so many people living on the surface of life and therefore have become isolated and alienated from themselves. I believe now, and have experience, that this prayer of the heart – meditation (Christian) leads me and has led me to the deepest reality I have known of Christian faith. Words are so inadequate to describe the awesomeness of this mystery. To enter into the deep centre of my being is to enter the consciousness of the Christus, the prayer of the Christians. It is almost too magnificent to talk about this experience. It may be described as the stream of love which flows in us constantly. This stream of love is the spirit of life. We also practise various other meditation forms, deep breathing, inner body, etc.

## Wednesday, 17 February – Ash Wednesday

I went into the office to put my raingear in. I told Laura Sage I remembered her today in prayer. I was so conscious yesterday of all she had to do, when Declan Calbaras was out, etc. What a very vulnerable situation she's in, in the Simon. She said, at times in the Simon, whether it's the new moon or what, there is an awful restlessness among the residents. This comes to them in phases, she said. Noah and George Faiss had a fight at the gate last night, she said. I could see Mel Lahive and Ursula Walk on the monitor. Mel is barred until Thursday. Ursula isn't.

Jerry Laar came along and asked Rosetta to 'push in', in the stool! His hands were filthy with mud, as if he put them into the muck, before he ate his beans on toast! He was quite comfortable sitting down near Rosetta on the stool. It said to me that he was growing in his own trust and confidence. I was happy to see it. Maybe, too, he sees we can accept him, no matter what his behaviour, *re* drugs, etc., is.

Alexis Obaris came over after a while. Alexis Obaris said he was not well with his nerves. In the space of the time, I saw Alexis Obaris had three mugs of cocoa, two sandwiches and three huge buns with jam on them. Later, Alexis Obaris talked a lot about himself and when Alex Peate said that he (Alexis) was washing himself several times and spending two hours in the bathroom doing his hair and washing himself, he said, "That is not good". I could hear Alex's real concern for Alexis Obaris. He would pick up a paper, if he saw it in the dining-room floor, pick up pieces of dust on his bedroom floor, take an hour to make his bed and have everything hanging down the

same length at each side of the bed. He shaved his eyebrows to make them
even, he said. When Alex asked him why he was washing his face five
times, he said, "Because Tanya O'Donaile's birthday is on the 5th". He
washed his hands then three times. He told Alex Peate it was to make them
soft. Alex said he needed cream for them and he said he had cream and
would give it to him. Alex said he'd need to snap out of the washing, etc.
Alexis Obaris seems to be a perfectionist and wants everything 'right'.
Alexis did not open his mouth for about three quarters of an hour. I said to
him I sensed different energy in him since he sat down. He seemed calmer.
He really listened, I felt. His big eyes were even bigger and more soulful, as
he sat there. He was totally helpless in his vulnerability. I kept reassuring
Alexis that he is a wonderful person and that regarding his goodness, no-
one could take it from him, but that he does not know it yet, i.e., that 'I am
good because I am'.

## Tuesday, 23 February - Ballygriffin

I said to Alexandra Bamidene we were privileged to have her here with us.
She said she was honoured, as it was just what she needed now. She said she
experienced peace in Ballygriffin. She questioned why she was taken on her
own. Was she so 'bad', that she needed to be on her own, she implied, I felt.

## Wednesday, 24 February - Ballygriffin

I was up early. The silence is awesome here now. I feel it in a very special
way. I'm unique in being held in reverence in that silence. The silence is a
person.

Alexandra Bamidene said that she was so happy to be here with us. I
felt, too, as did Rosetta, that it was a great privilege that she is with us. She
was very upset that someone in Cork seemed able to get at her vulnerable
spots. When she told the person she FELT like a whore, he kept throwing it
at her, she said. I talked to her about the daffodil's beauty later and how it
(the truth) was in the dark for so long and that it could not grow to such
beauty if it was not in the dark first. So, too, is her own potential, I said. Her
hurt is huge. She appears by her body language to have stuffed her pain.
Her darkness was very deep.

## Friday, 26 February

Declan later told me that Alexandra shared at the meeting *re* Ballygriffin. Declan asked her. I said it was good to ask her, as the experience of sharing this in a group could help her grow in her own self-confidence, too. I sensed here, the whole idea is that we are all partners on this journey, too.

## Tuesday, 2 March

I met five street-people at the back door, as I went out the door of the convent. Wayne Magee was there and Sean McCare, also his girlfriend, Aoife Teom, who is pregnant. He asked me for 50p for the bus. I said, "I don't have money for that". Kim Reaver and Keith Hamile were there, too. Rory Mano told Kim about Ballygriffin, she said. I said they'd be welcome to come to Ballygriffin and Wayne Magee said to the others, "You'd have to tell Declan". Rory said he was great friends with Declan. Wayne Magee was shook enough. He said he was fair enough. Rory said that we were very good to take them to Ballygriffin. "Why do ye do it?". I said, "We are better people for having met ye and our lives are enriched. The silence together is the deepest form of communication between human beings. We meditate together *to be*". Kim Reaver and Keith Hamile would like to go, too, they said, when I asked them. They come to the door, every day, for tea.

## Wednesday, 3 March

A tall man said, "Hello, Sister Catherine". I had no idea who he was. He said later had I met him before? I said, "Yes". I did not ask his name. He said to Andrew, "Sit there and talk to Sister". Andrew sat down and asked me what order I was. He said he's not able to eat at times with drink.

Next thing, William Caldwel came around at the other side – very full of drink but he did get great courage to talk. He said he stole a medal in a chapel. He was very upset about it. He said this twice and said he needed to say it to me. He said he has great time for me and he does not like to say 'Catherine', but would like to call me 'Sister'. I said either was O.K. – whatever he was happy with. He said, "At home a nun was to be 'Sister' and a priest, 'Father'". He said he was with a girl and had two children. He cried a lot and asked me if he could talk privately to me. He said, "I am an alcoholic and a drunk". His family don't want to know him, he said. He said he was with the British Army and he saw one of his brothers die. He saved another. He saw 15 people being blown to bits. He said all of this is with him for the past 25 years. He cried again. He talked a lot about this. He said he was in a mental hospital in Cork after it. He said he's a loner and likes being on his own. He wants to help Karen McAuton, he said. He said he loved Ballygriffin and would love to go again. He said, on two different occasions during his chat with me, that he 'found himself' there. He said he'd go for help. I said, "You're a good man – there's good always there in you. You are more than your drinking and your behaviour is not your best self. You're more than your behaviour". He said he was glad to talk – it was on his conscience about the medal, he said. William Caldwel shook hands twice. He had a need for tactility. William said he says 'Má – Rá – Ná – Thá. He loved the meditation.

### Tuesday, 9 March

Rosetta checked all with Declan. We moved on to Ballygriffin. Adeline is nearly 66 years. I chatted with her. She said when she was in hospital, there was no-one to identify her, she had no home, etc. We had lunch. We did meditation. I was very much aware of Adeline Bane on the way home, when she talked about the wall-flower. She liked the orchid and the camelia. I could sense her closeness to nature, as she spoke about the stars and moon. She used walk for miles along the roads at night, going from city to city. She'd not be afraid, she said – she may get drives sometimes. I could sense she must have experienced great freedom in all this. She said earlier that she had no clothes, only what she had on her. She had a lovely green coat on – black cardigan, black leg-warmers, and a green jumper. She had some jewellery, too. She had a good sense of humour. Apart from her nervous condition, she seemed happy and did not seem to worry much about anything, even though she had no home. She knew some peace in her life, she said. I was fascinated by the way she would look, not at, but through, me. I felt her eyes told me she had lived many, many lives in her 66 years. She was a learned person, I felt – had a deep gentleness, too. I sensed her free spirit within was / is alive and well. Her resilience was extraordinary. She has no one of her family left and she still goes on. She married a man from one of the islands off Norway. She is a widow now. She had a dog, too, in Mayo. Why do so many of the street-people do so much walking? Adeline said she liked Ballygriffin. She would like to bring her friend, Maud Keale, there. She does not like being on her own. "Ballygriffin is a nice place. It is a different experience to other places", she said. She would like her own home some day. She has no home now.

## Wednesday, 10 March

Karen McAuton came out. I took her hand and said, "I heard about your husband". It was Karen I could be with, as I sensed from Rosetta her concern for her children. She said she's glad her husband is dead, as he gave her 25 years of hell, raped her, beat her, threw bottles at her, etc. Leslie Sands got up and said to Karen, "Sit down there and talk to Sister". Her 10½ year old girl found him dead and she said she must be so confused as "I'm very confused". She has leukaemia but is in and out of remissions. She said they say, if you get it young, you can get over it, but she wonders. Karen has a boy, too, and her eldest girl, 15, she called Áine, her little doll, as she was tiny, when she made her First Communion, but has put on weight now and has grown. Karen cried and cried, as she remembered her children. She said she went to the social worker, the solicitor and the court since Monday. She can get a house in Cork when she sorts out about her children. Her step-daughter is 30+. Karen will meet her children on Saturday.

She said William Caldwel was brilliant to her on Friday when she heard of the death. She went to be with William Caldwel. They stayed up all night and talked. She slept later. It was the best sleep she had for a long time, she said. She went to church for the removal with William Caldwel and he went up the church, but her brother-in-law or sister-in-law would not let her into the church. She went in later, she said, and a little girl came over to her in the church (when nearly all the people were gone) said to her, "Are you Áine's Mam?". Áine is in first year in Secondary School. Karen said, "Yes" to the child. She did not go to the Mass or burial, as the in-laws did not want her there. She said William rang all her brothers to tell them to come to Simon, as Karen was there – none of them came. She said her step-daughter rang on Friday and she knew there was something wrong.

Molly Gaffey asked where was Rosetta? I said, "She's not in today". She said, "I know that!". Is that a politician's answer I gave?

A man, Edward Daunt, came out of the dining-room, linking a lady who was very badly able to walk. He took her to the toilet and sat down near me while he waited. He said she has a muscular condition – Huntington's disease – she has it 10 years and she has got worse. The two of them lived in Leitrim for a few years – the man who owned their flat demolished it and enlarged his supermarket. They had no home. Edward and his wife, Melaine, are from England. He did not like England. Her people have no time for her. He said they were in Kerry for a while and came to Cork. They could get no Simon bed last night, nor no B & B, so they both slept behind the bus office. It was heart-breaking to hear that they had nowhere to go last night to find a bed. 'There was no room for them in any inn'. The poor are victims. A worker said there would be one bed tonight – definitely, and maybe two. Edward said Melanie would have the first one.

## Friday, 12 March

Rosetta and I went to Simon. I sat in the hall, in a broken chair! Later, on my way out, I saw many, many beautiful mahogany or good wood chairs all broken up in the yard. How symbolic, I felt they were, of the brokenness of those who broke them.

Karen McAuton came along and sat down. She talked again, as she did yesterday, about what had happened at the time of her husband's death and since. It was nearly word for word as she had shared with me yesterday.

Cillian O'Carrag came over, when I said, "I admire your lovely clothes". He said he keeps himself clean. He looks very unsettled and sounds, too, as if he's planning a new adventure! He asked me had we any working boots? He told me he hoped to get a bit of work. He said he was going into hospital to have his teeth put in – an overnight. He said he'd be like 'Lord Gough' in there. He's still on VHI, he said. I sensed he's ready for off to live it up in some 'posh place'. All is well for *now*.

## Tuesday, 16 March

We went to Simon. A worker said he was working in a factory and said he preferred being with homeless people. I said, "You must be a people person". He said, "Definitely".

## Thursday, 18 March

We went to Simon. I met Noah McAlorey, being held up by the front of a car! He was in bad shape – his leg is probably sore at times, but I saw him walking very quickly into the kitchen one day lately. Maybe it gets good at times and not at other times. Whether it is sore or not – he is a 49 year old grown man, still drinking his bottle – the baby never really grew up. He was all dirt. He was barred and slept out last night. He has lovely blue eyes. His eyes illuminate and reflect his soul. There is an amazing light in his eyes. He said to me again, "Will you marry me?". I said, "Noah, it would be a bit cold sleeping outside the church!". He said, "I could get a house". He said, "You'd have to leave the order first". Noah said he was very fond of me.

We meditated. It was as if we were given this time there on our own today to ponder and reflect on our experiences. Awesome!

*Friday to Saturday, 19-20 March*

Rosetta and I left for Simon. On the way, I recognised John Hose as the young man who had spent some time chatting and sharing his life's experiences one day with me. I greeted him and he said, "Hello". John asked if we'd have a drink – herbal tea, etc. We agreed to go for tea. *The Quay Co-op* was near. We enjoyed the comfort of the coal fire. I was fascinated by John being so happy 'in' John. He said he'd gone to Glendalough for a few days. I told him I'd rang him one day to invite him to Ballygriffin but there was no answer. O.K.

He talked at length about Olivia Idris and him having two separate lives, even though they live together. He told me how inadequate he felt in school and growing up. He was the odd one out, he said. He never played football or went out with the boys. He asked me twice how I was. I told him I am well. I was in awe of his truthfulness and 'how he really is', but something is telling me that he has a big secret, somewhere, stored away deep inside. He has a lovely smile and could leave the table very graciously, when he feels he'd like to go. I noticed he put his hand on top of my hand on the table, at one stage, as he spoke. He must have felt comfortable in his own touch, to do this. It was not easy to listen to one person, when there were four of us at the same table. He asked me how often would I pray during the day – I said, "Four times" – he said, "*Rosary*, etc." – I said, "No, meditation". He talked of the Buddhists then and mantra meditation. At a deep level, the symbolism of *The Rosary* is powerful. Meditation in silence helps me to hear all of life with more reverence.

I could be there, though Samson McAlweer needed to talk almost non-stop – to be heard. I could hear him talking about himself a lot, even when he was talking about his family situations. His sister had / has some pain to deal with. I felt I could hear his mother and aunt, too, in pain. I was deeply moved by how he rubbed the dog outside the pub – his presence touched the dog. He was in the woods with squirrels, eating nuts, and a hare was running near him, etc. It was awesome. His stillness touched them. They could be themselves in his presence. Francis of Assisi, too, was very close to animals, etc. They could eat out of his hands. Samson talked today, and before, about Francis. He speaks to Samson in some way. Samson is an open person but is in the throes of an emotional attachment now. I'm glad he's allowing it live – I feel he's only at the tip of the iceberg yet in it. He talked about taking drugs and seeing the monster in the moon – which he could say later is himself. He felt he could not tame the monster, but it would calm in time. He was in England when this happened, he said.

Mark Salim said he was only out of prison. I said, "You had a rest!". He showed us his white runners, jeans and a shirt, someone up there gave him. The two-year old needed to say, "Look what I got…".

## Thursday 25 March

I went into the hall. Agnes Oates and Shaun Danaher asked me to sit near them. Agnes is a dote. She was in good shape. She was in care until 12. She ran away and left home at 16, then slept rough. She has six children: the oldest is 18, Eoin; John Danaher 17; Patrick Danaher, 10; Kevin Danaher, 4; Agnes Danaher, called after her; Denis Danaher is 3. The youngest is in care. Shaun's wife was murdered in Clondalkin. Sue was her name. Agnes is with Shaun 10 years. They lived in England and slept rough in London. Agnes was raped by a man from the North. I feel the children of 10, 4 and 3 years old are not Shaun's. I talked to Agnes for about one hour. Shaun called to passers-by, "Hi, a cigarette".

I saw Lee Dallyn and a lady I recognised. I heard Molly Gaffey call her Ruth Mannas – she's a lovely woman. I visited her home. I waved at her today and went over. She thought she recognised me. She said my hair was not as short, the last time she saw me! She said she was going mad, when I left the school in 1994. I'd always felt great pity, when I'd see her. She has a flat in Cork.

I said, "Hello" to Jessica Giles. She has lovely clothes. She said she's going to look for a flat. I admired her clothes – red beaded blouse, long red skirt, etc. She said so many people have died belonging to her – her mother, father and brother.

## Friday, 26 March

Later, I sat near Jessica Giles and Cameron Rasta from the North of Ireland. Jessica showed us her daughter's wedding in her own home. I thought it was a hotel, it was so luxurious. It had high ceilings and the curtains were very classy. Jessica showed us her ex-husband's photo. Jessica said to me, "Yes, love, no, love, etc.", a lot. Jessica knew *The Bible* very well. She said Job got a hard time, but he persevered – it was, I felt, about herself that she spoke. She said Abraham's faith was tested, too. I was amazed she mentioned Abraham, as I was moved by that lately, too. Abraham is a symbol for me of simplicity – at one – can be with what is.

Cameron Rasta read *The Bible*, too. He said the *Old Testament* is great. He said the *New Testament* is there only to make money! Cameron is a stone mason. He loved his work with stone, etc. I saw his energy changing when I began to affirm him. He said about the work of restoration: what is it? I said we do believe in the restoration and reconstruction of persons. He could hear a lot and said it was a very interesting conversation. Since he came in two days ago, he heard nothing, only lies, drink, etc. He worked in a hotel. He stayed in another hotel during the week. He was in a B & B opposite the station. His tools were taken. Some of these his father and grandfather made. I sensed huge anger in him. He was never in a place like this before, he said. I said, "Maybe you need rest". He said there's a reason for him being there in Simon. Cameron asked me why was I a nun? – when I first felt called, etc.? He prays at his bedside.

## Sunday, 28 March

Later, Deane chatted for almost two hours with me. He said he has been meditating since he was 16. Before that, he was big into the occult, witchcraft, tarot cards, cults of all kinds, etc. The buzz from these was only short-lived. He found through meditation a pathway into his inner being, which is totally reliable. He has now experienced his inner being as an energy, which is permanent, where nothing negative can reside.

He said, "That is the God in me. God lives and moves in me. I do a lot of inner body awareness also. I can experience the field of energy vibrating in my own hand, up my arm and throughout my entire body. It is the life of the spirit of the universe alive in me. God is almighty. This God / Creator is my best friend. This source of all energy never leaves me for an instant. I meditate daily, on several occasions during the course of the day. I can thus help clear my mind of thoughts and then this allows my inner being space to emerge to my consciousness. Life in depth is all about consciousness, awareness and attentive alertness. I've read Eckhart Tolles' *Power of Now, A New Earth, Stillness Speaks* and *Practicing the Power of Now*. On page 78, I remember he said, in his chapter on nature, 'In order to bring your attention to a stone, a tree or an animal, it does not mean that one has to think about it, but simply to perceive it, to hold it in your awareness'. I put a stone near a plant once and sat there, 'being with' the stillness of the stone and plant for quite some time. I experienced such joy in me, that is beyond anything the mind can think about. Once, I was in a state of pure joy for two and a half days. I wished it would never end. I've experienced other glimpses of 'being' along life's journey. I only have now. There is no past and no future. Now is where real life is. I totally believe, that everything I need is already given and all I need do, is be aware of this, believe it is real and not to doubt. Doubt comes from my ego or false self. This blocks the flow of good energy / real life in me.

"I don't believe in organised religion. What do most people in these institutions do? 1) They say to someone – you join us and you'll be saved – we're the true believers. 2) When people join the religion, some leaders say to them – now you'll obey this rule, don't do this or that, or you'll commit a sin, etc. 3) They ask for money. One day, I reflected on this and realised that the people who joined some of these groups were deprived in certain ways of freedom. I believe negativity can do a lot of damage to people. Believe something negative will happen and sure enough it will. In *The Bible*, I read, 'Fill your minds with all that is good, holy ...'. Also, 'Let this mind be in you, which is also in Christ Jesus'. Nature is my great teacher of stillness. 'Ask and you will receive' is mentioned also in *The Bible*. If I want, want, want, then my ego takes over and has a field day, so to speak. I am free now, so I can make choices. If I make a conscious choice, I will be enriched through the awareness. I am that awareness, at my core. Awareness becomes aware of itself.

"Once, a person asked me for a loan of money. I had €11 in my pocket. I gave him €10. He said he'd return it to me later. I said it was O.K., leave it. I went to the betting office to bet on a few horses. As I was about to bet, a person I vaguely knew, offered me €20, saying, "Keep that, I don't need it now". I thanked him then. I had €1 before he gave me the €20! his was to do me until I got paid the following week. I was in a hostel then, so I had food. My girlfriend depended on me for money, too. I shared with her what I had, €21! I felt fine, free, open to whatever arose, totally believing I'm being looked after and that life always gives me what I need, no more, no less.

"All the energy of the universe is interconnected. Look at the wooden bench we are sitting on. Because of the form / body we are in (so limited), we experience that wood as solid, but experiencing the wood from a deeper level, it is only 2% solid and the rest hollow-space made up of neutrons, molecules, etc. It is energy. Those who have gone ahead of us to the next realm are free of this form. They are in the spirit world. We could have already lived in many, many lives up to now and will continue to live in many more eventually.

"Now is all I need. We don't have to live only on planet earth. There are billions of planets in outer space. Is there life on them? Who knows? Death is a wonderful experience. All our thinking dies. Our soul / essence / spirit comes more alive. Some people have asked me to give lectures on my experiences. I choose consciously not to. I've had 'out of body' experiences several times. This was very sacred. In meditation, I sense my inner being more fully. 'I can do all things with the power of Him / Her who strengthens me'.

"Once, I saw a book called *The Third Jesus* in a shop. I hadn't enough money to buy it. Sometime later, I joined the library, went to the section on mind, body, spirit and what was on the shelf straight in front of me, *The Third Jesus*! This book looks at Jesus' life 'inside out', so to speak, at a deeper level, the contemplative Jesus or Jesus as the embodiment of Spirit, the enlightened one. The God of punishment in *The Bible* does nothing for me. That is a caricature of the true energy of life. I like to sit and BE. My thinking is much clearer, when it comes from stillness. I see what needs to be done more clearly and I can 'think' more purely and move freely, unhindered by the egoic entity. I can sense my father's presence in a more real way, who died two years ago, when I am clear of thinking, as a compulsive state, then our spirits connect on the energy of no-thing-ness".

I really believe this man, in whose presence was so honoured to be today, is a mystic. He is unknown to the world, but he can enjoy being unknown and regarded as nothing. He is a very deeply spiritual person. I don't know where he slept last night, or any night, but, whether he was in a bed in a room, which was cosy, or, in a doorway, or in a derelict house or on the pavement, this human being is a 'saintly' man, who is living life more fully, than many others, who say too much ABOUT their lives, but really don't experience the quality of presence, I sensed in Deane today. I don't know at all how long I was with Deane. That does not matter at all. Hours?

I felt so light, easy and grace-filled during the space of sharing, that it was like five minutes. It was as if time had stood still. It did, too, as I was full almost able to live in the moment. He said, "If I'm in unease, I get disease".

He was my real professor today – given as a total gift. In learning not to have expectations, I get much more than I can ask or imagine. I was privileged, as always, to have lived today in the presence of these great people.

## Saturday, 3 April – Easter Saturday

Agnes Oates could not make a roll-up of her tobacco! She said she makes one with a lot of tobacco in it. I helped her make it. I joked. I said, "It's like a cigar, it's so fat". She smoked it. Edmund Derham said he laughed at the nun making the roll-up. He never saw this before. He said he'll never keep Agnes in tobacco, if she made all her roll-ups with that much tobacco in them! He laughed!

Alexis Obaris came over for a long chat in the hall. When Agnes left, Alexis said, "No one cares about me in Simon. No one looks for me". How sad. I told him about Mary in Dublin. He had deep empathy. Earlier, Alexis said when he heard my voice, he came out of bed! He said, "The nuns are there!". He said, otherwise, he'd have been in bed all day. I said, "Rosetta and I will always be your friends". He smiled.

### Friday, 9 April

Cameron Rasta said, "Hello". He was peeling potatoes. I asked him if he needed help, so he said he was nearly finished. He looked a lot better. He had got the hat off and, in some way, did not look as angry as he did before Easter. I could sense his shame at being in the Simon, as he said, "I won't be here much longer". He said he had to buy all new tools. He had a paper, too, today and read it when he had the potatoes peeled. He said he used to go to school across the beach and he said he loves the sea.

### Tuesday, 13 April

I went to Simon. I had a very deep sense of privilege, today, being with my friends in the Simon. It was as if I could hear my own story being re-echoed in those people at times. I could sense my deep presence coming alive.

### Wednesday, 14 April

Sean McCare broke through the gate and came in, even though he's barred. He broke a cup on something in the dining-room. I could hear the crash. He kicked chairs, etc. Leslie Teaper said, "He's out on bail, spare him". I affirmed Mel Monst, the worker, later, when he sat near me at the table, on being so gentle with Sean. I sat around and observed 'the children' at play for a long time – the lobby is equal to the nursery!

Jerry Laar sat, too, and said to Jack Feeny, "Do you know what the Sister said about hash? She said 'Enjoy it!'". Jerry Laar was beaming from ear to ear. He said to me, "I won't smoke it in here". "Great", I said. I was just beginning to say about home and being 'told what do' and how one can resent it. He was gone before the end of the sentence!

A black man came in, named Aidan Bannon. Karen asked him if he'd like to join us. He did. He's from Scotland. He's homeless. He has a very, very cultured voice. He likes his job cleaning B & Bs / hotels. He walks a lot, as did Mel in Ballygriffin. He's very gracious and offered us a hot drink. He asked specifically if we would like a *hot drink*. He said that's a luxury for him to have a hot drink. He said that it was very poignant for him to see me drink *hot water*. He has travelled a lot and hopes to stay in Simon up to Saturday. Aidan Bannon has no time for material things. He had a plastic bag and one shoulder bag coming to Simon to-day! He said he loves nature in the environment in Scotland and Ireland. "Nature can speak, as much as people do", he said. He met lovely people, too, he said. He has beautiful, soulful brown eyes. I affirmed his gentleness. He thanked me and said he was happy to hear this, as many people don't often affirm that in him. He smiled a beautiful smile.

## Tuesday, 20 April

Rosetta introduced me to a lovely lad from Derry, called Michael. His girlfriend was killed in a car crash in September 1994. Michael's son died of heart failure in 1989 and his other son, a day old, died in February 1995. He has two daughters, 9 and 4, and his mother looks after them. He does not get on with their mother. He was born in Clare. He spent time in prison, since the deaths. He looked very clean and had a lovely face. He said, "With all the trouble I had, no one understood". That was the way he put it. I felt privileged listening to him. I was moved when I saw him giving Mark Salim a pair of socks – he had two and he gave one away. Surely, these are the people living the *Gospel*. He, who had been out on the street sleeping and having no bed, could be that caring of a fellow-man.

## Thursday, 22 April

I joined Rosetta and Alexis Obaris at the end table. I was so happy to be there, especially on the eve of Alexis's birthday and to spend some quality time with him. He talked about breaking out and seemed guilty about it. I gave him the birthday card from Rosetta and myself. He opened it later and was delighted with it, I could see. He also got a surprise twin-pack of drinking chocolate!

Benedict School sat down after a while and began to say he was on heroin for two years and did 'cold turkey' himself. He asked his mother and sister to lock him into his room and board up the windows, so he could not get out.

He said he had three buckets in there! He was given meals in there and the buckets were emptied. His family were admirable to support him in all this, for three weeks. He said he had a lot of pain, too. He was in prison in England and did two years. He was to do seven, but he came home. His mother met him off the boat. He smokes hash today. He said he does not drink.

We meditated later. As always, I wish these special people that 1) they will be happy; 2) they take care of their health; and 3) they may be free from harm. The present moment is the only time I have been given to live.

## Thursday, 6 May

Daniel Duns said, "Hello" and, when I invited him to meditate, he said he may be too young for that. I thought this was an amazing comment – he seems tuned in fairly well, I felt.

## Tuesday, 11 May – Ballygriffin

Abigail was happy with the day, she said. She is a gifted person in many ways, e.g., with flower-arranging, crafts, cookery, etc. She meditated with us at 6.00 p.m. We enjoyed tea, washed up and left to go to Cork. In Simon at 9.10 p.m., Abigail said we were doing great work.

## Wednesday to Thursday, 12 - 13 May – Ballygriffin

I felt it was a very positive environment Jerry Laar was in, being here, in the silence. He did not need to say anything, only be himself. Who can really rate whether a person of such infinite value is successful or not – our deepest self knows nothing of these polarities – success or failure. Our deepest self *is*. Jerry Laar *is* and his *real beauty* is in his is-ness. We had no expectations of Jerry these days. He could *be* in his own silence, gently. No one stood in judgement over him – but he was held in deep reverence, by Rosetta and myself.

Today, Jerry went for a walk through the fields. It was wet. I met him coming back and walked over to the chalet with him. He said he was dry. I asked him how he was here. I remember he said one day to me, that maybe he could come here for a longer time to Ballygriffin, and perhaps get off drugs. Today, he said he could get on without them, but he missed them a bit. I said he may need to go off and on them for a while. He said he may be able to get off them altogether then. I said he needed nothing here and he could be happy and he said he is happy and sees he doesn't need drugs here. He said, "People have to go to America and other places to get what I got here – peace / happiness". I said we all need places like this, now and then, to find out what's good in us. A nice peaceful environment, like Ballygriffin, can awaken us to our peace within. He talked about what's good within him and said that if he would be getting physically weak from the drugs, he'd be suicidal. He said there must be more to life than drugs and living this way. He said it is a slow process. You take drugs, don't take them, etc., etc. He could hear its gentleness as I said, "Jerry Laar, you need to be gentle with all this – enjoy the drugs in an appropriate place and not in Ballygriffin. Eventually, you may not depend on them so much". I felt, it may dawn on him one day, what's happening to himself through this addiction. He hears our reverence and respect for him, I feel, and in that environment, he can grow.

He took a shower and washed the shower room floor and swept the floor in the kitchen, gently. No one asked him to *do* anything and he gently did all these acts, out of his love. He could ask about the bed-linen, too, and take it off. He could leave the bin in his room at the door to keep the door open to air his room. I could hear how adult he was, in doing all the above acts. That he may grow more and more in his own love is my wish for Jerry.

I read this poem by Hafiz for Jerry:

> *Ever since happiness heard your name,*
> *It has been running through the streets to see could it find you.*
> *And several times in the last week,*
> *The Creator of your life has come to my door –*
> *So sweetly asking for your address,*
> *Wishing for the beautiful warmth of your heart's fire.*

## Friday, 14 May

Samson McAlweer sat down. He's doing some work there again, he said. He was asked by Declan. He did Tuesday, 3 May and today until midnight. He said he was 'upside down'. He got a job in construction in Cork. He said he'd do Simon for a while anyhow – maybe three months – he did not know. He said there was no violence the night he was on – it was very quiet. He said he heard things had been rough lately there. Samson McAlweer chatted about himself, about wanting to be a 'drop-out', going away like Francis of Assisi and getting lost for a while! He feels drawn to solitude, he said, and hopes to go to the mountains and for long walks during the next few months. He said he'd like to spend days on the mountain, etc., but he feels he's not meant to be alone on this journey. He said he does not want any advice on what to do. He has read so many spiritual books that he feels he has got no answers. Now he feels he has enough books read, because now he said he wants to see what Samson has to say and not anyone else. I said now is all he has. In 10 year's time, he'd look back and see this as so sacred, hopefully ... it would all fall into place. The confusion is good. He's open to all possibilities, which is great, but at the moment he's all over the place, he said. I said he may need many emotional attachments and need to live these over time – or he may not. He said he's not ready for any more, for now, anyway.

Kevin said he'd go for coffee and asked me to go for coffee with him. He offered me coffee. He got some, too, for himself. He drank it and I had coffee, too, with him in the café. Later, he began talking and said he doesn't care whether he'll get a flat or not. I said, "You are in pain, Kevin". He said, "Yes". He was hurting inside, he said. He also said he had lots of problems regarding his children, family, etc. I said, "You have a lot to say, Kevin". He said, "Yes". He was very gradually easing down. I never knew the second he'd roar out and break something, but he got so much calmer when he mentioned his mother and how he could love her. He cried and cried and cried. He talked a lot about his favourite brother, Terence, who died aged 18. Kevin was then 10. He was killed on a mountain. He said he wanted to be with him now. Why did he die and not another one of his 8 brothers or sisters? Why has he, Kevin, to live like this? His Dad, he said drank alcohol. He spent all his money on drink. Once, his mother bought Kevin a second-hand bicycle. She couldn't buy a new one, as his Dad spent all the money. His mother is still alive. He hopes he'll be gone before her, he said. He was crying for nearly half an hour. I encouraged him to continue. We were luckily sitting in a corner and no-one else was there. I feel it was all meant to be. I thanked him for the privilege of hearing his sacred story. I said how good he is. Why would I be still here, I said, unless I could see in him a person of such infinite value? About 5.45 p.m., he said he'd walk around, as he needed to be on his own for a while. He was fully calm by now. He even smiled and thanked me for listening to him and coming in for the coffee. My presence is enough here. I knew and was certain of that. I had not any other ammunition or anything to equip me for this very delicate situation. I was confident in that presence. I was very touched by his utter fragility, when he broke down and cried – this man with the 'tough exterior'. He was a child at heart, screaming to be heard. In just simply listening to Kevin, Kevin's anger softened. He spoke openly, and felt better.

I felt Samson McAlweer, too, needed to be heard over and over. He also asks for clarification and that's O.K. to share what I have already experienced and learned. It's more real then, as it comes from the heart. 'Head' answers are like chaff in the wind, I hear, but I need a lot of gentleness with these head ideas, etc., to enable them to be connected.

## Friday, 21 May

A lovely young lad, Harold Feliffe, told me he could not talk until he was 17 years old. He used to sleep with dogs. Humans were very cruel and mocked him, so his best friends were dogs. Dumb animals could befriend a dumb man, he said. He got speech therapy then and later married. He's separated and now lives with a girl. He asked me to visit him and asked could I have a chat with his girlfriend, Fidelma Eason. Her sister was murdered three years ago and she went heavy on drink since. He used drink, too. I said I'd go if it suited and see them on Sunday at 2.00 p.m. He said he'd ask her. I told him about Ballygriffin. He said, "Put my name down, and my girlfriend's, for the retreat". She needs help, he said, now. He said they would stay separately there. He is very fond of her. She's a lovely person, he said, but changes with drink. I remember Harold told me he used sleep, when he was older, with greyhound pups about two years ago, as they were very sick and he hoped by sleeping with them they would get better. They died eventually and he cried and cried, he said. He never had a dog since. I could hear he lost everything except the dogs, that meant something to him, up to 15 years. Dogs were his best friends then, now they, too, could leave him. I heard his total abandonment. He also abandoned himself, but he said, "Yes, I know there is goodness in me". He is the second man in one month, who told me how much he had cried and cried and cried. I felt honoured that both cried and cried with me. Their openness is setting them free, I hear. Harold said yesterday before I left, "Pray for me".

Tremendous hospitality has been shown to homeless people at South Presentation Convent for years. They get meals, sandwiches and many, many cups of tea on cold, wintry days.

## Tuesday, 25 May

I went to Simon. Tiffany O'Drisea left me in and chatted with me. She asked me how I got on the day after leaving her on the street with Kevin. She said she heard I took him for coffee. I said, "I offered him coffee". I said it was great, as he shared a lot with me. She said, "You were very brave as not too many more people would do that. You went one step beyond. You walked that extra mile". She said, "They were talking about it in the Shelter and felt it was so good of you to do this". Samson must have told her about the experience. I don't know who said something that led Tiffany to come up to me. I sensed their lovely care and concern – their love really.

Jerry Laar sat down. I said, "How's the hash going, Jerry?". He said, "I might give it up, because there is a lot of hash in me already, it takes time to clear, I don't need it". He said he sees now why he takes hash. It gives him a buzz. He said it to another man also. He, too, could hear what Jerry said. I said, "Enjoy it and in time you may not need it". He said, "That makes great sense". He said he'd be thinking about all I say and he comes up with his own ideas then. I admired him for this, I said. No-one need tell him *what to do* – he has all the answers in himself. His eyes light up when I say, "Enjoy it". He sat down and was in great form.

## Wednesday, 26 May

I listened very, very carefully for about an hour to Hubert Fay and I got a deep sense he may have been sexually abused. He said he hated his mother, etc. He was roaring and roaring, louder and louder.

Jack Balfry seemed very interested in the fact that I could stay with Hubert. I said, "In time, by staying with people and affirming them in their goodness, it may come to them that there *is* something good *inside* them and they may be able to say they don't need hash to *feel* good. What they need already is in there, i.e., their goodness within, but they don't know it". Jack asked me did I do counselling. I said, "No, but I began this journey on my own interior road six years ago". He said, "We're *all* looking for this good *in* ourselves".

Harry Fry, on Wednesday, thanked me for coming to visit *him*. He's about 35. He has a lovely face, but looks very deeply hurt. He needs to *feel* loved. Then, only then, can he truly love.

## Tuesday, 2 June

Jack Balfry sat near me. He said he saw a man asleep on the grass in the early morning, with a dog in his arms. He had no blanket. The dog was his blanket.

Brendan Wacami joined me. I met him with Chelsea once. They came to South Presentation. It cheered him up, he said to talk today. He said he cries a lot. He was married 15 years in September. He does not even know what his family look like. He has two daughters, one 21 and one 25. There is huge hurt in Brendan, I felt. He would love to go to Ballygriffin. I spoke about meditation. He would like to do it. He is very upset now, he said.

## Wednesday, 3 June

I said, "Hello", to Jason Gofield. He said he was a member of the Baptist Church and was a Christian. He showed me a book he was reading in French and the page he had out was the story of Abraham. I was interested when he began talking about Abraham, saying that he was a man of love and peace and God looked after him. He said his people used live wildly in the woods once and they were, I would say, from his gestures in describing them, of the 'savage' race. He illustrated this by making violent gesticulations, as he showed me how they ate their food. He said his people became Christians, too. He said he tells people about the good news – *belle nouveau* – my bit of French helped me understand some of what he was saying! He spoke quite good English. He said he's confused a bit now and needed to get a place to live. He said he'd do some of this work, if he settled down. He called God, 'Jehovah'. I talked to him about the God within him. He smiled. He said he likes people to be happy and at peace but not fighting. He wore European dress. He went to meet someone about accommodation. Later, when I asked him if he got a place to live, he said he got nothing. His energy changed from positive earlier to negative. Brendan Wacami sat for the next hour or so, saying intermittently, "I don't feel well". I can't count how many times he said that! He said he was very depressed. It came to me to meditate and I could meditate for a full half-hour, sitting in the hall – 'being with' Brendan. I could send him good energy. I felt compassion for him as he was in so much torture. His face showed huge anguish. I could be at one with the beauty of his creation, in spite of his almost 'zombie-like' posture and movement.

George Faiss said, "The nun is there and she knows I'm O.K.". His is really automatic and unintentional behaviour. I could say the mantra – be there.

I saw Edward Tassel writing one day and I admired his handwriting. He said he writes a daily journal – about how he lives, what happens to him and what other people do to him, etc. He burned 10 books recently! He has a small one to take around with him. He spoke very well and had a very cultured English accent. He was in university, he said and did a degree in Philosophy. He studied Zen Buddhism and Eastern Philosophy and could speak about all of the philosophers very well – Hume, Kant, Nietzche, and

Descartes, etc. I did Philosophy in my degree, so I could tune in to some of what he said. "The Church only teaches dogma. It doesn't touch the ordinary man in the street", he said. He had to go at 2.00 p.m. He said about community life that some are called to live celibacy, others are called to married life. *Live life* and it brings its own structure. He was an interesting character, but maybe a victim of subjectivism. He said he'd talk to me again another day. I said I would be delighted.

### Friday, 4 June

When I went in the Simon door, a lady ushered me in and began to search a lad, who had drugs. Eamonn and the boy with the dogs gave out to the lady for not searching me! I said, "I have no objection to being searched". He said, "It's them and us". I could sense his huge anger. He hurried past me. Jerry Laar said they found hash in his room when they went to tidy it – he was barred for one night. He was lucky, he said, as he could be out for six weeks!

It rained today heavily. Billy Pember, a homeless man, said, "Do you need the price of the bus?". How kind of him to ask. He said to ask Rosetta and myself to come to his new flat in Simon some Sunday and he'd cook a dinner for us. We'd have lemonade, too, he said! Billy talked about Ballygriffin. He said he'd go next week.

### Monday, 7 June

Alexis Obaris felt better, he said. He is hurting so deeply. I would love to wave a magic wand over him and make him well – a human being of such infinite value – so hurt. He seems at times removed from life – he appears dead to this world even, at times. Is he better here or worse off, I wonder when he's not in touch? I can be 'with' him.

### Wednesday, 9 June

Alex Base is a good man but does not know it – he may not even experience any at all of his own goodness, I feel. His body language seems to say he could be suffering from depression, maybe – how he carries his body or how his body carries him, etc. Alex needs to be heard a lot I feel, over and over and over again.

I feel lately I'm beginning to see / hear more and more the spirit of life in the street-people's faces. It is awesome to be in the presence of such greatness. 'The spirit of Him / Her who created the universe dwells in their hearts and in silence is loving to all'. *Always there* – this is what I revere. I sensed the deep reverence out of which I wrote these pages – I sensed very deep peaceful energy directing my hand in the writing. It is about each person first – who is a temple of the spirit of life. I sense I am more deeply aware of that in this unique now.

## Tuesday, 15 June

Greg Wald came with us to Ballygriffin. He seems depressed. The poor man must be very tormented altogether. He must be in terrible torture and agony. It must have been so awful when his wife left him 15 years ago and went away with his best mate. I went to walk in nature, 'being there', allowing the wind to embrace me as I walked on the soft grass. It was so comforting. We meditated at 3.35 p.m. and again at 5.00 p.m. All is well. I was touched by Greg Wald saying he felt safe with us. His fear is huge. He talked about pain so often, it seems to be killing him inside. How does he keep going at all? He's amazing! He keeps going in almost total misery. One has to go to the depths of misery and suffering, almost total annihilation at times, before we are fully awakened to our Being. Greg Wald is beautiful in his essence. It would be wonderful if he could hear it for himself. I feel he hears glimpses of it, but they seem to be very fleeting. I felt deeply in the presence of the Creator, our Source of Life, when Greg said: "I feel happy *now*". He mentioned joy. I felt he experienced a certain measure of joy. The more I can go into my own deep misery, the more I can be 100% with Greg. It is too awesome for words! Thank you, Greg, for awakening me to my deep source of life, through your misery and depression. I can hear the unique gift of my own Being in my misery, too.

I met Robbie and he said, "I have no time for money or material things, but what I have, I do appreciate it very much. It is far more important to appreciate what we have, than to have too much and have no value on it. Wealth does not make us happy. If I can enjoy peace in me and live simply, I'm a lucky person and rich, too". He said he believes that Jesus was a great teacher, but is not so sure about him being the son of God. He said he himself has been up and down many roads and he feels that in the areas of sex, we are all animal in our instincts. The man has a deep core with-in, he is *always* good in that core.

I shared the following with Robbie:

## A REFLECTION

*In some way, however small and secret, each of us is a little mad ... Everyone is
lonely at the bottom and cries to be understood; but we can never entirely
understand someone else, and each of us remains part stranger, even to those
who love us ... It is the weak who are cruel; gentleness is to be expected only
from the strong ... Those who do not know fear are not really brave, for courage
is the capacity to face life, face what is ... You can understand people if you look
at them – no matter how old or impressive they may be – as if they are children.
For most of us never mature; we simply grow taller ... The purpose of life is to
matter – to count, to stand for something, to have it make some difference that
we lived at all. We matter because we were created by the Source of Life. I am
good because I am. Each of us is unique, original and unrepeatable. Our sacred
presence is enough. Whatever action we take out of that zone with-in us (our
inner being / soul) is of infinite value. Each one's gift to this world is
inestimable. When we're aware of it, it comes more alive for us. Meditation
helps us to get more in touch with our being.*


## Monday, 21 June

I said, "Hello", to Siobhán Gorey, Cathal Carpet's friend. She's from Dublin.
Her mother, too, sleeps out. David Bagley asked Siobhán to make tea for
him. No, rather, he said he'd like it and Siobhán offered to make it for him.
He said, "Tea, milk, one sugar, stir twice to the right and twice to the left
and once to the right again". He said he prefers a mug. Siobhán said she
could not get B & B now. I told Siobhán she's a lovely girl. She's on the street
since she was 14. She's now 25. She went out then with Cathal.


## Tuesday, 22 June

I was very touched by Crystal Chaput's handshake. It was a very warm and
loving handshake. She held my hand very gently for a long time and then I
let go of hers, gently. I felt the energy of love coming through her hand. She
changed since I saw her. She would like to go to Ballygriffin some day with
us and said to let her know. She was in London for two and a half years.


## Wednesday, 23 June

On my way out, I met Adam Cafferkey. I greeted him. I said I was delighted
to see him. We had a long, long chat. He said when he was not brought up

in a family, he can't make friends. He said he was brought up in a school. People let him down so much, he said and he can't have friends, as he doesn't trust people. He said the let-downs he experienced are often the cause of him going back to drink to kill the pain. He said when people see the scars on his face, nose, etc., they won't talk to him. He said society has no time for people like him. No-one talks to him on the street. I would always talk to him, he said. I could hear his deep loneliness, rejection, hurt and desolation. No wonder he cuts his wrists, etc. He said the rejection might hit him later tonight. I said, "Rosetta and I are always your friends, Adam". I was a good hour with him, I'd say, or the best part of it. Adam held my elbow, shook hands and gently left. He said a lot, I felt. I said I felt better, because I met him. He was so honest, he touched me, I said. He made my day, as he touched my truth and awakened me to my own honesty.

Later, Liam Bailey sat on the chair. I moved near him. He was very chatty. He told me that, after leaving Simon the last time, having done the three-day retreat with Rosetta and myself in Owenahincha, he got a job as a labourer. A man gave him a week's trial, then took him on as a full-time scaffolding worker at £120 a day. The head man is only 26. Liam Bailey stayed in a B & B in Meath, where he worked. He said he never goes home. He said he may talk to them sometime in a couple of years' time! He will go to Kilkenny, as he always does at the August weekend. He came to Simon today, as he had nothing to do. He felt bored in the B & B. He stayed in Simon when the scaffold strike was on. He got no pay for six weeks then. Liam Bailey was in great form. Fourteen worked with him on the scaffolding. He hopes to be boss / foreman eventually. He would not like to go out on his own though, as there's too much hassle, too much money to handle, etc., too much responsibility. He's a lovely lad.

It was lovely to met Francis Fall, when Rosetta introduced me to him. He is in deep pain, though, and seems to have an awful difficulty with drink. The poor man is in bondage totally with it. Tears came so often to his eyes, one would love if he could cry and cry. It was lovely the way he said he was hoping Rosetta would be in Simon, when he came back from his walk. It did him a tremendous amount of good, he said to be able to talk. Rosetta listened so attentively to him. I could see how he was beginning to hear himself eventually. He experienced joy on being heard. It must have been a long time since he could talk like he talked to Rosetta. He's five years without seeing his wife or family. He said how understanding Joan, his wife, was. I found it hard to listen to him, when he said he did not know what points his son got in his Leaving nor what he is doing in college. A neighbour told him bits. I heard this man's hurt, his child's hurt.

### Friday, 25 June

Richard Hair said, "Hello". I chatted with him. He said he drank. I said, "Whatever way you are Richard, it's O.K. You are good, because *you are*". He said he had a lot! He was honest. I said, "Could you count them?". He laughed and said, "No, the pints or the women?". I said, "Both". He said he couldn't count the women!

### Saturday, 10 July

A new lad sat near the lift. Billy Jell was his name. He is in Simon two weeks and hopes to stay a couple of months. He asked me what I did here, etc. I told him I'm there (i) as a listening presence; (ii) to meditate with residents / homeless people; (iii) to do retreats with homeless people in the retreat centre; and (iv) most of all to learn from street-people, to help deepen my own sense of living in the now. He was very moved, I could see. He is about 24.

Later, Barbara O'Bradi came in with blood over her eye! She shook my hand with her hand all blood! I could touch the blood and receive her as she is in the 'now'. The ambulance came and she refused to go into it. She said she was very hungry. Later, Samson went with her in a taxi. She got four stitches. She said she would kill David Bagley when she met him. Why?

### Monday, 12 July

I met Melissa Kelers. I went over to her. She had left down her shopping bags on the path and said, "How are you?". She said, "Give me a hug". This request, I felt, was loaded. I was reminded of the Samaritan woman who said to Jesus, "Give me a drink of water that gives *life*". Love is what each of us needs. I was very conscious in giving her the hug. Maybe, it was the first embrace, out of love, she received in a while, who knows? I was taken aback that she asked *me*, a woman, for a hug. She has hundreds of men – sex, etc., but maybe no love. She's in the business of prostitution. Her dress at the back was open nearly to her waist. I asked her how her mother was. She said she had her two hips done. Melissa Kelers goes to see her. She said she told us that before. She goes to Germany. She has a daughter of 30 years old in Belgium, she said. I said, "You are a lovely lady". She said, "You are, too". She asked for Rosetta.

Leslie Jennes, a man who studied philosophy, talked about begging outside the church and said, "Christian people are really put to the test when they come outside the door after Mass and someone like myself asks for money and they pass by"! He said going to Mass can be a habit. People can be addicted to going to Mass, etc. I'd love to have had a longer chat with Leslie Jennes.

Some were throwing water at others – water went over my foot and George Faiss's. We joked – our feet were washed! George laughed. He's delighted after three years to hear that he needs no operation on his hips. He has some pain, he said, though.

I asked Leslie Teaper about Sean McCare. Sean got 10 years in prison and she hasn't seen him for six weeks. He drinks since he was 16. The longest time out of prison was six months ever, she said.

## Wednesday, 14 July

Alexis said he had no place to go. Alexis said he'd go away and get a holiday for a couple of weeks. He doesn't want to go to the flat on his own. He's not able, really. I feel life is hard for him. He said he'd be in the bookie's office and drink every day, if he were in a flat. He needs company, he said.

Colm Chamber came out and was mad with Alexis. He said he talks about nothing but drink, the past, the past, for seven months! He said, "Would he ever go away and do something". I knew Colm's form was not good at all and I wondered why. Later, he said his son, Mick Chamber, and grandson, John Chamber, were in a car crash yesterday. They ran into a bus. His grandson broke his hand. His son is out of the intensive care today. He was very upset. Colm said there was no-one here friends of his, only Amy and Alexis, he said, too. The Gardaí sent word to Colm about the accident. He wanted to go to Dublin. A taxi would cost £110 – one way! He said he would wait a few days – see how they are and go then. He got very down at times during the evening, I could see. He fell asleep at one stage – fed up, I felt. He chatted a lot then and I stayed until after 4.00 p.m. with him.

I met David Gabbay on the South Mall. He's on his own in a house. He looked O.K. It came to me, 'Jesus *stayed with them* and *looked at them*' – out of his deep love – what a privilege this call is.

## Thursday, 15 July

I stayed with a poor man, Gregory Lavo, who fell. He got a most awful fall, backwards, onto the road, off the footpath and hit the back of his head off the road. I thought he was dead. He was seeing could he walk. Another man rang the bell and I lifted him up and I held his arm then. I felt he wanted to walk on the footpath. A lady told me there was something / a seat around the corner. I held his arm and he was very wobbly. I could sense being there in my deep presence and said several times, "Gregory, you will be O.K. You are a good man and you will always be a good man". Some people see only behaviour, not the person. Eventually, he made to go across the road. I was still linking him and eventually he sat on the kerb near a railing at the river, and said he was fine now. "I'm alright", he said, "Thanks, Sister". I felt very privileged to accompany him to that place, where he was reasonably O.K. Whatever his circumstances, it was an awesome privilege for me to be with him in his total brokenness. I will keep him very specially in my heart now at meditation.

It was a special day in Simon for me. In the eyes of the world, it would be considered waste – I could be about 85% there in the midst of it all. My feeling even at one stage felt, "I'm doing nothing", but I could go deeper and my being said, "BEING IS ENOUGH. My grace – goodness (when I'm aware of it) – is enough for you". All is well.

## Friday, 16 July

Another boy, Felix Waket, is 25. For 10 years, he lived on the streets and was on drugs. His mother died when he was 10 and his granny came to live with them. She died when he was 13. He lived with an aunt and uncle then. He stole money from them. He went away. He had no contact with them for five years. He was in jail for the past three years in Mountjoy, Portlaoise, Cork, and Spike Island. If he goes back to England, he will go to Brixton Prison. He owes money to drug-dealers. He met a drug-dealer in prison. Felix had to get protection in there. He said he could not live in a house. He's more used to shelters, streets, etc., for 10 years. He will get a place at 30! He said he will be 26 in a couple of months. He said the time he spent with his mother and granny was brilliant. He said most people end up on the streets, who have family troubles, marriage break-up, etc. He likes Cork. I felt very privileged to hear his story. I said he is a good person. He smiled each time I said this and said it's much appreciated. He believes that he's good at times, he said. When he feels O.K., he goes for a walk. He said it's peaceful in Cork. In other places, people mock his accent. He's very sensitive and full of rage, I sensed.

### Saturday, 17 July

Ralph Seen offered to make me a cup of tea. Later, I invited him to mediate with me. He did and was delighted. He said he felt peaceful. He said he must do it before he goes to sleep. It may help him to sleep. I said if he could do even one minute or five minutes a day for a start, it would be good. Even one 'Má – Rá – Ná – Thá', said consciously, would be fine and then increase it gently. He could hear that. It can also help to listen to the breath, the in-breath and the out-breath. It can help one to come out of one's head and live more consciously.

### Wednesday, 21 July

I met another 'new' man. He smiled. Mel Sanborn, when he was cleaning Simon today, asked me for the piece of paper on 'How to Mediate'. He felt calmer since he began meditation. He said he used to do meditation all the time in his flat. He said he was in a flat since we met him last year. It did not work out with his friend in the flat, then, so he left it.

Ursula Walk came out dressed like the 'Queen of Sheba'! She wore a long multi-coloured skirt – ankle length – two big slits! It was made of very flimsy material. A 'plastic leg' hung off a button hole on her blouse! She was dripping with jewellery. I admired it and she said, "Wait until you see my necklace!". She got a white peaked hat from John Gabie. She wore a lovely red tartan jacket and a white blouse with embroidery on it. She looked lovely. She calls the tune here and, at her command, Mel Lahive followed her out with their bottles!

### Thursday, 20 August

Alexis Obaris said a man builds boats here. He talked about it.

Peter Mastare had huge pain. He shared about his grandmother dying. He was in prison at the time. He was led, hand-cuffed, to her coffin in the church. He felt such a criminal. He said the people must have been saying, "Will you look at the prisoner?". He said he was brought up a Catholic. They had the *Rosary* every night and were 'kicked' to Mass. His family had an addiction to religion. It could have done worse damage to them than an addiction to alcohol, drugs or gambling. I feel their essence / spirit could have been shrouded over by the compulsion of this addiction to religion. It is good to see these negative trends breaking down today among so many. There's a chance of finding the real person then, hopefully.

It is a very special privilege to be able to meditate in the Simon Community when possible, as I can send positive energy to all there on the spot.

## Wednesday, 1 September

Rosetta and I left here to go to Simon at 10.20 a.m. or so and, when I went out the door, I met a lady from three doors down. She walked along with me and I told her we remembered Julie Yeass in prayer. She was very grateful. I told her where I was going and she said, "I'd love to take those homeless people home and mind them. My husband has a nephew, Michael, who is on drugs and lives on the street. He's about 34. You probably know him". This lady is a very caring person, I could hear.

I met Jacob Gefenny on the street. Jacob said, "This is the love of my life", pointing to Gobnait Rael. He said they were getting a place. He gave her a hug and they both shook hands with me and went off.

I met Lee Dallyn today. He's like a person who has A.I.D.S. He is very poorly-looking. Wayne Magee was in hospital, suffering from depression. He said he felt very down.

I met Amy Ladde and her visually-impaired friend. I shook hands. Chris Carthon had a lovely, soft, gentle handshake. It was a velvet-like handshake. He could see nothing. Amy supported him, as they moved around to get fruit in the market. I said I was so delighted to meet Chris Carthon. Amy told him I said he is a lovely person. He smiled.

## Thursday, 2 September

Bill Glore came over. He lived in Italy for a time. He had a very, very pronounced American accent. He hoped to do biology at Oxford. He worked in Nepal for six months before Simon. I said he's great to do this work in Simon at 19. He was not sure what he'd like to do with the rest of his life. He'd like to work with children. He got on well here, he said. He'd like to see more of the country, go to West Cork for a few days now, etc.

Robert Seaton turned around to face me from the middle table. He talked a lot and smiled now. Before this, he was very solemn with me. He has two children in Sweden, two girls, 4 and 8. His father died when he was aged 8. He went to a home for two years in Dublin. He went to England then, and Sweden twice. His grandmother lives in Cork. He could be 'locked up' soon! He was very friendly. Robert Seaton said he often got soup / sandwich in Douglas Street. He did not go too often, as he did not like to take advantage of the people there, or take what they gave him for granted.

## Friday, 3 September

Samantha Caden is a 'skinhead' now. I asked how was she. She felt very sad. She said she had a baby four months ago. She had an illness. Maybe she won't talk, walk, or hear anything, she said. No-one is sure yet. She's in hospital in Cork. She was in Waterford first, and is now in Cork. She said she was very bad after the birth. She has a boyfriend here, Greg Fellard. She introduced me to him. Samantha and Greg are going to a social worker about fostering the child.

## Tuesday, 7 September

I went to Simon. I met Alice Jay. I asked her how she was. She said, "Same as ever". I wondered what that comment really meant?

Some street-people can be like children at times. Indeed, any one of us can act like a two year old. People – adults and children – do things, at times, to get notice, I feel. It often shows the depth of hurt in children, as they need huge attention. O.K.

Richard Manah said he had been in every prison in Ireland except one. He said how horrible it was in the basement of Mountjoy with junkies – heroin addicts. He's into hash, not heroin, he said. He was accused of doing something he did not do, he said. He will get them, though, he said, Gardaí, etc., who lied about him. He said he came from an upper middle class family. He went to a community school and he was expelled in second year from the school when he was 15. He got a job somewhere else. He went on the streets then. He's been in and out of prison since. He's an intelligent lad. When I said this, he had tears in his eyes. He said, "I have no patience to stay with anything. I was born with no patience". I said he has great patience deep inside but he doesn't know it yet, though. He said he'd like to get a place – start a new life and give up the life he is living now. He said he may need more time like this, though, on the streets.

## *Wednesday, 8 September*

I was at Chelsea Calcott's house for 12.55 p.m. I said in the card I'd be there between 12 noon and 1.00 p.m. She had not got the card and said only that if it was a wet day, she would be out all day. She goes early in the morning with the baby and Calum Cadoret. I knocked at the door. It was 'pouring out of the heavens', raining. It was a very dilapidated area, where there was graffiti on walls, etc. Attempts were made to make flower beds, but to no avail. Chelsea was delighted to see me. She gave me a hug. Calum was gone to the shop with Dana. Calum brought back chips, vegetables, kebabs and sausage rolls. He offered me chips – shared his, giving me a carton with half chips and curry. They were lovely. The serviette was the newspaper – newsprint, which was around the chips – fine! I chatted with them for a long time. Calum Cadoret, who lives with Chelsea, likes Ned. Their flat is nicely done up. Ned picked the paper for the kitchen – it was orange and red in colour with the word 'cocktails' written on it. The toilet was very dirty. The floor of the house was not very clean. I ate two of my own queen cakes that I brought to them. Calum made me lovely tea. I had two cups. I could see both Calum and Chelsea blossomed, when I accepted them and listened carefully to all they said. I held the baby in my arms. She is a lovely smiling child. I stayed about two hours. I was delighted I went up. They asked me where do I live now. I chose not to name the locality. I said, "I live in a place now, where I have more time for silence and prayer. As this work with street-people is so sacred and special, I find I need more time for prayer and quiet to have more respect for these special people". Chelsea and Calum looked fairly happy, I thought. They asked me to call anytime. I may meet them in town. Chelsea and Calum are lovely people inside. I said this to both of them. They are more than their behaviour

Samantha Caden had a photo of her baby. I said, "Would you like to show it to me?". She said, "Not yet". I could see the baby was wired up to something, in the picture. I asked her how Greg Fellard was doing? She said, "Up and down". She moved away. She said he has a lot to sort out in the coming week.

I said, "Hello", to Jessica Giles. She was on T.V. I said I heard she was very good. She said the government may do something for people on the street now. I asked Jessica what size clothes she takes. She said, "14". I told her I had very nice clothes I got from a lady. Her jacket is size 14. She smiled.

## Tuesday, 21 September

Tiffany O'Drisea said she could talk to me for hours. She said she gets such good energy from me. She said, "You do not drain me. Some people, telling stories in Simon, can drain me".

Nicole Manahane is facing the wall. She often sits there. I never yet heard Nicole talk. She has a beautiful face. I'm in total awe of her silent presence, her beautiful presence, as she walks around holding her breast with her hands, while rags hold up her skirt. The smell of dirt is severe enough, though the beauty within radiates through her face.

## Wednesday, 29 September

Clara Cassidy brought in her child, June. I called her over. She put out her hands and I took her up on my lap. She is a doty child. Cathal and Siobhán made a big fuss of June. I could sense Samantha Caden's anger, as she was probably remembering her own little child in hospital, who suffered from brain damage. Her anger was volcanic – I sensed it in her face. She's suffered intensely. When I said, "Hello, Samantha", she did not answer.

## Monday, 4 October

Richie Manah asked Marion for a brush, to brush his hair. She gave it to him. She shares everything. They have 'all things in common'.

## Tuesday, 30 November

The poor woman crying at the door upset me, too. She had no place to go. Abandoned, unwanted.

## Thursday, 16 December

I was delighted to meet Terence O'Donen and Jessica Giles. Terence is great-humoured. Jessica and himself went to Glanmire by taxi yesterday, had lunch, a free drink and came back again very happy last night after 7.00 p.m.! I enjoyed Terence.

Calum Cadoret said he slept on two blankets last night, in the freezing cold, in a warehouse, with three other people. He said he would not be happy at Christmas at home, so he won't go there. His mother lives in Leitrim. He's going to England for New Year's Eve, he said.

Rosetta gave out some more Christmas cards and it was lovely to see how the people appreciated them so much. I felt pain arising in me and knew there was something in me that needed evacuating – the pain of abandonment is so awful. It's like being dropped in mid-ocean and never being found again by anyone. It's a cold, fearful, lonely place to be. It's worse though, when I abandon myself.

## Friday, 11 December

I sat for one hour without almost saying a word – it was awesome to be there – I could be myself – no one had any expectations of me, nor asked me to talk or do anything. I could hear amazing respect, here in the hall full of people. I sensed great love there, in letting me be. I felt deep peace – people came and went.

It was an awesome day. It came to me that love only grows in opposition. In the eyes of the world, my time there today would be considered of no value, a failure, waste, doing nothing, no personal satisfaction, no success at the end, but deep, deep peace reminding me once more that being is prior to all action. Being is the highest form of all action. A few darts of fear hit me here and there alright, what would these people think of me? I felt one with them, when I could sit and be. I felt no different at all. That was special, too. Their being and mine is one. This is the deepest and closest communication one can have with any human being.

Living from the *centre* of our soul is awesome. Contemplation is a way of looking at ordinary life and seeing the extraordinary. It is finding the Creator in the midst of the everyday. Great art, music, literature help us to transcend ordinary time. Meditation is about being still, so that we can see more clearly. What we find there, we find elsewhere if we have eyes that see and ears that hear. Awareness is the key. Contemplation transforms our way of being in the world, being there in heightened awareness. *Being there by being here, now.* Now is the acceptable time. Contemplation takes place in the midst of an active life whenever we are *fully attentive to life.* Contemplation is fullness of presence and thus not a means to an end, i.e., Communion. Oneness. It is about NOW.

## Tuesday, 21 December

Richie Manah said he had a card for Rosetta and I, but it got soaked wet yesterday in his pocket, so he'd get another one. He said to be sure and tell Rosetta. He said he's making some resolutions for the New Year. He couldn't tell me one, as it is personal. Another one was beginning with a capital D – he said it's not drink. He was 'skippering out' for the last week. He slept in an old derelict house.

## Wednesday, 22 December

The *Emmanuel* at Mass was special. All the friends were there. I felt the Christmas Mass was the stable incarnate in the flesh, this year. I was moved by the birth in the hearts around me. I could hear the Christus present in John Gabie. He was searching for the truth – the birth took place in his heart – my truth touched his truth, I heard. It was a very profound experience.

## Wednesday, 29 December

A lad called Vincent Parle stood near me and said he was waiting for a flat. He was in a centre and said he got on great there. He did meditation and said that was brilliant. It helped him relax and clear his mind, he said. I asked him which kind they did and he said, "Má – Rá – Ná – Thá". He did lots of drawings, he said. His Dad was an artist. He used sit near him when he'd be drawing and learned a lot from him. His Dad died when Vincent was 12. That was the start of his own trouble, he said. Then his mother died. There were 13 in the family. He appeared to be solid. He said he takes photos of his art-work and has it in a portfolio. I asked him if he'd like to show it to me sometime. He said he would. He has a bed in the project room – one of the emergency beds. He said he can't meditate in there. I invited Vincent to meditate with us. Vincent Parle said he did a lot of work on himself in the centre and now it's all undone, being in a place like this.

Cameron Ballante told me he got the card for Christmas from us and said he's not used to getting a Christmas card. He said, "It is good that someone knows I AM THERE". That spoke volumes, I thought.

# 2000

I went to Simon. Ralph Seen was at the gate. He said he had been in a hostel and hoped to get in to Simon again. I said, "Hello" to Dylan Caball in the hall and a new man said, "Hello", and said his name was Rodger Mangaret. His house was boarded-up and he had nowhere to go.

Julie Joss was cleaning. She chatted a lot. She has three boys from 8½ to 4½ years. Her real husband left her three years ago. Her parents are very good to her. She'd love extra money to get a flat in a good area. It would cost £150. Welfare pays so much, she pays £56+. She has very little money to rear her boys.

Samantha Caden chatted with me for a long time. She felt very sad, as her little daughter, who has some form of illness, is now fostered. She wonders will she ever get her back. I said I'd call to see her if she wished if she was still in hospital. She was very, very sad. The child's Dad drinks and used to have drink taken, mostly, when he'd visit the little girl. Later, when Molly Gaffey, Samantha Caden and I were chatting, Samantha said she had made her mistakes and now she was going to get her life together again and make a fresh start. She does not seem to sleep on the street these times – she is in the Simon Community for a while now. Later on, she was very excited and said she was getting a transitional flat in the complex. She said, "When you come in next week, Catherine, ask one of the workers next Tuesday to come over with you and let you into my flat". I said, "I'd be very privileged to visit you, Samantha, in your new home".

Patrick Paschel said he reads a lot now. He may go swimming eventually, a couple of days a week. He's interested in organic farming. I said I admired how he could live with himself and *'not want to be doing'*, running away from himself – he stays with nothing (no thing) everyday. He had his last drink New Year's Eve and had none for 18 days since. I'm more in awe everyday at these special people's ability to be able to stay with themselves. How hard it can be for us so-called 'religious' to be asked to 'do nothing' for even one day. These people have a great capacity to *BE*. It seems to me that it's because they are so in touch with their woundedness – they are real and can talk about it, let it go for now and live now. It is awesome to be in the presence of these sacred human beings who are counter-cultural today. They don't, as they say, fit into the rat-race. It is as if they believe, deep down, that they are not made for that life. That is why I find that they are very interested in silence, solitude and meditation.

Nicole Manahane, the beautiful, silent presence who comes to work there three days per week and who, at times, drinks on the streets, was not there today. I missed her presence there. She's very tattered and torn-looking but what a radiant smile that lights up her face, as if to say 'My heart is always at home'. One could only see her clothes all tied up with old knotted tights around her, but that is not all she is. She is infinitely more – the dwelling place of the Creator of heaven and earth. This to me is the Christus born in her heart and living in the manger. The manger symbolises her humanity, a place of the limited unclean and woundedness – this is the mystery of the Incarnation alive today in our world. How awesome that our being / soul can be meditated through our wounded humanity. Rosetta's and my privilege is to be awakened ourselves to our own in-dwelling spirit and then to be able to accompany other people, as they awaken to their beauty within, too. Nicole is a means of awakening me more deeply to my own silent presence. These people are my teachers.

I met Chelsea Calcott's friend, Patrick Marah. He said he's grand now. He's working in a lorry and has a girlfriend. He used to drink a lot, but it seems he doesn't now. Patrick spent time in Ballygriffin, too. Later, he married and is now very happy.

## Friday, 28 January

Michael Baily told me about his mother. She could not talk, he said, but she was full of love. His eyes filled with tears. He said I would not understand about his mother. She's from Switzerland. His Dad was from an upper class. Michael worked in a big business. At 15 years old, he ran away from home. When he was very young, his mother and father did not get on. They lived in Austria and his Dad beat and beat his Mam terribly. He could later forgive his Dad. He said he gave his Dad a hug like he gave me today! I felt, when he hugged me today, that it was out of his needy need to give it. He was really hugging his Dad, I felt. O.K. He invited me for tea, so it was his place to pay. O.K. He said he was going to dry out. He paid for the tea then.

Jamie Rawle came over. He asked me could he meditate. I said there was no room for now available to us. He sat near me then and told me he was in prison. He was in a two-man cell. He was also in hospital for four weeks. He spent five months in a caravan in Youghal with his mother and Dad. Jamie was abused as a child. I said, "You're carrying a big load". He asked me to meditate with him, for a full half-hour. He did so very reverently. He felt very good, he said, after it. I thanked him for meditating with me. I said to him that I sensed my own peace come alive in me, from his good energy in meditation. I really did feel that so real – it was awesome. It was a time and moment of deep joy for me. I experienced his outpouring of goodness and peace.

## Thursday, 3 February

I was very moved when Cameron Ballante came over, stood near me and said to me, "You are very quiet today". He stood there with his face all cut. He wore filthy clothes. He had *seven* layers of clothes on, i.e., shirts, coats, etc. His ribs were cut, he said, and his knees were sore and still he could sense my energy. I sensed a communion with Cameron. I did feel some pain there today. I thanked Cameron for being aware of me today.

## Wednesday, 9 February

Another young, new man – Alex Jack – sat near the stairs and came over, when I saluted him, to Samson's seat. His face was hardly recognisable. He had a black eye, head scars, a face scar, his lips were all blood. Nearly all the back of his hand was tattooed. 'LOVE' was written across his four fingers on his right hand. He said his Dad 'topped himself' six years ago. He drowned himself near his home. His Mam and Dad had drink problems, too. He now has. He started drinking at 13 years, he is now 23. He said he's on drugs, too, and he gets very angry on them and beats up people and they beat him. He was only out of prison two weeks and getting on grand, when he was attacked outside his own door. He said they wanted to kill him, but didn't succeed. He said he can't go back there yet, as it would be risky. He said what happened was serious and he said he does not even like to talk about it. He has a brother of 12, and two sisters who are twins. They are 15. One sister is 9. One of the twins, aged 15, has a baby 18 months old. He showed me a photo of himself and her baby. He was a beautiful little boy, called Ryan Balfe. He said he's very close to his Mam and family. He got a barring order, as he was drinking and disorderly. He said he's responsible for what he does and he doesn't blame his Dad. He used to blame his Dad. I sensed he's beating himself up a bit, though! He was a pure 'skin-head' – a fine tall 6ft. lad, I'd say. Alex Jack said he's unwell, too, and was in hospital 37 times up to the age of 19. He was also in and out of prison. He had plenty of drugs in prison instead drink, he said.

## Monday, 14 February

I met Jerry Laar near the apartment. He said he feels very down and is nearly always that way now. He seems to be going down, down, he said. He hates getting up in the morning. He would stay in bed all day, only as he's so down, he could not sleep. He wonders will he ever get anything out of life. He said, "It seems to be passing me by. I can't get any kick out of it. Hash gives me a high, but then after I'm down again. I have no confidence. I'm like this, I feel down for about two years". His skin is very dry. I wondered what is *his* meaning in life at all? What keeps him going?

Samantha Caden will marry Calum Cadoret soon. She showed me her engagement ring. Later, I met Calum and congratulated him and said that he is a lovely man and Samantha is a lovely girl. I hope they'll be happy. I remembered that these two lovely people were in Ballygriffin at different times. Marriage is rare enough among the street-people.

## Tuesday, 22 February – Ballygriffin

Jessica Giles was with us today. She shared about her life and her family. In deep reverence, I can be in awe at Jessica's personhood in the silence. Thank you, Jessica for your unique and gentle presence with us today. Gently, reverently and respectfully, this is all that comes to me in this now, to write here, after this special day.

## Tuesday, 29 February - Ballygriffin

Greg Fellard came with us to Ballygriffin. I felt Greg was a bit down. He talked about his daughter on the way down. Her mother wanted to put her into a foster-home. She called after him 'Dad' in Brazil one day, when she was 14. He got custody of her, after five years looking for it. His daughter said she did not want her Dad to give up work, when he was looking after her. He said, "That broke my heart!". We did meditation with Greg in Ballygriffin. He shared a lot about his time at sea and fishing. He was an electrician on *Stena Lines*, too. He was fascinating. He worked in Rome. He was reading a book on the occult. I said I hope I did not disturb his silence. He said, "No, but I love to be silent at times". Something that struck me a lot about Greg yesterday was that when he said he did not go out in the middle of meditation, as he was 'being in the silence'. I sensed he discovered something precious in that silence. This is awesome. He awakened me to my own reverential silence – it is important not to injure it. I was in awe at Greg in his silence. The language of the Maker is the language of silence and no other language can adequately describe the Maker.

## Thursday, 2 March

I said to David Gabbay, "I have the medal you asked me for". He said, "YOU REMEMBERED *ME*". It was the way his face lit up when he said, "You remembered *me*", I won't forget. I feel he must have felt important, when I remembered *him*.

Greg Fellard, who was in Ballygriffin, talked about being very down at times. He said he was very good after the day in Ballygriffin still. He said he did a quarter of an hour of meditation last night before he went to bed, not to put him to sleep. He took no tablets last night, he said, and had a great sleep. He said it was great to do meditation with us, as it can be hard to do on one's own. He said in the silence, he could hear about forgiveness. He said he gets a bit disturbed about things he did. I said, "You are forgiven already. You only need to be aware of it". I said when we do meditation in Simon, would he like to join us. He said he would, but he'd have to be ready to do it. He'd need a day or two notice, he said.

I visited Samantha Caden in her flat. She made some tea for me and asked me to sit on her armchair while she sat on the other. We had a long, long chat about baby Austia Candon and how Calum would like to look after her with Samantha. She said he's heroic to do that. She said she could have other children like that, if she has other children. She said Calum would love a child of his own. Samantha said she's off drugs / drink for three years. She was on drugs since she was 13 – until three years ago. She's 29 now. She said they will marry in a registry office now – a church wedding would take two years to organise and cost £3,000 or £4,000 plus hotel, etc. She said, "We have each other". She said they had organised an engagement party but no-one turned up. There was a band there, a cake made especially, plus tea and sandwiches. Calum's Mam and Dad invited 25 people and no-one came! How terribly disappointing for them. They felt there is no point in having a big crowd at their wedding, or even asking them, Samantha said. She said Calum is marvellous. They were friends for a few months. He asked her to marry him at midnight New Year's Eve and she said, "Yes". He bought her an engagement ring before Valentine's Day. She said if she were to pick it out herself, she would pick that one. Calum said the sooner they are married, the better. The date is 26 May. Samantha said all her friends are in Galway. She may move there sometime. She was in Galway Simon and felt she was able to talk better to other residents there. She said she would like to go to the hospital to meet the staff, where her baby was born. She finds it hard to talk about a foster home. Samantha has great feelings for her child. She's very caring. Another person would give her up for adoption. She said people see her in a negative way. They say she can't mind the baby. Being with Samantha was a very awesome experience.

## Tuesday, 7 March

Jerry Laar also said yesterday something very profound, "I am the same now as if I were dead – things are no different whether I am alive or dead". I thought of the river he went into in Cork, asking it to take his life. In Ballygriffin, he could sit near the river and hear a call to full life here and now. He talked afterwards about it flowing along and he said he felt peace there. In time, hopefully, he will hear that this peace is in Jerry Laar. His energy of smiling and even laughing yesterday was positive. Good.

## *Wednesday, 15 March - Ballygriffin*

I said, "Hello", to Clare Scott and Greg Fellard. They said they were getting married in England. They are going there tomorrow. Clare had tears in her eyes. She said she'd love to get back her child. Greg asked me to say a blessing for the two of them. I did ask that they hear their own goodness. I said that separately to each of them. I then asked them if they would like to give themselves a blessing. Clare said she'd like to get her child, be happy and have a nice house. Clare and Greg asked me to bless the child's photo. I said I'd also remember them in my prayers.

We went to Ballygriffin. We meditated. Rory Mano was very aware of the silence. The meal was prepared by Rosetta. I spent an awesome time with Rory, when Rosetta went for her break – 1) stillness; 2) silence; 3) prayer; 4) silent Presence. I wrote each piece attentively for Rory. It struck me a lot how we all need to hear over and over those statements *re* prayer / silence, etc. We meditated later again and had tea. We brought Rory back to his place. It is a beautiful place. He has left the streets for now. Rory invited us to dinner some Sunday. He was so proud of his new home, he wished us to spend some time there with him.

## *Tuesday, 28 March*

James Ballard told me his brother of 16 has T.B. His brother is delighted, as he's out of school. He drinks, so do his uncle, mother and father. James is the only one who does not.

David Gabbay sat on the stairs near me. He had a long, long story. Teresa O'Fiache left him. She's with Kevin Saeen, he said. She's pregnant. She gave David an envelope, one day a few weeks ago, when he got off the bus in Cork. In the envelope was a Barring Order. It was on his birthday, he said. It was 14 March. David was very down. He said Teresa was gone from him for over a year now. She drinks in the streets. She showed David her face beaten by Kevin Saeen. Her body was badly beaten, too, he said. He was upset that she left him. He gave her too many chances, he said. She wound him around her little finger, he said. He said he was blind. He showed me a beautiful photo of his son aged 20 months. He's in care. He can meet him when the social worker brings him in. He said his son is the only thing that is keeping him going now. I said, "David, you are great to express your feelings. You are safe now to do that here". He said he had violent anger before. The violence has gone out of it now. I said he may need to hit the pillow or roar a bit at times in a safe place to get it out. He said he prays a lot for his mother, his baby David, and Teresa O'Fiache, believe it or not.

On the way up Oliver Plunkett Street, I met Marion Keleger sitting on a bag, with a red sleeping-bag around her. She had a tin whistle near her, a bottle of *Coke* in a brown paper bag and a container with a few shillings in it. She said she's out sleeping on the streets for the last three weeks. Sean Satch got very violent on drink, she said. He broke her nose. I wonder is she a traveller? She said if she had enough money, she'd go to a B & B. She was in a doorway of an old shop or was it a take-away?

## Friday, 31 March

I was talking to Suzanne Bulb and Pierce Pole about Ballygriffin. They'd love to go. Suzanne said it would be a change from Simon. Pierce said he was married and has one child. He said he lives in Cork. He knew Suzanne 20 years ago. He was doing a line with her. He met her again in August 1988. Pierce said they are not married. I said that was none of my business. "All I see is that ye are two beautiful people". They both smiled from ear to ear! Pierce Pole said, "You are a lovely person, too". Suzanne Bulb used to go out and feed the birds at 6.00 a.m. every day. She's a lovely, gentle person. They seem very fond of each other. Pierce said he was going out to collect the dole on Wednesday at 10.00 a.m. I said we go to Ballygriffin between 10.00 a.m. and 10.30 a.m. or so.

Ulick O'Flanny sat down. He chatted. He said he was at the University of Leeds. He did a Social Studies degree. He loves Ireland. I told him I was taking residents to Ballygriffin for days of quiet and meditation. He said he'd like that very much. He could not do that in Germany. It's too stressful. He was in Dingle once. He could get no bus back for a week. He sat near the sea and loved it. He loves sitting on the cliff by the sea, he said.

It came to me to meditate. I sat in the hall for an hour in practically total silence. I could *BE* there very, very well. I feel the good energy. I can smile at people who came in and out. I felt my own deep compassion awakened through today's meeting with the people on the street.

## Wednesday, 12 April

A man said, when I asked him where was he from, "I'm a knight of the road". When he realised I was a Sister, he said he probably got meals in convents.

## Good Friday, 21 April

After a while, Mark Salim came out. On his way back, he said, "Hello, Sister". He came over to me and said to put his name down for Ballygriffin. He 'moved me' over to half the seat and sat on the other half. Fine. He said he'd love if an angel would come down and say, "Stop", and he'd drink no more. If an angel could stop him drinking, he'd be delighted, he said. I said, "The angel is in you, i.e., the good in you. This, no drink can destroy". He looked at me and said, "Is there?". He said he was in a centre, broke out of it and went across a field to a pub. He had been in the centre for seven weeks. He held my hand and put his 'filthy with dirt' fingers on my hand. Through the dirt, I could see the Maker's creation. Awesome. He stayed a while, happily sitting down. He drinks 1½ bottles of whiskey during the day.

I met Aidan Callender. He had a lot of drink taken. There was a small drop of whiskey left in the bottle. He said I was a lovely girl. His pants fell down to nearly his ankles three times, at least, when I was listening to him! I met him again later in the corner of a road works barrier. He had no way out. He was banging at the green timber. I helped him out of his confinement. This was a very special Good Friday liturgy for me. These were real Stations of the Cross. Aidan Callender's pants falling down three times symbolised for me the three falls of a saint under his heavy cross. How humiliating for a beautiful human being to have to undergo so much suffering. The public, just as they made a laughing stock of the man Jesus, now mocks this poor man, who through no fault of his own is reduced to such a pitiable sight. I could really hear the crucifixion in Aidan Callender. Simon of Cyrene helped Jesus. These street-people support one another in Simon. The workers, too, are great. They, too, all carry crosses. I need no 'Church' liturgy today. This event was a total and very profound ritualisation of suffering for me with the street-people today. It was an awesome day surely. A blessed day. The Cross is symbolic of suffering. I went gently with the flow.

## Easter Saturday, 22 April

The man I met on Tuesday, who would not give me his name, said to me, "That man over there is a Frenchman". Later, I said, "Hello", to the man he called a 'Frenchman'. He said he was not French, but could speak French, Italian and had very little English. His name is Ross Ahere. He said he spent some time in Italy – 15 years at work. He said they are doing nothing for him in Ireland. He has no problem, he said. He doesn't drink or take drugs.

All he wants is a job and get money to buy a flat. He said he is not happy. I asked him if he'd like soup. He said he had it.

Mary Kaye is there one and a half weeks. She's from Sweden. She's a beautiful girl. She said she worked with orphans in Jerusalem for nine months, then went to Mozambique. She was there the time of the floods. She taught Portuguese to children. She began a pre-school for children. She lived in the bush with an Irish girl. She told her about Simon in Cork. The other girl taught maths and agriculture out there. She's home now. Mary goes to visit her family often.

*Thursday, 4 May*

I met Mark Salim. I said, "Hello". He shook hands. His hands were filthy. He said put his name down for Ballygriffin when we're going again. He said he was going to buy a naggin and drink it. He said he would then go begging to get more. He slept under the Savoy shelter in Patrick's Street last night. I said, "You had a roof over your head". He laughed.

Today, I'm invited at meditation to let go of everything. These street-people are so free in this way.

Later, a lovely young lad, beautiful-looking, about 19 to 22 years old or so, called me over. He is Clive Ceerp. He left the streets some time ago and went to live with his girlfriend, who already had a son of 3, before she met Clive. Clive's son is 15 months now and his girlfriend is expecting their second baby in April. He said he went back and studied for his Leaving Cert., but he fell by the wayside again. He said he never gives up and kept saying, "I'll bounce back again". I said, "I can send you positive energy". He said, "No, don't send me positive energy, say a prayer for me". I asked him what is his favourite prayer. He said, *"Our Father"*. I said that is my favourite prayer, too. I said, "Would you like to hear how I say it? This is what I say from with-in, out. "Our Father, who is in heaven ... The heaven is within-in me and the Spirit of the One who created the universe and all in it, dwells in your heart (heaven) and mine, in silence ... Hallowed be your name ... I am good because I Am – you are good, because you Are". He said, *"I am who I am* and you accept me with my faults, as I am". How beautifully Clive expressed his own AM-NESS. This was awesome, hearing this from this young street-person I met on the street today. How deeply he heard the prayer the *Our Father*. I went on, "Your kingdom come ... the kingdom of God, the Maker / designer is *with-in* us. May that kingdom / queendom come alive to our consciousness ... Your will be done on earth as it is in heaven ... the will of the Maker is inscribed our being, soul. May my humanity (earth) hear the beauty of my inner self, (heaven) … Give us this day our daily bread … all we need for today is already given to us, even before the day begins … Forgive us our trespasses, as we forgive those who trespass against us … our being is for giving back – we come to a sense of harmony within – or at least, experience that 'always there' harmony in ourselves and then we can't miss it in others. This is a journey into the *Now* … Lead us not into temptation … give you strength in time of the test you're enduring now, Clive … Deliver us from evil … the greatest evil is the evil of unawareness / unconsciousness". I said, "Clive, my prayer for you, then, is, that you may come to *experience* your own beauty, goodness, love, respect, wonder inside in you. That you may in time have *NO DOUBT* about that presence in you". He said, "Thanks". He said he's not interested in the past, nor the future, but today, the now, as that is all he has. He said, "That is enough for me". I said I would write down his saying about, "I am who I am", etc., and write it in this book that I'm writing. He said, "Thanks, I'll buy that book".

## Friday, 5 May

Dan, a Canadian worker, came to me and, in a very gentle voice, said, "Well, how is Sister Kathleen today?". He said he went for a walk in Fitzgerald's Park. He had his lunch and began the 2.00 p.m. shift now. He is very, very friendly.

I was very moved when Adam Cafferkey said today that someone said to him recently, "I heard you are off drink", and Adam replied, "I can only say I'm off drink *now*. I can't talk about tomorrow or any other day". Profound wisdom always moves me and inspires me. I said to him that he said something very profound. I felt he really heard what that 'now' is about. It is not a theory with him, I felt. It is a reality, a conviction. I hear he hears that *now is all he has*, really, the only time he has is *now*.

## Wednesday, 10 May

I set out to walk to Simon from town. On my way through a back street (facing the sex shop), at the riverside, I met Mel and Ursula. They were sitting on a door-step, sharing *one* bottle of wine in a brown paper bag! They said they have the first bottle there every day, the second one in an alleyway near the English Market and a third bottle on North Main Street! I asked them where they have the fourth one! They could not say. I said, "I suppose by then, ye hardly know where ye are?". Ursula smiled. She said a docker gave her a big bottle of sherry. She had it in her bag. She had the straw hat on with the black-coloured scarf draped over the crown of it. There was another bit of jewellery on it, a glass bird dangling! I asked her had she the Holy Spirit badge on at all today. She showed me a tobacco box, a flat tin box in which were some coins, one Canadian, one French, one Deutschland, some medals of Our Lady of Lourdes, etc. In the middle was one of the Holy Spirit. I can't remember how many rings she had. She had many, many rings, all sizes, big and small. Mel said little. I moved on.

Abigail Bancrow came out, sat and began to tell me her life story for all in the hall to hear, too. Abigail said her parents protected her. She grew up shy. They had a sweet shop and café. She was out in the park in Prague at 16 years of age. She went topless. She said she had a relationship with Victor Parry for 10 years. He beat her. She has a son, Joseph, aged 20, and, in her second relationship of 13 years, she has three daughters – Joan, 30 years, is the oldest. Abigail worked on a millionaire's estate, in Austria. Her boss gave her great presents. She said they had a very good hotel. Once, 50 people could be served. She asked one person once would she like more vegetables. The person said she got no meat yet! I wonder what other services she provided for millionaires on the estate? Abigail was in great, great high form. She's in Simon 18 months now. She had a flat in between. She said to look at her name on the Ballygriffin book. She wrote something special and unique. She said she'd love to go again. I admired her hair. She thanked me and said, "We all need affirmation".

## Thursday, 11 May

I sat on a chair last week that was perfectly upholstered. Today, it was all torn. It was symbolic of the destruction of people of themselves. Their humanity goes mad.

Hyacinth Feehay, whom I met later, sleeps on the streets in London. Hyacinth kept saying she was not able to get a place to stay. I wonder why. She looked pretty well. She talked, almost non-stop, for two hours. I was very interested to hear her story. I could see her, too, looking around a lot at people coming in and out. She said she likes Simon. After nearly two hours, she said she had a daughter of 18 now, whom she put up for adoption. Hyacinth was 21 then. She never saw her since. She told me I was like Mary McAleese! At another stage, she said I was like her uncle's wife! She's a lovely lady, she said. I felt I could be quite well there, with her. She bought *Readybrek* to eat. She asked me if I'd like tea. I said, "Yes, no sugar". She put sugar in! It was very, very sweet. She is very, very articulate altogether and very intellectual. I said it to her. She had a lovely smile.

## Monday, 15 May

It came to me to ask Samantha Caden and Calum Cadoret if they'd like to go to Ballygriffin on the 24th, two days before their wedding. Jonah McAlvey took me to Samantha Caden. She's number 4 bell. Samantha invited me in. I said, "Would you both like to go to Ballygriffin on the 24th for a day of quiet, rest, gentleness before your wedding?". She said she'd ask Calum. She said it to Calum. He was delighted. He'd love a quiet day. I said, "You are free to meditate, go to nature or whatever helps you to relax, during the day". She smiled. She thanked me for remembering them and she asked me how was my family. I asked her how was her child. She said, "One day, one moment at a time. In the beginning, it was very hard". She asked me to pray for her.

It came to me to wear my best clothes going to Simon, as an outward sign of respect for these special people. I felt that a long time ago, too. The best is not ever good enough for a person, the human being who is uniquely beautiful and is good inside, a reflection of the Maker, the Creator of all life.

## Tuesday, 30 May

I met Joshua McAllenor. He was delighted to talk, I could see. I felt great compassion for Joshua when he said he was an orphan. Even to use the word 'orphan' sounded so sad. He had no parents to care for him. No wonder he's on the streets. I saw his hand-tattoo 'Mary' and also a tattoo 'Joshua misses Jack forever'. His brother died at the door of *Brown Thomas* in 1989. Mr. Doolan used to foster Joshua McAllenor in Co. Westmeath. Joshua used to play lots of tricks on him, but he loved Joshua, I could hear. I felt he needed to hear that. He said he cried when Joshua left on the bus a couple of weeks ago. He said he will go back again there. The people all know him. Joshua needed to talk a lot, I felt. He'd love to go to Ballygriffin, he said, during the next month. It would be great if he could go once, even. He felt he'd like to go to his friends on the steps across the way then. He put his arms around us. I gave him a kiss. I remembered what Rosetta said about the gay man with A.I.D.S. The doctor said when she asked what helped him, "A hug, simple, but beautiful".

## Wednesday, 31 May

I heard my ego say, "It's a waste of time being here today". O.K. I caught it. I'm aware of the sacredness of each unique person with me. This is where I hear the wanting in me, wanting things to be different.

Pierce Pole said that some people think that in gathering things / wealth, etc., in this life, that they will last forever. He said they don't last at all. How wise, I thought. Street-people see life as it is, almost at times with the eyes of children, unadulterated. They are very wise really.

## Tuesday, 6 June

Jonah McAlvey said, "God has a plan for us all. Sometimes he says 'Yes', other times 'No', but we usually have to wait as we let the Creator's plan for us unfold". I said, "It must be hard at times doing this work". He said, "Patience is important". I said I like the 'wait' bit.

Susan Nadaya, a resident, said, "I hate this religion thing". 'Bible Bashers', she called them. Susan said, "I know ye do meditation". Susan gave an almighty roar later out of her, as she was walking up by the office.

Later, Noah McAlorey was giving out about the church forcing him to do things, with its rules and regulations. I said, "Nothing lasts, when done out of obligation". He said he doesn't believe in another life after this one. "This life is all there is. Enjoy it, die and go down six feet and end". He said he's doing his purgatory here. He said he'll be in heaven now, if he can get a bottle! It was the first time I ever heard him talk about doing purgatory here. Such suffering. I said, "You're always good inside, and all of us in the hall are good, but our behaviour may be off the wall". Noah said, "What is my soul?". I said, "The best part of you". He said, "Is it something like, he does the best he can and does not hurt others or ...?". I said, "I hear your soul talking now. You are expressing your truth and your truth is your soul". He said he's not really interested in the heaven thing. He said he has no time for hell and fire. He was told if he committed sin, he'd go to hell.

Terence said he loves to see us in here. I said to Terence today, "Your presence is your greatest gift". He said, "I know. It's what comes out. It's the best of me. What I say".

## Wednesday, 7 June

It came to me since yesterday that Noah McAlorey does live out of terror and guilt all his life. How many times did he talk about guilt and sin yesterday? What a huge burden to carry.

David Gabbay said some people said he'd make a great counsellor. I said, "Yes, you're a very good listener". David Gabbay said he needs to look after his own spiritual, physical and mental needs. He did meditation last night in his room. He was aware of lovely colours in front of him. David said his new lady friend reads the palms. She does tarot cards. He said what did I think of these. I said, "I'm not happy with tarot cards". He said he was not either.

## Thursday, 8 June

I went to Samantha's flat. Adam was there and so was Calum. I congratulated Calum. Calum and Samantha said Adam is very good and supportive of them. I saw the wedding photos. The suit looked lovely on Samantha. Adam wore a beautiful suit. Rosetta and I gave them a card. They did not offer me a seat. I sat eventually when Samantha got up. We joked about Adam getting married next! It was a very special day.

## Thursday, 15 June

We went to Simon. I asked Karen McAuton, "How's William?". She said, "Not good". He's in the T.V. room. He came from Cobh today. He got a lot of seizures, she said. He gets very weak afterwards. Karen said William is going mad, thinking of his days in the army in Africa, where 24 men were killed. William saw all that, she said, at 17 for 32 years. It's playing on his mind. He's 49 now. Karen was very worried about him. Karen asked me to go to the T.V. room where William was lying down to rest for a few hours, to say, "Hello, William". Karen asked me to pray that whatever God wants be done and they accept it. I sat near William and Karen for a long time. William chatted away. I said, "William, you're a good man". He looked at me and said, "That's what I'm trying to convince myself of". The poor man must be tortured from negativity, fear, doubt, anxiety, etc. He's now like a man of 80 in appearance. He is only 47. Karen called him 'love', 'darling' and 'pet'. She rubbed his back. She said his family approved of her. Hers do not approve of him. Both Karen and William were filthy dirty outside but I could feel great love there. She said he is so gentle. Her husband beat and beat her. She said William was always there for her. I gave them a card of Kate – one each. William cried and had to go out after reading it. Karen told me he lost two children, one at 7 months and one at 6 months. They were physically deformed, she said. She said Kate reminded her of her Gill. She said she prays to her. "She keeps me, directs me", she said. I suggested she put one card in William's pocket and Kate will protect him. Kate loved these special people. I trust her energy to help. She's now in the purest of all energy, which we can't even conceive of.

## *Tuesday, 20 June*

Connie Packer's hair was long. He has beautiful eyes. I said it to him – blue like the sky. He said he sees the Creator in the eyes of the poor. I feel he's called in a particular way, to be with the poor in a contemplative way. He seems to have very deep feeling for the poor. I feel he hears his own poverty very well. His shoes were only laced through the two bottom holes in one and the two top holes in the other one! He said he played the uileann pipes and guitar. I said I played the violin. I said I do meditation. He does 'Má – Rá – Ná – Thá', he said. He put his head down and was so still. I felt, I sensed, he could hear about 'being', too. I said, "It's not about being on one's knees all day that's important". He said to me, "You are very happy". I said, "Yes". He said he could see it in me. I said to him that he'd do great things yet. I sensed it. All life though is in the now. This man is 50 now. He gets up at 4.00 a.m. At one point, I wondered was he having me on. I feel he's in his first fervour, maybe.

## *Thursday, 22 June*

Adam Cafferkey asked me if he could have a word with me. I said, "Yes". He asked me could I get him a statue / picture of Our Lady and some nice flowers, not real, as he finds it hard to see real flowers wither, he said. He'd like to make a shrine in his room. The moon and stars in statues of Our Lady remind him of the time he slept out, he said. I asked Adam if he'd like to come now and get the picture. He said, "It's only a woman could get this for me". I invited him to come along with me. He picked out a nice statue and got some flowers. He said he'd write a poem to thank me.

## *Tuesday, 27 June – Ballygriffin*

Norbert Taffer was the 10th person asked if he'd like to go to Ballygriffin. He said he'd like to go. It was great to stay with the gentle energy that leads me on. It reminded me of the story in the *Gospel*, where Jesus invited people to the wedding feast. No-one responded to his request. He said, "Go to the highways and the byways and invite in those people you meet". Nothing in 'my plan' worked today! I issued the invitation, all said "No". I wanted the first person I asked to go! My ego would be happy with that. There was a far greater plan in place, which I'd have missed, if I was stuck in my own. The highways and byways are the unplanned territory in me, inviting those strong egoic energies I meet within me to come to my awareness. I may not like what I meet in this territory, but it's a place of most profound insight, i.e., the place I enter when I let all 'my plans' go. Pure peace and joy is found there in time. I'm really living from my inner being then. I can't sin from here. Awesome. There is nothing negative here.

## Thursday, 29 June

'The poor reveal our poverty'. How true. If I'm not in touch with my poverty, woundedness, how can I hear the poor street-people?

## Wednesday, 5 July

A group came in about 12 noon. I welcomed them. They wished to see what we were 'doing' with the street-people. I said, "We are being with the street-people". It was nice to see them. When Rosetta met each one of them, we invited them up stairs to the recreation room. Rosetta began her presentation and it was lovely, a very, very gentle approach. I felt it came across beautifully. I was looking at all the faces, as she spoke. Ray Rox, I felt, was very moved. I thought his eyes filled up with tears. I saw Ivers. I could see no reaction in him. Loe Stone was quite interested, I felt. She heard a bit anyway. Ann Andy, I felt had a bit of anger in her, or maybe cynical or …? David was interested. Chris Collins, too. David said to me, "Thanks for sharing your journal". Loe Stone said, "It was too short". I felt it would be very good if they could go out on the street with us. Then there would be a better focus and maybe feedback at the end of the day. Chris asked me what would a typical day be like. I told him briefly. Noah McAlorey loved when I introduced them to him. I thanked him afterwards for being so kind to them. I said they were from Australia, Chile, Ireland, etc. Dylan Caball was very open, too, to meet them. Arnold came over to me in the hall. He met the visitors yesterday. He said, "Rosetta and yourself are great people the way ye stay at this work". I said, "Arnold, it's because we love ye".

Terence O'Donen said, "There is a light at the end of the tunnel and that is what keeps me going". He said he feels great when he talks. I said it is part of healing. He could hear this, I felt, well. It was lovely to see his good energy here being awakened.

I was very moved on hearing Ritchie Manah's account of people who have died and are all around us. We can't see them, but we can feel their awesome presence though, the more we ourselves become purified of our ego.

I met Alexandra Bamidene, a resident, too, yesterday. I said, "You are a lovely, elegant lady". She looked at me and said, "Thank you. I'll remember that, as I often wonder how people see me". She said, "Is that true?". I said, "Yes". She seemed surprised to hear me say it. I told her I learned, and I am learning, that it is so important, to say these positive things to people, when I believe it and know it's true. "The person is always good", I said. She may not hear that part. She could hear something good, I felt.

## Friday, 11 August

I met James Rain. He's in A.A. for years. He feels some people don't bother to help themselves. He looks poorly enough. He said in the end, only the higher power can help each one, whatever that higher power is for them. I liked that – "whatever that higher power is for them". This did not confine them to following any religious denomination, so they were free to follow whatever path they were invited on by the source of life.

## Sunday, 13 August

I met Agatha Oakley. She's a sign of hope for all street-people, I felt, when I saw the big change in her almost overnight. She was very moved by the word 'truth' in Ballygriffin. She said when she's tempted to break out now, she remembers being in Ballygriffin and how great it was there, meditation, walks, too, etc. Agatha is about 38 or so, I feel.

## Friday, 25 August

Chelsea Calcott sat. She was very sad-looking. She was very, very silent. She barely said, "Hello". She had been drinking for two days, she said. She had not eaten for two days. I've never seen Chelsea so silent. She said her nerves were very bad. I felt Chelsea was more angry than in earlier days. She expressed it more now. Her impatience, too, came out more. She looked shook enough. She still asked me when were we going to Ballygriffin. I said, "You always loved Ballygriffin, Chelsea. We will let you know when we are going there again".

## Thursday, 7 September

I met the two friends, George Faiss and Aidan Callender. It was fun!

Lee Dallyn asked me to pray for him. He prays for Rosetta and I every day. Lee began to cry and asked for a pen and he said he wanted me to pray for his brother, Seán, Joe, and his Dad, Pete Dallyn, who died.

I met Mark Salim. He looked as if he had not washed for weeks!

### Friday, 8 September

Brigid Palmes said she does the 12 Steps. She's dry for 20 years. She said the 12th Step says, 'We need to be open to a higher power, through prayer and meditation, to hear what our call is from the Creator'. She needs to hear her call, she said. She'd love to do meditation the next time we do it.

What a day! Meeting wonderful human beings. It was a great privilege to meet all these special people today.

### Wednesday, 20 September – Ballygriffin

On the way to Ballygriffin, Brigid Palmes began chatting about her mother drinking. She had a child before her marriage and no one of her family knew this, until after her death. Brigid felt very sad. She did not tell her. Her son, born out of wedlock, was put in foster-care after being born, near her home. She never knew all her life that he was her step-brother. Her daughter (30) is addicted to drink for six years. Brigid goes to A.A. She feels she needs more now, to help her to get in touch with her spirit. She said she's very intellectual within, and tuned into what I was doing about meditation. She said thinking has her gone mad! Her daughter left home. Brigid's marriage broke up through drink. She said they had a farm. She used to drive a bus one time. She has two students staying with her now.

It was a fabulous day, out in the cathedral of nature. Brigid said to me that I was very encouraging about this journey. I talked about being attentive to eating, etc. Brigid said she needs to make the journey from the head to the heart. I gave her the big page on meditation. She said she'd put it on the wall of her bedroom. She'll keep the small page in her bag. I feel Brigid has lots of distraction at meditation, as we all do. She said the music was very relaxing. Brigid said she felt her head had eased a bit, as the day moved on. At 5.30 p.m., I meditated with Brigid Palmes. It was lovely that she could stay for meditation. She looked a bit different in her face, as the day went on. I said to her how much better she looked. She said she felt more at ease. She was able to say back to me what I said about meditation. She talked a lot about going from the head to the heart. She said A.A. talk about doing something with their lives but, she said it never, or they never, say how to do it! She said she found this day wonderful and it was a great help to her. She said she knew I was convinced of all this myself. She said I was so well able to explain. Brigid spoke a lot about nature and the gentleness of nature. I felt she needed to be exposed to more positivity. She said a lot of negativity gets at her. I said meditation can help here a lot. I suggested she get a plant and listen to it. "Let it be your teacher", I suggested. She could hear that. She said she likes solitude and silence. I said, "Brigid, you are one of the people who came to Ballygriffin from the street-scene, who could be so silent for so long – straight after going there". It takes some people more time to get into the silence. Everyone is different and Brigid has different needs. Brigid talked a lot about the breeze blowing. She felt it on her face and said it was so beautiful. "Stay with the breeze", I suggested. She was very taken by the hens, slowly moving around and in no hurry! I never felt so aware before, at this deep feeling level, of the effect (in a real way) of the positive environment on a person until I saw with my own eyes how Brigid could change! Tremendous. A very, very, very special experience.

## Monday, 25 September

Samantha lost the baby she was carrying. She wanted to kill herself. She was very, very, very, very fragile.

Adam Cafferkey was painting the crib figures. He could 'be there' very well. I was in awe of him. I affirmed him on his patience in painting the figures. He painted them so very gently, even the very tiny figures. I could hear and see Adam's great care of Samantha.

## Monday, 30 October

Jim Lorst is a lovely person. He said how he organises his day. He takes time off during the day. He was taking one hour off when I met him. He said he only does one job at a time and then he goes onto the next. He finishes one first. Even when I was chatting with him, I was amazed when the phone rang, he did not answer it. He had respect for Jim. I could hear that. He also stayed with his free hour and enjoyed being free. He does his work very gently. He is able to do it very well. He said he was working in a factory for over 20 years. He was a resident of Simon once and helping here is a way of saying thanks, he said. He awakened me to my own attentiveness and 'being with' what I'm doing in the now.

Gerard Racke said he'd like to meditate with me. He said he'd need to go over and freshen up – he'd be back in 10 minutes. He was on drugs for 32 years and is now off them for months. He does not want to commit suicide. He'd like to do well. "It's hard to live with myself", he said. He told me about the ego and about the seven things the ego can do to the inner good self. He talked about behaviour and person. He said, "I'm not just my behaviour". I remembered that Michael Baily told me Gerard Racke murdered someone. He said he loves meditation. He asked me how do we do it. I explained what we do. He said he'd remember. "One thing", I said, "everything is O.K. in this now". It seemed to help him.

## Thursday, 9 November

Samantha Caden was going to leave the apartment as there were too many bad memories. She said she'd let me know if she'd like to meet me. Samantha was in deep pain. She was in a very negative mood.

Wayne Magee, a very young man, died – hanged himself in his garage at home. He had been in Ballygriffin for three days the year before he died. Wayne Magee sniffed ladies' nail varnish – went home and hanged himself.

Nicholas Lavis (29) injected himself with heroin and died.

It looks to me at times as if some of those who are going to Ballygriffin with us are preparing for the next life. It seems that, through the Ballygriffin experience of sharing, quiet and meditation, we enable some people to come to a sense of their own dignity before they die. Perhaps it helps them to die with some dignity within and, even though, at times, it is in awful circumstances they die, that's beyond anyone's control. We only get one chance to accompany any precious human being on their road to heaven – in the next life. If they do not discover it in this life, hopefully they will in the next – awesome. It would be wonderful if a person could come to a sense of their beautiful dignity, while they are alive.

## Wednesday 29 November

John Gabie and Abigail Bancrow came to Ballygriffin today. We had great craic on the way down. Abigail was quiet enough. I could hear how very, very, very kind John is – he has a beautiful nature really. He is so kind to Abigail – he told me Abigail is on medication. Some people think she ought to be locked up but he says "No". I could see that John is very fond of Abigail. I could see John today living a lot out of his soul, being / spirit. I could see a very, very genuine, caring, kind person in John. We went for a walk after dinner towards the river. John washed the ware. He was very helpful. I showed them the video of Nano Nagle, as she walked among the street-people in Cork. He said his brother was an atheist. He himself believes in a God – he signed the visitors' book, 'John Gabie had a very relaxed day here – thank you, God'. Abigail wrote 'peaceful'. She had a more radiant smile as the day went on. I felt, at times, she's in great emotional pain. I'd say, in fact, she's probably is in so much emotional pain, she could hardly get to the end of it, she's so full up with it. I remember hearing she carried a knife for protection. I wonder is she carrying it today? Later, we went to meditate in the little oratory. It was great, it was so peaceful. I said it's healing for someone when someone listens attentively to them. John said Abigail needs no drugs! Abigail did not say much to me there. I feel she'd talk to John on her own. She shared a lot with me another day about her home, etc. It was a privilege to be with Abigail and John there.

### Wednesday, 6 December

I was happy with my visit to Samantha Caden and Calum Cadoret – I find her very real in expressing her feelings always. I really felt strongly today that I was in one of my essential activities (i.e., what I'm meant to do in life), being with the street-people. We can have more than one essential activity. What an extraordinary journey.

### Tuesday, 12 December, 11.30am

I sat near Ruth Mannas. She sat on her own – she was very down. She said Luke Joel was gone – he was minding her bank card – he took out all her money Sunday night in the middle of the night. She has no money, she said. It struck me that the most likely thing she could do to get some money for Christmas was to go into prostitution. These women are so vulnerable. She said she was crying when Luke took her money and went off with it. She said she stopped the card now so no-one can take anymore. She had fallen out with him already in the summer.

### Wednesday, 20 December

The crib frame and figures were made by some residents. It was on the table in the hall. There was a blanket under it as a table cloth. How significant. The white crib figures looked lovely in the wooden crib.

David Bagley began to sing – *Silent Night*. I joined in with him. He has a beautiful voice. He sang *A Long Time Ago in Bethlehem*. He went over near the crib, as he sang. I joined in with him. He sang *Danny Boy* beautifully then and I joined in with him. I felt Danny was there near me.

*Christmas Eve, 24 December*

I was at the church at 8.30 p.m. In the talk, the priest said that, "Of all the groups who went to the crib, the shepherds were on the ball!". He said the angels told them about the birth, but they said, "Let's see for ourselves". The shepherds were the first to have the birth revealed to them – the poor, like the shepherds, heard it, too – they were able to have space within to allow the birth to take place in them. They were free of their worldly goods. 'Let's see for ourselves' speaks to me of experience. No amount of talking about something can replace or bring one to the deep place of experience. Meditation enables us to experience the good within us.

Now it's 12 midnight. I take the baby to the manger now in the hermitage, as a symbol of giving birth to my true self in my own place of poverty. The poorer / emptier I am, the more deeply I experience this birth within myself. This is real joy. I lit a candle on the four front windows, symbolising the welcoming of the new birth within me and others. I feel very, very deep peace now – the real joy of Christmas. The star led the shepherds, after the angels told them of the birth. It was a starry night. They left behind the darkness and went into the light. We are called to face the new birth – to let go of the old and move forward.

# 2001

## Tuesday, 9 January

Ruth Mannas slept out on the quay last night. She was attacked. She asked a tall skin-head lad to wait for her as she's scared of going out now. He was quite young. Martin Kava was his name.

Jo Raza said he felt he himself was sinking fast. He would love to go somewhere for a month. He asked me about Ballygriffin again. He said one day or two are no good to him. He said he'd like to talk to me privately some day but there's no room here to talk, he said. Another thing struck me, there is no room in Simon now for meditation either – we're surely being stripped of everything. The 'success' of failure speaks.

### Thursday, 11 January

In the dining-room, I saw a lady eating chips. I asked her would it be O.K. with her if I joined her. She said, "Yes". I heard someone call her Evelyn Schiess. She said she was a rep with a clothing company for two years. She speaks very well. She said she had a bad cough. She asked me do I read *The Bible*. I said, "Yes". She asked me what was my favourite part of *The Bible*. I said St Paul's writing and St John's *Gospel*. She said she loved the story of Lazarus, Martha, Mary and Elizabeth. I felt she could have been quite a 'posh lady' in her day. She seemed to know all the people's names who came into the kitchen. She said she's very good at remembering people's names.

### Wednesday, 17 January

Zita Pesneau came over and sat near me, when I went into Simon. She said she was very sick – she was out in the streets about a month. She has a room now. She doesn't like sleeping on a bed. She feels safer on the street. She sleeps under the bridge where Frankie Kanza used to sleep. I asked her would she be afraid she'd fall into the river. She said, "You could fall in, but I HAVE NO FEAR – I DON'T HAVE ANY FEAR IN ME".

Joss Morat is 23. He said he found it hard when he was trying to help some friends come off drugs and drink. Some young girls went into prostitution in England and they did not appreciate his help. He said the people in Peru, Ecuador and other South American countries appreciated more what was done for them. He has friends there to help the people plant trees, build houses, etc. He built a bridge when he was there. He said one of his friends was murdered there. He has a girlfriend there. Herself and her mother asked him to go out to her again. He was there six months. I could hear deep, deep compassion in Joss Morat and he will do great good yet, I feel. It was a terrible heart-rending story he told me of being told to leave his step-father and mother's home at 14 years of age. He's on the streets almost since then – nine years. He slept in the South Mall last night. Joss Morat travelled to Amsterdam, London and South America. He would like to go back to Peru if he had the money, he said. He met his natural Dad, he said, on a work site once. He did not know him then. Later, when arrangements were made by his step-parents to meet him, he recognised his father as the same man who worked on the site. He stayed at his Dad's house for six months, but left as they did not get on. Joss Morat is a lovely young lad.

## Wednesday, 24 January

Aoife Calvey came over to me and chatted for a long, long time. She asked me if I had heard about Arnold, her brother. I said, "What happened to him?". She said, "He took too many tablets and drink together with them, on purpose, because he said he wanted to end his life, as he had too many problems to deal with". She said he's in hospital. He's 22 years of age. He's like a vegetable, she said. He is on a life-support machine. The doctor said it would be a one-in-a-million chance if he gets out of it. She doesn't think he will, she said. Aoife Calvey asked me about the meditation. She said, "Would it help me relax?". I said, "Yes, it can help to empty the mind of the clutter of things that can fill it". She said she'd like to do it at 1.30 p.m. I said I would give her a page on how to do it. She said, "That's good". I feel Aoife is in denial about Arnold, her brother.

## Friday, 26 January

I went to Simon. I listened to Fabian Pards talking about his life story for an hour and a half. I left Simon at 5.00 p.m. It was a great day with these very special people. It is like going into another planet, when one goes out and sees all cars 'flying by', etc., etc. These lovely street-people value time and see the violence of hurry and rushing. Some have all day to do nothing really, eat, sleep, maybe work, drink, pray and do drugs! They are all as special in their essence as the person doing a day's work from 9 to 5. I wonder who has chosen the better part – like Mary in the Martha and Mary story? Who knows? The better part surely is the life that is more consciously lived. There is no consciousness / love in running and racing around. It can be a violence to the person, too.

## Wednesday, 31 January

Andrew Hampson told me he was going to get a radio for Christmas but then he said, "No, I won't get a radio, I'll give *myself* a break". He is so wise. I was very touched by that. I said, "You would have found it a burden" – he said, "Yes". I always feel I can learn so much simple wisdom from these very wise people. Here, in making a conscious choice from his being, he became free of wanting another material object, which at first he felt would make him happy. No material object can ever make any of us permanently happy. They are only a temporary relief. All lasting happiness and peace comes from deep within. When he finds that, he can say, "There is nothing I shall want".

## Wednesday, 7 February

Richard Hair met a wealthy lady. She had €1,200 and, in eight days, they had it all spent on drink – vodka. He stayed with her in B & Bs and hotels all over Ireland. She left him then. He's now back in Cork, living with another lady. He left her, as he said he could not be seen with her. Her behaviour and reputation isn't so good. He can go back to her anytime and she'll take him! I said, "You are such a handsome man, the women would be around you like flies"! He saw his family at home last week. He drinks after visiting them, as he can't handle them. His two daughters are working – one of his daughters has a baby.

## Tuesday, 13 February

The project leader said once respect is lost, it's very hard for it to be restored by street-people. These people have built up trust in Rosetta and I over the years. He said, "It's like confession". I said, "Yes". "It's all about respecting the dignity of the person", he said. I affirmed him in his own lovely presence there and lovely approach to residents. I could see how he listened.

Ruth Mannas passed by me and she was at the window table with Jos Gatt. I asked Ruth how she was. She said, "Not too bad". She said she'd love to go away from Cork, from Jos Gatt. He won't let her away from him. She said he gave her an awful beating again in the street. She must have been unconscious. She woke up in hospital. The ambulance took her, she said. Someone must have rung for it, she said. Jos Gatt came in a taxi to take her out after two days or so. She's not supposed to be out, she said. Her face was black and blue, she said. She wrote to her daughter who is making her Confirmation. Jos came in, she said. He hit her with his fists! Terrible! I feel she's probably a sex plaything for him. He seems to bully and dominate her. She said when she's with him, he never touches her or beats her, only when she leaves him. She said she only went out to buy a pair of runners one day and he beat her. She's his slave. Terrible!

## Tuesday, 20 February

Pete Penn said he has three children, two boys aged 10 and 14 and a girl of 20. He said they were taken off him and 'his missus', because they drank when the children were young. He sees the two boys by arrangement. The girl is in England. His face looked as if he had been battered for years. His nose was going in three different directions, north, south and west! He said he says five *Our Fathers* and five *Hail Marys* every night.

Terry sat at the table. He plays the guitar on the streets, he said, near the Grand Parade Banklink. There are lots there at night, he said. A man set fire to his flat. He lost clothes, all his belongings, etc. Terry was mad. He turned over on his guitar and broke it!

## Wednesday, 21 February

I went to Simon. I had a long chat with Sue. I called Kevin to go with us to Ballygriffin at 11.25 a.m. in the car. It was an awesome day of quiet, meditation, nature, sharing and savouring the fruit of the earth. Rosetta and I were deeply moved by these street-people's capacity for silence and stillness.

## Wednesday, 28 February

The Simon workers must have extraordinary patience with the street-people. They get a bed and then go out and drink and then come in again some days later looking for a bed again, even though they are not able to keep it when they had it! 'No reward, no success' on a surface level for workers. We all need to do this work from a very deep place. Otherwise, we would not last.

## Wednesday, 7 March

I met Ruth Mannas. She said Jos Gatt burned the caravan. She said he's a psychopath. He assaulted her. She lost her job over him. He put a brick through her daughter's window, and also through her brother's window.

## Wednesday, 14 March

I asked Bill his name. Bill Blar was very, very interesting altogether, telling us about his time in Eastern Europe, etc. He was in Africa, too, where he lived for a while. He was in Yugoslavia, Romania, etc., also. He said he saw the place where Mary, the mother of God, was buried. There's a church there now. He said he was in Antioch. I said Paul preached there. In Antioch, the disciples were first called Christians. He saw the underground hideouts in Turkey. No arrows could get in where Christians fled to, the time of the Roman invasion. There were lots of murals on the walls. These were decorated by Muslims. He said Muslims there today have no time for Christians. He said he married an Australian lady. He said, "Ameribow" is Turkish for "Hello". There were lots of people on the street in Istan but most of them were amputees, as they had no money to go to hospital. What they do then is cut off their limbs if they had any trouble with their feet or legs. He said people beg on the streets, too. They are not violent. He talked about his first wife. She was an Polish lady. They have two children, one 22 and one 27. He did not see them for 20 years. He's afraid to make contact, in case they'd say, "We don't want to see you". His eyes filled up telling me this and, eventually, he cried and was overwhelmed with the painful emotion. He quickly stopped crying then. He has a son by the Australian lady. His name is Bill. He said they tossed a coin to see would it be his Dad's name or Mam's name they'd give the boy. His Dad's won! His wife's name is Sarah. Bill Blar said the Australian lady is here since he came over. He's here 10 years and he loves Cork. He has friends in Cork. He was in a flat and had trouble with the landlady. He was with a woman and they had an argument. He likes men's company, and women's, too, at times. He likes a drink.

### Wednesday, 21 March

Ursula Walk said she coloured her hair, 'deep rose' she called it! She got lovely shoes. They are black suede. She showed them to me. They are lovely with a dainty bow at the side of each shoe. She said she boils an egg in the electric kettle in her room! She makes jelly, too, in her room!

Katy Coone came in. She carries weapons, knives, etc. She's Pat Casor's wife. She'd even use them on him, Ursula said. She looked very, very tough when I saw her close up.

Ursula Walk told me Jonathan Cass murdered a man.

### Thursday, 22 March

On my way past Ballyphehane Church, I felt I'd call in at 11.10 a.m. I saw people outside the door. I sat inside. There was Mass being celebrated for James Moos, who died. There was a huge flower arrangement. James nearly always lived in a caravan. Pete Prade said he knows him for 10 years. He said he had gone through a lot of caravans, because of fires, etc. He lived in a tent for a while. He was always on his own. He used not talk to people much. The Corporation built a wooden hut for him. James was 49 years old. His sister was very upset. She was very good to him, Pete said.

## Wednesday, 28 March

Lee Dallyn sat on the chair later when Alexandra moved. After lighting a cigarette and letting it burn out fully on a saucer, he said to me, "Will you pull in my chair please? Can I talk to you?". I said, "Certainly, Lee". He began talking about his time in Africa. He was 20 then. He was in the army for three years. His Dad was in the army 38 years. He said it broke his heart when his three mates were murdered by a man from another army. It was hard at times to understand the words Lee was saying, but I feel I got most of them. He said that man got life in prison. He said if he went into him, he'd kill him. He told me a very heart-rending story then of how his best mate was shot by a member of the British army. His best mate was called Zaceria Zenith. He was a half-caste and was only 17 – a child, he said. He said his skull went in two parts and before he died, he looked at Lee and said, "I love you", and died. I could hardly contain my own sorrow and sadness as I listened to him. I could be there 100% though. He began to cry and got very upset. He said he was ashamed to cry in front of me. I said, "It's very good to cry Lee, as there's healing in it. It eases pain a bit". He never got over that, he said. He said, "No-one wanted him (the half-caste man), nor had anyone any time for him, but I had time for him". He told me the same story all over again later and I said, "Lee, it's very, very good to talk about all this". He said, "You are the first girl I ever spoke to about this, since it happened". He said that to me twice. He said he felt very relieved after talking to me. He said again, as he was very upset, "Why did they not shoot me?". He got very upset. He said, "I could have killed myself but I have two children, (1) Lee Dallyn, 12 years and (2) Mary Dallyn, 15 years". He sees them at times, he said. He has a wife, too. He does not want to die, because he has two children. He said he feels like going into the river though. I asked him was it when he came back from the Lebanon to Ireland that he began drinking. He said, "Yes. I did not drink in the army. I left the army after my three mates and best mate were killed". Then his twin brother died of a heart attack. He was very shocked at this. His Dad died later. I invited Lee to Ballygriffin with us some day. He said he'd like to go. We meditated then. I could hear great gentleness and kindness in Lee. He said, "I've an alcoholic disease". I said, "You can't help that, Lee".

Later, I met Denis Dere. Denis talked a lot. He said he lost in five minutes a permanent professional job he had for 22 years. He said he's married 10 years. He lives in Kerry. He has two children, Saoirse, aged 4, and Susan, aged 5. He said two years ago, he went home from work and his wife and two children were gone abroad to his wife's relatives. He said the Easter eggs he bought them were still on the table at home. His eldest daughter asked the Gardaí abroad to ring Ireland and see could they find her Dad. Two weeks ago, he said his wife's new boyfriend came to Ireland. Denis went to see them yesterday. A row broke out. He was accused of trying to kill his wife and her boyfriend. He can only go to certain parts of Cork now or he'd be arrested and get jail if he moves outside those areas. When Denis Dere asked me if I worked in Simon, I said, "No. I come to listen and learn from these wise people there. I also sit, chat and listen to people (homeless) on the street". He said, "Some most intelligent people pass through here and I am enriched, too, by their lives". I said, "Yes, they are lovely people". He said, "You'd hear about all of life here".

### Wednesday, 4 April

Alexandra Bamidene's clothes were taken off her in the park and she was raped, when she had a couple of cans and fell asleep in the park.

John Gabie showed me his sore leg. I never saw anything like it. It must be something like leprosy is, from the pictures I've seen of it – big, big sores – weeping – he was drying out the pus from the wounds when he was showing me his leg. It is good when pus (emotional) comes out, too, through the painful feelings. John Gabie said that others said to him, it's like he was shot in the leg. It will take four months to get better, he said. He was in hospital for 18 days.

We went to meditate. Julie came with us. The chat with Julie after, was wonderful. Her sharing was moving. She has had a hard life herself. She is great to keep going. In a special book, I write the names of people to whom I need to send positive energy. Her face lit up when Rosetta said, "We'll write your name in the book". She was delighted. Rosetta and I listened to Julie's story for over two hours after meditation.

### Wednesday, 11 April

I went into Simon. Rosetta said Suzanne asked her could the staff do meditation. It sounded like a great idea that staff could come together to meditate at 2.00 p.m. Four staff members meditated with Rosetta and I today. It was a very special day in Simon with our very special friends.

## Wednesday, 18 April

I saw two people covered in blankets outside the dole office. As we walked towards the Shelter gate, there was a person wrapped in a blanket near the gate. I couldn't see a face!

I met Frank Mal coming out of the Holy Trinity Church. He's not on the streets now. He has a job in insurance. He is beautifully dressed, brief case and all! Lovely to see that he spent 20 minutes in the church. He said he was sorry to hear about my niece. He said he prays for her.

## Wednesday, 25 April

I went into Simon. Adam approached us as we went through the hall. He asked us to pray for him. He said he never before in his life asked anyone to pray for him. That was astonishing and very moving altogether. He was so open, truthful, gentle and humble sharing his pain. I felt deeply moved by his sharing about himself and his sister. They are only beginning to get to know each other over the last five years. She was not able to talk to him. She did not know what to say. She was so sad. It was lovely to hear how close they grew over five years – wonderful. He was great to express his emotions, I felt anyway. I felt deep compassion for him.

On my way to the market, I met Ursula Walk. She called me over and asked me to sit on the steps with her. I did and she began to cry and said she was very upset. She was out last night and someone hit her. She said to me, "Look at my nose". She showed me her leg, too. On her shin, where she showed me the sore spot, was tattooed 'Mel Lahive'! She took out a photo of Mel Lahive from her bag – framed. She said she misses him so much. She kissed the photo and said, "I love him". She had about half a bottle of *Europa* wine taken before I had arrived. While I sat with her she took another slug! I stayed awhile, sitting on the street step, chatting with her.

## Wednesday, 9 May

Fiona Cass asked me if I would be there tonight. I felt she thought I was a resident. She said to me another time, that I was like a nurse. She said my face was familiar. Fiona came over and sat near me. She did not guess I was a nun, I'd say. Great – she seemed very much at home with me, in my company. Fiona had a 3½ year old son, James, fostered by her sister. She was setting out to see him on the bus at 11.00 a.m. Moss Mels got her a bag of bananas and scones from the counter for the bus.

Nilo came along. I thanked him for putting the article on the meditation in the newsletter. He smiled. I said, "It was lovely to see it". He gave the article the title, *Cool Meditation*. I asked him where did he get the name, *Cool Meditation*, from? He said, "A band from the 70s wrote it and sang a song called *Cool Meditation*". He said, "The band was called *Third World* and the song talked about the energy and relaxation of meditation". I said, "We have meditation with the staff in the workers' quarters in the Shelter at 2.00 p.m.". I said he'd be welcome. He said he'd like that and thanked me.

## Wednesday, 16 May

I went to the Simon gate. A new person called Sam left me in. I notice when I'm in 'my being', I can be in Simon 100% with the people there. When I'm not in 'my being', I'm not able to be there. A person came over to take a photo. I do not like to be in these photos. This is a hidden ministry.

Jo was wrapped in a blanket at the door. Aidan went out to him and Sam also took care, gently, of him. The workers are saintly people to wash the sometimes very dirty toilets. They do it quietly.

## Wednesday, 23 May

I felt drawn to stay on my own today. No-one else came to sit with me before 11.30 a.m. Many passed by outside. I felt very well sitting there, 'being'. On the wall a poster read, 'Today is a small piece of time, to manage, where we do not need to allow trouble overwhelm us. Then our minds and hearts are freed from the heavy weight of yesterday and tomorrow'. I could hear this as a Now. *Hodiae*. The moment of the day. Now is enough for us.

## Friday, 25 May

It struck me today it would be a pity not to write a book from all my journals on street-people. It is so precious. People would love to read it, I'd say! It had sad stories and very funny stories, too. A balance!

Richie asked me to pray for him to help him keep off drugs. He wonders will God give him any more chances, as he has been given so many chances already. I said, "The Creator never stops giving you chances. He / She loves you as you are and never stops loving you for even one second". Richie was happy to hear this.

## Saturday, 26 May

The Simon Community residents are very like, in a way, the first Christian community. We are told they shared everything. They gave their goods to the poor. In many ways, I see similarities. I would say some of the first Christian community were not any angels either.

## Monday, 28 May

There is great freedom in being completely open on this journey. I could hear very much more deeply the gift of the street-people on this journey. I hear, too, there is a great new creation emerging in me after evacuating pain. It is only then I can be free to come alive. Giving birth to a true self is always an ordeal within. Job said, 'When you face the truth, prepare for an ordeal'. It also struck me today that with diversity, I need great gentleness.

Alexis said no-one else sent him a card, only ourselves. He said, "No-one cares where I am. They don't even look for me any more". It must be very, very painful to live with that.

## Tuesday, 29 May

Dave introduced me to Don as 'the Sister with the street-people'. He said he rescued two women from the river. One lady he rescued told him she was too upset to go on and live. The other lady told him the reason she went into the river. He said he can't say this to anyone. She asked him not to say it. He said (and this touched me) that they were two human beings. That touched me very deeply. The compassion of that man on the street. He then said, "And I had to sleep on the street / footpath that night". His story was on the *Independent*, the *Echo* and the *Sunday Mirror*. He had these papers in his bag, he said. Don has a lovely face. He has a very gentle expression.

## Thursday, 31 May

On my way down Drinan Street, I met Alexandra Bamidene. She said she was helping a man to find a doctor. She said it keeps her going, to go around and help people like these people and they help her, too, in many other ways, she said!

## *Wednesday, 6 June*

Bríd said she has a son in Belfast. He's 24. She saw him Sunday – he has two children, one is two months and the other is 6 years old. Bríd said she did not go to counselling last week. She said meditation did her no good. She hopes it does more good for her son and daughter than for herself because it did her no good. 'Instant everything', I feel, some people need! If it does not work instantly, they say it doesn't work! I said one needs to practice it regularly, as effects happen slowly and you'd be surprised.

## *Wednesday, 20 June*

The room was ready for meditation. Again, these special street-people remind me so much of the early Christians – caring and sharing all they had. They held all things in common, we are told.

Pierce Pole was out on the footpath. He was so attentive to feeding the cat with milk. He had put some milk on the cover of a plastic cup and gave it to the cat. He watched the cat so attentively as she drank the milk. He had put three stones into the carton of milk so it would not blow away or over turn. As the cat finished one cover of milk, Pierce poured more milk on the cover for the cat. Pierce sat almost motionless on the step. He was totally in the moment, I could see. I asked him, "Where did the cat come from?". He said, "She is a stray, she is lost". That word 'lost' struck me a lot. He said the cat is pregnant. He saw the cat around at other times, too. I asked him did he like cats. He said, "No, I am a dog man". When the cat was finished drinking the milk, it lay near him on the road. He said, "That cat was not always a stray cat". I could hear his own story reflected in what he said about the cat. This was surely real living – real Zen, as Christians call it – in the present moment. Awesome! I moved on enriched and energised. Pierce was my teacher today.

## *Wednesday, 11 July*

I met Nellie Ness, whose relatives were living in tents in Kilworth when I was young. I said my Dad used to bring me along to meet them. We used to chat a lot with them. Even as a young child of 8, I felt very drawn to them then. I felt there was a freedom in them. They were real. I was a bit afraid as a child, in case they would take me away. Daddy was so protective of me, he made sure they would not. I associated them with very carefree days at home when I used to go out with Dad meeting people, walking and driving in the country.

## Wednesday, 1 August

I met Suzanne Bulb. She said she's having a baby in three months. She said, "What harm!". Both of them are in the Shelter again – Pierce and herself.

Bríd Bens said, "It's hard to get peace. I say that word you gave me – 'Má – rá – ná – thá'".

Twelve street-people we know died since January.

## Monday, 6 August

Corina said since she got to know the street-people, she has learned so much from them. She said one heroin addict in Dublin was asked how meditation helped him. He said he looked for peace in drugs, it was temporary; meditation gave him a deeper experience of peace without drugs. I remember a person in Ballygriffin, who once said he used drugs to calm him. He said the quiet time in Ballygriffin brought him to deeper calm. Meditation helped, too. Corina said she finds it hard to switch off in Simon but if she's free some day, she'd love to do a day with us in Ballygriffin.

## Tuesday, 7 August

Jamie Jor looked at if he were deteriorating physically. He, too, could sink quickly, I feel. He said to me that he could tell me many, many stories about himself. He said God is looking after him now. I was very moved on hearing this person's deep trust.

## Wednesday, 8 August

I went to Simon. I met Bill from the U.S.A. He was a landscape architect. He got arthritis in his hands and could not do garden-work anymore. He was in the Marines and then he was in the Vietnam war.

Terence O'Donen is 87. He said me he never gets depressed. Someone asked him was it because of his sense of humour. Terence is nearly always very pleasant, I noticed alright.

Sophie, a new girl, came to meditation today. She liked to sit in the position – cross-legged on the floor. This was the staff meditation session. I was standing up ready to go out. Sophie started chatting about meditation.

She feels Rosetta and I are well into meditation. She said she felt distracted today doing it. At times, her work is hard-going. She said she's very sensitive to people and finds the sadness of people terrible hard to hear. She said she began this work once but had to give it up, as she was not able to take the sadness of it. I felt privileged listening to her sharing.

## Thursday, 9 August

I met Conor Cass. He has a hearing impairment. He has a very penetrating look in his eyes, a very gentle, peaceful expression, as if he is totally aware of another person's energy and respects each one as he or she is.

## Friday, 10 August

Bernard O'Byre said it took him nine months to find out that his girlfriend was a lesbian. He loved her so much he could not leave her. He thought she'd change all the time. Emily, his girlfriend, wrote to Bernard and said how much he had done for her. She never felt so loved by anyone before that. Bernard asked me to read the letter she wrote to him. At the end she wrote: 'You are fine, kind (yes), loving (yes), gentle (yes), understanding (no), caring (maybe a bit?)'. Extraordinary. He said he goes to the park after 2.00 p.m. to sit there and to reflect quietly. He said he'd like to go to Ballygriffin.

## Monday, 13 August

I met Adam Cafferkey near Cook Street. I asked him how he was. He said, "I'm not in such good form, another person passed away in Simon, Jack Leer". I could see Adam was in shock and I felt he does not realise this man has died yet. He said he was related to Adam. George Faiss is related to him, too.

> *Written August 2001 – after 13 street-people died through suicide, drugs, other substance abuse and natural causes. They all died within 10 months. To all of us who continue, daily, to walk the streets and roads of this life.*
>
> *No words can tell of that big sadness in our hearts,*
> *These many months passed,*
> *When to their death our friends did step.*
> *No call will bring them back,*
> *There is nothing now they lack,*

*But we have still our task -*
*To do what, you may ask.*
*Promise on this new day,*
*And in this now,*
*If others walk away,*
*Let them be somehow.*
*Even if people crush and step on you,*
*There is nothing you can do,*
*Man is not your enemy,*
*So let him live and die with dignity.*
*In your compassion and loving kindness,*
*Show this world, you at your best,*
*Invincible, no limit,*
*Is your true name this minute.*
*Hatred, how can you respond,*
*To the image of the Maker's hand,*
*One day when you are by yourself,*
*Listen to your own awesome deep respect*
*Your calm eyes when full of love,*
*Echo the smile of your friends above,*
*As you are reborn each day,*
*Even if your smile is only one ray,*
*Let it blossom as a flower,*
*In solitude and with great power.*
*Alone again we go along,*
*Maybe still imprisoned in our frozen pain,*
*Still we can sing our song,*
*Of love eternal and not in vain.*
*Let love have room,*
*Within the tomb of iceberg wounded,*
*Lonely one,*
*To walk again the lovely path of compassion and that hath,*
*For its touch, your great and loving heart.*
*Be brave, everyone,*
*As you look at the sun,*
*You are precious and dear,*
*Our loved one says, "please hear".*

Adam said he's not able to take much more himself. I could feel his terrible anguish, pain and sadness, deep suffering, despair, weariness. Such a sad sight was Adam, where there were crowds of people all around him totally oblivious of his pain. Poor Adam, I hope he will be O.K. I feel called, to touch into hope these days in Simon, while not ignoring or belittling people's pain. Let joy come alive. We need a balance.

## Tuesday, 14 August

Siobhán said that there was good, positive energy from meditation today. Too much negativity can drag people down. They need a lot of the positive, especially as there have been many deaths recently.

A reflection on death poem by Rabindranath Tagore:

### WHAT WILL YOU GIVE?

*What will you give,*
*When death knocks at your door?*
*The fullness of my life –*
*The sweet wine of autumn days and summer nights,*
*My little hoard gleaned through the years,*
*And hours rich with living.*
*These will be my gift,*
*When death knocks at my door.*

## Wednesday, 15 August

Suzanne and Pierce had a huge disagreement about an issue. They gave tit for tat. What touched me was that Pierce could smile at Suzanne eventually and let go of his own point. I could see and hear great compassion in his face. Suzanne seemed a bit tougher, I felt, but in time, too, she seemed to soften out.

At the gate, I looked at two bouquets of artificial flowers on the rail. There was a note in the middle about Jack. George Faiss and all the lads had pages with their own messages stuck together with elastoplasts. Myra Mee said, "That's the other side of them". It's lovely to see this. There was a sash with 'Boston' on it and a glass cloth beside it with 'Cheers' on it. So simple, yet so full of meaning, and a Rosary beads was wound around one lot of flowers.

Today, five years ago, 15 August at 9.30 a.m., Declan Calbaras, the then Shelter Manager, invited me to speak to residents, during Thursday's meeting, about why I felt drawn to come into Simon and meet street-people. The year was 1996. Great. It was a special day. It's nice to be here again this year, five years later on 15 August 2001.

## Wednesday, 29 August

I went to Simon today. I sat near Mark Salim. Mark was in an awful condition. His face was cut. He was filthy dirty. His hands and his clothes were very dirty. I was privileged to gaze on the Maker's creation in Mark, beyond all the dirt that was on the outside. He held my hand every time I said the following: (1) "Mark, you are a very good man"; (2) "You are my friend"; (3) "It is always lovely to meet you and have a chat with you"; (4) "You are a great person". He smiled every time I affirmed him. He was like a cat with cream.

I read about the arrangements for Ursula's funeral. It was in Dublin. I remembered her especially at 10.00 a.m., as her funeral Mass today was at 10.00 a.m. in Dublin. Some people went to Ursula's funeral.

Andrew Hampson said there was a big part of Simon gone, when Ursula was gone. We all meditated. I felt very sad today in Simon. I missed Ursula very much. I saw a wreath at the gate – a nice gesture. I cried tonight when I remembered Ursula died. She was so kind, so good humoured and so very entertaining. She took people as she found them. She was well able to express her feelings about other people, mostly, never much about Ursula, maybe very little, I felt. I feel privileged to have known and met her and enjoyed many hours in her company, over the years.

## Wednesday, 5 September

I walked gently to Simon. I met Mel Lahive near Parnell Place. I felt so sad to see Mel on his own. He stopped and said it will take him a long time to get over Ursula. He said she was his best friend, his girlfriend. He said he was in Dublin at the funeral. His sister and nephew went with him. He was very sad. He seemed to have some drink taken. I cried when I left Mel, I felt so sorry not to see Ursula with him. He looked like a lost man.

Alexandra Bamidene came along and I asked how she is. She said, "Very well. How is Rosetta?". I said, "She is well". She said it helps her a lot, especially in her darker moments, to know that Rosetta and myself are two people, *for sure*, who really care about her. She said if she did not see Rosetta, to be sure and tell her what she said.

I sat near Susan Carld. She showed me the bandage on her leg. She had it dressed today. She was in school in the North Pres. and then in Strawberry Hill. She later went to some school for girls in Blackrock in Dublin and was there until she was 16. I liked to sit with Susan and give her quality time.

I take great care writing these notes down, when I meet the street-people. Many hours are spent meeting these people. Many more hours are spent writing and recording their stories, which are so precious. It comes from presence.

When I told Jeremy Malcome today I'd write his name tonight to remember him in prayer, he said, "It's nice to know somebody remembers *me*". It means an awful lot to people, I can hear, when I say I'll write their names and *remember them* in prayer.

## Wednesday, 12 September

Rosetta was talking to Jenny Rone. It was lovely to see Jenny and Rosetta. I chatted with them for a while. She asked me to read her letter. We read the letter she wrote to Diarmuid, her boyfriend. She gave it to Rosetta.

I sat near Rachel, Suzanne, Grace and Alexandra. Rosetta was there, too. I felt that listening to the women chat – some, at least – they would hop in and out of bed with anyone.

## Wednesday, 19 September

Bernard O'Byre came in and looked as if he had been in the wars! He said some people (homeless) attacked him last night outside the Shelter. He had only come out of hospital that time. He could not stay in, he said.

## Thursday, 20 September

Having checked with Maura, Rosetta said Ruth was going to go to Ballygriffin. Great. We were on our way maybe before 9.30 a.m. When we went to the car, we drove to get our groceries. We moved on to Ballygriffin and it was great to be there at 10.35 a.m. We went up for the box to the store. I asked Ruth to come in with me. Rosetta and Ruth walked down towards chalet C, while I drove down. I was taken aback when I smelled drink from Ruth. As Rosetta wisely said, we need to mention that to Maura. Ruth was 'all talk' on the way down and giggling a lot, too. O.K. She seemed pretty relaxed, I felt. I checked to see was it chalet C we were in.

Yes, it is. We brought in the goods from the car and I put it (car) up behind chalet B. I drank a mug of boiling water, which Ruth had very kindly poured out for me. Ruth asked for holy water for Colm. I went up to see if the sisters had it. When I went back down, Ruth and myself went to see the hens. They now have 148 hens. We went in for meditation before 12.00 noon. We went to the kitchen at 12.40 p.m. to help prepare lunch. We enjoyed a lovely lunch, carefully prepared by Rosetta. It was delicious. Ruth talked again a lot at the meal. About 1.45 p.m., we began to move. Ruth is such a cheerful person, in spite of her huge suffering. We would both have a one-hour break in the afternoon. Rosetta left and Ruth washed the ware. I asked Ruth if she'd like to see the centre. She said she would. I took her around it and invited her to sign the visitors' book. Her address was put down by her as 'Cork'. Her comment about the day was 'Beautiful', which she wrote, too. She asked me could she buy a card. I said, "Yes". I could not see prices. She said she put in £1 but it looked like 20p to me, as she was putting it in! I gave her some free literature available there for anyone. I took her to see the top building there, where the new dining-room is. We were at chalet C around 3.00 p.m. We met a member of the Ballygriffin staff and I asked him were the black and white fowl ducks? He said they were. During my 'free space' time, I went to the river for a walk and sat on the seat next to the river for about a quarter of an hour. It was lovely and peaceful there. After 4.00 p.m., I got up to come back. I needed to be in for 4.15 p.m. for meditation. I was in the room for meditation before 4.15 p.m. I went out to organise my goods for going home at 4.50 p.m. I did not go back to the sitting-room, as I sat for 10 minutes in the lovely peaceful surroundings at the back of the house. I then went to collect the car and sat again. When I heard Rosetta and Ruth in the sitting-room, I did not like to go in, as I thought they were chatting – perhaps. Ruth needed to talk to Rosetta, in particular, at that time. I could let it be. Near 5.30 p.m. or so, Ruth and Rosetta came out. We got organised to go. Sometimes these people can take a while to open up. They need to trust us, test us out for a while before they can share their pain at times. Ruth chatted about her family of origin, and her own family, too. We'll remember the court case especially on Monday next at 10.00 a.m. It was lovely Ruth stayed for the two meditations today. It was a lovely fresh day out. The chalet was heated. Poor Ruth, I felt compassion for her, having to live out her life in this way. Ruth thanked Rosetta and myself for the lovely day. One person – a human being – is of such infinite value. Awesome. I was happy to see her go safely in the gate.

### Wednesday, 26 September

I sat near Seán Caste, Chloe Costel and Nora at the table. Chloe was crying and said her court case was adjourned for one month, as her ex-partner and herself had the same solicitor today in the court. She has to wait now for a month to know whether or not she'll have access rights. Her child, Jane, would be 5 soon. She has just started school. She lives with her Dad. I admired her being able to cry there. She went to her room after a few minutes. She came down later and seemed much better.

### Wednesday, 3 October

I went to the lobby and looked at the photographs of the people, who have been in the Shelter for the last while. I was amazed at the energy in their eyes. Sadness in some, confusion in others, roguery in others, a deep loneliness in yet some more, torture in some, too, contentment in few, I felt.

### Thursday, 4 October

It was great Scott Bacon came to Ballygriffin for the day with us. He's 21 years old. He seemed to have been in the 'wars', by the look of his arms. They looked as if they had been slashed. It was lovely for him that he had such a good relationship with his granddad. I admired his ring later and he said his Dad gave him that for his 21st birthday, 14 December 2000. He also gave him £200. The ring cost £170. He said he is very close to his Dad. He came here to see him on St. Patrick's Day, he said. Scott writes to him all the time, he said. When his Dad came to see him, he said he'd stay in a B & B or hotel, but not in his flat. It was good we had turns to be with Scott, as we had decided. In my hour 'off', I began to write for five minutes only – as the ink dried up in my pen! O.K. It was good Scott could sit for the two meditations. It was a very good day with Scott.

### Wednesday, 10 October

I met Adam Cafferkey earlier and I asked him how he was. He said, "Don't ask me". He passed on later before 2.00 p.m., in the dining-room. He came over specifically to me, put his hand on my shoulder and said, "I'm sorry for what I said". I said, "Thank you, Adam for that". No more. I was tempted to say there is no need, but I let it. My inner being had understanding, for Adam said it from the heart.

Jill asked if I would meet Steve Piny who was new, when I was finished. I sat near Steve Piny, who said he was in London and went 'to the edge'. The poor man started crying and said he starts crying very easily. I said, "It takes a strong man to cry". I remember saying that to Lee Dallyn one day, too, when he started crying, as he was telling me about his dear friend and comrade who was with him in the Middle East. He was shot in front of Lee. Steve Piny did not seem to have any drink taken. He appeared very emotional. He showed me a letter from a nun who befriended him and helped him. He hasn't had contact with her for a while, he said. She used say to him how well-dressed he always was. He was beautifully dressed, I thought, today. I nearly felt like crying myself, when I saw him crying a second time. The tears rolled down his face. He said he used to do farm work with his brother. He said he was promised something to eat today in Simon. He got a nice meal from Jill. Steve talked almost the whole time without stopping. He said before he went out, "I have enough said now". I felt deep compassion for him.

Laura Sage came in. It was lovely to see her again. She was nearly always a very cheerful presence around, I felt. Rosetta came along. Great to see Rosetta. I invited her to meet Laura.

Jeremiah thanked me before I left. He said, "You helped me. You have such a Christian approach". He stood up as I was leaving and held my hand. I met him later after the meditation, before I went out. I shared some of my own woundedness with him. I said, "I confess to you now". I found this a very liberating experience. I could be open, truthful, gentle and humble with him. I thanked him, too, for being so honest.

## Wednesday, 17 October

I said to Joseph today, "It is good to do the meditation in the building here, as positive energy is sent out to people living here then". He said, "That's very important as the morale is low at times, as there is a lot of violence".

Thomas Caffrey talked to me for a long time. He said there were 20 of them in the family. He was on the streets at 6 years of age. He said he was with his sister's family recently and they robbed him. He said his own wife robbed him. He began to cry and cry and I could feel his deep hurt and pain. He said he wished he was never born. He repeated that twice, "I wish I were never born". He tried to commit suicide. He was in the river and said, "It is a mortal sin, so I came out again, after going under twice". The poor man, I could see and hear he was in great, great pain. A tear can be more powerful to heal, than a thousand words. The tear heals. People need to cry. Thomas was hurting. I said to Thomas, "It takes a strong man to cry". Thomas said he'd go to Ballygriffin tomorrow with us.

Pierce passed by and said, "Are you saving souls?". I laughed and said, "No, they are saving me!".

I felt very, very deeply peaceful there today with my special friends. In particular, I felt a deep empathy with Thomas Caffrey, as he shared his truth.

### Wednesday, 31 October

I saw a new man sitting at the table near the counter, so I joined him. His name was Austin Ross, he said. I had a very, very long chat with him, for about one and a half hours or so. I found him a very serene man. He said he was agnostic. He was from Slovakia. He talked about his travels all over the world. In Bolivia, where he was recently, a man killed his neighbour's bull and a friend of the bull's owner murdered the man who killed the bull. He said he slept rough in Bolivia, but one could be chopped up by the natives if they found a foreigner there. He was in Afghanistan. He said it was a beautiful country, but the women had to cover themselves up, if they saw a man coming along the road. He said it was overdoing the whole modesty thing. In India, when he dined with a family, all the men ate first out of a big dish in the centre of the table, then the women ate, etc. He said a person was meant to finish completely the first helping, before they put a second helping on their plate. Once he left some food behind him, as he took too much and he was reprimanded, he said. He has sisters in Canada, he said. He said there would be no flowers like those in the Shelter garden in Canada now as the frost would have taken them. He was amazed to see the lovely fuchsia in the Shelter garden in October. He was in Africa, Pakistan, Australia, Europe – in every continent. He slept rough in Cork last night, he said. He did not know the Jazz Festival was on. He was setting off today.

### Wednesday, 19 December

Con Corl was found in the river. Ross was asked to identify him. He was two and a half weeks in the river. His face was very swollen. He had no eyes. His bones were broken. They think he was murdered, as he owed thousands of euros for drugs. He was addicted to cocaine. He had to have it. He was on the streets very young. He used to hang around the Peace Park, when he was very young. It struck me that Con Corl was in Ballygriffin with us, too. It could have been meant to be his preparation (unknowingly) for death. Some who came to Ballygriffin with us have died. Con was only 26 years of age. He is resting in peace.

## Monday, 24 December – Christmas Eve

It was a great opportunity to meet and chat with people before midnight. It was a very moving experience, as always. I feel I would not have celebrated Christmas at all, if I did not go to Midnight Mass with the street-people. It was very, very moving. As I hear this, for me, the real message of Christmas is found in poverty and misery. Christ can only be born in me, if I let go in a symbolic way, in my life, through living the experience of poverty, misery and weakness. Christ can only come to birth in me, I notice, at a very deep level. Its an awesome privilege being in Simon at Midnight Mass. The street-people are real. No one is worried about their image.

Stan Mager thanked me and said he appreciated very much that I would come in to be with the street-people, homeless, on Christmas Eve. He said it three times how deeply grateful he is to me and others, who come in to be with the homeless for Christmas Eve.

## Wednesday, 26 December

I met Con Axe, a German, who is 21 years old. I asked him was it hard for him being away from home at Christmas. He said, "Yes". I admired him and what he does for these people at Christmas, being far away, too, from his family. He said that he misses his family. I'm amazed by the generosity of these people. It's extraordinary.

Nonie Ner is very generous, too, away from her family at Christmas. She did not seem as upset being away from her family as Con did. He was also away from them last Christmas.

I met Cory Car, another young American worker, who was giving himself to the care of the homeless this Christmas.

These three I met today really inspired me. They are wonderful young people.

# 2002

## Wednesday, 2 January

I put up the meditation notice on the outside door. I put on some gentle music. Jerry Laar came in as I was just about to begin the half-hour's silence. I said, "Jerry, you are welcome to stay if you wish". He sat down opposite me. I trusted the good energy of meditation that Jerry would be O.K. there. He stayed for the whole half-hour. I said, "Jerry, you had a rest". I was very conscious of directing good energy towards Jerry. Afterwards, he did not move. I asked him how he was. He said, "Alright". He feels depressed nearly all the time. He said, "I get 40 seconds of peaceful time, when I meditated. I experience peace then. I always hope I can hold on to it, but, I can't, as it's gone again". He was very quiet today. He had very little to say, I found.

## Wednesday, 9 January

Jerry Laar sat at the table. A young man, Stan Apse, sat near Jerry. He was chatting about society. He said it is so materialistic. He said he took L.S.D. It was his first time seeing the 'real' from the 'unreal'. He said the only things that were real were people, birds, animals and trees, but all the man-made things – houses, buildings, etc., were crumbling in his field of experience while on LSD. He said ignorance leads to fear. He asked me was I afraid of people on drugs? I said, "No, as I've met so many beautiful people who were on drugs and, when I got to know them, I could hear they had various reasons to be on drugs". He said, "Yes". I said, "They are good people". He said, "Were you ever afraid of people who are on drugs?". I said, "Yes, before I got to know them". He said, "That proved what I believed – ignorance leads to fear". I felt he'd have been a great teacher. I said to him, when I met him, "I'm delighted to meet you". He said, "How could you be delighted to meet me, when you don't know me?". I said, "You have a soul / spirit and I'm delighted to meet that in you". He asked me, "Why do people take drugs?". I said, "Because they don't believe in their own goodness enough". He said, "Not because they don't believe in their own goodness, but that society doesn't believe in their own goodness".

It was lovely to see Zita Pesneau's baby – the poor little pet, what will it's future be? The innocent child never asked to be born. The baby's name is Nicole, Zita's sixth child. Her other five children are in care. Her mother, at times, minds them, too.

I met Katy and Ollie on the Grand Parade. Katy spoke and said they were doing street-work now – they had the Shelter as a base only. This is new. They go to see are there people sleeping rough who don't avail of the Shelter services. They go to hospitals and prisons, too.

## Tuesday, 15 January

I met Rosy Benor, a lady I used help some years ago. She had a difficulty with drink. She's a lady in her 50s. She has a beautiful face.

## Wednesday, 16 January

I was passing along by a residential house door and, as it was wide open, I went in. I went into the kitchen and Terence and Bill were there. I greeted Terence and Bill. I told Terence I called to see him a few times since Christmas, but he was not around. He said they told him I called. He said it is hard to catch him. He goes out now everyday, he said. He'd be bored inside. He goes to meet his nephew sometimes. I stood for a while and then I said I'd sit down. Terence said he was going to ask me to sit down. He asked me would I like some breakfast. I said, "No, thanks". I was very taken by the lovely gentle way the meals were prepared and presented – very attentively, I felt. Batt came in and had a bowl of porridge. Terence and Bill had a lovely fry! I could see how very caring Ned Orld is of the two young lady workers. He is very gentle with them. He was telling the lady about herbal tea being good for a person. It is a nice homely place in this residential house. It is lovely the workers can spend so much time with the residents and get to know them. Terence said he's very happy there. It is hard to beat the personal touch.

I cried tonight when I thought of Essie being dead. Essie was 28 years old. I remember she came to meditation with us in the recreation room one day recently. Also I cried when I remembered Basil was dead. Terrible – such very, very young people.

### Thursday, 17 January

I met Daniel, Stan, Doris and Jay, a Dutch lady, walking along the quay. They stopped to talk to me. They said they were friends of Essie's and that they could not sleep last night in the Shelter, they were so upset.

### Wednesday, 23 January

Ruth Mannas told me Zita's baby's name is Blueberry! She told Ruth that was her name. The baby was taken away in the paddy-wagon, as Zita was drinking on the street and I suppose the poor child was neglected. What a life beginning for a little innocent child, who never asked to be born. Essie used to mind the baby for Zita when Zita had been drinking.

Ruth asked a man, who came in, for a cigarette. He not only gave it to her, but also Vince gave her some, too. How good these people are to one another. They share almost everything they have. They are not possessive, I notice, of any goods and most of their worldly goods would often fit in their pocket or in a small plastic bag! How free. They have a good heart, I hear over and over again. All their behaviour is automatic and unintentional.

Adam joined Rosetta and I. He is amazing. He does not plan anything – he lets each day happen. How wise! He said there is a purpose / reason for everything. How true. He said you can say "Yes" or "No" to anything. He wishes he could say, "No", at times, to things he says, "Yes" to.

### Tuesday, 29 January

I met Pat Carl outside the side door of *Roches Stores*, on Maylor Street, today. He was drinking a can of beer. When I asked him how he was, he said, "I'm fed up". I said, "What would help you not to be fed up?". He said, "Two cans of beer". I said, "You know you are good, don't you?". He said he does. I asked him does he like this life. He said, "No, but I have to live here and I hope to get another 50 years out of it".

### Wednesday, 30 January

A new man who called himself 'Cando' introduced himself to me. He said he was 18 years in London in hostels for homeless people. They could stay there for 12 months. He felt he needed a change after 18 years. He said he studied Theology and was in a seminary to become a priest for a while. He asked me was I living here. I take it he thought I was a resident. O.K.! I told him I was living in the city. He asked me where I was from and I said Co. Cork.

Alexis Obaris sat near me and talked for one hour solid, without almost taking a breath. I could listen well and, at times, enjoy Alexis, too, as he's fun.

### Wednesday, 6 February

I was very moved listening to Jer Sheed – whom Rosetta knew. The poor man – he had suffered a lot. His mother died. He was not told for one week afterwards. His niece and her boyfriend were both killed on the road. I think these tragedies happened over Christmas. He seemed pretty down at Christmas. He was looking after his mother, who had Alzheimer's. When it got too much for him to care for her, he had her brought to a home and used the money he had in the house to pay for her keep there. He ended up homeless. His girlfriend died next to him. He was such a gentle person. I felt very privileged to listen to Jer with Rosetta. I felt the sacredness of his story.

### Wednesday, 13 February

Scott came over and sat at our table. He said to me that he is an unwell person and he's on the streets. He said, "It's terrible that the people have to be left out on the streets. There's no bed for them. They all have problems". Suzanne said, "Only that they had problems, they would not be there".

I said it was Ash Wednesday. I saw the ashes in the saucers. I said, "That is what we all are – dust / ashes". Pierce said, "We are all one, all the same.

At soul level, we are equal. All we have in common is our humanity. This will turn to dust in all of us". Sobering! They really listened with great attention, I could see. Awesome.

## Thursday, 14 February

A man came over to me and asked could he speak in private to me. Jack Japor is his name, he said. Jack started off by saying: "I am an alcoholic". What a pity these people are so judgemental of themselves. He said he has health problems and is on medication. He said he's 35 now and wants to commit suicide. His arms are all marks under his coat, he said. He lost the tops of about a half or a quarter of the four fingers on his left hand. He lost his total small finger. He said there are no bones in his fingers, as they melted with the fire. When he was 10 months old, a fire broke out in his own home. His mother was never well mentally and his Dad solved everything spiritually. His Dad did not drink. When Jack used to be drinking in Dublin near his home, his Dad used to ask him not to drink so near home as people used to go up to his Dad and say "Your son is down the road drinking". It used to upset his Dad, he said. He said his brother, 14 months, died of a cot death. That deeply upset his Mam and Dad. He said when he's alone, he weeps a lot, when he thinks of who and what he could have been. He said he often feels a failure. He has no sense of his own worth, he said. He reads *The Bible* and he could quote wonderfully well out of it. He quoted about Jesus in his agony and said he suffers like Jesus. He said he hopes Jesus will say to him when he dies, "When I was hungry, you gave me to eat, when I was thirsty, you gave me to drink", etc. He said he believes in being good to people. He suffers from depression / anxiety, he said. He can get very low, he said. He would like peace and quiet. He can cook and he likes cleaning. He said he cleans the house here in Simon, and the workers are delighted with him. He's neat and tidy. I told him we meditate here on Wednesday at 11.45 a.m. He said, "Is that 'Má – Rá – Ná – Thá'?". I said, "Yes". He said he used to do that before and he liked it. He asked me to look for him on Wednesday next and he'd go to the meditation. I could see that the *Scripture* really spoke to him. The word of life / God / the Creator is *alive* and active for him. He believes, he said, that he's looked after by God, all the time. It was so beautiful to listen to Jack. He is a truly spiritual person. I felt he is much saner than many other people, who call themselves sane. He said he did not hear much of his own goodness yet in himself. He's discovering it bit by bit, he said. Good.

## Friday, 15 February

I met Mel Sawborn on Patrick Street. We had a chat. He said he was off drink for seven weeks and was just coming from his counsellor. I admired his beautifully-polished shoes! He had just polished them earlier, he said. I said, "Your lovely polished shoes say a lot to me about you, Mel, they speak to me of how you look after yourself, how you have respect for yourself".

## Friday, 22 February

On the Nano Nagle Bridge, I met a lovely young lad, Kieran Calse, about 19 / 20 years young, sitting down with a cardboard behind his back, to keep the wind from him. He told me that he was not from Cork. He's on the streets three months. Things did not work out for him, so he came to Cork. He spoke beautifully. He said the hostels were booked out and he, a girl and another man from Dublin sleep at the back of Anglesea Street, on a black bag with some blankets around them. Then they pull some bins around them to keep out the elements. He was gathering money to see could he get a place to stay. He said he doesn't drink. He doesn't want to get mixed up with the street-drinkers, he said. They can be violent.

## Tuesday, 26 February

I met a young man this morning on Nano Nagle Bridge. He sat on a pink blanket, soaking wet, with his dog under the blanket, too. His own name is Batt Bond. He said his dog is pregnant and expecting pups next week. I rubbed the dog's head. When I was coming back before 3.00 p.m., he was still there and there was another lad with him. I saluted both of them and kept moving.

## Thursday, 28 February

Today, I met Miles Bur on the bridge. I stopped to chat with him. He said he was able to buy a car with the money he got on the bridge! He said he's determined to get away from this way of life. One day, he won't be on the bridge.

Alex Ardor, a very young lad, sat near me. I greeted him. He said he was 20 years old. Alex was in a centre for three months. He did not drink for six months now. He was there again for drugs for 19 weeks. He said he watched the Ireland and Iran match recently. He drank *Coke* all night until, at one stage, he went up to the bar and got *Coke* and vodka. Thus began a bad time of drink, he said. He's very violent on drink. His girlfriend is pregnant and is expecting their baby in June. She lives on her own. He, when drinking one night, broke cups and plates in their house. She threw him out, he said. He said he was a good runner! He got a scholarship to the U.K. for sport. Also, he was on a Dublin soccer team. He let it all go. He smokes now. His Dad and Mam are separated. If he met his Dad now, he or his Dad could kill each other. They never got on. Alex was so chatty. He's a lovely, friendly, young lad. It's so sad. He said he'd love to get a flat here for a while, to see can he make it on his own. He'd get back with his girlfriend, hopefully. He is drinking since he was 15. He left home at 16. He never liked being at home. I really enjoyed listening to Alex chatting.

### Tuesday, 5 March

A very young girl, called Susan Carr, is on the streets, too. She asked me could I read for her the names of places, where she could get accommodation and tell her where they are. I did the best I could. She's a lovely, very young girl. Her hand was burned.

### Wednesday, 6 March

I was delighted to sit on my own, by the wall, for half an hour after meditation. I sensed in a small way what it must be like for a person on their own in Simon, when they go in there first, and don't know anyone. They must feel totally on their own. I'm sure they can get very lonely and then they drink or go on drugs, sex, etc. I felt very deeply peaceful there today.

I was very touched today while talking to John, who quoted this in French for me: "We must only take what we *need* and not be greedy". He referred to getting €8 busking for about one hour or so. He said, "That is enough for me, for now". His face moves me to tears. In his eyes, I see a long, lonely road.

### Wednesday, 13 March

Derry Gayn sat with me, for – I'm not sure how long – three-quarters of an hour or so. He bought candles. He said he loves candles. He said they create a nicer atmosphere with a fire than artificial light. He has a most beautiful mind. He said he was living in the country now. He has a garden and likes the experience of going for a walk, he said. He's very aware. He said he used to be very self-righteous, but now he's not. He hears that the Provider can take his life at any moment. He said it's a great privilege to have life – a life, his life. It doesn't matter whether one belongs to a church or not. What matters most is, *how* he lives his life now. He said its about 'being' and 'presence'. He's 27 years old. He's really an inspiration listening to him. He is so very gentle. He has grown in great maturity since my last chat with him. He said his life is graced. He does not worry whether anyone likes him or not. He can *be himself*. He slept rough on the Continent for five years and was never short – the Provider, as he calls the Maker, looked after him. He travelled through India, China and Siberia, too – over a six-year period. He lived in tents. He said now he could live in a hut! He said he has no expectations of people and does not depend on them now. He learns from every single person he meets. He asked me about myself. I told him. He was getting ready to go. I left, too, with him. I asked him does he meditate. He said he does and he does three hours' exercises every day. He does one hour of silence every night with candles. He's a very open, lovely person. He emanated pace and tranquillity. I told him that. He said his aim is to be peaceful himself and contented. He does bits of jobs, he said. I'm not sure what! It was lovely to have the chat with him.

## Wednesday, 20 March

Kyle said he felt weak. He said he has diabetes. He talked again about the sex abuse. He prays for someone who upset his night. In the *Our Father*, he said we say, 'Forgive us our trespasses as we forgive those who trespass against us'. He said he's a Catholic. He's impotent, since his last son was born. He went to Confession one time. He said that he had been drinking. The priest said, "Again! You'll go down under". He said that that frightened him a lot, but he went to another priest and he asked him to make an *Act of Contrition*, which he said he did. That second priest said he had no more to worry about. Kyle told the second priest what the first priest said and the second priest said, "Don't take any notice of him. He's one of the old traditional types. Hell fire!". It's still around, alive and well! He said he's not afraid of dying, but he's afraid of meeting God. I could hear that. I said, "He has forgiven you everything and is all loving and kind to you, always". I asked Kyle can he (Kyle) forgive Kyle? He said, "No. I did awful things". I said, "The good lives *in* you, too, that never changes".

   I sat near Abel Casser, who appeared to be asleep. Eventually, he woke up. He said he is drinking since he was 12. He's on the streets eight years now. He was sexually abused at 5 years. He said he drinks three bottles of vodka some days – two most days. Abel has a good sense of humour. He said he was in a centre for drink. His family disowned him. He lost his house and wife.

## Wednesday, 27 March

I was at Simon around 9.50 a.m. Karen Carp left me in. I saw flowers – primroses – on the gate and hoped another person had not died. To my horror and shock, when I asked Alice in the hall, she said it was Ernest Exor. I felt so upset on hearing this news. I'm crying now as I write this. This is so awful. There were conflicting stories as to how he died. Someone said he got a fit and died in hospital. John Gabie told me he broke his neck near the Opera House. Someone else said he had drugs taken – whatever the cause was, it's so very, very sad. I recalled the day, only very recently, that he was at the table with Andrew, Joe and myself and Joe was offering the *Rolos* around and Ernest said, "I'll have the last one!". Was it the last *Rolo* he was ever to eat? Little did he know!

## Tuesday, 9 April

A young man, whom I did not know, lay flat out on Nano Nagle Bridge, when I was going along. I went over to see if he was O.K. I could see him breathing, so I let him be, trusting he was O.K. Maybe he had too much drink taken or something.

## Wednesday, 10 April

Paul Pawn brought me a mug of water. I was very touched by the gentle way he turned the handle towards me, when he brought it to me. I sat for almost two and a half hours learning more about people and life on the edge.

## Friday, 12 April

Kevin Kend said he felt the biggest addiction in Cork now is not drink, but prescription drugs. He said some people – street-people and others – go to two or three different doctors and get medication from all. He said an awful lot of people in psychiatric hospitals are far too long on anti-depressants, they keep on needing them more and more and get addicted to these.

## Wednesday, 17 April

Paul said he was on the dock drinking last night. He could not get out of bed this morning. He said a man approached him (for what I don't know) but he refused him. He said he saw the prostitutes there. Some were fine-looking women, he said. Colm said there are three kinds of women: 1) prostitutes; 2) hoars; and 3) other women. A hoar would not get as much as prostitutes. Paul knew one lady who makes two grand a week without any sex! Rosetta arrived then. We continued the chat. Paul and Colm were so open about all this – I wonder was Colm himself ever involved in it. Interesting – Paul said that one lady he knows is a 'hoar-master'. I know her, too. I thought she'd be pretty upmarket, by her appearance. I'm solely going on her appearance. Paul was very relaxed with us, I could see by his face.

## Friday, 19 April

I really enjoyed listening to Derry. I felt sorry for him. Seán came over to Derry and myself. He bent down near us. Derry said to Seán, "I had the most wonderful conversation of my life with Catherine!". I'd believe he had. No one ever listened to him for so long before, he said, without giving out to him. I really listened to him. He said he only told his mother and me some of his secrets.

I heard Karen McAuton died. She used to be with Dave. All the care she took of him and how she used worry so much about him, poor Karen. She was a lovely soul. It is sad to hear of one more of our friends dead now. Karen was in Ballygriffin with us, too.

## Sunday, 28 April

I met Aidan under a shelter in a dry spot near a church. I said to him that he had a lovely dry spot. He said, "The Lord looks after his own". How well said, I thought. I said, "You look very happy". He said he prays. I felt before that Aidan is a spiritual person.

## Wednesday, 1 May

I sat for a while, just observing the people around me at the table, saying nothing. Great. Just BE - ING. Later, Mary Rald on my right-hand side began talking to me. She said she has lived a bad life. Her mother had a deformed baby before Mary was born. The mother went dancing while she was expecting that child. She lost the baby. When Mary was born, she committed suicide, hanging herself in the shed, as she thought Mary would also be deformed, and she could not take that. Mary's father was a very angry man. Her eldest daughter stabbed her Dad and later she herself got a phone call from her eldest daughter saying her Dad had died. Mary has three children – two daughters and one son. One of her daughters is doing 15 months in prison. Mary does not get on with her son. She said she was brought up in an Eastern church and they were very rigid – no drink, no smoking, no music on Sundays, etc. She said her Dad was very rigid. He felt very guilty one time he played music on Sunday. She said she left home and went drinking. Then she met the Mormons. They used to visit her, so she joined them and gave up drink, as the Mormons don't allow drink, or smoking either. She said they discontinued calling to her and she went back on drink again. She said the years she was with the Mormons were the happiest years of her life. She said she was lonely and on the street when she met Dave. He's a street-child, she said. I asked him what was the cross on his forehead. He said he's an atheist. The cross is an upside-down cross. He said it means 'Out with religion – No to religion'! I felt in my feelings that I was sticking out like a sore thumb at the table. My feelings don't want me to be associated with an organised religion. Spirituality is what we all need most.

I met Laura Sage. I gave her a hug and asked her how is she. I chatted with her then. She was lovely to me, when I came in, in the very, very early days to Simon.

Dave said to me today, "It is nice you come in here and talk to us".

## Friday, 3 May

I said, "Hello", to Donie, Molly's friend. He held on to my hand for a while. He was sitting on the seat on the quay, near the river. A man named Steve, at the end of the seat, said to Donie, "You must introduce me to that lovely lady". Donie said, "That's Sister Catherine". The man stood up and said, "Catherine Fenton, are you?". I was stunned and said, "Yes". He gave me a very warm hug. He lived in a town near us long ago! His name is Steve Ricle. He said, "I fell in love with you, but the Church took you"! He asked about my family and how they are. When I was going away, Steve said to me, "I still love you". He gave me a kiss.

## Wednesday, 8 May

Molly Gaffey greeted me. I asked her how was she. She said, "Bad". She then proceeded to tell me Jonah, her partner's brother, died. I got a shock. Poor Jonah. He was a great character. The last thing he said to me on 26 April at 10.40 a.m. near the bus office was, "Will you marry me?". I said in my own mind, "It is not everyone asks me to marry them at 10.40 a.m. on a Friday morning"! I cried in front of Molly and gave her a hug.

Jonah is resting in peace now in his heavenly home – no more drink or sex needed now. I felt so honoured to spend time with Jonah last night. I rang the funeral home and asked if Jonah's remains were there. Yes. I asked if I could visit them. The caretaker said, "Yes, they close at 9.00 p.m.". I walked over and sat on my own in silent meditation in front of Jonah's remains for a half-hour. The silence was beautiful in the funeral home. I kissed his forehead and put a lovely bunch of flowers with some of their green leaves on the shelf beside the coffin, at the caretaker's request. They were from the garden. I said to Jonah, "These are from Rosetta and myself. Thank you Jonah for having known you, for your good humour and your stories. Thanks for the gift of yourself. Thank you". I went on my two knees on the floor out of deep respect for his beautiful soul – always snow-white, like the lily of the valley flowers. They symbolise the purity of his soul. That never changed amidst all the drinking and angry moments others may have *only* seen in Jonah. I kissed his forehead again before I left. I felt so honoured to be there and all by myself with him. It was a special time for me there. I felt he made it possible for me to be there on my own. He liked me in life and now in death. He wanted me near him. His total brokenness and fragility brought me to the realisation of the impermanence of the apparently permanent in this life – his humanity. Yet, he needed his fragile frame to mediate the mystery of the Creator alive within him. No words can describe the marvel or splendour of such a sacred journey, the journey of the soul.

## Tuesday, 14 May

I met James Walor in *Eason's* today. Jo is a great person. He is a very dedicated, gentle and loving person. He still does the soup-run, he said. He said they need some more places to take in people off the street. It could be a shelter where they can lie down for the night and go out again the next day. I said the original Simon idea was always to take in people who were intoxicated off the street for the night. There isn't enough accommodation for that in Cork, he said. There were two people out on Sunday night in the pouring rain. Their blankets were very, very wet. He said there is one good staff member called Miley and he let the two in and put them somewhere?! Others keep too rigidly to the rules, he said. Jo said another street friend of ours died. I told him what I did on Wednesday night, being with his remains. He was at the removal, he said.

### Wednesday, 15 May

Grace said she's off drink. Today is her first day and she finds it hard. Benedict Balor, her partner, went away with his Dad last Thursday and she has not seen him since. She was with him 10 months and she said he never told her he was going away. She said he's very good with her children. She has three children, one aged 8, one 3 and one 2. The 8 year old girl made her first Holy Communion last week. Grace's Mam and Dad brought her for it. Catherine saw the clothes. She can't see the children when she's drinking, she said. She said, "I'm an alcoholic and so is Benedict".

### Friday, 17 May

I remembered James Walor saying that when he, James, was passing the church on Thursday night, it reminded him that this was Jonah's first night inside the church! Many, many other nights he used to sleep outside the church door! He used to give out that the lights were on and that he couldn't sleep!

### Monday, 20 May

I asked Alexandra how was she. She said Ned, who died, talked to her for four hours on Thursday. He said what he was going to do and how he was going to do it. She said she thought he would not do anything after talking to her. "What good did it do him talking me?", she said. I said she listened and she could do no more. She was probably the last person he spoke to before he went to the river. He went out that night, Alexandra said, and never came back. He had some domestic problems, Marty said. I said he's at peace now, in heaven. Alexandra told me she went into the river, too, a while ago and six people took her out! She got cards from the people in the Shelter, she said, who expressed to her their sadness on her friend, Ned's, death.

Simon Community is a great school of growth – a gift for me, today and many days. My only prayer today was at the end of my meditation, "Give me this day my daily bread". One takes on huge responsibility when one says these words. Everything that happened there today was exactly as it was meant to be. Everything that I *needed* today was handmade and given to me from the beginning. It was part of my unique life's journey.

## Wednesday, 22 May

Joseph talked to me for a long time. He said he used to be depressed and was on medication. He still takes a yellow tablet, he said, as otherwise he'd be very nervy because his nerves aren't good. I found him very gentle – mainly.

These people are so caring of each other. They have such big hearts. Pete said to me, "You meet all kinds of people in these places. One word you say to them could cause them to ponder it up in their room, and maybe help them a lot". That was so comforting to hear that. I felt I was 'being there' today. He said you may never know whom *you* yourself help any day. I found his insights very moving and very encouraging, really. I said to him, too, he does a lot for people himself in life. He said he does. He said when they see him nice and neat and clean, they think he's grand, that he has no problems! He said he's no different in behaviour to those who are dirty and wear raggy clothes. He said he likes to iron his clothes. He was then going for a shower and getting nice clean sheets for his bed. He was always very kind to me, too, offering me tea, etc. He liked me, I could see. He said he must drink some boiling water like me. He said, "The poor are the people in town who will give you money – the rich pass by".

## Friday, 24 May

There don't seem to be as many people in now in the Shelter as there used to be before, since the Day-care Centre opened. It seems quieter, now, at times.

## Wednesday, 28 May

My heart nearly broke, when I saw poor Chelsea Calcott on the Grand Parade with another woman. She looked so down, poor Chelsea. I shed tears on seeing how very bewildered she was and how awfully sad she looked. It was heartbreaking to see her in this state. I stopped for half a second to say, "Hello, Chelsea". I felt by her that she was going to keep walking. She did!

I was delighted to meet Ciarán Cumor during the week. He said he's doing very well now – works in security three or four days a week and is married. He has three children, 2, 4 and 6. He said, "Thanks to you, I stayed out of prison. We went through madness those days. You were good to us, when we had nowhere to go, only sleep rough on the streets, take drugs, drink and get ourselves into big trouble always. You saw the good in us and, in time, we saw that good in ourselves. We turned our life around and we're very happy today". I said, "Ye needed to live well those teenage years".

## Monday, 3 June

I met Sive. She is from Turkey. She has meditated with us for some time and found it very good. She meditates about three times a week now, not every day. Sive said, "Street-people don't lie. They have nothing to hide – ordinary people do hide. They can lie, too".

## Wednesday, 5 June

Tadg talked a lot about going to Glenstal for quiet space. He already spent five days there. He said he has a cousin there. His cousin is 82. Tadg went to a help centre for three months. He got a job after, was back with his girlfriend and had a luxury apartment! He went to West Cork to do fishing – got €2,000 per week and went on the drink again and drank it all! He's now in Simon.

Rosetta and I met poor Amy Ladde on the road. Rosetta and I did what we could to help her, by holding her hand and letting her cry on my shoulder. She put her hand firmly in my hand and put her other arm around me. I, by 'being', gave her love from my being through my body. Rosetta also was there in her being with Amy.

## Wednesday, 19 June

I was out in the street early this morning. I felt very at peace there. About 8.20 a.m. or so, I saw David Gabbay walking around the garden. He stopped at the Crucifixion and prayed. This moved me.

Mark Salim sat with us. He was eating his lunch. I invited him to meditation with me. He said he would come along. The two of us came along together. We began before 11.40 a.m. Mark sat for the whole meditation, a half-hour, as quiet as a mouse. He said after, "I *felt* goodness in me. It was great". He said, "There is someone looking after me". He said,

"Má – Rá – Ná – Thá". I could see him saying this at the start. I felt so moved by him. He said his Mam and Dad gave up drink for him. His Dad prays for him every night. He said his Dad said he doesn't know how Mark is alive at all from the drink! He said he'd come up now every Wednesday, to do the meditation. I told him after that I felt honoured that he was with me for the meditation. I said it made my day! Mark's clothes looked to me as if they were not changed for weeks – months maybe! Nor had he washed, for quite a while, I felt. Still, his inner beauty shone through. He thanked me. I felt he was so very grateful. Mark also said to me earlier, "God nearly put me to sleep". He told Teddy, "I felt something in my stomach. Goodness. A tickle in my chest, too". Mark, who has spent most of his life on the streets sleeping rough, could hear this goodness (his true self) alive in his body. How beautiful. Beautiful, such simplicity.

## Monday, 24 June

I won't forget Ray Jey's kindness to me and to others, too. He suffers from rheumatoid arthritis. He had a crutch. Still, he could totally forget himself and get a mug of tea and two sugars for Aidan and give some roll-ups to George Faiss. There was such compassion in his gestures. He was just beautiful. He told me then he was a Brother for 20 years and was addicted to the altar wine. He used to give out clothes, etc., to poor in America and now he's at the other end of the pole – in need of these clothes, etc., himself. He studied *The Bible*, he said. He said three score and ten is our span and anything extra is a bonus. I quoted the Psalm, "Our span is 70 years and 80 for those who are strong. Most of these are emptiness and pain. They pass swiftly and we are gone". He got some toast and cheese and made some sandwiches to take with him. He was going to Spain, as his sister was ill. He had not seen this sister for 30 years. He was going on the boat. He showed me his ticket. The poor man. All he had was a plastic bag, with his few goods in it. I was honoured to talk to Ray.

## Wednesday, 26 June

I met Alexandra Bamidene near Simon and she said she had bad news – Aidan Callender died. He was taken from the river near Blackrock. David Bagley was beaten up and was on a life-support machine in the South Infirmary. I felt so sad on hearing this news. I felt my eyes fill with tears.

It came to me today that it is so important what we say to people every day – it may be our last time ever meeting some of these people. On

Monday last, it was my last time ever meeting Aidan again. He is now forever resting in peace.

I meditated in the staff quarters. When I came down, Molly said the prayer was in the recreation room. Pete, Susan, Dolly, Jack, Adam, Cian, Tessie, Pam, Molly, Alexis, Roy, Ruth, Seán, Jessie and a couple more, were there eventually with myself. About 16 of us gathered for prayer. Someone asked me to lead them in it. I thanked Pete for suggesting it and said that why we were here was to pray for David who is in a coma and to remember Aidan, who has gone to his home in heaven. Pam, David's sister, was very upset. She said a little. I thanked her for her prayer. Cian said he wanted David to get well. He said this beating will have to stop on the streets. He knelt on the floor, facing into the seat of the couch (like when we used say the *Rosary* at home long ago!) and cried a lot. Susan shared that her brother was in a coma and came out of it. He's now very well, she said. I said we're praying here together and the love from our prayer goes to David, to bring him peace. I said we would all like to see David well again – Pam's brother was Adam's friend. Paul said one *Hail Mary* at the *Rosary*. Pete suggested we say a decade of the *Rosary* for David. Pete said an *Our Father*. Molly said the second *Hail Mary*, Cian the third, Adam the fourth, Paul the fifth, John the sixth, Mark the seventh, Ruth the eighth, Alexandra the ninth and Penny the tenth. I said the *Gloria*. It was so real from their hearts, it moved me very deeply. I thanked them. Pete suggested we say *Our Father* together. We held hands, as a sign of our oneness. Penny said, "We're like a family". I began the hymn, "Bind us together God with cords that cannot be broken, bind us together with love". Because we are *all* broken, we need to be bound up – our being is the cord that cannot be broken. Our in-depth love *always* holds us together, when everything else fails. That is the love that binds our humanity (brokenness) together. I felt very honoured to be part of such a sacred celebration.

## *Saturday, 29 June*

I saw Chelsea Calcott and Barbara O'Bradi sitting on a bench near the Courthouse. They were in a bad state. Chelsea was putting her hand out to the passers-by for help. It was so sad and pathetic to see this poor young woman on the edge.

Tess and I went to see David in the intensive care unit. He is very, very ill. Tess and I prayed with him. Later, we met John, Ken, Julie, Pete, Tammy, June, Jill, and Seán Bagley, David's brother. Seán said he has no time for nuns or religion. He said the family was separated and sent to different places, when they were young. Now, he can't find his family. David's brother was angry, saying, "What good are the prayers now, when he's not going to get better?". Seán apologised to me for being angry with me and he began telling me his story. It was a fascinating story.

## Tuesday, 2 July

I met Dave Dant. He told me David died on Monday – when they took him off the ventilator. I felt so happy I went in on Saturday and prayed with Tess and David and remembered Barbara, his partner, too. It was such a special privilege. Dave Dant said Barbara was very upset. She was David's partner. She's not left alone at all at any time now, he said. Poor Barbara, it must be heartbreaking for her, as it was she hit him last Tuesday and knocked him over. He hit his head against the concrete bin. Awful!

## Wednesday, 3 July

I met Alexandra on my way to the Shelter. She told me about David. She said Adam said he'd ask the street-people for a donation for flowers for David. He did, and collected €60, Alexandra said. She said someone was saying they only had a little money and Alexandra told them the story out in the *Scripture* of the widow's mite. She gave *all* she had, whereas the rich man did not hardly miss what he gave, he had so much. The widow trusted and gave all, trusting that she would not be short or in want – such heroism. The person today then gave Adam what he had, a few coins. Alexandra told me all this so gently, on the path. She was going to meet Jimmy further up the footpath, who was drinking. Dolores was going along, so I went with her. Terence was there. Terence said he was still very lonely after Colm, his friend. He said he has Colm's walking stick – a blackthorn. It was offered to him. He looked at Colm's cat curled in a ball on the chair nearby.

Molly said there would be Mass on Monday in the Day-care Centre for Aidan and David. We had very spontaneous sharing from Pete, Susan, and Adam. They expressed their feelings very clearly and openly to us. We recited one decade of the *Rosary* at Pete's request – he asked me to start. I did and said the *Our Father* from deep within. Each person said a *Hail Mary*. I said the *Gloria*. They thanked Rosetta and I for joining in with them.

*Thursday, 4 July*

I met Judy Rye, David's other sister. The two of us went to the funeral home
for 5.50 p.m. There were a mere three or four people in the funeral home,
when we went in. I met Mary Resor. I thought I smelled drink from her.
O.K. She said she was at the funeral home and would go to the Eucharistic
celebration tomorrow. Later, the priest asked me in what way did I know
him. I said Rosetta and I visit – listen to people and do meditation in Simon.
This is part of our work. Cillian, Joe, Seánie, Ambrose, Joan, George and
Julie were there. Ambrose and Julie were crying. David's sister, Josie, came
in and his brother, Anthony. The church ceremony was simple. I felt very
moved at the door, the outside door. There was a sheet of plastic on the
ground with some words written on it. On it, there stood a wine bottle, with
some simple wild flowers in the bottle. There were no flowers near it.
Written on it, the plastic, was 'To David from Bessie'. Bessie is 17 years old.
She lives on the streets. Anthony, David's brother, came over to me
specifically to thank me for being there. He held my hand with both his
hands. I felt comforted. Josie, David's sister, said she is trying to keep the
younger generation away from the drink, her own and Judy's daughter. She
said, "We could not have the winos, our brother and sister, near our
children, but ye took our place and looked after them for us". I said I felt
honoured to be given such a privilege. I was so deeply moved to tears. She
thanked me again. Poor Andy, David's brother, was inconsolable.

*Friday, 5 July*

It came to me last night to bring *As I Leave You* to the Mass today. I would
not like to read it, as I felt it was more appropriate that a street-person ought
to read it.

### *AS I LEAVE YOU*

> *I leave my thoughts, my laughter, my dreams*
> *To you whom I have treasured*
> *Beyond gold and precious gems.*
> *I give you what no thief can steal*
> *The memories of our times together,*
> *The tender love-filled moments,*
> *The successes we have shared*
> *The hard times that brought us closer together*
> *And the roads we have walked side by side.*

*I also leave you a solemn promise*
*That, after I am home in the bosom of God,*
*I will still be present*
*Whenever and wherever you call on me*
*My energy will be drawn to you*
*By the magnet of our love.*
*Whenever you are in need, call me,*
*I will come to you, with my arms full of wisdom and light*
*To open up your blocked paths,*
*To untangle your knots and to be your avenue to God*
*And all I take with me as I leave*
*Is your love and the millions of memories*
*Of all that we have shared.*
*So I truly enter my new life as a millionaire.*
*Fear not nor grieve at my departure,*
*You whom I have loved so much*
*For my roots and yours*
*Are forever intertwined.*

I felt Danny asked me to bring that today and give as much comfort to the street-people and David's family, as it has been for the Fenton family. I asked Alexandra Bamidene, a 'lady of the night', would she like to read the reflection. She said, even before she read it all, that she would. When she read *As I Leave You*, the first bit only, she said, "Of course". She said, "It is a long time since anyone asked me to do anything like that". I believed she would be fine. I found the celebration of the Eucharist a lovely experience – very gently and sensitively handled by the celebrant. I felt he has suffered, as even he was remembering all David's friends. He asked the Source of Life to remember us, too, "who are often disillusioned and fearful". He said in his homily, that David used to spend time in that church and that he was locked in one night, as no-one knew he was there! I found it so moving to see the street-friends receiving Holy Communion. It was, as I experienced it, symbolic of the holy / whole common-union with one another. The receiving of the piece of food sacramentalised that inner reality beautifully. Alexandra read the reflection beautifully. Andrew said with tears in his eyes, "All the street-people are nearly dead. Fifty died in a very short time". So sad.

## Monday, 8 July

A man from Norway sat next to me. He said he has an Irish wife and two children, who live in Cork. He can't go back to Norway for six months. He is now on the streets, he said. He was a very, very good-looking man. He said he is a house designer. Some generations of his family are in that business, too. He showed me his photograph. He looked unhappy in it. He said he hopes to get a bed in the Shelter. He will get his money tomorrow. He was very well-dressed. I pitied his poor wife and children. Their suffering must be awful. He said he had very little English. I could understand him, though, quite well. His wife and family live in Cork. They all lived in Spain for 10 years. I saw a very sad look in his eyes. He had a gash on his face over his right eye. He was looking at my clothes and asked me was I staying here. I said, "I visit".

## Wednesday, 10 July

I sat near a man called Batt Bank, who had a big cylinder – silvery – as an 'arm' from his elbow down. There were some screws at the end. I felt such compassion for the poor man. He said his hand was like this for 36 years and he's now 42. He was only six when it happened. He said no more about his arm. He was born in Brazil. He was in England for a while. He said it upsets people to look at this (his silver cylinder) more than it upsets himself.

I greeted Alexandra Bamidene. I said how good she was at the reading at David Bagley's Mass – the *As I Leave You* reflection. She said that, before she went up, she was very nervous, but when she was going up the stairs to the altar, she felt a great peace come over her. She said, "That is God". I said, "Yes". I said, "That's always in you, Alexandra, but you may not always be aware of it". Other things get in the way of our peace emerging. Alexandra said Samson gave her a hug. He said, "You were brilliant at the reading. You were so calm and sincere and felt what you read".

Rosetta, Sammy and I meditated together. Sammy talked for a long time after. I feel it was for about an hour. It was lovely listening to him. He's a lovely person. He was a student in a religious group in Holland. He also qualified in psychology and was not happy in it. He left and joined another group of people who were searching for two years. This group was based its life on: act justly, love tenderly, and walk humbly with their Maker. They had a deep spirituality. He could quote the *Scriptures* very well. He loved the quote from Jeremiah – 'my plans for you are peace and not disaster'. Also, he quoted from the *New Testament* something about even though we go through great sufferings, God never lets us down. He said even if we are homeless and sleeping on the street, God is always with us. He never leaves us. He said he's working now in Cork. He said he could feel the presence of God in the room. He said he felt it helped him to have this chat. He quoted on death from Tony de Mello's *Wellsprings*. He seems to be about 38 years of age. He quoted from Thomas Merton, on *Silence*. He talked about feeling being neither right nor wrong. If a person is down because of drink – it could be he feels anger, fear, etc. – but a lot of Shelter people can't face those feelings. He said he had handed over his life to God to do whatever he wished with him. He is being open, he said. That means, he said being open to whatever he asked of him. He said Jesus is holding him in his arms, as he goes along life's way. Rosetta and I clarified for him, at his request, as we went along. We talked about personal growth, meditation, etc. Sammy has faith in what is given, I could see well. It was a joy to listen to Sammy.

## Wednesday, 7 August

I went to Simon. I went into the dining-room, got a mug of boiling water, asked Betty Bass could I sit near her. She said, "Yes". She chatted a lot about drink and asked me did I ever drink? I said I did when I was young. She was surprised at that. She said she sits on the window sill in Patrick's Hill and watches the people go by. I sat listening to Betty for an hour. She is such a fragile person. She said she has only one set of clothes now – what she had on her! Her deep gentleness touched me. She was able to keep so calm and dignified in the midst of such hustle and bustle around her. She was centred beautifully.

## Monday, 19 August

Jill showed us the black eye which her partner gave her. She also showed us her badly-bruised arm and leg and said he hit her with the handle of a brush. She showed me the marks he put on her, when he tried to cut her legs with a saw. Horrible. She said she's six months pregnant – the poor girl. How does she survive? She and her partner met in a help centre. They were together for about a year. She was in the hospital with her injuries. Ruth was taking her to her flat with her. She said that her partner said that it was not his child she was carrying and that she's around with other men. He goes mad when he drinks, she said. He takes drugs, too. It was around 12.30 a.m. when he did this to her. Her son, 11, is with her mother in Cork.

I met Kylie. She was just back from the Buddhist centre. She said the meditation was good, but she feels mixed about the experience. She's not comfortable with it – Buddhism. I said the Dalai Lama said to stay in your own religion and take what is best out of the other religions. I invited her to meditation on Wednesday. She said when she was at the centre, she was encouraged to keep her eyes partly open, looking out at the waves in the sea.

## Tuesday, 3 September

I met Georgia Mars who is from Cork. She's 36 weeks pregnant. She was on the streets and now she's in a flat with her boyfriend. I said I would remember her in my prayers. She held my hand gently and said, "Thanks".

I had a longer chat with Michael Deers, when I went to wash my cup. He said he does a 39-hour week. He can break it up, i.e., eight hours a day or four hours, etc. He said there are many people between the ages of 18 to 26 around. There are too many of this age group on the streets. He said if a person can help *one person* out of 12, then that's great. He said the services are not adequate to back up what some people are doing. The young people have childhood issues, which need to be dealt with. They won't often follow an education programme. He looked pretty worn out. He was a caring person, I felt.

## Monday, 9 September

Agatha came along then. She asked me about being a nun. She said how long does it take? I told her about the various steps – postulant, novice, professed, etc. It takes six years before a person is finally professed. She said Mark Salim's birthday is on Friday, 13 September. I said that was the date of my final profession – 33 years ago! Mark Salim will be 30 on Friday. He looks every bit of 50. Today, Mark was just there, sitting down, doing nothing – he was just staying in the present moment – awesome. I watched him – he could do 'nothing' – all day and every day. He's a beloved child of the Maker, whatever he does – nothing or something. Mark was just being – being himself. Beautiful. He is my real teacher today, me, who can be bored doing 'nothing'.

## Wednesday, 11 September

I said the Shelter was quieter since the Day-care Centre opened during the day. There were only three women in the emergency Shelter four years ago.

Now, there were lots of young women. When I looked around, I saw Annie,
Lily Lex and Grace Daams.

## Wednesday, 18 September

I met Ciarán on my way in. He said his sister had a cot death. The eight-
month-old baby died in her arms – her heart, etc., was tested. There was no
reason given for the child's death. What suffering! It really tore at my heart-
strings to hear Ciarán describe the night the child died, when they stayed in
the hospital all night. He said they had to take off the clothes that the baby
died in and put on other clothes in which to lay the baby out. His sister has
seven other children. I invited him to the meditation.

Barney Bird asked me earlier would we do a slot / workshop on
meditation at the National Simon Conference in *Shandon Court* on 16
November. I said I felt that would be O.K. but I'd check with Rosetta. He
said he came up with the idea as we do it here, with street-people and staff. I
invited him to meditation on the days we do it and he said if he had time,
he'd love to go. He said he does it himself at home and it's 'a life-saver'. He
needs space, he said.

## Wednesday, 25 September

I saw on *The Irish Times* on Friday, 'Dying for a drink: a society in denial of
an alcohol abuse epidemic'! How true.

## Thursday, 26 September

Zita said, "This is an awful world". I said, "It is, when we let our emotions
and mind take us over. When we live from deep within, i.e., our true self,
we can have heaven on earth". She's with another partner now, too.

Pat Puny said the staff need to be very spiritual people to do the Simon
work. He said they are well-educated people, who have given up good jobs
to do this work. How loving they are to offer their lives for some of the most
vulnerable people in society.

## Friday, 27 September

Robert asked me my name. He said he's Robert. He was eating the food first
with his hands – salad, in an animal-like way almost, then he used his
cutlery. He had some drink taken. Mucus from his nose ran down his

clothes and maybe onto his food. He wiped it on his sleeve. I said, "You are a good man, Robert". He said, "I am. No one else ever said that to me before". He later asked me, if he could talk to me. He said a few words. He said he had troubles. He thanked me, held my hand and left.

## Wednesday, 2 October

Samson said his doctor said meditation is good for the heart! It relaxes the body. That is correct. I said we were just finished our meditation. I met him later on the stairs. He said *he* wanted to get back with his wife before, but now that *she* wants to get back with him, he doesn't want to go. How complex the human is.

Gregory Ryl sat next to me. He asked me my name. He has lovely eyes. I could smell alcohol from him. He said, "I'm a good man when I can get a woman to smile!". He said, "I got you to smile".

## Friday, 4 October

Vince Pox said in the winter, he sleeps in the woods – he makes a home of the bushes and all the animals come to him, he said. He said it's people we need to be more afraid of, than animals. How wise.

## Wednesday, 9 October

I found the energy negative in the Shelter today. I was drawn to the garden and found great energy in just looking at the fuchsia flower – good energy in the midst of such pain.

## Wednesday, 16 October

I met Thomas Caffrey. He said, "My name is NOBODY – I'm going to the river. There is nothing here!"

## Wednesday, 23 October

I greeted Grace, JoJo, Pete and Robbie. We talked about Sean who murdered poor Richie. Poor Sean. I went to meet the street-people and staff before they went to the funeral. I sat with Steve and Ronnie for a while. They were very sad. Steve used drink with Richie, he said. Ronnie said he thought he'd die himself, when he heard the news. Jack Restor joined us later and shared on death. His cousin's Dad died. He touched me again, talking about his friend's child who was four weeks when he died. He said he reads Tony de Mello, *The Bible* and goes to churches – this gives him strength. I was very moved by Redmond saying, "All in life is gift … to be able to get out of bed in the morning is gift. Eternal life is *NOW*".

### Thursday, 24 October

Ger had only four hours' sleep last night, so he did not feel he would go to Ballygriffin. After thinking about it for a while, then he said he would go! He washed and got ready. We left Simon at 10.00 a.m. We got our groceries then. We were in Ballygriffin at 11.40 a.m. We had a chat. Ger was very interesting, as he was telling us about the drug trade in Holland. We meditated with Ger. Ger said his mother lives with his sister in Cork. His mother teaches in the Middle East. He seems to be close to his grandmother, to whom he goes for Christmas. He has one sister. Ger spent time in England with his uncle, he said. He had lots of tablets to help him deal with depression. He lost €30,000 in gambling and got depressed. Ger has learned a lot in his 27 years of life. He slept under the shelter in *Páirc Uí Chaoimh* for a week with June, Robbie and Kevin. He said they had nowhere to sleep and he went to join them for the company. He said they kept his bed in the Simon for him. We had tea. Ger was delighted with the day. He shared a lot. He said, "I felt in the morning like as if the whole world was down on top of me but, now, after the day, my head is clear. I felt I could go outside myself and it helped me see myself from another side – time for myself. I feel great after the day". It was a great day with our very special friend, Ger.

### Friday, 25 October

We met Benny today to talk about the National Conference. We gave him an outline of what we hoped to do.

Zita was very wild around the place. She jumped over the chair and later I saw a glass breaking near her. She changed her clothes and washed. Poor Zita, she needs so much attention. She's like a two year old child. Zita said about me then to Jonathan, "It's alright, as she had a boyfriend before she became a nun. She is like us … she's grand!".

Con came over to me and said he was with a girl for a while. He thought she was having his baby … instead, he said, what popped out was a black baby! He said he was heartbroken. He went on drink after that – he hit the bottle. He said he did not know where to go or who to turn to. He said there is always a reason why people are on the street. They are not there for nothing. He had tears in his eyes. I thanked him for sharing his story with me.

### Wednesday, 30 October

Jerry was around. He later thanked me again for being there to listen to him, at a time that was very important to him. He said it was not forgotten and "he sent up a few" for me, not only himself, but his family as well – prayer, he meant! I really appreciated him saying that to me. He was so sincere saying it – I still don't know where I met him. That is O.K.

Amy left us up to the meditation room. She gave me the impression she was pretty much 'all over the place'. Rob meditated with us. He said after, "It was very relaxing. It's good to do meditation when you are working here". Rosetta and I had a chat with Rob afterwards.

### Wednesday, 6 November

#### NAMELESS AND UNMISSED

*Homeless and desolate these people you would have passed. With distaste, fear and maybe even disgust. Some of you may have taken pity, tried to ease their hardship. But only having lived with and depended on these people could you possibly understand their kindness, their friendship, their unending love and understanding.*

*I will have to live with the grief of their passing, and the knowledge that they will remain nameless and unmissed by a city they loved.*

### Thursday, 7 November

Poor Jo was in an awful state outside the gate. He cried later and said Jack beat him. It was so sad to see him crying. I said they may be able to help him in the Day-care. He asked could I help him. I did. He went over towards the Shelter and sat on the ground. He then cried and cried. Liam helped him, too, and consoled him. He was so compassionate towards him.

#### GRATITUDE

*If I wrote what I really wanted to say, it could be difficult because I always want the best for everyone, no matter where they come from. I'm a middle-aged African man. At present, I'm unemployed and homeless but, thanks to Cork Simon, I* have a place where I can sleep and I have something to eat. I came to Simon for the first time when I lost my flat, which was caused by my drinking. It's hard to say how many other Africans were in the same position. The Africans I've met in Simon have had similar problems: alcohol, loss of accommodation, being on the street – and have also had enormous help from the Simon Community. I have to say that it isn't really the same. However, when I lost everything and I had to live on the street, someone told me about Simon. I asked for a bed, which I got without any hassle. The next day I went to the Day Centre, where I got all the help I could ask for. To make a long story short, Cork Simon Community helps you a lot with getting your life back on track. I'm sure Simon have plenty of problems, because there are many people from all types of backgrounds and each with different personalities, but I think, even though they are divided by all those differences, they also have a bond. If we talk about things we wish for, I would like people to be able to stay in Simon accommodation until they get a job and, in my opinion, if Simon wasn't there then I, and many of my countrymen, would probably be lost. I don't know if they share my opinion on this but what else could a homeless person do, without the Simon Community's help? For the small piece of goodness we get from Simon, I would like to thank God and Ireland for such a place. I've met lovely people here. The staff put all their hearts into their jobs, and they're ready to help at anytime. If I could work with such a team of people in the Shelter and the Day Centre, I would be very proud. Thank you for everything from the bottom of my heart. I won't name anyone because I'm afraid I might leave someone out. Finally, I would like to mention that I wouldn't be here if it wasn't for Cork Simon. I wish that more Africans were grateful for Simon's help. Grateful for everything.

**An African immigrant**

## Thursday, 14 November

I will never forget Sam's smile yesterday, when he was giving me the gifts of the pear and banana. It was truly heavenly.

## Wednesday, 20 November

I met Andrew Hampson and we had a chat. It was with deep sadness I learned from him of Terence's death. I was so happy to have sent his last birthday card – 88 years old on 2 November. I had one small regret that I did not visit Terence at the time. He knew, I hope, he was in my heart. I felt so happy, too, that I visited and met him so recently.

## Friday, 22 November

I met Joseph sitting under the bridge. He said Chelsea was in Limerick – he did not say 'prison'. He said she would be going to a clinic and hopefully get help there. He said she may learn to read and write. That would be good. I heard Chelsea got seven years. I don't know if that is true or not. I asked Graham could I write to Chelsea. He said I could. He has not been to see her, as she does not want to see anyone. Poor Chelsea. It is so sad for her. I can remember her daily in my meditation, sending her the best of good energy – the poor darling.

## Wednesday, 27 November

We / I had good fun at the table with Paul, Essie, Grace and Batt. They were very witty. I said to Essie that she ought to be on the stage. She laughed. Grace said, "Yes, she could scrub it". Essie is like a comedian really, I feel.

Poor Jo and Jack were on the ground wrapped in blankets looking shook enough. They are human beings there lying on the concrete, who are in such a pitiable state.

## Monday, 2 December

I sat near Mark Salim. I said I wrote what he said about meditation on the sheets / hand-outs I gave people at the Simon National Conference. I said they went around Ireland. He was delighted. He said, "When I did the meditation, I felt something inside in me – like when you have Jesus. I knew there is someone looking after me". These very saintly people can be refused Communion in the Catholic Church today. Who can judge? I asked Mark was he afraid to die – he said, "No". I said, "Mark, you are very close to God, the Creator, as you're not caught up in material things". He had one pants and one pair of runners – all second-hand! He said to me, "These will do me for Christmas". The pants was not even ironed! The poor man! He patted me very gently on the shoulder going out and said, "Thanks". He is such a lovely gentle soul.

## Thursday, 5 December

I had a few words with Redmond, who sat near the river drinking vodka! He asked me was I a social worker. I said, "No". I said I was being accompanied by, and was accompanying, street-people on their life's spiritual journey. I said, "We talk about what's important in life, we feel". He said, "I love God". He held my hand. He said, "We're friends, when I shake hands with you".

### Sunday, 15 December

Today is the Christmas party. There was about 70 to 75 people, I'd say, at the party, 85% to 90% of young people. I knew many, many street-friends there, both women and men. Louise put glitter on our faces. I thought it was jam! I met Allie. He said there were 64 more young people coming out of care next year. Allie looked well. Andrew Hampson sat near me. He sang later. The food was lovely – Bar-B-Q-Pig! I felt the man who went to such great trouble cooking could have got a big round of applause when he came in with it. His son and daughter helped him. It was delicious. It was like very moist turkey. There was a lovely meal given, turkey, ham, pork, apple sauce, roast and mashed potato, brussels sprouts, carrots, turnips, with trifle and fruit cup after the main meal. There were minerals on the table, too. I saw the soul of each person. That was awesome. Each person has a soul – made in the image of the Creator – each one's behaviour may be totally off the wall, but they are made in the image of the Creator, beautiful beyond words. Nothing could describe adequately the beauty of the human soul. It is more radiant than the sun. I saw. The sing-song was good and the dance after. The karaoke is very good, as the words to sing are on the screen. The street-people could enjoy the party and go then. I hope they appreciated it. A lot of trouble went into the preparation. *I was very happy to have gone and been with the street-people, as they celebrated Christmas.*

### Saturday, 21 December

Soup-run. We went to visit Edmund Bell. His flat was in an appalling condition – the landlord had taken away the one table he had in the kitchen. There were mice in the kitchen! He had two traps set. The dirt of the flat was terrible. It must be so depressing for anyone to live there.

We went to Jonathan's caravan. It was all boarded up – he was not in! We were told by Joseph that Zita was there one night. We called to two people, sisters, later. They did not invite us in. The food was handed in at the door. We went to two lovely old darlings, named Betty and Maura. They had a lovely fire. Betty and I sat at it. Their dog, Spot, is such a friendly dog. The two of them looked so happy in their completely and utterly miserable surroundings. There was great love there. I felt it so tangibly.

We went to Stephen and his sister. Their place was in an awful state, too. A complete mess! Everything seemed to be in the one room, but they were so happy and good-humoured. I was very touched by that. Stephen is off drink now and is going to A.A. He said he needed to get something for his children for Christmas. We went to Caitlín then. She was on the radio one day, being interviewed about her condition. I notice they are not slow in asking for anything. Joseph was so lovely with them. He is so gentle with them. He was doing all he could to meet their needs, so lovingly. We met two more people in blankets near the bus office at about 2.10 a.m. or so.

I felt I got a great broad view of some of the most 'materially'-deprived people in Cork. It was an eye-opener. I noticed how very patient Joseph and Sue were going on these rounds – very caring. They lovingly met the people – it was love in action. I could see the spirit alive in these people last night – as it is the same spirit that gives me life – awesome. I was in here at 3.00 a.m. or so. It was a wonderful experience to accompany these very special people at night this time. The night scene is very different to the day!

## Tuesday, 24 December – Christmas Eve

A priest came for Mass and he was so lovely to these special street-people. Mel Lahive reminded everyone that his Ursula died during the year. The names of those who died were called out.

Martin read very well. June did, too. Fr. had some lovely little reflections. The whole experience was simplicity personified.

## Thursday, 26 December – St. Stephen's Day

Jonathan Carlo's poem on loneliness was very moving – so real. These people need their physical, spiritual and psychological needs met, too, as do all other human beings. I hear how spiritual these people are, too, how they, too, need support on this very deep spiritual journey.

# 2003

## Wednesday, 8 January

Andrew Hampson was all chat. He said people are like many different-coloured threads. Each colour invites. I found him like a guru or someone who had very recently taken, or was on, some kind of drugs!

John sat beside me earlier and said, "I must sit near my friend, before I go to meditation". June, Eleanor, JoJo and Sue sat with us, too. We had some laughs. It was sad, though, for Eleanor, who lost her home in the floods in Blackpool. She's just got a new place.

## Wednesday, 15 January

A lady sat next to me, who had writing across her forehead. It was, I could see, written with a biro. She moved to a side-table later and fed the birds out the window.

I sat with Grace Daams for a long time. She could have the baby any day, she said. It is a girl! She saw it on the scan. She showed me the photo of the baby in the womb. They are going to call her Saoirse, which means freedom. They went to see two houses yesterday – Bart and herself. They got none. Bart went out last night and had a naggin of whiskey. He was so upset when they could get no house. He went to the doctor today to get something to help him cope. The baby kicks a lot at times, Grace said. The baby in her tummy was asleep today, when Grace was talking to me! I offered Grace tea. She did not accept.

## Wednesday, 22 January

Marty Feestor is so honest. He said to me that I ask too many questions. I said, in defence, that this is my way of understanding him. He said, shrugging his shoulders, that he didn't want my understanding! This was his need for now. I felt I wasn't totally present to him. I was not meeting his need, but only my own. These people, in their honesty, have so much to teach me every day. What a gift, when I'm ready for it. Marty is my teacher today.

## Thursday, 23 January

I stopped to greet Benedict Croler on the bridge, who was playing the flute. What impressed me so much was that, when someone dropped him a coin on his mat, he stopped playing to say, "Thanks" to the person who gave him the coin. He knew my face from another time. I chatted with him. He asked me my name. I said, "Catherine is my name". I had no money to put in his hat, but I was very touched by the respect he had for the people who put in a coin. What an inner core coming alive. How beautiful inside he is. His heart was / is full of love. His face looked sad at times. My gift to him was not monetary, but respect and reverence for the person.

## Friday, 24 January

I met Seán Eller, a young man about 25, I feel. He had a story and was so well able to tell it. When he was 6 years of age, he stuck a knife twice in a boy his own age. The boy lived! Seán was 'put away', as he said, but was too young to stay in the centre. He was only 'there' six months. His mother suffered from a mental illness, he said, and he himself was pronounced manic-depressive. He was walking the streets at night, since he was 6 years of age. His parents gave him a hard time, he said. He has been in and out of prisons and hospital all his life. When he was in prison, he used to be kicked by people, sometimes for about an hour at a time. I said that was no way to treat a human being. He said they used to be stripped also as a punishment. He was let out of it at times but, due to his unacceptable behaviour, was put back in again. They were allowed only a book there, no T.V. or radio. It was a 23-hour lock-up. He could have exercise after the Court of Human Rights intervened, he said. He spent some time in Bulgaria and was in hospital there, too. He said he has children everywhere! He doesn't know how many, or what they look like, or where they are even. He said one wish he has is that he will see his 8 year old daughter, Julie. Only that he has seeing her to look forward to, he would have done away with himself long ago. Julie's mother sent him photos of his four children. He doesn't know whether to believe her or not. She would like if he would go to see them for a week-end. She was in Cork around Christmas. When I asked him what keeps him going, he said, "The Spirit". Seán held my hand later, before he went away, and I said, "I am delighted to meet you. Thank you for sharing your story with me".

## Wednesday, 29 January

Ernie came in to say, "Goodbye". He was going to London, Copenhagen and, eventually, hoped to go to Mozambique, Angola, Malawi, to work in the villages. He'd like to go while he is young and had good health. It was lovely to see Ernie in such good form today. Healing seems to have taken place in him. Good.

Liam Seerl asked me could he sit near me. I said, "Yes". He calls me Mary and that is O.K. He thought I was a nurse. He said he was one year in Korea. He has a daughter there. She's 12. It was 12 years ago since he was there. He never saw his daughter, he said. were many hurricanes there, about eight every year. Once, there was five feet of water outside his house, cars were turned upside down and houses were knocked down. When the hurricanes come, people say that the best way to cope with them is to get a bottle of rum, drink it and go to bed! Liam said he asks God to help him and he said he doesn't help him at all! I said what would you like Him / Her to give you? He said, "Patience and a flat in a peaceful place". I said someone said once that the purpose of life is to practice patience. Liam said he's never patient. I said I'm often feeling impatient myself, too. I said, "God is maybe helping you in other ways, i.e., you have a bed for sleep, your meals are cooked for you every day, and you have company – people around". "Oh yes, that is true". I asked him had he any friends in Simon. He said his friend is Andrew Hampson, who sleeps next door to him. Poor Liam is such a gentle soul. His being is alive and well within. Nothing can violate that. He said the only time he was patient and happy was when he was in Korea.

We listened for as long as was needed, to people who were very troubled today, I felt. It was a very special day with these special friends of the street. I never go in there that I don't come out feeling so enriched. These are my real teachers.

## Wednesday, 12 February

Abel Jester is a fisherman. He's in from the sea now for the Spring and Summer and will go home later to Donegal. He has one daughter, aged 17. His wife lives in Leitrim. He said he works out at sea for six weeks at the time – he goes to the Azores, Africa, etc. He can live on the fish, so he lives cheaply. He said fishing is far more relaxing now – it's all electronically worked. One even knows when they have a catch of fish, without having to watch out for it all the time, as in the olden days.

We meditated. Sam, I felt, had drink taken and was a bit 'jiggy' – all over the place! I showed him the charts I had used at the Simon National Conference where Rosetta and I were asked to speak, on 16 November 2002. He said they would be brilliant for his presentation. I offered him two charts: 'How to meditate' and 'Starting meditation'. I also gave him the typed notes on how street-people found mediation in the Shelter and in Ballygriffin. I also gave him an account of what Ballygriffin is about. He said he was very grateful for all the invaluable help.

### HOW SOME STAFF MEMBERS EXPERIENCE MEDITATION IN THE SIMON COMMUNITY: MEDITATION – WHY DO I DO IT?

*Favourite time is when I'm able to get up at dawn. A peaceful and gentle time of the day which really goes well with meditation.*

*It helps 'recollect' my energies, i.e., it is grounding, centring; it gathers 'me' together for 20 minutes and leaves me feeling refreshed and rested. It works by focusing on one thing (rise and fall of the tummy or mantra) and during the many times that the mind is distracted, just gently bringing it back to the breath / mantra.*

*By constantly 'letting go' of the mind, a sense of peace and calm arises (and this can continue in daily life).*

*'Tis a great balance to the speed and busyness of modern daily life. Also, occasional retreats are a lovely antidote to daily life.*

*For me, the weekly meditation sessions provide a welcome opportunity to take time out from the hustle and bustle and stresses of the daily work routine.*

*What I think meditation is: you quieten your mind, so God can hear your soul.*

*It helps me get in touch with my body. I find myself getting in touch with my body. I'm more aware of my body. The work is so stressful here – meditation helps me to get in touch with myself and my spiritual self.*

*I feel the mediation group has helped and still is helping me in the following three areas: to learn what it means to be silent, really silent on the inside, amidst the hustle and bustle of daily life; to use this silence in becoming more aware of who I am and who God is in my life; to learn what it means to be vulnerable and broken and that it is O.K. and part of being human. This I have experienced in many ways in working with the residents of the Simon Community. They have been a tremendous inspiration in this area. To learn more about the meaning of my life, relating to others. I'm getting to know in a deeper sense, the person of Jesus Christ, the risen Lord.*

## HOW SOME STREET-PEOPLE EXPERIENCED MEDITATION IN THE SIMON COMMUNITY

*I read in a book, 'Be still and in time the sunlight will shine through the mist'. For a fleeting moment, I feel happy. It will be meditation and stillness that people would be looking for in the next millennium, 2000+. I am beginning to hear my own spirit come alive in me. I'm filled with joy. I would like to experience more of nature's life and would like to be drawn to it as I used be when playing as a child in the garden.*

*I felt better after doing the meditation.*

*It is brilliant, very, very good. The more I do it, the more I'm learning the way to do it.*

*When people meditate enough, they can experience total peace in this life before they die at all.*

## SOME COMMENTS FROM STREET-PEOPLE ON HOW THEY FOUND IT BEING IN THE BALLYGRIFFIN RETREAT CENTRE

*People said to me when I came back to the Simon Community, "You look so calm and so well". I advertised Ballygriffin in the Simon – all over the place. It was wonderful. I meditated twice a day in my room after coming back. I was in Ballygriffin for three days. I experienced peace there. I would love to go there again.*

*I found it good to go to Nature and stay with only one thing, i.e., a tree, a flower, a bird, etc.*

*I love the freedom of it and the peace of it all.*

*I never thought I could live without the radio or T.V. but I did not miss them. The silence helps you to be yourself.*

*I will send the Ballygriffin brochure to my mother to say I was there, in the hope she'll see some good in me.*

*It's the freedom there I love. I love it.*

*People have to go to America and other places to get what I got in Ballygriffin – peace, happiness within.*

*It is like Paradise being in Ballygriffin.*

*I had a very relaxed day in Ballygriffin. Peaceful.*

*I felt in the morning like as if the whole world was down on top of me but, now after the day, my head is clear. I felt I could go outside myself and it helped me see myself from another side – time for myself was good.*

## Wednesday, 26 February

I met Jim Jacor, a new man, drinking a bottle of *Southern Comfort* near the Day-care Centre. He said he would drink the bottle in one and a half hours. He said after drinking, he sleeps and then he gets up and starts drinking again. Jim said he'd like to get off drink and asked me was there anywhere he could go. I was stunned when he told me Mark Salim had died. Mark was only 30 years. Thirteen days exactly after he had been in the Ballygriffin Retreat Centre. I sensed the shock in the people around, after Mark's death.

## Friday, 28 February

I went to Mark Salim's removal. I spent quality time there in his presence from 6.00 p.m. to 7.30 p.m. I meditated for two half-hour sessions. The removal was at 7.30 p.m. Ruth Mannas came over and was very sad. Ruth wrote a lovely tribute to Mark, saying how he cheered her up when she was in despair, with his laugh and how he dispelled her anger. She said he was a loveable, likeable rogue. Many sent flowers. Some Church leaders were at the removal of Mark. He was a great person.

## Saturday, 1 March

I spent one hour in the Church today before Mark's Mass. I met his parents, brothers and sisters. I told them about Ballygriffin and that Mark did a day's retreat there on 13 February last. I said they would be very welcome to visit

Ballygriffin to see where he made the retreat and where his name was written by himself in the visitors' book, also after it, his comment was 'A good day'. His mother was delighted to hear that and his sister said she'd go there.

## Friday, 7 March

Trevor told me his friend, Sean, slipped into the river yesterday and he jumped in to save him. Another man went down the steps and held both of them for 20 minutes until the fire brigade came along! Sean is Trevor's best friend, he said. It was on today's paper. Trevor is only 23. They recovered in hospital later.

When I asked Jim where he was going for the rest of the day, he said, "Drinking". He said, "I don't want this sort of life". He tried to get into a help centre, but it was full, he said.

## Thursday, 13 March

Clement Hax is doing very well at his growth work and meditation. He is now able to get in touch with feelings of shame, guilt, fear, lack of self-esteem, inadequacy and inferiority. He's doing meditation as well as he can. He did one day's retreat with us. I trust the path Clement is on. He's a gentle soul. His tears began to flow during the one and a half days he stayed with shame. He said he felt like coming in today and bawling crying. This gentle approach helped him come out with his pain and that was very good.

## Thursday, 27 March

The three young men who were to go to Ballygriffin, were not going this morning. They said yesterday that they would go! We are used to that – when people change their minds. I met JoJo and I said he would be welcome another time, when he could go. He said, "Thanks, Sister". He was the only one of the three who said he was unable to go, because he had to get his dole. Of the 10 lepers who were healed, only one came back to say thanks!

## Wednesday, 2 April

I got out the books I got from Auntie Joan (which Auntie Sheila sent from Alaska for the street-people) and put them on the table. Abigail was interested in some of the pictures and took them. Dessie, from Dublin, took some for his children. Sophie took some, Tessie took a picture, Suzanne got some books and said she'd give one to her son. Austin was reading *Christ Denied*. Pete later took some books, so did Ellie. I saw Jean reading one book – said she belongs to the Pentecostal Evangelist Church.

I went to find Pete, to give him the watch that Perpetua's uncle, Ned, gave her to give to some person who'd appreciate it. Peter suggested that Pete would get it. Rosetta and I visited Pete in his apartment. He made tea for us. He took out the best china for us, like Mammy used do long ago for only special visitors. We had a nice chat with Pete. He had a lovely welcome for us. He thanked me for the watch and said it was beautiful. He said he did not think a homeless man / person would be given a gift like that. He was surprised Peter Restor remembered him, because he did not think Peter even knew he was there. He was delighted to be remembered, I could see. He said he'd wear it on Sundays, as he'd wear his other watch in the laundry.

### Thursday, 3 April

I met Joseph Hogal in the South Mall. He was going to Mass, he said, in St. Augustine's. He said, "It's the only thing".

Séan is back on the drink and was disgusted with himself, as he was off it nearly five months – the longest ever. He was going to go back to A.A. again.

Lily Lender was down from the North and slept in a doorway since last Saturday night. She said looking down at her clothes, "Look at the cut of me".

Larry Lyor said he is very touched by 'the silent work' Rosetta and I do in the Simon. He said he told his mother about us.

### Wednesday, 9 April

Poor Liam was 'in bits'. He sat near us after meditation and said June, his girlfriend, went away and prostituted herself. He said what was worse was that it was someone else who told him about her. She went off with a lorry-load of men! He said whatever happened her in her life, she's doing things he can't understand. He loves her and when he can, he'll meet her and talk to her, he said. He can forgive her – what a heart of gold he has, to be able to say that. He was heart-broken after June.

### Thursday, 26 April

Ned and Ciarán came with Rosetta and I to Ballygriffin. It was a retreat day. Both meditated with us. We had two sessions. Deane did not turn up. There was no contact either. We went to nature. It was lovely. We enjoyed lunch and chatted. It was good to have an informal sitting. It was more relaxed, I felt anyway. Ciarán said he enjoyed the day. He said it was a lovely place – very relaxing. Ned said he liked the day. Ned was in a light-hearted mood. It was so nice of Ned to share his scones with us, on which he had his mother's lovely homemade jam! I felt very at home with them both. They will be able to do more, I'd say, on all this, meditation, etc., in time, when they are ready. We gently, very gently introduced them to the notion of retreat for the day and said next time, if they came along, it would be more structured. I felt it was a very gentle day today for all.

## Wednesday, 7 May

Mona was chatty. She said she has no time for priests or nuns, but, when she meets one whom she can talk to, she doesn't see her / him as a nun or a priest. She sees each of them as a person. She said she was in a home run by nuns, when she was young. She did not like it. There were too many rules – they had to go to Mass every day. Mona is about 18 years old or so. She said people go to Mass and then come out and give out about their neighbours. She said, "That makes no sense". She said she gave it all up. She has a little girl called Medina. She's 15 months old and she's in foster-care. She can see her two days a week. Mona said a teacher said to her in school, that she was 'a child of the devil'. She said she was proud to be a child of the devil! She said, "I'm evil". I said, "So are we all, in part, in our own wounded humanity. You are good because you are you. If you do nothing, you are still good inside". She's going to college. She has first aid exams to do. Mona has a beautiful face and sparkling blue eyes, full of the life of the spirit – the windows of her soul.

## Wednesday, 21 May

I saw poor Mel Lahive asleep on a blanket, his head on a pillow and he was covered by another blanket. I found it sad that a bird had crapped on the blanket. I felt this is how so many people see these street-people, as crap and the only response they often have to them, is to crap on them, too, through rejecting them, despising them, etc. On the other hand, the bird may be giving Mel a blessing, saying "You are good, I know"!

Edmund said he met some friends and they said to him that they did not want to see him on the streets any more, but to ring them and they would have a bed for him. He was not happy about this, because he said he was there with them four times and broke out on drink, so he'd be ashamed to ask them to take him again. He said it was lovely and peaceful there, in one of his friend's houses.

## Wednesday, 28 May

Horace did well on his growth journey yesterday – he's growing gently. It is not an easy road to discover 'who I am' – but it's possible to find it out, not by analysis, but by awareness. Horace feels fear a lot and feels unwanted. All can be healed.

## Wednesday, 4 June

Robbie told me, when he was on his own, he's from Offaly. His brother is living in Clare, etc. His father was the manager of the factory and was moved around from place to place. He himself has four children, aged 7, 10, 17 and 20. He talks to them all the time on the phone and can visit them anytime, but if he meets them, he feels so sad. Afterwards, he takes to the bottle. He feels being addicted to drink may be genetic – who really knows? I felt even more compassion for him then, as he could even have been born with an addictive personality. The poor man, he hadn't a chance. I have great admiration for the way he keeps going, in such very difficult circumstances. These are the saints today – all their behaviour is automatic and unintentional. Could it be destiny or what? It's so easy to see this from my in-depth love. It is only from this zone I can hear this. Poor Robbie. I wonder how do these people really keep going?

The two ladies were in to do the mosaic in the garden wall. I went to see it. It was beautiful and I sensed a lovely energy from it. I loved the flowers and I asked the artist could I make a flower. She was happy to let me make a flower. She allowed me choose the colour. I chose a pinkish-red colour. This colour was not unlike my jumper. It is pink. I love pink. Regina Ring broke up the tile for me. She put on the cement, too. I made my flower on the cement thus, saying, as I was creating it, "I need space in my life – hence spaces in-between the petals". The centre is heart-shaped. I did not see this, when I picked up the white shape. Then the symbols spoke more, i.e., everything grows from the centre out – when I'm living from my centre, soul, essence, being, I can only radiate positively, i.e., I noticed the petals pointing outwards, too. Later, it came to me that these are the fruits of living from that centre, love, joy, peace, patience, kindness and gentleness. I see these already being so well lived in the street-people's lives – their kindness, gentleness, love, patience, etc. I witness this on a daily basis. Awesome.

## Thursday, 5 June

I sat near Jerry Dunor, whom I had not met before. He was very chatty. He lived in Cork growing up, he said. The seagulls used drop food off in his mother's back-garden, every day, on their way from the dump! We talked about pollution here. We talked about the Dalai Lama and Tibet. He had heard about the Buddha under the tree! The Buddha found enlightenment under the tree – by sitting, breathing and being still. He had looked outside himself for a long time and could not find enlightenment. He found it when he looked within. He is supposed to have spent six years doing fasts but he did not experience enlightenment. Jerry asked me if I saw the painting on the wall. I said, "No, I had not". I asked him about it. He said it was on a screen and they transferred it on to the wall. It showed Nano Nagle Bridge. There was a lady walking on the pedestrian bridge, with her umbrella open over her. It was raining obviously. A person lay on the bridge. A street-person there looked as if he / she were asleep. A 'blue'-coloured horse was running from the bridge. Jerry told me that the horse symbolised freedom. Being free was the dream of the man lying on the bridge, he said. This was his interpretation. There could be many, many more, of course.

## Tuesday, 10 June

A person sat near me. Con is his name. He's interested in music. He was in Simon in Dublin for two years. He said when he was there, he was fearful. He had no respect for the other street-people. Fifteen years later, he now wished to come back again to Simon and did so with fear and trepidation. He said he's in a different place now to what he was in 15 years ago. He's O.K. to 'be' now a bit more. I shared about how difficult I found it being in the Shelter, when I first began. I, too, felt fearful – very much so. I can 'be there' now pretty well, most of the time. Con does yoga and meditation and finds these good. He asked me what kind of meditation we do and I said we do Christian meditation, but were open to other forms, too. We use a Mantra meditation. It is about stillness. To be still means to accept ourselves as we are. I said we do it in the Shelter and the retreat centre in Ballygriffin. Con comes in on a Tuesday morning. We talked about the four vital centres. We can live out of any of these four: intellect, feelings, body and being. From what zone in me am I living now? From which of the four above do I live now? I was going to leave, when no one was talking to me earlier, and go. I could hear it was my head saying, "You're wasting your precious time here – go away". I did not let my head lead me, but listened to my being, which said, "Stay where you are, Catherine". Then Con came along and we had a most wonderful chat – very awesome.

## Wednesday, 18 June

Marty showed me the piece he did on the mosaic. It was the map of Ireland, he said – tiny in the midst of the universe. The yellow tile he did was in the midst of the green hill. I said, outside, we can look tiny, but there is a vast world of good within us. I showed Marty my flower and explained its significance. Today, I saw how nice and comfortable my flower was lying on the green. It also represents for me today that we are but a tiny flower in this vast universe and still we can transmit love, joy, peace, patience, kindness, gentleness and trustfulness through our wounded humanity and deeply to touch those we met. Our presence is all we need. It is our most precious gift to the world. Awesome! This is the real, true you and the true me.

Marty told me he did a thistle on the mosaic, in memory of his brother who died. My flower on the mosaic also represents Kate, my lovely niece, who died of cystic fibrosis at the tender age of 11. It was Kate who always inspired me to "Keep with the street-work, Kathleen", when I often felt like giving up. She transmits love and joy to me from her home in heaven and I, in turn, touch others out of the good energy. Red, too, was Kate's favourite colour. The tile was a pinky-red colour.

## Friday, 20 June

I went up a side street to see who was lying in a doorway. It was Adam lying in the hot sun. There was one large, and one small, empty bottle of vodka and an empty cider can next to him. I said, "Má – Rá – Ná – Thá" and touched him on the arm with my good energy. Poor Adam, he was a pitiable sight.

## Thursday, 26 June

I went to the barbeque last night, which was held in honour of the unveiling of the mosaic. The mosaic took six months to do. It is really beautiful. Henry Hugo was talking when I went in. He thanked Rosetta and myself. I felt so proud of my little flower on the mountain. Marty read a lovely poem and he also cut the ribbon. The mosaic was officially unveiled in the garden of remembrance. The garden is in memory of our street-people who had died there and outside Simon.

## Wednesday, 2 July

I went to Simon and on my way I met Marty. He said he was on his way to Cove Street. He said it was the *first time ever* he felt the effect of someone praying for him. He said he knew it was my prayer helped him, as I said I'd remember him when he shared his painful story with me, last week. He said he felt a glow all over him. He said he thinks of me now as a holy person. I said I'm a weak instrument the Creator uses to mediate His / Her presence / gift to other people. That is my privilege. The important thing is to be aware that it is all happening only through the power of the Creator – nothing happens without His / Her strength and mediation. I can do nothing of myself from my humanity – my being (God) guides me, through my humanity. My humanity can do nothing on its own. It is the spirit within, the God within, that gives life. All these are only words, unless I am in touch with that spirit in me. Thanks, Marty, for enabling me to be also awakened to my spirit within me. Truth begets truth. Spirit begets spirit. Love begets love. Having gone through such a dark night, Marty deserves to be comforted in the Creator's love.

## Wednesday, 9 July

I went to Simon. I sat at a table. I got some boiling water. Two people left the table when I sat there! A man called Ronnie Rule talked to me for one and a half hours. He had been in an institution as a six-month-old child. His six brothers and sisters were there, too. His mother has a drink problem – his father, a vet, was a womaniser. His mother is still in denial. She can't face the fact that she abandoned her baby of six months old and the other six children. It is so sad. Ronnie said his father used to ring up the institution and say to the Sister, "I hope you are taking good care of my children". He'd ring at 9.00 p.m. at night, he said. The Sisters used be very annoyed. He talked about having got counselling over the last five years. He was beaten as a punishment, when his Dad used to ring up so late. He said one person was a sadist. She fancied a man and when he did not return her love, she left to go abroad. She protected him up to the end. He, her fancy man, was also involved in abuse. I'm in awe of the street-people how they don't blame their perpetrators – they have an amazing capacity to forgive these people. He said he felt anger, but that is over for now. He may not be able to deal with any more, I feel, for now.

*Friday, 1 August*

I went to the Day-care Centre today. I greeted Alexandra, Abigail and Amy. Austin sat near them. Amy Ladde didn't seem to be so well. She was in a very angry mood. Poor Alexandra seemed to have got the brunt of it. Abigail left. She barely saluted me. I felt Amy's viciousness across the table. This same evil is in me and each human being in this world. The only difference is that I have got a chance to get to the root of it and deal with it and therefore prevent myself from letting it all out on another. I can feel that way at times, but where my anger is expressed in a safe place, then it can hurt nobody else.

Garry asked me to read a questionnaire he filled in on Simon. It was very honest, I felt. He loves the street-people – they are so honest and real, he said. He is now off alcohol, he told me. He's going to A.A. He smokes and hopes to give them up soon. That is his only vice, he said. Garry had done his Leaving Cert. The reason he gave for going on the streets first day was: 1) family problems; 2) drugs; 3) alcohol. He said he would feel honoured if I read his answers. I felt very privileged to read them, as the questionnaire was confidential.

I saw some new people today, too. One man was very grateful for the service provided in the Day-care Centre. He thanked us all.

Annie and John had a 'sparring match' – each calling the other names – very angry verbal assaults were made by each to the other! It was getting more angry. John came over near Annie and struck her with his hand. He and she were roaring at each other. I felt orange drink being poured down my back and neck, over my hair and the front of my dress. John poured this over me – or it spilled out of his hand as he was going forward to attack Annie with his hand! The chair I sat on was all wet! Poor Ruth Mannas, in her great kindness and compassion, said I ought to get a change of clothes. She went into the office and got me a jumper. She got some clothes for herself, too. She had a plant in her bag and probably all her worldly goods in that one plastic bag. Her heart is overflowing with kindness. Her inner beauty shone forth in her lovely smile. It lit up her face. The spirit of life and love was so alive in Ruth – she was the pure emanation of the glory of the Almighty. There is nothing negative in her soul, spirit, being. I felt honoured to sit with Ruth.

I complemented the staff on how well they handled the difficult situation. They were very calm. Anyone of us there at that time could have been hit. I stood calmly in my own presence.

## Wednesday, 20 August

John Gabie said he was shy growing up. He went to see Elvis in America –
Elvis was sick. He could not see him. His life changed when he was 27 years
old. He felt life had nothing to offer John. He felt he had no value in himself.
He lost his sister for 15 years. He found her again. Joseph told me about all
his travels around Kerry, etc. He loves travelling around. His father used
take him and his family out driving when he was young, too.

## Saturday, 23 August

David Gabbay was lying on the grave, as I passed in Presentation Garden! I
left him be. Later, he came over and sat beside me in a seat in the garden. He
asked first could he sit near me. He said he knows what Jesus suffered as he
looked at the crucifix in the garden. He said, "HALT: **h**unger, **a**nger,
**l**oneliness, **t**hirst". David said he talked to his mother in this garden today,
who died three years ago. She said, "Cop on and get off the streets". He said
he looked at the river and it was attractive. God looks after him, he said. He
asked me what kind of a family background I came from. I said my parents
were good people – they had enough to live on. They were selfless and did
all they could to help us in life. David said he will be 42 years old on his next
birthday. I felt very privileged listening to David. He said he would not
share what he shared with anyone, only me. I felt honoured. I felt at one
with him – oneness with him in his vulnerability, utter fragility. I said to
him that I experienced the presence of God in him. Also, I learned to leave
what seems so important to me and listen to a precious human being. David
said he comes to the garden for tranquillity. It is a tranquil place, he said. It
helps him to sit quietly, meditate, walk and rest in this lovely garden. He
asked me what is the difference between faith, belief and trust. We chatted
about these three words and their meaning. He said to me one needs to trust
oneself first. He said he knows God looks after him. He said, "Maybe I'm
meant to be dressed in raggy clothes, smelling and living like I am now".

## Tuesday, 2 September

I greeted Monica Macor. She and Eddie Eags sat at the table. Monica said
she lives in a caravan. Her father lives in a barrel-top caravan and her
mother lives in another one of these. Her brother suffers from depression
and spends a lot of time indoors in bed, too. His niece died at 4½ years and
Monica was very close to her. Her own father backed his car by accident on

top of her. The family also had a cot death with another family member. They now have six children. Her brother, Tony, has been suffering from depression for three years. Three years ago, the child died. Monica wore three sets of earrings on each ear. The big ones were like curtain rings. She said she likes the big ones. She had her face painted, too. She used live in Galway and has moved to Cork. She gets the bus from her own door to town. She said there is a lot of traffic on the road. Monica said she likes to go to Mass and say her prayers. She took her mother to Knock last year. She said she loved it.

### Thursday, 11 September

There were five people sleeping outside the Shelter this morning – Grace Daams and Bart, with three others I did not know. What amazed me was that they could stay so sound asleep, in spite of all the noise that was going on around them! They seemed to have plenty bedclothes for sleeping on the footpath. Bart and Grace even had a table-cloth over the bedclothes.

### Wednesday, 17 September

I asked Grace about Chelsea Calcott. She'll enquire for me where she is. Poor Chelsea, I hope she's O.K. What I admired so much about Chelsea was that, when she fell so many times, she could get up again so many times. She'd begin again by doing up new flats, settling into so many new places and then everything would go haywire, when she began to drink. She was back in square one, so to speak.

I wished Adam Keenol well for the race on Sunday. He's running for Our Lady's Hospital for Sick Children in Crumlin. He said he's doing it for the children. He's not doing any training today. He said all the great runners take days off before these big races. He said, "This marathon is five miles". Adam Keenol looked well.

### Friday, 19 September

I met Craig Baine during the week. He's from England. He had lost his children, he said. He began drinking. I met him in the garden here. He said there is something special about the South Presentation garden here. When he came up the cemetery, he said he got goose pimples. He said, "There is something here". I said there was prayer said here for over 200 years – there was much pain, sorrow and joy shared there, too, indeed. He said, "It's tranquil here". I said, "Yes, it's a place for people to be quiet, to walk, sit and meditate". He said he wouldn't bring crowds in here.

## Wednesday, 1 October

I greeted a man on the bridge and I gave a *Kit-Kat* bar to another lad, who sat begging. We had a long chat about life on the bridge, when you became nameless and even faceless to so many passers-by.

## Thursday, 2 October

We went to Ballygriffin with Lulu L. and George. It was a great day indeed. Lulu was in the bath when we arrived and, when a staff member went to call her, she had fallen asleep in the bath! When she was eventually ready, she looked well and was all spruced up with many, many Rosary beads around her neck! She got a new wig – had washed that, too. George was asked by Lulu to dress himself properly, as he was going 'with the nuns'. He had a lovely sports-coat and matching shirt and pants. He was wearing a leather waist-coat also. We got our groceries. We were in Ballygriffin around 11.45 a.m. It was a truly beautiful, sunny day.

Lulu has two sons, Deane is 23 and Kevin is 19. Lulu is very sensitive to life and people. She has an eye for beauty. She said "It is *the me* I see in the beautiful" (The soul *that* is mine). She has a lovely mind. She's in love with George, and he with her, for 11 months now. How they met! George found a dog straying in town and Lulu came along and met George with the stray dog and said, "That's my dog!". Later on, she asked George to mind her dog. The dog disappeared. The dog stayed away – they looked everywhere for the dog – no luck! But Lulu stayed with George and thus began the romance! He would not leave her out of his sight for a second. The love-affair seemed to have brought out the very tender, loving and sensitive side of George. Lovely. We enjoyed a lovely lunch. I showed Lulu and George the centre. George was very taken by the picture of Nano Nagle talking to the street woman. George and Lulu did meditation with us today twice. Their stillness and silence was special. George has a great sense of the sacred. It was a great day with these two very special people.

## Wednesday, 8 October

I went to the Shelter. I did not recognise Zita Pesneau. She had her hair tied back. She talked about being a nun! She lost her eighth child after five months' pregnancy. She took the baby home and was happy to hold the baby during the night before the burial. I felt very moved and in tears almost, when she said the baby was cold, so she wrapped him in a blanket. She dressed him. I thought my heart would break, when she said all this. I remembered Kate when she died and how we dressed her and Mary wanted to put on her socks. This was very painful for my feelings today. Zita asked me for a medal. I gave her one. She said she would put it on her son's grave. Her two sisters had miscarriages after she lost her son. Zita laughed nervously a lot.

## *Wednesday, 15 October*

Johannes Jappe joined us for meditation. He is Belgian. He likes silent time on his own. He meditated before in school and in the training day. I notice some young people, both street and staff, like silent time on their own, to balance the time they spend with people. This is good. It is very important to take some quiet time when working with homeless people, as this can be very difficult at times, for young people.

## *Wednesday, 29 October*

I forgot to bring my scarf today and Tiona offered me her scarf. It was so kind of her, on such a freezing day. I did not accept it. The kindness of these street-friends baffles me.

## *Wednesday, 5 November*

Victor Petch said there are nine in his family. He said his parents are wealthy now. They can go on three holidays! He said it's his own choice to be on the streets. He and Tessie went for some nights to a B & B. He owes over €1,000 for rent. He has a sore leg, so he is allowed in.

I was really interested in the talk about the way people live today. Some people have big houses, beautifully furnished, two cars and have to work around the clock to pay their debts! Some young married people have a single bed in each room, as they can't afford to have a child. How sad to hear this is Ireland today. Wesley Cron, 27, was away for six years in Italy and he could hardly believe it was the same Ireland in 2003 that he left six years ago in 1997. He said people hadn't money then – now it's all money, he said. He could live much more cheaply in Italy. Ireland's prices compared to Italy seemed to be much higher. We seem to be getting ripped off here, Sally said. Sally said, "There is no compassion today. A lot of people are just doing their own thing". The street-people, I find, are very deeply compassionate people. Today, they shared their time, themselves, cigarettes, lighters, money, too, with others.

## Wednesday, 12 November

I sat with eight young lads for a long time. They were very honest. Some were there when I went in. Most of the Simon group were there after lunch again. We had fun. Abigail Bancrow said to me, "You're happy now, getting all the attention!". That was her perspective. She was entitled to her view. I felt annoyed at the remark, but I could respect her opinion.

## Wednesday, 19 November

Samson told me his story. He went to a hostel to get lodgings. He said 1) the man in the hostel said, "Why don't you go back home where you came from?". Samson said he can't go home; 2) when he went to get a flat, the person said, "The cost was €139 – but that's too good for *you!*"; 3) he started a job on Friday and was left off today (Wednesday). He went to work at 8.00 a.m. and was told there was no work for him today! 4) he was ashamed to say where he was living, when asked at work. I felt for Samson who experienced so much rejection. He said he's 36 years old. He was out sleeping rough last night. He may go back fishing.

## Tuesday, 25 November

Basil Pyne was vomiting into a plastic basin, which was laid on newspapers. He lay across two seats. His feet looked as if they had not been washed for a very long time. It was so sad to see a human being so down-and-out, neglected by himself, as he seemed to have no control over it. The poor man, I felt so sorry for him, as I looked at him.. He looked awful.

Compassion grows in tragedy. It needs silence, solitude and stillness to blossom forth. It's about having nowhere to go, but where one really is now. I feel more and more that this very awesome journey with these street-people, for me, is one of enjoying being unknown and regarded as nothing.

## Wednesday, 3 December

There is a very precious person behind this / these outwardly very broken person / people. This is what draws me / attracts me to these street-people.

Once I've discovered this precious person / soul in myself, it is so easy to see it in Pierce, Joshua, Katy and so many more I met today. Awesome. The spirit of life and love lives in each one of the special people's souls.

### Sunday, 7 December

I greeted Cathal O'Callan and Joshua McAllenor on Sullivan's Quay. Both of them held on to my hand and would not let it go. I felt the deep loneliness in their grasp. It felt to me like a dead man's grip. They are killing their pain in drink. It has them almost deadened – the poor creatures – what deep loneliness. No one can enter into that lonely place in their heart. The loneliness in Cathal's eyes was overwhelming, such a look of despair, hopelessness, helplessness. It came to me that they possibly always live in the unknown. They are the special people today. I have so much to learn from these great souls. I feel so very privileged accompanying them and in their accompanying me on life's journey.

### Monday, 22 December

I went to the Crisis Shelter at 11.07 p.m. or so. Caroline came in from the street with her duvet. She went into bed. I chatted with her for a long time. She took off her boots and said, as she left them beside her bed, "They won't be gone when I wake up?"! She said her son of 18 years of age is on the streets, too. Her children are in foster-care. She was two years in Scotland. She's happy she's in Ireland now, as she can see her children. She said she's 'an alcoholic'. She was sleeping outside *Jury's* gate last night. She was moved then and was brought to the Crisis Shelter. She was delighted with it. She's a lovely lady. She said she feels bad having a bed, when so many are sleeping out. She prostitutes herself to make money. There is a 'skipper' under the bridge near a pub. There are Rosary beads hanging up there in memory of all those who have died. She said there is another 'skipper' under the iron steps in front of the big houses in another part of Cork. Caroline went to sleep later on. I stayed two hours.

### Tuesday, 23 December

I find it hard leaving the warm room here and going out in the cold tonight. How must the street-people feel sleeping out in the cold?

## Wednesday, 24 December

I was in awe of the way the altar was laid by Alexis Obaris for Midnight Mass. I found Susie's taking over hard to take, but later, I realised she was my teacher – it was myself I saw in her – my control – and that was very painful – it was this wound having being exposed finally brought me to the stage of giving birth to my true self on Christmas morning. I missed the simplicity of other years. I found it all too organised – the street-people could feel threatened, as they let life structure itself, and they are not happy with a rigidly structured life. We need great gentleness and patience with ourselves to let life structure itself. Great trust.

## Thursday, 25 December – Christmas Day

I went with Sean Sheer to do the soup-run. We stopped to chat with Mona, Julie, Susan and Paula. A deaf-and-dumb girl was among a group of very young people. We went to Robert Row. I had lemonade and a sweet. Josie Jorr was in, when we called. Three other people were in, when we called to their home. Two of them were ill. One poor man had a very bad chest infection. The boy was unwell. The fire was so warm. They had a lovely warm welcome for us. Stan Story was at home. I gave him three days' dinners! Sean had more food for him. We went to the Crisis Shelter. I met Rosetta. I stayed about 50 minutes or so. It was awesome, on Christmas night, to see so many where the 'Inn' was open to them. We spent three hours or so out on the street-round. It was such a privilege on Christmas night to be there. A holy place.

# 2004

## Friday, 2 January

I went to the Crisis Shelter about 10.30 p.m. Joshua was sitting near the fire. He said he has only four months to live. He asked for soup and sandwiches. He was not so well able to hold the soup, so I held it, while he dipped his sandwich in it. Poor Joshua told me he had cancer. He was 33 years old on 27 December. He asked me to say the *Hail Mary* with him. He said, "I'm saying this one for you". He said, "Jesus, Mary and Joseph, I give you my heart and my soul. Jesus, Mary and Joseph, assist me in my last agony. Help me in time of need, etc". He asked me to say the *Our Father* with him.

## Saturday, 3 January

I went to the Crisis Shelter tonight. Joshua was there. He said, "I'm a holy man". Later, when he lay on the bed, he asked me to pray with him. I felt so honoured. I saw on Rosetta's card, 'praying for you'. He said the *Our Father* slowly again. It moved me to tears. He said he loves God and He looks after him always. Joshua's eyes lit up when he asked me to say the *Hail Mary*. I can't forget his face, such love in his eyes. I could feel my own abandonment in Joshua's eyes. It was my privilege to spend this quality time with Joshua.

### Wednesday, 14 January

Alexis said Joshua was beaten up. He was in the intensive care and there was no hope for him.

### Tuesday, 20 January

Alex Ando came to chat with me. He said his father was English and his mother was Spanish. They lived in Cork. He was on all the drugs one could be on, "Been there, done it all". He felt he was not understood by his family. He went to a help centre for ex-drug addicts. They prayed and fasted there. He was in the help centre for seven weeks. He had a disagreement with someone and left it. His father died when Alex was 2 years old. He spoke about never having *felt loved*. He said he could not love anyone, until he began to love himself – then he could go out to others, out of his love, as then he'd have something to offer people. He said all the people here are beautiful people. He used to be out on the street like them, himself, one time, he said. He said God directed him to come here today. He hopes to set up some place to help people. He is about 25 years old, I felt.

### Wednesday, 21 January

I was shocked to hear of Joshua's death – Joshua McAllenor. Grace Daams told me he was found collapsed on the street – someone said outside Simon. He was taken to the C.U.H. Hospital. He surely lived his 33 years in poverty and suffering. He was buried on Monday, 19 January. He died, Grace said, either on 15 or 16 January. Poor Joshua, all his troubles are over and he is at home in heaven forever.

### Tuesday, 27 January

Denis Ron said he was on the radio and some people rang to say he ought not to be drinking, when he was on the street. He said he needed the whiskey to keep him warm! He said good came out of it, too, as he got an offer of a flat and he hopes to get a job soon.

## *Tuesday, 24 February*

I chatted with Ruth Mannas on Washington Street. She said she got a flat in Cobh – brand new. She was very happy about it. She said Samson is in hospital. They were not sure whether he got (a) an alcoholic fit; (b) an epileptic fit; or (c) a diabetic fit. She was going to see him in hospital later. She said he will move in with her.

## *Wednesday, 25 February*

I met Karl on my way down, he said he hoped to have a film made of the skate-board boys outside the Opera House on 6 March. He said one gets to know these young lads and then you can 'evangelise'. He said you don't go up to one of these young people and start talking about God to them. He said God guided him to go to these people. He said it came to him recently from the Creator, not to pray for anyone, but 'to be alongside a person' – in other words, 'to wish for the other person what I would wish for myself'. How very profound this young man of 28 years is, who spent so long on the streets sleeping rough.

## *Wednesday, 3 March*

I read today on the wall in the recreation room, 'The world never has a place for saints, visionaries or reflectors'.

I went to the dining-room earlier and had a mug of water. James Beept was sitting there, so were Alexis and Ross Abass. Ross Abass and I chatted about the Passion Play that will be in cinemas shortly. He asked me how would you define death by natural causes? I didn't know. He then said that, "We breath, don't we, to give us life and when the breath ceases, we die. What is the breath?", he said. I said, "The Spirit". He said, "Yes – the Spirit leaves the body, then the body is only left. It is just a mass of bone, tissue, flesh, etc., when that Spirit is not there. The breath / Spirit alone gives it life". I felt so touched by this description. How wise and in touch these wonderful people are – true contemplatives – so many of them. They see things often as they are, because of their clarity of vision, unpolluted by material things of any sort. Awesome. He sure was my teacher today.

## Thursday, 11 March

Robbie was ready to come along with us to Ballygriffin. It rained and rained and rained and rained! We got some food. Robbie was a lovely, gentle, reserved, quite young man about in his 20s or maybe early 30s or so. He mostly, in the beginning, answered in monosyllabic responses, "Yes", "No", "Yeah", etc. That was O.K. He went from England to France and back. He said he spoke Welsh at home – he's a native Welsh speaker. He said some words in Welsh for us and they sounded very like Irish, e.g., *llapel Bwyn(w)* = white church, in Irish it is *séipéal bán*! It seems Welsh words have a string of consonants like *bnyf*. It is the third most difficult language in the world to learn. Chinese is the most difficult. Robbie had sessions of therapy to help him come off drink. He also had counselling. He lives in a hostel now. We meditated together for sometime in stillness and silence. Robbie liked the meditation. He said, "That was nice", after it. We enjoyed a lovely lunch beside a lovely open fire. We dried our wet boots and coats. Robbie's socks were wet. He opened his runners with the greatest care – very slowly, he opened each part down along until he had them all opened up – so gently. I was in total awe and wonder at him opening his shoe laces. He awakened me to my patience, gentleness and I learned today how to untie and tie my laces in a new way, being *fully* attentive to what is – now. In no hurry – he was going nowhere. He was living totally in the *NOW* of opening and closing his laced shoes. He was a saint in that now and in each now he lived today. He looked at the fire, too, with deep attentiveness. He said, "Thanks" for his meal. It was clear he could see the gift in food – how he reverently ate it. He could also receive the gift of the day given to him. Robbie smokes the pipe. He would like another day in Ballygriffin. He said he would put his name down in the Day-care Centre book, for the next time. We did a second meditation together later. Robbie had a lovely gentle presence. He was so gentle, one hardly heard him move around. He was my teacher today indeed. I feel, I'm only *beginning* to know how to tie my shoe laces! I *started* learning today. It was a very special day with Robbie. His energy of reverence, respect, gentleness and gratitude pervaded the chalet. Earlier, he offered to make us some tea and we accepted.

## Wednesday, 24 March

One person sat totally silent today in the dining-room. I have not ever heard him speak one word. He seems and looks comfortable in his own silence. He has a pleasant face. I felt a good presence in him. He seems to sit on the same chair, in the same place, every week. I sat today, too, myself, for quite a while in my own silence – awesome. *BE-ING* there – in awe of my own deep silence, peace, love, joy and radiating that to the people around me. I sensed the awesome presence of each person in that dining area. I found, today, that my deepest response to these people's silent presence is my own silent presence. I felt a deep harmony and one-ness with them. Awesome. The deepest bond / relationship I can have with anyone is *SILENCE*. What a gift these poor homeless people awakened in me today. The presence of the Creator.

## Wednesday, 31 March

A man sat in total silence next to me. He's been there for several weeks now. This man never spoke to anyone, while I was around. What is going one in his mind? When I sit like that at times and just observe – as no one seems happy to chat with me, I can *be*, maybe I'm being prepared for something very special – a very special meeting. This, at times, happens. On these occasions, one is immersed in solitude, deep in the mystery of the Creator, in order that one may be sufficiently empty of self to make space for the other, through the open doors of one's being. And so, when these times arise, in which no one feels drawn to chat with me, I've got a sense of being called to stay in my solitude (even when there are crowds around) and hear it as an inner preparation, a kind of self-emptying, so that at the moment of meeting, I can allow the street-person, or whoever it may be, to enter freely into my space and perhaps feel less burdened by his or her pain. I can truly see the Spirit alive in the street-people – they manifest the glory of the Creator for me. But in order for such meetings to take place, one needs to be a person of meditation / reflection / prayer. We are more open to these meetings, when we allow the Creator time to prepare us for them, so that when the moment comes we have the interior liberty to allow others come in to our life. If I am moving too fast, if I'm on my guard with people, these meetings won't happen. It is a gift sometimes not to be welcomed by others! Savour and taste the time of solitude given to prepare our heart. The task in accompanying / journeying with these very special street-people is to uncover the beauty of each human being, that is often buried under years of abuse and neglect. It doesn't matter what their history has been, each one is 'brother' or 'sister' and needs to be greeted and treated as such. No one has to make them beautiful, they are already beautiful as human beings, it's just a question of awakening them again to that which is beyond (in them) what has been traumatised. They are always more than their behaviour.

One street-person said about sleeping rough, "One who sleeps on the streets lies on cardboard and fear is his / her blanket". Another said, "I'm so afraid to sleep on the streets, that I can only do so, when I've drink taken, as without drinking, I can't sleep". Fear, for street-people, is an integral part of sleeping rough. The more they sleep on the streets, the more fearful they become. Some pray and can discover peace of heart, to enable them to live with this fear.

## Wednesday, 5 May

I went to the Shelter today and got some water. Frances was there and I gave her the page, *Celebrating You*, and painted the flowers at the end of the candle. I painted the wick, too. It looked lovely, when I had it finished. She will put it up on her wall.

### Celebrating you

You are worth celebrating.
You are worth everything.
You are unique,

in all the whole world.
There is only one you.
There is only one person
with your talents, your experience,
your gift.
NO ONE CAN TAKE YOUR PLACE!

God created only one you,
precious in His sight.
You have immense potential to love,
to care, to create, to grow, to sacrifice.
if you believe in yourself.

It doesn't matter your age, or your colour,
or whether your parents loved you or not.
(May be they wanted to but couldn't)
Let that go.
It belongs to the past.
You belong to the now.

It doesn't matter what you have been.
the wrong you have done.
the mistakes you have made.
the people you have hurt.
You are forgiven.
You are accepted.
You are OK.
You are loved in spite of everything
So love yourself and nourish the seeds within you.

Celebrate you.

Begin now. Start anew. Give yourself a new birth. Today.

You are you and that is all you need to be.

You cannot deserve this new life.
It is given freely, gift.
That is the miracle called God who loves you.

So celebrate the miracle and celebrate you!

### Wednesday, 12 May

The same man sat silently in his usual corner. I've not yet heard him say a word. He has a pleasant face. I never heard his name. How does he feel inside him? What does he think? Is he happy? Who knows? Does anyone know? Does he even know himself? Does it matter?

### Wednesday, 19 May

People spoke today about how kind the street-people are and how they have such regard for all of us, whom they feel are there to 'be with' them on their journey. I still have so much more to learn from these great people, who often have 'nowhere to lay their heads'.

### Saturday, 22 May

Today, I stood to look at a little boy give a street-person money on the bridge and the street-person shook the little boy's hand. The little boy looked back twice at the street-person, as he crossed the bridge with an older man. He won't forget the street-person's handshake, I feel. A second child passed later and looked again more than once as she crossed the bridge. What did each child see, I wondered? Could the child be awakened to compassion, I wondered?

### Wednesday, 2 June

I was privileged today to accompany some street-people in the Simon and on the streets. I was happy to meet Ursula and to give her the 21st birthday card for Ken. He was not there today, himself, but he rings her every day, she said. He rang her last night. He calls her 'Mammy', she said. His own mother is dead. Ken is a gay person, a beautiful human being, who is in search of love. I trust Ursula to give him the card. She said he would be very touched when *someone remembered him*. There were tears in her eyes, when she was saying this.

### Wednesday, 16 June

Dinny gave me a copy of the poem he wrote about Noel. He told me later Noel Lam had been in an institution – no one knows what goes on inside anyone's head, he said. He said he himself never said he was in an institution until two years ago, when he began counselling. He was very angry about the rape and abuse he experienced in the institution. He said he thought of suicide. He even had the rope got. He said when a man throws himself into the river, as Noel did, it was not a cry for help – it was the end of the road for him. Dinny was suffering a lot. He needed a lot of love today. He showed me some lovely poems he wrote. I felt so honoured talking to Dinny and listening to his sacred story.

We met the Director, to evaluate our ministry with street-people today in Simon. That was a very satisfactory meeting. She showed great appreciation for our ministry with street-people. We appreciated that very much.

## Wednesday, 23 June

I met poor Anthony Sorr today near the Day-care Centre. Anthony is 33 years old. He did not know me. He was very intoxicated and I felt, too, he was on drugs. Poor Anthony, his pants were wet. What a humiliation for a noble soul – a person of such infinite value – the Maker's creation – a breath of the power of God, pure emanation of the glory of the Almighty, made in the image of the Creator and here he was – a nobody, a drop-out, outcast in the face of society. They miss the beauty of his beautiful soul. I wished well for Anthony and hoped he would travel safely around.

## Monday, 28 June

David Gabbay came along. He always has some words of wisdom. He said, "Jesus ate with the down-and-outs". He said he would be going to hospital on Wednesday. I said I'd remember him in prayer.

## Monday, 5 July

I was very privileged today to be at Matt Morrow's funeral in the South Parish. Matt was deaf-and-dumb. He used communicate by writing down what he wanted to say to people. He spent time in prayer in St. Francis Church. I was very moved at the Eucharist. There was no family there. I felt so sad seeing three Simon staff only – wonderful people, no doubt, in the front seat, but no family – the priest said, "He belongs to God's family always". Molly Gaffey sat near me. There were 10 people – Simon staff and friends at the Eucharist. A wreath of flowers was placed on his coffin. Molly asked me why was the white cloth on the coffin. I said it can be to remind us that he was a good man *always* in his soul (inside). The flowers symbolised for me that life is only for a short time, then it withers and fades away, dies. Putting the coffin into the earth touched me deeply – that is all I am in the end, in the flesh – dust – my Spirit goes on.

## Tuesday, 3 August

I went to Simon today. I felt 'at home' with these, my very special friends. They accepted me totally as I was – no questions, no reprimands, nothing about, where were you? I felt loved by them, deeply loved and respected and I could confirm my own love and respect in me. Then I could touch them. They awakened me to the very best of me. Thank you, my friends.

After my day of fast, my heart was more fine tuned to the hearts of others. I'm sure many street-people could say with John Paul II, 'They try to understand me from the outside, but they will only come to an understanding of me from the inside'. It is the silence that teaches. It is only in silence that human beings can hear in their innermost beings the voice of God, which truly sets them free. I'm free then to see the beauty, listening, presence, goodness, love and compassion in me and then see it in my brother or sister.

## Tuesday, 31 August

Poor John Dess, aged 35 years, died, I heard. He was a lovely soul, but drink and prescription drugs had him beaten down. He lived in his own place. He took an overdose and died. He has two children. One son by one lady and one daughter by another. He used say to me on the many occasions I met him on the streets, "You always say 'Hello' to me", and, as he was saying this, his face would look happy. I picked him up from the street once and he went in the ambulance later to hospital. This was just before Christmas Day, Christmas Eve. John's *Rosary* and removal was at 7.00 p.m. tonight. I met his poor Mam and Dad, son, brother, sisters and aunt. His uncles were there, too. His coffin was draped with the Liverpool F.C. flag and on his chest was the Liverpool scarf. There were many photos in the coffin – some of John. His son was in one with him. A friend of his told me later that John gave some drugs to Batt, his friend. Batt began drinking also and he was found dead last week, when he choked on his own vomit. John felt badly that he had died and blamed himself a bit for giving him the drugs. John's son, John, too, is on dope, drinks and is taking 'E's' (Ecstasy). He is 14 years old.

## Tuesday, 7 September

Just a few minutes ago, a word came to me for the title of my book, *Beauty*. Exactly, at that moment, a beautiful autumn leaf (yellow and green in colour with an amazing sparkle on it, as if there were diamonds shining on it) gently floated on to the ground near me. It is very vulnerable now, I feel, as it has only just let go of the security of the tree and it is all alone. It is the first time this individual leaf was experienced being totally on its own. It must feel lost, as if, perhaps, no one cares, its only destiny now is death. The poor lonely leaf, how can it survive in this big world cut off from its comfortable home, where with its other brother and sister leaves it laughed and played and cried. The leaf symbolises for me the plight of the homeless sister or brother, son, daughter, when they leave wherever home was and take to living rough on the streets. It can be such a frightening place to be. The sparkle on the leaf represents the inner bright core of these great people – which is always good, always beautiful. Nothing negative can ever enter that precious zone – the home with-in. This is a *totally safe* place for anyone who has found her / his true home – the *only* safe place one can be in this world. We are, when we rest in our true home, in the arms of the Creator. 'Make your home *in me*, as I make my home *in you*'. This is the beauty I see, when I look into the eyes of these very special people.

## Tuesday, 28 September

I saw Mike Moro today out at the Lough just walking around, sitting and looking at the water and the birds. I saw he could be there for a long time on his own in silence. I felt moved, as I watched him sit there this evening by the Lough. Peaceful.

## Wednesday, 29 September

I met Ken begging on the bridge. He had made €160 at that stage, which was about 3.45 p.m. or so. He was there since 10.00 a.m. One man from Dublin gave him €50. He had been in London for six months and when he would have enough money made today, he'd go back again. He is only here since Saturday. He met a lovely person in London who put him up while he was there. He had to get a new flat then, so he gave Ken the money to go to Ireland, while he was looking for a new flat. He said his friend misses him, so he hopes to get back as soon as he can. He said London is his favourite city in all the world. Some days on Patrick's Bridge, he makes up to €250 and he spends €50 and saves the rest. While I was chatting with him, two people put money in his carton. He was wrapped in a blue blanket – sitting on it in the rain. It was such a privilege to meet Ken. He is only 21 years old.

### Tuesday, 19 October

I'm still in awe at the experience of communion I had with Jarla*th*. My name, I heard since, is a symbol of my unique-ness – my individuality. He, too, is *handmade* by the Creator. I, too, am a gift to myself. This com-union is the presence of the designer of life in us.

### Monday, 25 October

I felt deep with-in me, today, that everything and everyone I need to make my life's journey, is already given to me as a gift – each day is already mapped out, even before I live it. All this is the Creator's work – my Creator's design. I don't create anything, but I watch creation / the Creator at work in life, in myself, in people, in nature, etc.

### Thursday, 4 November - Ballygriffin

Sean shared a lot about himself, the time he worked in England in the Old Folks Home. We worked there for two and a half years and he said he loved that work. When he was 15, he went to England with his Dad to visit and stayed there for six months! He came back and finished his secondary school. He sold electrical goods for a while, etc. It seems Sean was not able to keep a job for too long. The poor fellow, this must be hard on him, as he seems a very intelligent lad. He reads a lot, has joined the library, and gets books in Simon Library and in second-hand shops. He reads for a couple of hours before he goes to sleep at night. He seems to have a good relationship with his parents. His youngest sister has scoliosis and has three children. Her husband is in England. Sean has a good sense of humour. Later, Sean signed the visitors' book in the Centre. He was very happy with the day. I told Sean I felt enriched by his presence today.

### Friday, 5 November

Today I spent one hour in the funeral home where Mel was laid out. I felt privileged to be able to spend that time there on my own. The silence was beautiful – not a sound. Mel is in his eternal home. It probably is the first time Mel has a real home. I meditated there. Ruth Mannas and Peter came in at one stage and they talked out loud in their own words to Mel. Ruth brought a bouquet of flowers and had Mass said for Mel. She wrote on the card, 'Mel, you were a mate, I'll miss you, but I won't ever forget you. I love you, from Ruth' – how sincere, simple and beautiful that is. Louis cried a lot and told me Mel and himself were best mates.

## Monday, 8 November

Today, I travelled on the bus to Gurranabraher Church for Mel's Funeral Mass. Ruth and Peter were on the bus, too. Ruth called out loud in the bus, "Catherine, are you going to the church, too?". I said, "Yes". When it was nearly time to get off, she said, "Catherine, this is the stop now". She was so kind. A lady beside me had already said to me that she heard me saying I was going to the church and said to me, "Your stop is the second next one". How kind people were. It made me feel cared for, warm inside, safe and secure. I got out at the Church with Ruth and Peter. Ruth lit a cigarette and Peter said he would like a drink, but would drink in the field, as he would not drink in the church area. Outside the church, Ruth said, "He has respect. He's a good person". He was beaten up outside the hostel last night.

I met Joan, Mel's sister, in the Church and she said, "They got 50 cent and a Miraculous Medal in his pocket when he had died, no more". How beautiful – such simplicity, I felt. I said to her that I was very touched that he was not caught up in the material things of this world. He died, as he lived, in utter simplicity. Poverty. Joan said, "We were his first family, and the Simon was his second family – he loved them. He went for treatment about 10 years ago and stayed off the drink for one year, then, he missed the street-life and went back there again. That was his life, they were very good to him". I was touched by the readings on death at the Mass. The soloist sang very well – *Eagles' Wings* – 'I will raise you (Mel) up on eagle's wings, bear you on the breath of dawn, make you to shine like the sun and hold you in the palm of my hand'. How comforting this will be eventually for Mel's family. I felt very moved to tears when his sister read a poem about 'Do not weep for me for I am free'. The final hymn was *The Rugged Cross*, sung with such reverence and feeling by Mai. I went with James to the burial place for Mel, his final resting place. Susan, Mel's other sister, said, "Thank you, Sister, for being good to Mel – for looking after him".

## *Friday, 12 November*

Kieran sat down. He said that he had stayed in the Himalayas. He had a house there. He was living quite near the Dalai Lama. He liked the Tibetan Buddhists. They are people of compassion, he said. He spent time in the Ashrams. would like to go back to India and study some meditation ways and come to Ireland and teach it. He has also been in Africa and South America. He would love to go back again to Bolivia. The weather was lovely, he said. He meditates every day. He had a very calm expression – peace-ful. He is 42 years old. He said he has no wrinkles! The meditation helps him, he said. He said he would call himself a Christian – he doesn't follow the Catholic way. His mother is very religious, he said. She opens the church every morning. She is over 80 years old. She does not understand Kieran's ways, his beliefs, etc.

## *Wednesday, 24 November*

I met Steve McDoone later on the street and he was sitting on a step, relaxing, as he read the paper. He said, "You should see the people's worried unhappy faces in the morning going to work, how can they work when they are not happy?".

## *Wednesday, 8 December*

I felt the goodness in these very broken people today. "I am good because I am". Each person is good because they are, even if they *do* nothing good, they are still good in their essence. This is what the majority of people miss in life, I feel.

## *Sunday, 12 December*

I met Cathal, Declan and Oliver at the Christmas dinner in the Day-care Centre. Mel and Noel and Andrew enjoyed their meal. Alexis Obaris was very quiet, but he looked very well. I handed him a cracker to pull it. I asked him if he would like me to put on the hat on him. He said, "Do". I put it as carefully on his 'jelled' hair as I could! He looked like a king, complete with beard! I moved around to say "Hello" to various people. It was once again my special privilege to be among these 'real' people today.

I went into the street and saw artificial lights, people weighed down with shopping, doors open on Sunday and no one satisfied with their lot, but kept on wanting more of this world's goods that will go in the bin soon, when they get fed up of these things. Do they feel so unimportant that they have to fill their lives with *things* and more things, *doing, actions*? Emptiness – where does it come in? To be filled with love, joy, etc., I need to empty out first. The street-people own nothing, as they are free of material possessions – what a gift? How heavy the weight (mental and physical) of material goods, people, possessions. What a contrast – so much real love is found in me when I'm poor, so also in poor people materially, what love is there no one can estimate.

## Wednesday, 22 December

Mary McAleese said in a speech recently that one of her dreams was that our most marginalised would be encouraged to have more self-belief.

## Friday, 24 / Saturday 25 December

We were in a derelict hut. Someone asked me to pray at midnight. I did not feel it was appropriate. We allowed what would happen spontaneously to happen. It was awesome. I felt on this Friday that I was in the stable at Bethlehem in 2004.

Jack said, as he went on his knees at 12 midnight, "I am nobody, I have nothing, I have nowhere to go and I don't know where I am going in my life. I can't be with my children on this night, but Father-God you will look after them. Thank you". It was from his heart. Joe knelt, too, in reverence and Paul began to cry and cry. He laid his hand on Jack's hand when he was sharing his pain; later, again after about a minute, he laid his two hands on Jack's hand in such a compassionate and loving way. Jim was silent and Mark was still. We sang *Silent Night* – the only response after that was silence. The experience in the cold weather shelter was one of giving birth – it awakened me to myself and enabled me to give birth within me to my vulnerability / fragility. I wept.

# 2005

*Monday, 31 January*

Jimmy seemed to be very annoyed with me. I asked him how he was and he said, "You don't care about me or anyone else only yourself". He then said, "Look at your fine clothes, you care about no one". I asked him how his brother David was, who has T.B., and he said equally angrily "You don't care how David is. Why ask me?". I felt how hurting poor Jimmy was inside himself and left him, sending positive energy to him.

## Thursday, 10 March

Arthur, Aidan and Craig came with us to Ballygriffin. It was like a summer's day. The weather was glorious. We ate out and did both meditations out-of-doors in the lovely environment of nature.

Craig talked about the present moment and said that is all he has. Craig was in a cell in an English prison for 12 months and he had no book or radio. He was only left out daily to get his meals and to do his hour's exercise, walking around the yard in a circle with the other prisoners. He learned patience there, he said.

Aidan started to drink at 9 years old and was seriously drinking at 15 years old. He's now 28 and is off drink now for seven weeks and hopes he can stay off it. He goes to A.A. He did the psychological test to enter the S.M.A. Missionary Order of Priests, because he would like to help the needy. He was asked to come back again when he felt better. He was 17 years old then. He used to sleep a lot on park benches. I told him about what I was reading now, *The Power of Now*, by Eckhart Tolle. The man who wrote it lived on a park bench for three years. He said he'd like to get that book.

The three of them really appreciated the beautiful day in the country.

## Wednesday, 6 April

I was touched by the number of Sisters (nuns), who told me they now speak to the homeless people. They are not afraid of them anymore. They give them time and find these homeless people so real. The birds on the trees have a home, these people don't, so are they not following in the footsteps of the Creator, who, when on earth, said, "The birds of the air have homes / nests, but the son / daughter of man / woman has nowhere to lay his / her head". These homeless / street-people are very special.

## Thursday, 5 May

Maurice said he has four half-bags of *Bibles* at home! He said he reads them and knows what is in them. He said a man called Judas dipped his bread into Jesus' plate of gravy and Jesus said, "Where are you going, boy?". According to Maurice, Jesus said, when he spoke of his parents, "You know my father and mother were older than me!". I was interested in his interpretation of the *Scripture* passages! It showed me how people can *really believe* what they say and how they speak to them. O.K. who knows what was the 'original' of what came down to us in the present *Scripture* form?

This is the danger of fundamentalism. Maurice went beyond that even, and heard it as Maurice's version – a good Cork version! New translation!

Poor Agatha was in a bad way this morning, as she sat half-naked on the steps of the Courthouse. Her face looked cut. I rang 999 and the ambulance was there in record time. The ambulance man was so courteous and said, "Leave it to me and I'll look after her. Enjoy your day". I hope she feels a bit better tonight. It was such an undignified way to see a poor woman on the streets. If I were there in that situation, I would like someone to come along and be kind to me. We were on our way to collect some street-people to take to Ballygriffin, when I saw poor Agatha. It would be lovely to take her for the day but I felt she needed hospital care today. It would be nice if she could come some day with us.

## Friday, 13 May

Norbert Taffer was so lovely to meet. It was something new for me to see his face. I had never seen his whole face before. He has a lovely face, but is inclined to put his hands over his face quite a lot. Is it shame or shyness I wonder? He said he would like to do meditation again and also he said he would like to go to Ballygriffin some day. Norbert likes the peace of his new home. I felt deeply honoured to spend time with Norbert. He wore a glove on his left hand a lot, but he took it off at one stage when Rosetta and I were talking to him. I remember I gave him a purple glove, one time, when he had lost his own glove. I gave him one of the gloves I myself was wearing. He said he cannot stop losing his woolly caps!

## Friday, 20 May

My heart went out to John, Austin, Alex and Rob, all of who are under 25 years of age. Each one's girlfriend is pregnant and they all have left their girlfriends. How sad. They spoke beautifully, were very well-educated, I felt. Alex and Rob beg on the bridge. They said, instead of calling it 'Patrick's Bridge', it ought be called 'Alex and Rob's Bridge'! They sleep rough. Austin has a place to live.

Johanna and Jimmy looked so happy. They looked radiant. They did not seem to have a care in the world! They slept on the streets for five months in the icy cold weather. Did they get a cough or cold – certainly not? No 'flu' either! How can they survive like that?

Barry said he slept in a toilet for five years. He got a caravan at one stage. He had not slept in a bed since December 2003 until May 2005 – 14 May was his first night in a bed for 17 months. He had a most beautiful, serene, calm expression. He looked very thin, though. His feet were sore. He used walk 11 hours some days, when he was in France.

Amy gave some goodies to the street-people. How kind she is. She is from Thailand. They did appreciate what she gave them. Ruth, John, Rob and Abigail were happy with their gifts of biscuits and sweets given from Amy's heart.

It was a privileged day being with my special friends. I felt my compassion came alive, as I listened to their stories.

## Wednesday, 15 June

I met Louis Ballagh yesterday. He was put out of home when he was a teenager and younger. His parents used give his bed to his uncle. Louis slept in the snow many times. He went through a tough time in his early years, but today he has done well for himself. He has a taxi business. He has two lovely children, Cian and Dillon. His partner, himself and his children are very happy today. It is so good for others who, maybe are on the streets today, to know that one *can* get up and be very happy in life. Louis took drink and lived it up in his day, as most teenagers do today. It was then I first met Louis. He said when he looks at his son today, he thinks of himself at that age out on the streets. He said he can't understand how a parent could put a child out in the freezing cold and not care. He could not do that to his child. I was delighted to meet Louis.

Cameron Ballante died. I went to his removal tonight. I heard that he never liked when the clocks went on and the bright evenings were there. He preferred the dark evenings. He died on one of the long summer evenings. He was a very private person. Years ago, I remember when he used come to South Pres. for food. He had a dog. Kate Fenton was fascinated when Ann used to lovingly give him his meal. My memory of Cameron is of someone infinitely gentle. The last time I met Cameron was when he was having a drink with some friends on the bridge.

## Friday, 17 June

Cameron 'looked well' as he lay in the box. It came to me that this is where we will all end up. I will be put in a box and 'locked' in there by four bolts! What a sobering reflection! I cannot come out, nor can I bring with me any of the possessions, material or otherwise, into that small box. It is a very small box really. Cameron did not have many of the world's goods – I wonder had he actually anything at all that he could call his own? As someone so wisely said, Cameron was not attached to life, so he was, perhaps, better able to let go of it, and move on to the 'fullness of all life' in the end.

Cameron lived a lonely life since his parents died 10 years ago. His father died in January and his mother died in March. He used get sad around March for about a month and pick up again then. It was said that when his mother was in a nursing-home in Cork, the staff said she was the best cared-for patient there, by her family. Her only son, Cameron, came *every day* and stayed lovingly with her for hours. He loved his mother dearly. He could not live in his home any more after her death. He went on the streets to live then. He and his new companion, the dog, walked the streets as he began the lonely journey of a man, whose best friend had left him to live in her heavenly home – her true home really. He quietly drank to ease his pain, day after day. It temporarily eased his pain, but never took it away. His friend, Joe, 72 years old, said Cameron said, "I'll be dead before you". Sure enough he was. Drink probably took his life. He was called 'Cameron the can', because he'd always have only one can of beer with him in town! Cameron won't sit anymore on his favourite seat in the North Mall or by the docks, where he loved to wander. He is sitting on a more solid seat in a more secure realm in his new life. He is at peace. Thank you, Cameron, for gracing us with your lovely presence in this life.

### Wednesday, 29 June

Today, I read on an 'exhibition park bench' (to be put in one of Cork's pedestrian streets shortly), the following quotes:

> *"One, just one short life and nothing to prove".*
>
> *"Most of the people who are homeless, and are seeking shelter at the moment in the Emergency Shelter, are under 35 years".*
>
> *"The average life span of a person who lives on the streets is 42".*
>
> *"Each homeless person has her / his own individual story of homelessness".*

### Thursday, 14 July

Seven street-friends sat in a very sheltered place out of the heat today. I greeted them, as I knew them all. Lucy Lander was with Leslie Lacey, Marty Lagrue was with Susan Ling and Agatha Banks was with Jerry Quayt. Mark

Katfaman was on his own – no partner, I mean. They were very pleased to see me, I could see. Marty asked me to "Take off the shades" (sunglasses), as he said he couldn't see my eyes and said, "I can't talk to someone who has her eyes covered". He surely is my teacher. It helped me realise that my eyes are such a big means of communication between me and another person. I removed the shades gently.

## Friday, 15 July

A friend, Molly Jennes, told me she was very privileged to massage / pour oil on her homeless friends' feet in San Francisco. What an honour for her. Each was attended to with loving care by Molly, I have no doubt. Each homeless friend got a lovely new pair of socks then, after the care was taken first of their feet. What a beautiful way – the way of touch – to minister to and be ministered to by these homeless friends. Molly was blessed and her friends were blessed. Homeless in the area of touch – so many are not at home at all in this area. The good touch can heal. The touch some of them are used to in their bodies is not so good, it can be destructive, even fatal at times. When we can lovingly touch ourselves, then we can lovingly touch another. Healing comes. One day later, Molly met a homeless person selling a magazine and she could see him looking at her. He said, "You washed my feet and gave me new socks. It was I who ought to have washed your feet". What joy Molly felt on meeting the poor (rich now, inside) person – so his home inside began to emerge. He felt cared for, loved.

## Tuesday, 30 August

I said to Sam Dunne that he is my teacher today. He said, "How am I your teacher?". I said, "Because you can go down so far and rise up again, be happy then and make a new beginning". He said, "Yes, it is good to be able to do that".

## Wednesday, 7 September

Liam Janny sat with us for meditation. He shared his story with us at the start. He loved trees and plants, he said. He used to work with a gardener. He loved taking the small plants from the tiny pots and putting them very gently into the next size pots. He liked this gentle work. I could hear how present he was in the doing of this work. When they were fully grown, the plants were very carefully placed in large pots. I could hear Liam's deep reverence and respect for this element of nature – the life in the plant. He himself qualified as a tree surgeon, so that he could know how to cut trees in a caring way – for the tree. He worked at this job for many years in Australia. He began to take drink then and discovered he had an addiction to it. He spent 16 years in treatment. He is off drink for three years now. He believes he can make it in life now again. He has more confidence in himself. He said he's learning now to find out, as he says, "Who I am and what my life is about. I'm 33 now. I can live again and get my life sorted out". His mother and father were separated when he was young. Liam felt heard by Rosetta and myself, I could see by his lovely happy face energy. He was then ready to be silent and be more fully in touch with the holy – the good self within. Liam enables my compassion with-in to come alive for me. I could look on him with the eyes of compassion.

Norbert Taffer still has his glove! He has blossomed as a person. He never could look at people straight in the face before. Now, he has his hair cut beautifully, he no longer has his woollen hat pulled half over his eyes and I can see a beautiful radiance shining through his beautiful shining blue eyes. I could see that gradually he's giving birth to his true Norbert with-in. His outward glow is a manifestation of his inner beauty. He feels at home in his new external home, he feels wanted, loved and recognised as a person, I can see. He is peace-ful. He gently went to the garden for quiet. He left us chatting at the table in his new home.

I never spoke to Nathan Cahoon before, but I was privileged to do so yesterday. He always sat on his own and never spoke to anyone before. He has a beautiful gentle, soft-spoken voice. As I listen to this gentleman speak, I'm reminded of the words of the Sufi mystic, Rumi, who writes, 'Out beyond right and wrong, there is a field, I will meet you there'. I was not ready to enter this field until now and listen to this gentleman's gentleness, his being.

Last night, I felt so honoured on being invited to the launch of *Mosaic – A Poetry Anthology*, where I listened to heart-stirring poems read by Sam Cafferkey, Thomas Caffrey and Fraser Cairne. They said what they had to say, as they felt it deeply. Their honesty touched my deepest zone with-in me. They were real. I feel my words totally fail to convey what I really felt, on hearing such openness, truthfulness, gentleness and humbleness. I just noticed that *I* was privileged to make 'a flower' on the mosaic that's seen on the cover of this poetry book! The mosaic was a ceramic mosaic done by street-people in the Shelter garden. Some of us were invited to put our tiny gift there, too. An open flower came to me, symbolising the beauty with-in each person. A flower, fully in bloom, is really seen by us from with-in, when we are fully living in the moment. To look reverently and attentively at a flower is oxygen for my being. Just as the body needs oxygen for life, so does the soul / being. With-in each of us, is that flower. This inspires a possible name for this book, *For You Are Beauti-full* – sounds good and fits with-in my soul.

## Wednesday, 21 September

The meditation we invite the street-people to take part in freely is based on three ancient practices:

◊ The *repetition* of a sacred word or phrase – this, according to the 6th-century writer takes our mind off self and helps give our whole attention to our Maker.

◊ The *poverty* of a single word brings us to simplicity and to unity with our Creator who is one.

◊ The *abandonment* of thought allows the source of our life to be itself (allows God to be God, to use other terms), sheer mystery and not a Creator / God we have come up with from our imaginations.

It can be helpful to offer some clarification for people who are beginners. We are all beginners every time we sit to meditate. By beginners above, I mean, those who are new to this experience.

## Wednesday, 5 October

Robbie was in a wheelchair. He had some disagreement with his family and now finds himself homeless, but a homeless person with a difference – a wheelchair-bound, homeless person. I felt sad.

I met Kyle. His father died some weeks ago. He said he drank when the funeral was over. He had not met his sons for 11 years. One was a grown man. He did not recognise his own son. He must find that terribly hard. He said the disease of drink is terrible. It has such control over him. He said he does not want to drink. It takes over at a moment's notice and rules one's life. He feels helpless in the face of it. He lost everything in life, his professional job, wife and family. I always feel Kyle's deep, deep loneliness, isolation and his sense of being abandoned. He does not like the city at all. He can earn good money, when he feels well.

## *Sunday, 9 October*

I met Agatha Oakley on the bridge begging people for money. I stopped and had a chat with her. She said she lost her house and was now sleeping on the streets. Agatha is a lovely young girl, who has had a lot of suffering in her life. Poor Agatha, she is so lovely to her children when she is well, but when drink takes over, she's incapable of looking after the poor darlings.

## *Tuesday, 11 October*

I stood for sometime watching a child of about 12 years old cross the bridge. She put some money in Basil's hat. She then went to the other side of the bridge and proceeded to give the birds some bread. She gave an occasional look back at Basil and continued to feed the birds. She then went over and offered Basil some bread from her hand, which he accepted. She fed more birds and eventually, after, as it were, sussing out Basil, went over and offered him a nice bag of bread. He had eaten some of this and shared more of it with Missus later. I was so moved by the kindness and compassion this lovely child had for this very young man (about late 20s, I'd say), who sat homeless on the bridge today. She responded beautifully to another's need. I hope it helped Basil to feel loved by the child. I wished I had met her, to say how touched I was by her gesture. Perhaps I was not meant to, as maybe I'd embarrass her.

## *Wednesday, 12 October*

As I meditated today, in the Emergency Shelter, I became so aware of the beauty with-in myself and others around me. By being conscious of my breath and listening to its sound, it came to me that this very simple exercise can awaken the Spirit alive in me. Only through in-depth awareness, attentiveness, consciousness, can I be in touch with this limitless field of energy. Meditation is the key that unlocks the inner door. This is what we invite our street-friends to, every time they sit with us, to meditate. Awesome. What a treat when some of these people can discover the hidden treasure with-in them.

## *Friday, 14 October*

Liam said, "Aren't ye great to keep coming in here all the years and listen to us being so angry and even violent at times, too". I said, "It's because the person is always good. Underneath the unacceptable behaviour, there is a beautiful soul made in the image of the Creator, a place that has no violence nor anger, nor anything negative in it. This is the part of us that is *always good*. That *never changes* in anyone of us".

## Thursday, 20 October

I met Molly and Joss on the street. Joss and David sleep in a 'skipper', that is, a derelict or disused house. They have light, but they do not turn it on! David, now in his early 40s, has to wear protection, as he's incontinent. David was missing this morning so Molly and Joss were looking for him. They cannot get David to wash himself or have a shower. He said he wants to die in peace. Molly was drinking her bottle. Joss did not look that well, I though. I was happy to have met them. I said to Molly that I was so happy David and Joss were not sleeping out in the rain these very wet nights. The rain is torrential these times. It is good to know they have a roof over their heads.

## Thursday, 3 November

An old street-lady, Molly, went to Mass one day and received the bread. When she went back to her seat, the two people near her said, "You are so lucky you can receive that Eucharist, as Jimmy or I here can't receive this". The old lady said, "Why not?". The young woman said, "Oh, Jimmy and I are living together, and we're not married, so we're not allowed by the so-called 'Catholic' institution to receive this bread at Mass. We feel sad about this". The old lady took her bread (Eucharist) she had received at the altar, broke it in two and offered it to her two friends. They received it with love and gratitude. What has this institution done to Christianity, I wondered? She re-echoed the words of the great teacher and what was more, lived them, as I hear it – "Take this *ALL* of you and eat it". Neither had that old street-lady any dinner that day. Later, the next day, the three met again and shared another 'Eucharistic meal' in her humble shed. How awesome. She shared ALL she had. She surely was their teacher.

## Thursday, 10 November

All I need is deep with-in, waiting to unfold and reveal itself. All I have to do is to be still and *take the time* to seek for what is with-in and I will surely find it. This is my call today. Nature is there to provide that environment in Ballygriffin. The sheep are my real teachers. One sheep in total silence chews its food. Another sits silently, 'doing nothing'! Another sheep is standing chewing the food. They did everything in total silence. They walked attentively, in no hurry. There was such deep silence in the field. The sheep were my teachers: calm, still, silent, gentle.

## Wednesday, 16 November

Conor joined Rosetta and I at meditation. He had spent 14 years in prison. He went on hunger strike for 60 days. Then, he went to prison again for seven more years. When he was there, he did yoga and meditation and said he found the meditation very good. "It was very relaxing", he said. When he came out of prison, he got a shock when he saw a bus, panicked and had to call his sister to take him off the street, where the bus was. In prison, he had no recourse to books or T.V., when he was in solitary confinement. At another stage, he was entertained listening to stories told by fellow prisoners. He liked the silent meditation today. He'll come again next Wednesday, he said. Hopefully, Conor can come for a day of solitude with us to Ballygriffin sometime. I was in awe of Conor today.

## Saturday, 26 November

I was very privileged today to be invited to view the private screening of the film, *People, Places, Things*. It's a Cork Simon Community / Cork 2005 film project. Its showing today took place in the *Capital Cineplex*, which closes its doors to the people of Cork on Thursday next, 1 December. Some homeless people spoke on the film.

Molly spoke on the film about her life. She's a lady of about 28 years of age. She said she spent most of her young life up to now institutionalised. She was in orphanages. She went to get flats then and thought she could live on her own, but she couldn't. She said loneliness is her biggest problem. She said when she was in the flats, she felt so lonely, that she'd invite her friends in. Then there may be trouble, fights, etc., when they would have drink or drugs taken and often things may be broken. The landlord would ask Molly to leave then. This was a recurrent pattern, regarding her flats over the years. "Loneliness is my biggest problem", she repeated. She needs company.

Alexandra Bamidene said that, even though she lives now in a hostel, she still is homeless. All this staying here and there for them is temporary. Some people sleep on the streets together for the company. They do not even like to be in a bed on their own in a shelter or hostel, at times. Alexandra Bamidene told me today that she was in awful pain in that film –

when she was being interviewed. She said she hoped it would not be noticed. She was only out of hospital to do the interview and went back in again the next day. Alexandra thanked me for sitting beside her at the showing of the film today. I said, "I feel honoured to be sitting near the film star!". She laughed.

Patrick from Italy was involved, too. He was really looking forward to seeing himself on the screen! It was a great experience to be there, sharing in the joy and sorrow of all involved.

### Wednesday, 30 November

I met Ruth Mannas today in a pitiable state. Her face, at this stage, is almost disfigured through having got so many beatings and fallen, etc. The Christ fell three times under the weight of the cross. Ruth, I feel, could not count the number of times she has fallen under the weight of her cross. Later, I met her and she looked an even more pitiable human being. She cried and cried and said she feels so bad now that she wished she were dead. She hugged me very tightly – her poor body needed an embrace of Love. She said her heart is broken over her family, her son, Joe, her grandson Jim, her daughters June, and Sheila. She does not see them now. She said she still has got the birthday card Rosetta and I gave her. She said in all her suffering that she would get a card for Rosetta and myself at Christmas. She has such beautiful kindness in her lovely heart. I can bow in deep reverence before her presence, her deep and radiant essence. This is the spirit of life and love coming alive in her very battered and broken body. Awesome.

I experienced the real meaning of Christ-mas today with Ruth. The incarnation means that each person's goodness, kindness, beauty and reverence can be mediated through their wounded humanity. This is what the mystery of the incarnation is about. God, or the source of our life, became man / woman, so that man / woman could become God / Goodness. Ruth mediated that God / Goodness to me today. Ruth, a lady of the night, was God / Goodness for me today. Awesome. Her truth set me free. In some churches, it is believed that God / the source of all living beings and things is present in what is called a tabernacle. This is awesome. Ruth's tabernacle opened up for me today and touched me profoundly. Presence. The tabernacle of one's being is almost too sacred to put into words. I find the words are very limited, when it comes to attempting to talk about the mystery that is the person. One person like this in a day can be so energising. Today, I was honoured to meet so many more.

We meditated later.

## Wednesday, 7 December

I went to Simon today. It was our meditation day. Mary and Joan shared a lot. It was very awesome. I felt very energised, listening to them. We spoke about *Human* and *Being* – awesome. They were my teachers – how?

(1)   Their openness enabled me to be awakened to my own openness – open space with-in me.

(2)   They enabled me to realise that my own gentleness is a gift.

(3)   Being aware of Now also is a gift and letting what is BE is gratuitous. I do nothing to deserve these gifts. They are gratuitous – already in me, but if I don't know they are there, what use are they to me?

(4)   Awareness is the magic key that unlocks the door of unawareness. Awareness is very, very gentle – cotton-wool gentle. It is the small, very faint voice with-in me that cannot be heard, if there is too much noise in my head.

(5)   Silence, Solitude, Stillness are basic – without this atmosphere I cannot hear the gentle voice. It never shouts! St. Augustine says, 'Eternity lies in wordless silence'.

(6)   I was aware of my gift of humour, too, today.

(7)   Their truth set me free to express my own truth, openly, truth-fully, gently and humbly.

(8)   It awakened me to new depths of aware-ness, in myself.

(9)   It helped me to be *attentive* to the positive and *aware* of the negative. It is only, with the strength of the positive, that I can diffuse the negative.

(10)  Trying can be a violence to the human being. *Anything* done out of duty / obligation does not last. I hear that now, at a deeper level.

(11)  There is *no thing* I shall want – 'My being is my shepherd'.

Cotton-wool treatment for myself and then I can have that same gentle cotton-wool care of other people in time. 'The divine in me greets the divine in you'. *Um nama shiva.* This time, I found, that Rosetta and I spent with Mary and Joan, was very sacred – inspiring.

*Friday, 9 December*

I went to Shandon to see the photographic exhibition done by the street-people, during the summer. They were given 30 disposable cameras to go out with and take photos of Cork. *How We View Cork* was the theme. I spent some time this evening 'being with' the photos.

Thank you, my friends (some whom I know personally), for doing these lovely photos for our enlightenment. The story behind each photo is *their* story. We only need today to *walk* the streets of Cork and see reflected the brothels, the alleyways and the dark places in our own humanity, to meet our Creator / source of all life / God. We can see this face in places where we did not believe we could see it. The Christ is reported to have *chosen* these broken people and gone to these undesirable places, on this planet, when here. How gently can I embrace the dark place in myself? *The Gospels* are the most radical documents we can read. We read out of our experience and act on it, or we dilute them to meet our own comfortable needs.

*Wednesday, 21 December*

Adam called Rosetta and myself. He was begging on the bridge one day recently. A mother and a 3 year old child passed by him. The child pulled the mother's sleeve and said, "Mammy, give the man something". The mother who was very annoyed said, "No, stop". They walked on. The child began to cry, saying "I want to give him some present for Christmas, in case Santa won't come to him". The mother, hearing the depth of the child's compassion, gave her €2. Adam said, "The little child, Joan, came over to me and put the two Euro into *MY HAND*". I knew, from previous stories Kevin shared with me, that he loved children. He told me one time, that *seeing the smile on a child's face* one day helped cheer him up *all* that same day.

*Saturday, 24 December ~ Christmas Eve*

I was walking down the South Mall at 10.00 a.m. I stopped to see who was wrapped in a white duvet at the unopened door of the *Allied Irish Bank*. I very gently uncovered the face, careful not to awaken the person, who may have only just gone to sleep. I recognised that the person under the white duvet on this freezing cold morning was Sean Bakala. I saw a person dropping in a €10 note under the duvet – there was also another €10 in with it, when I looked in. A few minutes later (which I was happy to witness), a man called Jim came along, took out €50 and put it under Sean's duvet. Sean woke up then. I greeted him and introduced Jim to him, who had put the €50 under the duvet on this cold, freezing Christmas Eve morning. Jim said he's doing well in his business now, so he felt he could share some of what he had with a less fortunate brother. What Sean does with the money is Sean's business. How Jim was thanked – the happiness I was privileged to see in Jim's face was his reward. I could feel his joy in giving. "But", Jim said, "look what he did for me". Jim brought a homeless person on another occasion (who was standing, in the middle of Patrick's Street, with two bags, having nowhere to call home) to a Shelter to get a night's lodging, recently. Jim may never know his own greatness, but he *IS A TRULY SPECIAL PERSON*, who wished to remain anonymous. He then asked me, what could one do to help these people on the street. I gave him the simple answer "Talk to them, let them see someone sees them in their dignity as a human PERSON, of infinite value". Jim thanked me and left. It was a very special experience.

# 2006

*Wednesday, 11 January*

I saw a young man sitting on the street today. He could not look up at the people, but held both his hands over his face (as if he were used to being cared for), but now seemed full of shame to be seen in this pitiable state – helpless, begging on the street. He had some money in a box, some sandwiches (that probably some generous soul offered to him) beside him on the ground, and a card in front saying, 'Please, dear people, could you spare some money for me for food, as I have no food. Thank you'. I went over to him and said very gently to him, "It is O.K. to be where you are. You don't need to have your hands over your eyes, as you are a *good* person inside". People, unfortunately, often only see one's behaviour and miss the beautiful person with-in – the Soul, essence, holy spirit, non-conflictual zone, where there is always *ONLY* peace, love, joy. *Nothing* else can exist in that realm in you. "There is nothing negative here". He said, "Thanks". He was a gently-spoken person of about 20 years old or so.

## *Friday, 13 January*

Today, I'm remembering, is the 60th birthday of the lady who washed the street-people's feet in San Francisco. I hope she has a happy day.

I met Stephen, Connie and Charlie. They were sheltering under the front of a business. Stephen said he, his wife, Jennifer, and daughter, 2½ year old Chloe, were moving house soon. He said he does not go home when he has had drink taken. "It's some time since I was at home. I will probably stay drinking for the whole week-end now. I can't stop when I begin". It is so sad to see three young men today in the 'gutter', so to speak. Each soul is of unique value. They are more than their 'off the wall' behaviour.

## *Friday, 20 January*

Today, Pat joined me in the street ministry. She is a Presentation Sister from Iowa, U.S.A. We chatted for a while, while she enjoyed a cup of coffee at 10.30 a.m. We then meditated together before going out to do a street trip. The sound of the bell before we began was to remind us that now we are leaving the place of words and talk and moving into a SILENT SPACE. I explained to Pat that I need to do this, in order to be worthy to enter the sanctuary of the street-people's lives. We moved along gently and met Lyr, Ere, Ros, Est, Dar, Isl, Jaco, Vico – all from Poland. They did not have a lot of English. I offered to make tea or coffee for them – Lyr would like a cup of coffee with two sugars and no milk. I made it gently and gave it to Lyr. He thanked me. Joseph welcomed Pat. He was very gracious towards her. She is a very gentle and caring person, I could sense.

Pat and I then went for some food to Mattie's. I had some chips, peas and fish. Pat had a can of *Club Orange* and a batter burger. Mattie is very kind to the street-people. He gives quite a few of them free meals. He has a special part of his counter reserved, to serve those who don't have money to pay. How kind and generous Mattie is. I could savour and taste the food. We went to visit Mill House and June very kindly offered us tea, which we enjoyed. She said Ruth Mannas is in hospital. We asked if it would be O.K. to visit Ruth. She said, "Of course". We walked gently to Ruth. She had an operation for a brain haemorrhage. She said her daughter, Jade, her daughter, Susan, and her son, Dick, came four times to see her. She said it was good that happened, as she had not seen them for six and a half years. She was so happy to see them. Her friend, Jerry, would call later today. Her sisters were also going to call to her. Ruth's head was a bit sore, so we did not stay too long. There was a nice homely environment in the ward, I felt.

It was a special experience, today, to walk with Pat, from the U.S.A., on the streets and meet so many friends in all these different places. Pat was such a lovely presence today with these special people. It was my privilege to walk with her. When we came back here, we shared a little. It was such a sacred day of deep experience, that words were not adequate or appropriate to describe it. So, as the only and deepest response was SILENCE, we sat in silent meditation for a while, to sacramentalise the experience. Pat thanked me and went away about 5.30 p.m. Thank you, Pat.

## Wednesday, 25 January

I met Chloe Yago today. She took one drink after 25 years and was back on the streets again begging. She did not realise that even one drink could lead her back again to the lowest rung of the ladder and lower. She said it is very humbling. I said I am privileged to accompany people who live on the streets. "I've learned so much from them", I said. She said, "That is a very spiritual work". She looked a bit shook, I thought. I found her very open, truthful, gentle and humble. She said, "I had no self-esteem. I was running and racing keeping everyone happy and I could never be good to myself, or look after me. It is the hardest thing of all to be good to myself and to love myself. My marriage went, too. I'm now a different person. I have the support I need. When I went through the pain, I felt freer and came out feeling much better in myself. Someone who hasn't gone through pain, finds it hard to hear this. I'm glad I did. I went to a help centre". I was delighted to meet Chloe, she was so real.

## Saturday, 28 January

I felt very, very privileged to sit with and be with the street-people who gathered together to show their respect for Craig Baitson, who died. A Mass was celebrated – Eucharist – well-gifted – can I celebrate my own giftedness at this? About 20 people sat reverently and silently in the recreation room. Joan read from *Paul to the Romans* that no thing, persecution or anything, can separate us from *LOVE*. We have that love in us *always* and nothing can take it away. We can lose the awareness of it only. It was a very real, lived experience for me today to live this – persecution – rising to new life with-in. The priest / celebrant or co-celebrant with the people had great feeling for the street-people. He called them "My friends" on many occasions, which was very moving, as he meant it.

Joachim said he liked it and it went to his heart what the celebrant said at the end of Mass, that we're all so lovely peaceful and calm. Joachim said, "This affirmation went to my heart. I felt God in me. The rest was ritual". So well said by Joachim, who was quite intoxicated by drink. One of my favourite *Scripture* passages came alive for me here: 'I was found by those who were not looking for me and I clearly revealed myself to those who never asked about me', *Romans* 10, verse 20.

Craig used come to our meditation sessions and he said they used help him a lot. He liked the meditation a lot. He shared some of his life's story with us, too. Craig, who died, seemed to have been very well liked by the street-people, who said of him that he was "so gentle, kind and quiet". What a lovely tribute to be paid to Craig by his friends. His life of depression was not easy, still he did his best to live every day well. I'm happy Craig died in a bed, in the comfort of his room, among friends and that he did not die alone in some lonely city lane or hovel. I noticed most of the people at the celebration of Craig's life and death today were quite young people – most under 45 or some even 35 years of age. Craig, you are resting in peace now.

## Tuesday, 31 January

Pat from Iowa was here very punctually before 10.30 a.m. It was lovely to see Pat. After a chat and a cup of coffee, we meditated. The sound of the bell symbolised the letting-go of outside distractions and allowing ourselves space to enter our own centre, soul, being – inner sanctuary. From there, then, we were ready to set out and walk the streets to be inspired by the street-people, homeless people mainly.

It was an awesome day. Pat's company was so gentle and she has such a lovely presence. It was a truly contemplative experience. I was in awe at Pat's love, respect and reverence for these broken human beings. I felt a deep oneness today with those I met. Pat inspired me, when she said, "To be able to let go of the need to be doing". Pat inspires me, when I hear her saying that she doesn't have expectations. She said that again last week and it helped me to feel very much at ease. I learned a lot about pleasing people, too, during the last days. I noticed today, Tuesday, as I walked along the street with Pat, that I was oblivious of what was going on all around me. Even though there were lots of people and a lot of traffic up and down the streets, I felt I was very much anchored in my still centre, as I walked around. Awesome.

## Tuesday, 21 February

Michael Baily greeted us and I invited him to sit down, which he did. It has been quite sometime since I met Michael. I introduced Sister Patrick to him. He was so gracious. Patrick has such a lovely, caring presence with the street-people. She can *BE THERE* very well, I feel. Michael said, "I'm an old tramp, but I dress well. I like to walk the roads". He said he's separated from his wife. He loved his wife. He said he and Simon Tannes loved the day with Rosetta and I in Ballygriffin some time ago. He said they experienced contentment and it has been with him since.

It was great Patrick could accompany me again today on the street ministry. I love the day Patrick comes along, as she has such feeling for these special people. Her presence is a great gift to me and them.

## Wednesday, 22 February

Rosetta and I crossed the road to see our other friends, Juliet, Steve, Kieran, Mark, Larry and Alex. Lloyd was there, too. They sat on a step at the back of the hotel. The Gardaí came along and gave them 30 seconds to move, or else they would be arrested! We said we could all have been arrested! Lloyd said it would have been fun if we were and it would be on the front of the *Echo*: 'Nuns arrested with their friends'!

## Wednesday, 1 March

I shall, in my day of silence and solitude, tomorrow, remember Andrew Hampson, with deep gratitude, many times during that day.

## Tuesday, 7 March

I feel such deep peace, ease, lightness and joy with-in me now, having spent time with Sister Patrick from Iowa on the streets.

Terence asked Sister Patrick if she would give him a hug. I helped him to stand up from his sitting position. It was such a lovely experience for me, to see that Patrick could, so gently, offer Terence a hug, when he asked for it. I could see she could accept Terence, as he was – exactly as he was – as a beautiful person inside, for now a little bit intoxicated. Perhaps too many people were not able to hug him (maybe he could not ask even), when he was in an intoxicated state in the past. In accepting Terence *as he is*, perhaps Patrick could be instrumental in helping Terence to accept Terence as he is –

*always* good inside. There is nothing *negative* in his inner being. They are one at that level. Patrick's *presence* was her gift, to Terence. These street-people need so much *good* touch from special people like Patrick. I also believe Terence was living from his good energy at that moment. I sensed the presence of *PRESENCE. AWESOME.* Terence sat on an empty, or almost empty, bottle. His clothes, all he had, were in a small plastic bag under him on the ground, too. He had a few coins in the end of a tea carton. He said he attempted to hang himself twice from a tree and twice he was cut down. He said, "I was not meant to die". Patrick and I gently sat Terence on the bridge again. He loves his mother dearly, he said. Terence smiled beautifully at us, as we set off to go. He held each of our hands and said, "Thanks". I said, "Terence, you are a good person". The *person* is *always* good *inside*. The behaviour is always to be separated from the person.

We enjoyed a simple meal of potato, burger, peas and sausage where the poor dine. We paid money for it. Simple. Today, was a day of deep awareness for me. It is often our willingness to accept the hard things in our lives, that we most 'want' to get rid of (because of our impatience) that makes us most interesting as people. Our acceptance and struggle with these very elements is the way we become our true selves. Awareness offers a different way of relating to our suffering; encouraging acceptance rather than resentment, approach rather than avoidance, patience rather than impatience. It is about a waking-up to life, your life, so that you or I are fully living it in this moment. Using the breath as an anchor to bring your attention to the present moment. Awareness encourages an attitude of acceptance and kindness towards one's experience, instead of one of self-criticism. It's a way to be with one's bodily sensations. It *OFFERS A WAY* to handle feelings and thoughts, without becoming overwhelmed by them. The foundation of awareness is a compassionate attentiveness to one's experience, so that you can begin to be present to what is actually happening in your life in the here and now. Awareness meditation, is essentially about *taking time to be in touch with YOURSELF / MYSELF*, so that one can be embodied and grounded, instead of disconnected and alienated. This is what the street-journey is all about – the energy from which all the action flows. We meditated before and after the street experiences, symbolising the touching of all the experiences with deep love and gentle strength. It also enables Patrick and myself to be more present to the sacredness of the human being. What an awesome day. I felt deeply energised by it all.

## Wednesday, 15 March

It was so sad to hear of Steve McDoone's death. Sister Patrick and I had a lovely chat with him recently, as he was sitting on the steps in Patrick Street. He was enjoying a beef and tuna sandwich – I wonder was it his last? We met Steve on Tuesday and he died on Thursday, from internal bleeding. He had told us he was in hospital for bleeding. He had lost a daughter and had one son of 12 years old. Steve was 42 years of age.

## Saturday, 25 March

Today is Mona's funeral day. Sister Patrick arrived here this morning. We did our seven minutes meditation time as usual, only this time was a little different. Patrick presented me with the most beautiful gift of a pink photograph album of street-friends, Rosetta, Patrick, myself and some (beautiful) moving nature pictures. Coupled with this was an account, in her own handwriting, of how the time she had spent with me, on the streets, spoke to her. It was such a thoughtful and special gift. Thank you, Patrick. You are such a wonderful person, who has been so open to 'going with the flow' in whatever situation we found ourselves over the past couple of months. I felt enriched by your presence. In the silence, I read the script, through many tears and laughter and admired the photos for one and a half hours, in Patrick's presence. How awesome. What a moment, to be treasured and pondered in my heart.

## Wednesday 5 April

I attended the celebration for Steve McDoone's departing this life and entering his new home in eternity. It was very awesome to see so many very young street-people at the celebration. I could feel how well liked Steve was and how much he'll be missed. Later, Benny took up Steve's photo and the crucifix and said, "Hip, hip, hurrah", symbolising and celebrating the end of Steve's very heavy cross in this life. His sufferings are now over.

It was a very special day. I felt honoured to walk among these special people, who in so many ways today taught me how to be real. Most of all, I learned that each person is *more than* his or her behaviour. They are *not just* their behaviour. There is a sacred being in each person, where the spirit of life dwells. This is our common bond with all people – our deepest communion.

### Tuesday, 9 May

I saw Sammy and Sox sitting on the path in Emmett Place today. Sox, the dog, was resting on Sammy's lap. Sammy said he would stay there for an hour and a half. It was lovely to meet these special friends today.

### Wednesday, 17 May

There were some new young people around today – lovely young people, who seem to be drifting a bit lately. Fiona said later that she would like to see them get work. They need to go to bed at a reasonable hour and get up to go to work. Some who have jobs don't get up in time and can lose their jobs. They may need some training in being responsible for their life. Perhaps, they are at the adolescent rebellious stage and will grow through it, hopefully.

### Sunday, 21 May

I met Jonah McAlvey near a phone box on the street. I asked him how he was. He said, "I'm good. I don't be able to say that I'm feeling good too often. In fact, it is the first time I've felt good for many a long day. My son, now a grown man, and his girlfriend came to visit me last night. It was great, as I hadn't seen him for years. That was why I had to keep the pain of hurt and being rejected repressed by taking prescription drugs all my life. That, too, was why I was homeless. I couldn't cope". I thanked Jonah for his sharing of this. I said, "I rejoice with you, Jonah, on this great occasion, when your son and his girlfriend called. I'm happy for you. You deserve that. You are a very good person, Jonah". Jonah thanked me. I felt enriched and energised on hearing his truth.

### Wednesday, 24 May

I met Robbie Reen. He said he was just back from England. He spent six months there. He has a 3 year old child there. He was with a girl for seven years. Robbie said if he wrote or told me all the stories of his life, he would fill up a book of pornography! He was very open and honest. He used write a lot of poetry, when he was in prison. He'd write poems for the prisoners about themselves, their girlfriends, their families, etc., on their request. He sleeps rough and lays down in the evening, when he gets tired, wherever there is a place to lay his head. He said he may need to spend five more years on the streets in order to find out who he is. He is searching for sometime, he said. Robbie could be about 38 years old or so. He was very jolly. Robbie wrote this for me:

> To Catherine, God bless, with love. I'd rather be led blindly,
> Than to see the destruction of light all around me.

He said, "You inspired me to write this, when I looked into your eyes". I said, "Thanks, Robbie".

## Wednesday, 31 May

Garry Punch said, "Hello, friend", as he approached him. I felt we had met already. He said he was interested in finding out about St. Patrick – who he was, etc., and particularly, he wished to visit St. Patrick's wells around Ireland. He visited one in Sligo, he said. He spoke of the mythology surrounding the St. Patrick story. He asked me could he drink the water in the wells. He said, "I have a seed of faith in me and, when I drink that water, it helps my seed of faith to grow. I believe that water is good for me, water is life".

Joe Dere came in after the meditation and began a long session – two hours – with Rosetta and myself. He is a very clever man and seems to me to have natural skills for dealing with people in a very respectful way. He said he has a problem with drink. He said he always had feeling for the street-people. One night, when he was on his way to stay in an emergency shelter, he met three people, who were going to sleep out that night. They asked him would he join them and he said no, he was not into sleeping rough. They offered him some drink. He refused. One of the biggest of the three men stood up and Joe was afraid he was going to attack him, but, instead, in a very gentle voice, the man said to him. "I admire you. You are a very honest man". Joe was amazed. He moved on. He used read The Bible a lot in the past, he said. He said one time his daughter of 10 asked Joe if she could give some of her 'change' to a man sitting on the street. He said, "Whatever you're happy with". She gave the man some money. She took out some small change and said, "Fifty cent is too small". Joe said, "It's not how much you give that's important, but if you give from the soul, that is love". It is such a tragedy that such a fine person as Joe could be caught in the addiction of the substance called alcohol. I said, "You're in touch with your strength it seems, and that speaks to people of a genuine person". I asked Joe what keeps him going and he said, "I do believe in a God and that

I'm looked after. There's a reason for everything, even though, I don't know what the meaning of some things is yet". I felt, on listening attentively to Joe for two hours, that he can accept others, who are different, very well.

## Tuesday, 13 June

I saw a person 'hunting away' a very shabbily-dressed, poor man from outside the bus office. I felt sorry for him the way he was 'driven away' like an animal. I wondered how this poor man must have felt. He looked very vulnerable altogether.

## Saturday, 12 August

I met Seany Sorr on the quay. He shook my hand and invited me to sit on a beer barrel near him. He sat on one himself outside a pub, too. I said, "Seany, are these barrels full?". He said, "No, if they were, do you think they would be there?". I said, "No". Seany speaks very well. I enjoyed chatting with Seany today sitting on an empty beer barrel!

## Wednesday, 6 September

I stopped to chat with Chrissie, Mick Sun and Ken Dawe, who were on the pedestrian bridge today. Chrissie held my hand and said she was feeling suicidal. She had many medals around her neck. She feels they symbolise her being protected by the Creator. Her brothers died and her mother. She prayed the *Our Father* and part of the *Hail Mary*. She was, I felt, fervent in her prayer, her plea for help. Chrissie looked about 32 years old. Her friends could have been about the same age, I felt.

I realised today I cannot be with people, unless I spent quality time in my hermitage space. This hermitage is set in a lovely garden, a sacred space, which invites me or whoever enters it to connect, link up with one's own inner being, inner self. The elements around it can be stormy, rough, fragile, gentle, symbolising the vulnerability at the core of the human in each of us. Our being is permanent, never changes, but our humanity is very fragile. The hermitage is hidden away, symbolising the hidden nature of this sacred call. It is the call of

the centre – the core to come alive to my consciousness. The hermitage also symbolises the call to go into the hidden place with-in and find one's true home there, at the deepest core of one's being. The wood makes the hermitage part of nature and still set apart from it. The garden around it reflects somewhat the 'world outside' as do the car sounds on the road. Some street-people can live lives of a hermetical style. Awesome.

## Wednesday, 13 September

A street-person said about helping those in need, that there are many people cutting at the branches of evil, to maybe the one who is striking at the root. It could be that the person who gives the most time and money to those people in need, could be doing it unconsciously, most of her / his way of life, to produce that misery, which he strives in vain to take away. We need to love purely, with the energy of the stars – bright, clear, free, twinkling and diamond-like (precious). Am I, today, as a Presentation Sister, the one who dares to claim my irrelevance in the contemporary world, as a divine call, that allows me to enter into a deep solidarity with the anguish underlying all the glossiness of so-called 'success' and bring light to that place? I need, for this, I feel, a spirituality of contemplative co-creation if people are to be treated as persons of infinite value and sacredness. What an awesome call.

## Tuesday, 3 October

I was walking down Patrick Street today when David Gabbay greeted me with sad news that he had H.I.V. and had not long to live. He said, "I want to be with Joan. My son, David, will be alright". I felt compassion for poor David. I hope he doesn't have to suffer too much pain. He looked very, very thin. He said he'd like to go to heaven. I felt like crying in front of David, when he told me the very sad news.

## Wednesday, 4 October

When I called Mark by his first name, he looked at me from the depth of his gentle soul and said, "YOU REMEMBERED MY NAME". I feel he felt recognised as a person. He was worth remembering. He was important enough to me to address him by one of his external forms of identity. He heard my respect for his uniqueness, I believe. His name, too, is special to him, I could see. That someone / me / I remembered his name meant he, too, is special. He looked very pleased about this. Sometimes, I feel people may pass by these special people, not realising that they have a unique identity.

## Wednesday, 18 October

It came to me that some of these special friends can find it very difficult to 'fit into' this world. Some are fortunate enough to find protective space for themselves, where they can be on their own and not be too much involved 'in the world'. Some people drop out completely and live on the margins of society – a society, with which they may feel they have very little in common. Some of these friends on the street, may turn to drugs, because they can find living in this world too severe and painful. I've met such deeply contemplative people on the streets. Some of these special people, by their gentle presence, can affect the world much more deeply than we can see on the surface of their lives. Often, those who don't have 'eyes to see' can only see behaviour and miss the person.

Andrew Hampson said to me today, as he observed six beautiful young people who are on the streets, ranging in age from 17 to 23, "They are in search of their soul".

## Friday, 20 October

Jessica Murphy said to me, "I will never forget what you said about one person being of supreme importance. It changed my life and my way of seeing one person at the time. I was always more interested in numbers for the sake of being able to say that there was a big crowd at such a meeting I had. Now, I realise if there was one person there, that is enough. I can sit in respect before my own essence and the essence of another. Thank you, Catherine". I felt moved by this affirmation.

## Wednesday, 1 November

I was very sad to hear of Karen Kerr's death, too. I met Karen a few times recently. She looked awful. She did not see much point in living in this world. She was looking for a blanket to keep her warm. I did not have one for her the day she asked me, but the soup-run people, hopefully, were able to give her some. They take them out at night. I felt badly I could not comfort her there and then. She had lots of drink taken. I heard today she had organ failure. Poor Karen is at peace now and hopefully on this day, 1 November, when we remember especially all our loved people who have gone ahead of us, Karen will remember us, who travelled some of life's journey with her, and that she will pardon me for not being able to help comfort her with a simple blanket, on the Nano Nagle Bridge on 3 October this year.

## Wednesday, 8 November

Reflecting on the death of some of our friends lately, I hear, for them, it was their moment of truth. They have now come face-to-face with themselves. In death, we cannot escape from who or what we really are. Our true nature is revealed.

Today, James Mel said he was very down. He said, "I won't be here in 12 hours". He said he slit his arms, as he said, "I needed attention. I don't feel loved. No one ever loved me. I'm looking for love and I can't find it. No one is helping me. I have pain. I haven't been good for the past two weeks. I want to die. What is the use going on?". Rosetta and I listened from deep within ourselves to his pain. He said he had not eaten for three days. He appeared to me to be quite weak, too. Lots of people in Simon would have been very kind to James. He said, "I don't like being very down like this when I meet ye". I said, "James, whatever way you are, Rosetta and I are happy to see you". I feel he did not believe me. He did not seem able to believe me. His faith helps him a bit, he said.

Later, I met Betty Blue, who said she was in her 40s. She looked a lot more, I felt. She was eating some cheese. She said many times to me, "What brought me down so low? What brought me to this place? Why did this happen to me? I stood out for four and a half hours before I got a bed last night to sleep in. I lost my flat. I used be a respectable woman, who worked in solicitors' and accountants' offices in various parts of Ireland. I don't know what happened me. I'm now on the streets. The staff in the Day-care Centre are very kind to me. See how I can still dress so well. Why am I like this now? I'm homeless. I helped so many people in my life and not one of those people help me now". She cried and cried. I encouraged her to cry and this may help give herself some emotional relief. She was a very sad lady.

## Wednesday, 22 November

Peter Coole greeted me and asked me how long I was a Sister. I said 43 years. He remembered meeting me a long time ago and said we used take people to Ballygriffin. He said he could do now with some peace and quiet. He's from County Louth. He lived in the slums once. There were 10 in his family. They had two rooms there at the time. One room was the bedroom for the whole family and the other room was where they ate their meals. They were happy, he said then. He got married and later his wife left him. They had no children. He said he had lots of issues since his childhood, which he did not realise he had up to some time ago. He began to work on them then and found that helpful. He said he has an acute feeling of being abandoned. He said it affects many aspects of his life. The poverty of Africa and Calcutta, etc., is felt when these people don't have enough to eat. He said the poverty of the West is loneliness. He feels people out around don't have time for one another. "It is such a gift when someone listens to my pain. I feel important that a human being felt I was worth listening to. It is not easy to feel good about oneself at times. We keep going", Peter said. He said he has gone every road – the road of drink, drugs, women, etc., and nothing satisfied him. I said, "Peter, if you can *feel* your own goodness inside you, that is peace-ful. Even if you can take one conscious breath in a day, that can be a peace-filled experience. One breath taken with awareness is more power-filled than many taken in unawareness". I felt he could hear some of this.

Alexandra Bamidene, who died, had been many years addicted to prescription drugs. She was even as young as 18 when she began. She was an adopted child. I wonder had she ever met her real mother? She kept in touch with her father.

Chelsea Calcott called my name as I crossed Castle Street. I hadn't seen her for a long time. She said she's back in Cork one year now and lives with a new man in the north-side of the city. She does not see any of her eight children now. She asked me to let her know when we were going to Ballygriffin again, as she'd like to go with us. Chelsea had been, in the 'eyes of this world', a complete failure, as she was into drugs, drink, prostitution, etc. Today, I see a lovely person, whose soul shines through her lovely smile. She can begin again. She has an amazing capacity to get up and begin again after being in prison, sleeping on the streets, etc. Life for her now is about beginning anew. Each moment she lives is a gift of life given to her, she realises. Her story is a great 'success' story at the level of her inner self. Our inner self needs no 'success'. It is already successful and this may sound paradoxical or even contradictory, but all she needs is already in that zone in her to enable her to begin anew. It's her acceptance of 'failure' then that can bring her deeper, as she searches for something permanent with-in. She has come to emptiness, no-thing-ness, God, because God is no thing.

It was a special time with these people of such infinite value.

## Wednesday, 29 November

It was special later to be introduced to Alexandra Bamidene's Dad, who came from France for Alexandra's funeral tomorrow. He is such a gracious person, just as I remembered Alexandra was, too. I was touched deeply by his handshake, when I introduced myself as 'Catherine'. He said, "I remember she talked to me about you". I felt his appreciation and deep gratitude that she was so well cared for by us all who knew, respected and loved her as a kind-hearted and loving human being.

## Wednesday, 6 December

Rosetta and I attended Cillian O'Carrag's funeral ceremony. Cillian, whom we had known for many years, was found dead at the end of Oliver Plunkett Street on Sunday night. He was the young age of 56. It appears that he was dead before he fell. He had brain damage, lung and liver failure. He has now done his suffering and I hope he's at peace, in a safe dwelling and enjoying a holy rest. It was a very special privilege that we could meet his wife and three lovely sons. They were sad on his departure from this life. He was a very kind man, very generous and caring of other people, especially of those "worse off than myself", he would say.

## Sunday, 17 December

Today was party day in Simon. A beautiful meal was provided. It was carefully prepared by kind people whose work reflects the love they have for some of the most vulnerable people in our city. Some enjoyed the food, others could not eat, as they were sick from either too much alcohol or too many drugs. Some others would not come along, as they preferred to eat their burger in the seclusion and isolation of some doorway, some back lane or somewhere where no one could join them, as they wished to be on their own. Others drank alcohol all day and were oblivious to what day it was. Others again did not want to meet people who were not their family, as the only people they longed to be with were their own family. In many cases, this could not be, as family feuds, barring orders, estranged relationships, etc., prohibited them from being with their family at this time of year. I went along as the meal was ending. At the time I went in, there was lovely music being played by a man on the accordion and another person playing the guitar. A third man sang. It was very lively. It was so good to see these young people, most of who live on the streets, being able to enjoy themselves in a safe place, where they were totally accepted. They could *be* themselves. There were about 100 dinners served today. Someone donated several dinners. How beautiful of people to show such generosity to those less well-off. What joy was awakened in them, as they share their gift with so many made poor. I, too, felt the experience for me of being there awakened my compassion and joy.

## Monday, 18 December

I went to join 15 more people this evening, for a celebration to mark and remember the lives of 23 street-people who died this year. I felt some street-people present were very, very vulnerable altogether and did not wish to talk to me. I respected this totally. Some sang nicely and other read some readings. There was one night-light lit for each person who died and each person's name was very carefully written on their own card next to the night-light. This was done by Pete and Joseph. It was lovely to see their respect for the street-people, who are now in another realm, where they can enjoy a better life than the one they seemed 'forced' to endure on this planet.

## Sunday, 24 December – Christmas Eve

Street-people gathered for Mass. I found the reading of *Scripture* very unsuitable for a group of such vulnerable people. It seems to me that a different type of para-liturgy (where the ritual could be more simplified and the texts more meaningful) could be held. Some of these people write and compose lovely poems and songs, and I felt it could be very meaningful to include some of these in the ritual. Sixteen street-people attended the ritual today. We had a sing-song and dance after. That was fun. Some Sisters came to sing and play music.

# 2007

*Wednesday, 11 January*

I heard the sad news today of the deaths of three Emergency Shelter residents. Sonny Harl died in Dublin. He was getting on very well and had his own place. I don't know the circumstances of Sonny's death. He would be about 35 years old, I'd say. Steve Ryer died in hospital. His liver had failed. Tom Crew hanged himself in his room in the city. Steve would be mid-50s, I felt, and Sonny was in his 30s.

## Wednesday, 17 January

I met Noreen Nard today. She showed me where she had got stitches in her jaw, in the inside of her mouth and on the back of her head. She is 18 years of age. She had a child of 6 called Jade. Her parents have barred Noreen from their home and from seeing her child for a year or more, as she used be drinking and causing trouble in the home. Noreen's brother died two years ago at 29 years of age. Noreen left school at 11 and cannot read or write now. She began to drink at 16. She lived on the roads once. She said, "One night, I wanted to jump into the river to end it all". She showed me about 16 slash marks on her arm, as she attempted suicide many times. She said some of her family have a chronic heart condition. She was tested for it today and said that she hasn't got it. She said, "I wonder is that true, as I would be better off dead if I had it. God won't take me though, until my day comes. He knows me and no one else does". She was a beautiful-looking girl. She had lovely blonde hair. Noreen said she always wished she could go to Ethiopia to mind the babies there. She has been wishing she could do this for some years now. She got a bottle of cider later and took it out to drink it on the street.

## Wednesday, 24 January

I asked Joseph if he would be happy, if someone bought a helicopter for him. He said, "No". I asked, "What makes you happy, Joseph?". He said, "The sun on my face makes me feel happy. It's the simple natural pleasures I treasure. They are the best". What a joy to listen to Joseph today. The Creator's spirit was / is alive in Joseph, I could hear. I moved on, enriched and energised.

## Wednesday, 7 February

I met Cahill Cann. He looked about 70 to me. He said he was 26 years on the streets in England, Ireland and the U.S.A. I was in awe of Cahill being able to endure the hardship of this way of life for over a quarter of a century. He did not look too robust, but he had endurance, it seemed. I said Rosetta and I would be meditating soon. He said he does not like meditation. Cahill said, "I'm not a Catholic, nor am I a Protestant, but I am a Christian". He believed he was being cared for by a cosmic source of life.

It was an awesome day spent in the presence of God / Creator / cosmic source or whatever name each one is comfortable with. The name is the symbol, which again is meant to express the underlying reality. If this word does not point to a deeper reality beyond, it is empty and has no value. It is respectful of ourselves, too, to say a name / word that can express for us even in a limited way, the Maker. The language of the Creator is silence and *no other language* / words can adequately describe this Being. It is a wordless entity, I hear deeply.

## Wednesday, 14 February

I felt deep compassion today. Compassion gives life, power and meaning to mere words / symbols. True compassion can bestow a power-ful force of life on our words. Today, on a day known as Valentine's Day, this compassion / love can be more powerful than any love represented by a flower or a material gift. Of course, these can represent at times a gift of love from the heart, which is beautiful. True love is about oneness. Asked about love, St. Augustine replied, 'What does love *look like*? It has the *hands* to help others. It has the *feet* to go to those in need. It has *eyes* to see misery and want. It has the *ears* to hear the sighs and sorrow of people. This is what love looks like'. It takes deep compassion to love people as you love yourself. Can I feel another person's pain as my own? Can I feel another person's sickness as keenly as if it was my own body that is sick? Can I feel another's grief as if my own heart were breaking? Can I, too, share their joys as my own? Can I share another's success in whatever way I am called on to do so? Compassion is the gift that can enable me open up to others. My call here is to be open to it. The street-people in a special way can enable this opening of my heart to come about. Thank you my friends.

## Wednesday, 21 February

Jo Lane and Jim Jor slept in a shelter on George's Quay. They were covered with duvets. Jim had his boots taken off and they lay beside him. It is raining a lot today. At least, they are in a sheltered area. Hopefully, they are dry. How sad to see that there is no place for these very young people to go into overnight yet, when hostels are full. In a country like Ireland, growing and growing in affluence, could such a service not be provided for some of the most needy of our society?

## Wednesday, 28 February

Rosetta and I meditated. Joseph Jorr joined us. It was peace-filled, sitting in stillness there. Joseph was reverenced in that sacred space, as a human being of infinite value, in the serene and gentle atmosphere of meditation. He chose not to speak later. Our deepest communication with him is stillness and silence.

Jim Joss from Poland committed suicide yesterday. He was not into drugs or drink, but was a bit down. He had settled into a flat and begun a job, and was doing very well, when his tragedy occurred. It was his way to the light, perhaps.

## Friday, 4 May

I saw three street-people sitting in the sun today. They could sit all day and do nothing, it came to me, and not feel guilty about it. How free they are really in this way.

## Tuesday, 8 May

Batt told me today that he never gets bored. He seems to be able to spend quality time listening to and being with nature, the perennial teacher. It is said Jesus spent about 85% of his time in nature and drew much of his deep wisdom from listening deeply to the flower, the lake, the grass, etc.

### A REFLECTION

*But what is justice? And what is holiness?*
*And who is that hungry?, I cried to the city.*
*We are, the people called back.*
*We have spent all our money on things that don't last.*
*We are hungry with a hunger that is deep inside.*
*We are hungry with a hunger that won't be silent.*
*We are hungry for something whose name is*
*Everything Holy*
*Everything Gentle*
*Everything True.*
*We are hungry for all that matters*
*for all that is lasting*
*for all that is right.*
*We are hungry for*
*broken bread*
*and answered prayers*
*and kept promises.*
*We are hungry, cried the people.*

*And trembling beneath the burden of such a hunger, I asked:*
*But what have you done to the prophets?*
*And the people grew silent*
*And the silence swept over the city like a wind.*
*Then a woman stepped out of the crowd.*
*We are too sophisticated to stone the prophets, she said,*
*and so we just ignore them and our hunger deepens.*
*If you are wondering what to pray for*
*We are hungry for new hearts.*
*And I bowed my head in the city streets*
*And I wept for sheer joy*
*And I announced Good News*
*To all who would listen.*
*And the news was this:*
*Blessed are you if you are aware of hunger*
*so deep as all that,*
*for God will surely feed you!*

**Anonymous**

## Wednesday, 18 May

It was so awesome to sit in Bessie's silent presence in her own temporary dwelling. She sat there in such lovely energy – I could feel it so tangibly energising me. She hardly said one word for nearly three hours! She did not need to, as her radiant presence spoke clearly and with dignity. Paddy, too, sat in his presence, listening out of his deep presence. Good energy begets good energy. They were my teachers of presence today – awesome. They awakened me to such deep stillness with-in me.

## Wednesday, 23 May

It was lovely to meet Mary Sallower again after about nine or 10 years. She said she had left Joshua McAllenor before he died. She was with a man from Galway for eight years in Spain and has three children, Joan aged 7, Mel aged 6 and Suzie aged 6. They are being cared for now by some family members until Mary is well enough to look after them. She drinks, she said. She was 17 when we met her before. She is now 27. She is a sweet girl, with a lovely smiling face.

When I see animals with street-people, I hear more and more how wise they are. I'm reminded of Job 12:7-10 in the *Old Testament* book of *The Bible*, when I read, 'But ask the animals and they will teach you; the birds of the air and they will tell you; ask the plants of the earth and they will teach you; and the fish of the sea will declare to you. Who among all these does not know that the hand of God has done this? In God's hand, the Designer's / Maker's hand, is the life of every living thing and the breath of every human being'. Much of Rosetta's and my time is lived in attentiveness to what is in the now. Believing that one's presence in solitude is *AN ACTION FOR PEACE AND JUSTICE*, we become one with the street-person's life, and expect nothing from anyone. We are privileged over many years to have provided sacred space for any street-person who felt called to quiet and rest. These people in their own quiet and hidden way make the Creator a reality – one needs 'eyes' to see this, behind their 'not so pleasing' behaviour at times.

## Wednesday, 13 June

Rosetta and I send good energy out to all in the Simon, when we meditate there. It can appear (sitting in stillness / in meditation) that we are doing nothing – but real doing nothing, when we are in the state of intense presence, is a very powerful transformer and healer of situations and people. It is very different from inactivity in the state of unconsciousness, which comes from doubt, not sure of oneself, indifference and fear, etc. When our minds are quiet, an intelligence greater than thought operates, in which, when we are open, a deeper and deeper dimension of being manifests itself. This is an awesome journey into the now. The now is who I am in essence, who each one is at their core. If I resist this, I can miss it.

## Wednesday, 27 June

We meditated. After the session, Jack Jee chatted for quite some time with us. He had been away for sometime and had a few drinks at the week-end, having been off it for several months. I said, "Jack, it's about beginning again. It is a great person who can fall down, then get up and begin to walk again. That can take a lot of courage. It can take more courage in fact, to get up and begin again". He said, "One must remember that the good is inside me always and no one, no drink or anything can rob me of that. I must go from my mind to my heart, my soul. The soul is the important one. That is the best of me. I must keep remembering that there is a good part in me that never changes. This is the *real* me". It was lovely to hear Jack speak like that about himself. He used to meditate morning and evening for some time back and found it good, he said. Jack met his family recently. He was very pleased with that. He must have slept on the street last night by the look of him. The poor man was in poor shape. Jack's story reminded me of the fern I saw recently in the wood, from which I learned. It unfolds very slowly, one little green curl at the time. It is usually in hidden, unlit places in the wood. It grows from within out. Jack's journey is slow, too, and he can spend a lot of his time in hidden dark places, drinking, etc. Still, he is aware that it does not affect the dignity of his noble soul.

## Wednesday, 31 July

Brian Bello greeted me. He said he is on the street again. I said, "Where ever you are, you are *always* good inside. Even if you drink all day, that good person inside never changes". He said, "Thanks for the encouragement". His smile was transparent and I saw the gentle, playful, carefree little boy inside him, the curious adolescent and the loving young man, now bruised from beatings. I felt deep compassion for him.

I met a woman whose family spent many years in the business of prostitution. I have experienced deep love in that family, whenever I visit them in their home, or meet them on the streets. I'm inspired by the love they show to their parents, their own children now, and also to their sisters and brothers.

## Wednesday, 5 September

On the street, I met James Jerl, who was in Ballygriffin with us on a few occasions. He now has successfully completed his Leaving Cert. with 2 As, 2 Bs and 2 Cs. He is going to U.C.C. on 24 September to begin a degree. I have great admiration for him, that he could leave the drug-scene and move into studying. He said his biggest problem always was being bored, so he had to temporarily get rid of the bored feelings, by going into drugs, etc. He felt he was going nowhere fast. He stopped to take stock of his life, and where it was leading – into a cul de sac, he found out. James said he could go to meditation and other groups that would be on in U.C.C. He asked me if we were going to Ballygriffin and I said, "We haven't gone while they were doing the renovations". He said, "It was a great place to go to".

## Wednesday, 26 September

Rosetta and I were joined for meditation by Joss Ryal, Sheila Cany and Jer Lyne. The stillness was real. It is always enriching time spent with these friends. Now is all I have, now is all I need.

## Wednesday, 3 October

Alexis has a great big heart. One time, when someone blessed Alexis, he felt something happen inside him, he said. I said, "The goodness of the person who blessed you, Alexis, awakened you to your true self inside – to the goodness within-in you – that is the God / Creator / source of all life, of birds, of the fuchsia bush outside the window, etc. – that lives in you. You began to hear your own good through the goodness of another person". He smiled a lovely soul-smile then. I said, "Alexis, you are a good person inside, you always were good inside and always will be. Sometimes, it is only our outward behaviour that people see. You are more than your behaviour. You are unique and there is no one like you, anywhere in the world". He felt good, too, on hearing this and said that people don't be 'at him' as much at all like they used to be before. He's glad of this. He may get some confidence back, re-discover what is already there and which he once enjoyed.

## Wednesday, 24 October

It felt good for me inside not to stop and chat with seven people I know today. Before, I would have felt too guilty to do this, but today, in deep gentleness, I could move along in my own joy and, out of that good energy, send good to all seven people individually. When I accept *what is*, there is peace, no matter what that *IS* happens to *BE*. I hear that *IS* now as the Creator / source of life – 1) Be *still* and 2) *know* that *I AM*. I don't feel one shade of selfishness in me, but rather, I feel true liberation.

## Wednesday, 31 October

We, Rosetta and I, meditated at 10.30 a.m. or so. Ryan, Rosto, Jim, Jer, Pete Cast and Sean Sols joined us. It was a time of gentle relaxation and quiet. Paul came in and said he needs this relaxation. Then his friend arrived and went away, so Paul left, too, with him.

After the half-hour, Ryan shared about himself. He is from Belgium and is very unwell now. He showed us his two arms. On one arm there were about six razor marks. On the other arm, there were three or four. The cuts looked very raw. He tore the plasters off them to show us the scars. Rosetta then very gently asked him, if he'd like her to put them back on. He agreed. She put them back on very gently over the scars, where they had been earlier. He looked very happy that Rosetta helped him put them on. I felt he could feel her good energy, as he smiled a lovely smile then and was so grateful. He said he feels like harming other people now, too, especially his family members. His granny is very ill now and he is very upset. He said he was always close to her. He feels like killing the partner his mother had, as he sexually abused him. He smoked a cigarette and when I said, "You need the drugs for now", he did not disagree. I don't know which drugs he was on, but they seemed to 'calm' him a bit. He liked the relaxation / meditation time earlier. Later, he appeared very restless. He said he slept on the streets for some days now and it was not easy. Ryan looked about 27 or 28. He said he does not have good feelings now towards himself or other people. When I said he is good inside, he could hear this a little, I felt. He smiled. I said, "Rosetta and I can see the goodness in you". He said in surprise, "Oh, can ye? I feel good for very brief periods. Then, everything changes and I feel bad feelings again. I wish the good feelings would last for a longer time". Ryan was going away from Cork tomorrow, after sleeping out again tonight. He said, "I am not able to take compliments and I don't like being told what to do". I found Ryan very, very open and truthful. I send him good energy now, wherever he is tonight. May he be safe. I could see he blossomed when he got so much attention. His face changed from looking very aggressive, violent and threatening, to being more at rest inside. He had a most beautiful smile. When he smiled, his face would light up. Poor Ryan, it was tragic to see such suffering in a young man.

## Wednesday, 14 November

When I returned here later, I recalled my lovely experience on the 'Coach Road'. It moved me to tears, it was so touching. I could visualise all, as if it were only yesterday, when Daddy and I used stop and chat with the man in the tent. It brought back very happy, carefree days of my childhood to me, when there was no rush, no hurry, only lots of time to sit or stand and chat with our friends, heat ourselves by the camp-fire and wait patiently for the next yarn or story that would be told. I loved the glow of the fire, as it lit up our faces. It was the only way we could see one another! It was magic.

## ON THE COACH ROAD

*Mammy said, "Come home straight from the shop and don't stop to talk to anyone today". I did not want to waste too much time on the shopping, so I came home quickly, as I knew I would be going for a walk with Daddy later. One of the highlights of this walk was our visit to our travelling man, Sam. He moved around a lot, so we never knew when he'd arrive down the Coach Road. He was a kind of a mystery man to me as a seven year old. His name was Sam, Dad said.*

*We set out this day anyhow and whose tent did we see along the way only Sam's. He was nearly always in the same spot on the roadside. He used to mend tin objects, Dad said, that was why he was called a 'tinker'. I loved to go into his tent and, of course with Daddy close by, take a good look at what he had inside. He would mend a milk can that leaked and it would be guaranteed never to leak again! He always invited us to "sit down and rest for a bit". We did.*

*There were holes in the wall of our field, where he parked, that held a saucepan, a gallon, an old broken picture and a few more things I could not fully see. They were higher up and I was too small to see them properly. "Dad", I said, "lift me up 'til I see what is on the high part of the wall". He did. I was amazed to see a coin, a necklace of pearl, a key and a little cup, which I loved to look at and gaze at in wonder. He hid his money in a hole in the wall, which was on the tip of the wall, where I could not get at. Sam spoke very little. He did not like us to talk much either. We'd sit and enjoy his company and, of course, I'd have a look at 'my' cup and necklace, when I got a chance. I loved the china cup.*

*"Why is Sam always on the go?", I asked Dad. "Could I move around like that too?". Dad was aghast! He said, "He is a man of the road and he likes the freedom of being able to take off and be by himself". Has he children like me, I wondered. What does he eat?*

*One of my favourite times was when Sam lit a fire outside the tent. I warmed my hands at it, so did Dad. He told Dad about some of the places he'd been to. I loved looking at the expression on Sam's face. At times, it seemed he was unaware of either Dad or I being there. He made us tea in one of his tin cans. Dad always said, when I'd make a face, "Remember, it is the love in Sam's heart that is so precious for you to realise. The giving to you of the tin mug of tea is an expression / a gift to you from his lovely heart". I hated the tea, but I took it.*

*One day, I was asked to go to a lady up the road to buy some of her eggs. Mammy gave me some money. I was so happy to be allowed go up that road on* my very own. "All my Christmases have come together", I said to Sam. "Glad to see you, girl", he said to me, as he smoked his pipe. I looked up and saw the cup and the necklace on the wall. I was nearly eight now and I was grown up, I felt. Sam asked me to sit on the tree trunk, which I did, of course. He looked at me, smoked his pipe, looked at the donkey and cart outside and said, "Where is your Dad?". I said, "He's at home". "Will you ask him to call over to me?" I ran as fast as I could the half-mile or so up the road, past the cemetery and in home. I was breathless. Mammy was glad to see me and said, "Where are the eggs?". It was only then that I realised that my original mission was to buy a dozen of eggs! I asked Dad to call to Sam, that he needed him. He duly went and so did I. We sat in our usual spot. Sam went out and had four gifts for someone, for whom we did not know. He would trade things usually for a favour. He looked at me and then Dad and said, "I have this nice necklace for your missus, a coin for your son, the key for you and the cup for the child". I nearly fainted when I held the cup. He gave Dad a warm handshake with both hands and gave me a hug. I thought I was in heaven! We thanked him and, as we were about to leave, he said, "I love you both. You have been my best friends for many years. Thanks". We left. I felt sad, as I wondered why he shook hands with Dad for the first time ever and gave me a hug.

Later, two days later, we called again. He was gone. I cried. I never saw him again. Some time after that, Dad told me he had heard from his cousin, Jamesie that Sam had died on the road one day. He told him also that he had four treasures: a key, a cup, a necklace and a coin. The coin, a sovereign, had belonged to his mother, Sue; the key belonged to his father — it was the key to a locket he got when he got married; the necklace belonged to a girl Sam dated and who died on the roads; and the cup was a gift he made from tin, hoping that one day he would have a child of his own to give it to. The cup was bright and shiny. He had painted it white. Dad's eyes filled up with emotion, as he shared this story with me. I said, "Thanks, Dad. I loved Sam, too. I believed I was this lucky child of his dreams". My Dad was a great friend always to the people of the roads.

## Wednesday, 28 November

I was privileged again today to walk among my dear friends and be enriched by their presence. There is often more joy in the street-people, than in some people in institutions today, such as church, convents, governments and other so-called 'respectable' organisations, where joy is meant to be the hallmark or echo of the Creator's life in us all. Who is the truly spiritual person in today's world I wonder? The street-man or -woman or the monk? Who is most real? Who lives more out of a false sense of self-image? The answers can be so clear at times, I don't need to elaborate any further! Who is the freer person? What does freedom mean? I felt deeply energised and enriched and much better for having met these great people today. Yesterday was the feast of Our Lady of the Miraculous Medal and today is the feast of Catherine Labouré (my own feast day), to whom Mary appeared and asked her to have a medal made in the form she had experienced her in one of her apparitions. Thus came what we call today the Miraculous Medal, which is used at times by homeless people as a symbol of protection.

My name, Catherine, which I personally chose to be my new name (as a symbol of letting go of worldly attachments, i.e., my baptismal name chosen by my parents was Kathleen) has great meaning for me today. Each letter has a deep meaning for me, e.g., **C** – contains, **A** – all, **T** – things, **HER** – her, **IN** – in, **E** – essence. At silent meditation, one day a long time ago, the meaning read – **CATHERINE** = 'contains all things in her essence'. Today, on this special feast, that word became flesh with the lowly young street-man, in the performing of a simple action very consciously. Dylan was totally still – awesome. He had so much deep respect and reverence, the sacred could not but be felt deeply in the exchange. It came to me today my special feast is a call to celebrate my *being* / essence. What a magnificent celebration I had – too awesome almost for words. The beauty was felt in the sacred exchange, which led to oneness / communion. Our common-union became flesh and is living, alive and transformational. 'The Word became flesh …'. Today was extra special for me. Nothing was planned, yet all was given as total gift, more so when we were open to receive it. A simple action was transformed into something beautiful through presence / awareness of presence. This was a heavenly day.

Kate, too, was celebrating with me all day in her deep presence with me here. Thank you, Kate. You are 24 today. What is that like in your heavenly home? Your new realm of living? Thank you for you. You inspired me 13 years ago to stay with these street-friends and not to leave them, as 'They are your *special* companions, teachers and friends on your life's journey', she says even today. Peace. Love. Joy. All upset, disappointment and worry seem to have dissolved in the love I felt come alive in me today.

## Wednesday, 5 December

A Mass was celebrated today for all those who died over the last few years on the streets. Some street-people and staff attended. One man felt so proud of himself when he was asked to go up, as he said himself, "where the priest was", and read out all the names of the people who died. Jack was dressed in a black shirt and black jacket with blue jeans. He said, "They will be calling me 'Fr. Jack'!".

A lady came to chat later about herself. She hadn't an easy life. She is on the road to finding herself, she said. We must be lost, so that we can be found.

## Wednesday, 12 December

Rosetta, Andrew, Jonathan and myself meditated together. The silence was very moving. The energy of peace in the silence was so real. I felt a great oneness with the group. Meditation with a group is very powerful, because we energise one another and we go out very enriched, as the good energy of even one person can energise all. This inner energy is that powerful, far more than our physical energy, even. We light one candle each symbolising our presence and, when we end our session of meditation, we put out the flame of our own candle, the outer symbol only when we feel we can move out in the energy of our own presence. We wait until we feel ready to leave silently.

## Monday, 24 December – Christmas Eve

Teresa Rolds lay on the pavement beside her bag of beer. She had four cans. When I asked her if she were going to drink them, she said, "Oh no, they are for Christmas". They would probably have been her breakfast, Christmas dinner and tea, tomorrow! She would be on the street for Christmas. How must she have felt, really felt deep inside, to be homeless on this night, when so many people were inside in their warm homes sitting beside their warm fires, later going into a warm bed, or was she oblivious of it all?

Christmas literally means the festival of Christ. It is really a celebration of our inner Christus, as it is only in experiencing our inner festival of love, joy and peace, that we can come to know who we are, beyond any other form. The more we are experiencing what is deep with-in, the less the external forms make sense, in fact they make no sense to me now, only if they awaken me to my being. The street-person comes closest to soul-living, as they have no material possessions and never boast about it.

# 2008

## Tuesday, 8 January

Today, I met Joseph, who is 39 years old. He was a perfect gentleman in his being there in his lovely presence. He came from a very well-off family and lived in a large house in a very 'posh' part of Cork. His family drank and then everything seemed to fall apart on them. He himself had a serious illness and has, as yet, not fully recovered. He spoke with such a beautiful, cultured voice. I could see he had such deep respect for the food he was eating slowly and very attentively. He appreciated the little he had. He had a large family, was close to his brother, but not to some of the other members of the family. He would like to be able to work again, but is not able for the moment. He has a very kind friend, who looks after him very well. These January days are bitterly cold on the streets.

I saw Ruth Mannas and Josie walking in torrential rain today. Will they get a cold? No. They can allow the rain to bathe them with a wide-open and waiting soul, with no desire, no judgement and even with no view or opinion on it. They can let it be as it is. It was a very awesome experience watching these two ladies of the night walking the streets in the rain. I've rarely seen a street-person who uses an umbrella!

## Monday, 21 January

I met Pierce, whom I was happy to see had work now and so can earn his living in a dignified way. He feels better, too, now, that he is off the streets and doesn't have to beg anymore. He has a good job now, one in which he needs to be very reliable. He drives a lorry. I'd have met him over some years now begging on the streets, especially on the bridges and lanes. I said to him that I was saying to a person during the week how he got a job and was doing well. He said, "Was what you said about me good?". I said, "It was very good, Pierce". He was delighted to hear that. He would be about 42 years of age, or so, I felt. He is a lovely gentle person.

## Monday, 28 January

Anthony asked if he could sit with us. He is a song-writer, poet and brilliant guitar player. He sings a lot of songs about love. He speaks with a very cultured voice. He said he is living on the streets for some years now. There was something very sad about his eyes. He felt so bad one day on the street, it helped him to write a poem. He used the word 'dream' many times during the conversation.

Once in his life, he found the streets very, very tough going, because there was so much violence, so he moved for three years to the woods. He said, "God, look after all those people who are aggressive, and if you have time after all that, look after me!". He slept in the woods under the trees and he said he never got wet! He wrapped up in his blankets and slept soundly. He was never afraid there. He said, "I am in a place of great harmony, so I can't fear anything here. A fox would come often to greet me and we'd have a chat. He was my friend. I met him every day. I went to a garage nearby to get some bread for the birds and my friend, the fox. They had food and I had none! My drink was my food. I listened to the birds' song every day and I was very contented in myself. Some birds were high up on the trees and others walked around the wood near me. The sound of silence was everywhere to be heard, as darkness descended. Stillness was my companion. I was not lonely. The trees, birds and animals were my brothers, sisters, my family. They respected me, loved me as I am and I also could let them be. Harmoniously, we all lived together. I found it so peaceful there. There is more harmony there, I found, than among humans. It is a naturally harmonious environment, where nothing is forced. All the trees, plants, bushes, undergrowth, in total silence deep in the forest. I felt very safe there. I was aware of the sacred harmony. I was in good company. This is God's own territory. At the dawn, we all woke up early. Each one of us invited the other to awaken gently to greet a new dawn. Our morning prayer was sung in harmony, as each of us gave thanks that we awoke to greet the new in us and in all around us. At night, we slept in the silent embrace of this mysterious place. Of course, new life was being born in me and around me, as we rested. Our night salutation was one of deep gratitude for yet another peace-filled day". I was almost in ecstasy listening to Anthony's experience in the woods. It was a mystical experience for me to hear Anthony. His transparency moved me deeply. Such a noble soul. His outward appearance was not great, but what beauty of soul was expressed through his unkempt body. I bade farewell to Anthony. He said to me, "Thanks for bringing kindness to this house". Such a lovely greeting to receive.

## Tuesday, 29 January

### AN INDIAN LEGEND

*According to an Indian legend, the gods were discussing where to hide the secret of life, so men and women would not find it, not until they are ready for it. The Creator gathered all of creation. He consulted with them about where he ought to hide the secret. 'Give it to me", said the salmon. "I will hide it at the bottom of the ocean". "No", said the Creator, "One day they will go to the bottom of the ocean and there they will find it". "Give it to me", said the bear. "I will take it into the mountain". "No", said the Creator. "One day they will dig into the mountains and they will find it". "Give it to me", said the eagle. "I will take it to the moon. They will never find it". "No", said the Creator. "One day they will go to the moon and they will find it even there". Then Grandmother Mole rose. Everyone became quiet. They knew that, although she has no physical eyes, Grandmother Mole lives in the breast of Mother Earth and see with spiritual eyes. "Put it inside them", she said. "It is done", said the Creator.*

And so the secret of life is hidden within us. It can take time to discover it. Some people never do. Here is one person's account of how he discovered it.

## LIVING ON THE EDGE

*My name is Joseph Deerle. I first came into contact with meditation in 2002, when I had slept rough for five years. I always found it hard coping with the world I lived in. I heard about meditation from a street-man like myself. I said, 'I'll give it a go and see what happens'. I was worried all the time, but something about this meditation appealed to me. I joined a group and realised how simple it was to meditate, but not easy, as I learned. I felt my troubles were suspended, while I concentrated on a simple exercise of sitting still and being aware of my breath. Up to now, my thoughts would be all over the place, like monkeys on a tree, hopping around and making a huge clatter! I did not realise at that group what lesson I learned, which was going to stand to me through some of the worst times I was to face in later years. I was beaten on the streets, robbed of my money and did prison sentences. I was not fit to associate with the others in the American prison, in which I was held for 10 year, so the prison officers told me. I felt isolated. I had remembered a bit about the breath meditation and began to practice this. I realised now that there was something good happening me. I felt some peace in me.*

*I left prison and continued saying to myself that I'm really called now to be faithful to my breath meditation. I practised music meditation later. I felt more easily able to focus on what I was doing in the present moment, the only moment there is, where real life abides. I felt that up to now I was lost in some unreal world of my thoughts. I began to wake up, I felt, from this unreal existence, real hell, no more. I felt better around people and they, I felt, seemed to have some kind of a 'strange' respect for me now. The good seemed to shine through me now and I could see it more clearly in them then, of course.*

*I meditate now before an important choice. It gives me a clarity I never previously knew about. I was always confused and mixed up. My mind is only one part of intelligence and can lead me badly astray, when I get caught up / enmeshed in it, as I did. I, too, had read the 'Indian legend'. Now the Indian legend spoke with deep resonance for me. As Augustine, many years ago, wrote, 'Late have I loved thee, a beauty ever ancient, even now. I have looked all around me outside, to see if I could find you, never realising that all the while, you are alive in me'. Sometimes, I still live on the streets, but that is O.K. I am happy inside, what a gift. I may never have a home of my own but I am 'at home' within. I don't drink or smoke hash now. I move around as a free man. Did not Jesus of Nazareth move around? Are we not told, 'He had nowhere to lay His head. The birds have nests, but He has not'?*

*His journey, too, which he shared with us, as our great itinerant teacher, was
to find that home with-in. 'Make your home in me (awareness /
consciousness), as I make my home in you'. I know that the Creator of
everything, my source of life and the creator of the entire cosmos lives in me
now. I am a lucky man, No one can take this life from me. I continue to make
my faltering human journey, moment by moment. I am happy to have lived
in this world. The trials brought me 'home'.*

## Wednesday, 30 January

I met Alexis Obaris before I left the street-people today. He is getting on
well. He said, "Thanks to you and Rosetta, you both have helped me greatly
over the years. I can remember the words of encouragement ye said to me.
They come back to me all the time and they are a great help to me now, as
things are looking brighter for me, even brighter than ever before. I'm
beginning to feel better in myself and I have lost a stone and a half. I don't
drink any more and I'm down to nearly half of the cigarettes I used smoke.
Rosetta and you have helped me greatly. I pray for your family every night
and then for Rosetta and you. I never forget ye". I thanked Alexis for his
kind words. He meant what he said I could see and hear from how he
shared with me. It was lovely to meet Alexis. He's about 40, I feel. We
would have accompanied Alexis and been accompanied by Alexis for
many, many years now. He is a very sincere young man. I hope he
continues to feel better day by day.

I met Gene today, the young man in his 20s, whom I met for the last two
weeks with his three friends, Joanie, Jeff and Liz. He looked great and said
he was very good now again. I could see his goodness shine through his
lovely smiling face.

It was a wonderful privilege to have had such fascinating conversations
with such special people today. I felt deep peace come alive in me, as I
listened attentively to their sacred life stories. I feel I'm *never* in a position to
listen / be with a *HUMAN*-BEING unless I have come from a place of deep
solitude myself. *Only there,* can I again and again deeply be aware of the
inestimable dignity of the precious HUMAN-*BEING*. I've had the privilege
of spending time in silence and solitude very often to listen to my own
demons and 'being', too, and go from that still-sacred zone to meet and
embrace the brokenness, pain, joy and happiness of all those I feel honoured
to meet each day.

I was delighted to meet Andrew Hampson today. He is off the streets for now and is happy in his new place. He said, "I went to *bed* last night at 8.00 p.m. in a real *bed*. I slept until 7.45 a.m. this morning. It was great".

## Wednesday, 6 February

I went to meet David, whom I had met at the check-out on 17 January last. I said, "David, I would like to apologise for the way in which I so badly treated you on 17 January. I found, going through this experience afterwards, for me, was a very pain-filled time. I am making no excuses for my behaviour that day. I felt a hypocrite". He looked deeply into my eyes, tearful eyes, and said from his noble soul, "Catherine, that is water under the bridge now". I felt so relieved, healed and whole again. His gentle acceptance of my vulnerability, brokenness and fragility, enabled me to feel loved for who I am, in this moment and, what I did, seemed to have melted away in the light of David's radiant presence. Awesome. In the *Scriptures*, when a woman asked Jesus for water, he offered her living water springing up into everlasting life. I was offered that living water today from David. The prodigal daughter (me) came home and, from afar, I was received in love, by this great soul. David became my healer.

Rosetta and I were invited to sit with him in his own small room space then. He offered his chair and bed to us to sit on. We were with him for about two hours. He was most inspiring. There was a spider in his room on the wall. It had not moved from the one spot on the wall for *four* days. It lay there curled up comfortably. There was a very gentle atmosphere in David's room. He had got a new coat from a person and he said, as he looked at the second coat he had on the bed, "I will hand that back now. I don't need two coats. Some other person might be glad of the second one". I felt moved deeply. How many coats have I on this Ash Wednesday? He opened his bare wardrobe. There was so little in it. He said, "Once when I lay on the blanket on the concrete at night, I looked up at the star in the sky and thanked God that I was *ALIVE*. I told Him / Her that I knew He / She was taking good care of me always and I had nothing to worry about. I always believed that I was being very well looked after every moment and no more. I am happy now. I can get cross on drink and give out to people too. I have little or no control over my anger then. The drink talks. I could never say that I was sorry (to a person whom I had offended), if I had drink taken, as it would not be a peaceful regret, but what I would call Dutch courage and that is no good for me or the other. I don't bond or connect with the other in that way, but there is separation. No real healing occurs then. What is loneliness? I feel lonely sometimes, but I don't say it. There is an isolation about it. I am at a loss now, as I can't go far with the cast on my leg. I am off drink for one week. Can you remember the day I was in the Lough, Rosetta, and you came over and sat beside me? Not everyone would do that. People would say mostly, 'Look at the wino'. You saw *me, the person*. I remember when I was in Ballygriffin with my then girlfriend. We had a wonderful time. Ye asked us what *we* would like to eat, when we went to the shop to get the food for the day. We felt honoured as persons. That was such a lovely day".

### Monday, 1 September

I met Moss. He is well now and said he and his friend, Jerry, were looking for a place to live. They were both in to visit Nano Nagle's grave to pray, as Jerry said, for a friend of his who lost her little baby, who was only a few hours old. Jerry slept out for one week before I met him today. He said he likes to come into this peace-filled place in South Pres. He said, "We all need the peace and quiet. It is only in the nice quiet garden that I can find myself. How can I know myself if I don't have peace and quiet?". This was very profound coming from a young man of 24. We parted company then, as I allowed both of them remain in their peace there.

I met four more street-people later on their way to the grave also. Two of the girls were only 18. They were beautiful girls, but very, very vulnerable indeed. Two young men went in with them. One man finished his cigarette before he went to the grave, out of respect.

### Monday, 8 September

One person called Louis, who gave up a good job with house, car, etc., went to become 'a gentler man of the road' at 28. He said he did not wish for the wealth his father had (as he was to be handed over his father's big business), so he said, "I need to find nourishment in wandering. I need to seek emancipation for my heart and release for my spirit, as I free myself from all family ties and learn to live with the minimum possessions for a few years. I need to be even free of washing myself and being too respectable for a while. I need to waste time, to do nothing, expect nothing and feel my new real self come alive. Free to be me, only myself and not what anyone wishes me to be". He was a very handsome young man. I admired his courage greatly.

## Thursday, 11 September

Pete Golder greeted me at the lights in Patrick Street. He said, "You and Rosetta were always so kind to me. Ye are lovely people, who do nothing but good for other people. We all do bad things, but ye do so much good. Ye have helped an awful lot of people in their lives. I feel very rejected now by other people. I'm just finding everything very hard at the moment. I say what I believe to be right and then I get belted for it later. I would like to have a career, do something good with my life. Who knows when that day will come – hopefully, it will be soon". I was very moved by Pete's sharing. He has a lovely soft gentle face, but eyes that seem to 'belong nowhere'. I could feel his inner homelessness in and through his eyes.

## Thursday, 18 September

I met Ruth sitting on a box enjoying her bottle of whiskey! She said, "Will you please pray for me that I will give up drink? It is destroying me. I can't even work at times, because I can't get up in the morning with my hangover. I'm O.K. now in the morning these times, so I can do my work. That is good for me. I'm glad to see you". After a while, I left Ruth.

## Tuesday, 23 September

I met Sean, who was sitting on a window sill. He said, "I'm here enjoying myself under the shade of the old oak tree! The warmth I feel from the sun heats my body. I buy my orange juice! I thoroughly enjoy this juice! I'll stay around until later on. I walk, I sit, I walk, I sit, I drink. This is what I do all day. I'm very peaceful". He always seems very contented, whenever I meet him. I bade him farewell and I moved on.

## Wednesday, 8 October

As I walked along by the river, I saw a very sad-looking young man, sitting on an old coat, with a bag on his lap, out of which was peeping a bottle of cider. He looked troubled. I sent him good energy. Behind where he sat, the river was totally still. My wish for him is that he will uncover that place of stillness, peace and joy in himself.

## *Wednesday, 15 October*

Recently, someone sent me the following: she said, "I have never before found myself as much in the arms of the Creator. I wished always that I would experience this comfort now, I don't depend on myself anymore, but on the Maker, She / He who made me and keeps me going when I make choices, they can often come from my ego, then there is no value in that choice. Now I leave it all to the designer of my life, He takes charge, I see, when I have allowed Her / Him and Her / His plan for me is far more wonderful than any plan me in my limitedness could make. She / He is entirely and totally in charge now of my life. I leave my life in the loving arms and embrace of my God". Letting go of egoic plans was greatly freeing for this one person. I feel she could almost say, "I live now, not I, but the source of life in me". The ego is about wanting, wanting and wanting, what I want. Freedom from wanting is freedom from struggle.

I once read the following: 'Early one morning, a young man is walking on a beach strewn with hundreds of stranded starfish. As he walks, he picks up starfish and puts them back into the water. He is asked by another walker why he is doing this and what difference will it make when there are so many starfish. The young man looked at the starfish in his hand and then put it gently into the safety of the waters saying, "It makes a difference

to this one"'. One could say the same about 'being with' the homeless / street-people, when there are so many everywhere today (from all parts of the world) on our Irish cities, footpaths, in derelict houses, on bridges, on railways and roadways, etc. We can remember that we love one street-person and can be there with her / him in total reverence and respect that 'it makes a difference to this one'. If could behold the infinite value of one human being, we would be perpetually bowing in awe before their magnificent soul.

## *Wednesday, 22 October*

I heard recently that a man was in Dublin city one night, saw a girl begging on O'Connell Street and said, "Why are you sitting there in the freezing cold? Have you any place to go to sleep? I have a family but there is an empty bedroom in our house and you are welcome to it for the night". She said, "Thank you, but all I need is €1.50 so I can go to the hostel. I'm from Eastern Europe and I can't claim any benefits in Ireland yet". The very kind gentleman had already given her €5, went away and on reflection offered her another €5. It was after the further chat with that he gave her the final €1.50 for the hostel. He reflected later on how comfortable he was with a car, nice home, warm fire and many other material comforts and here was this girl with nothing. It was very disturbing for him. The street-people are among our greatest teachers.

## Wednesday, 29 October

Rosetta and I had our meditation session today.

It was wonderful to meet Jimmy again today. He said the reading helps him to go to sleep. He likes to meet us each week, he said. I offered him a book to read on *A Christian Community for Young People*. It is a place where young people can go, who may be feeling depressed, anxious or despairing for one reason or another. It caters for young people between 18 and 30 plus. They can stay for six months or more if they wish. What touched me on reading about it was how they totally trust on the Creator for staff, for funds, young people coming there, accommodation, etc. Prayer is central to their whole mission. They spend quality time in prayer each day. That is their source of strength and inspiration. Jimmy was delighted with the book.

We met many more lovely young people, Pedro, Julianne, Joe, Jack, Ronnie, Steve, Sean and Jeremiah. Ronnie is from Somalia. Julianne is from Sweden. They were all under 25, I felt. In all, we met 13 young people today in the space of a very short time. They were all homeless for one reason or another. Some are the children of previous homeless people, who may have been fostered and at 18 can leave their foster home. Some have nowhere to go, only on the streets. These nights are bitterly cold to sleep out.

It was a great privilege to meet these wonder-filled people today.

## Wednesday, 12 November

We, Rosetta and I, had our mediation / relaxation session as usual. Freddy joined us for it. He said, at the end of it, "That was very beautiful. This is a very special moment in my life. I have not felt this peaceful for about 10 years. I've lost everything, wife, house, because I drank. I've hurt a lot of people too, but I did apologise to them when they told me how much I did offend them. I did not realise what hurt I had caused. The drink was acting and saying what I would never say. When I'm not on drink, I'm a quiet man, who was well-respected in my job. I had a very well-paid job. I've slept on the streets and was feeling so intoxicated at times that I did not care whether I lived or died. I have no work now, but hopefully I will get back on track and put the pieces together again. It may take awhile, but that is O.K. I'll make it one day. I know I'm sick now and need care. I have good parents. I don't wish them to see me like this. I have a lot of growing up to do. That is O.K. Today was a good start for me with the quiet time and sharing of my story with both of yourselves. I feel better already, as I haven't been able to share this with anyone else. I feel a release of negative energy now. I can cry and be allowed cry. I can be myself with you. Thank you."

Rosetta and I listened to Freddy very attentively. There is a soul in there, a person. This being soul / essence is indestructible and nothing negative can enter there. We are being and human. In time, we hope Freddy will see this inner love himself. Even one glimpse of it can be plenty. It was wonderful listening to Freddy for such a special time. It was like five minutes. Several hours can be just like five minutes, when we sit and listen in presence. He repeated several times, "I have faith, I have faith".

Today is the 29th anniversary of Daddy's death. I felt his presence so real with me today with our street-friends. He was my first means of contact with these lovely people over 50 years ago. He loved them and spent a large amount of quality time in their lovely company. In the country, he invited me to go with him at times, to sit with them and listen, chat and warm ourselves at the fires they lit in the open air. At times, there was a cup of tea for us. Once, I remember saying to Daddy, when the cup my tea was made in was not too clean, "Dad, I can't drink out of that cup". He looked at me with great tenderness, as he said, "Kat, my dear, it is not the cup, or the tea in it, that is the most important thing here, but it is the love in the heart of this poor man who made the tea for you that counts most. Can you feel that?". I said, "Yes, I can". I drank my tea and it tasted good.

## Wednesday, 19 November

I met James, who said to me, "Happy Christmas". I found this greeting very real, as I felt the presence of the source of life within me. There is no point celebrating an external event, like Jesus being born 2,000 years ago, if the Divine is not born in my own heart. I wished James well and hoped that he may get some glimpse of his own goodness being born in him this day. Every day can be Christmas, if I feel that love, tranquillity and gentleness deep within me. Thank you, James for that greeting.

Ger said he was loving it, just walking around. I was reminded of the verse someone wrote once. It went something like this and I write it as best I can. You or I do not have to look for anything, just to look is enough. I do not have to listen to specific sounds, just to listen is all I need. Anyone of us does not have to be compulsive about accomplishing anything, we only need to be. I'm just looking, listening and being. One can then experience the creator of all things. Ger was living that, it seemed to me. Awesome. He helped to awaken me to the mystery of being here and to savour and taste the quiet-silent immensity of my own presence. He was my mentor of being. Ger spoke with such 'authority' from his nothingness. I'm reminded that the blood, the life, in me is sacred, and this also true for all the people around me and for all of life.

Rosetta and I did the meditation session.

There were mostly young people in our company today. Their ages ranged, I felt, from almost 20 to maybe 30 or so. Some are seeking further help, while others seem to be going further down the dark road of drugs and drink. Some have felt deeply neglected by some well-known institutions in Cork. This has hurt some people badly. A few friends, who have not been on drugs or drink for years, have gone back on them and seemed to have got more caught in this terrible addiction. These victims of drugs are mostly beautiful young men and women in the prime of their lives. I felt we stood on holy ground today with all these special people. Being aware of standing on the external ground, and hearing it as holy, awakened us to the holy ground within each one.

## Wednesday, 3 December

Rosetta and I held the meditation session today at 10.30 a.m. as usual. The silence was deep.

I met Aggie earlier on the street. She had been with us at meditation some weeks ago. Aggie is 25. I said I wrote her name down after my first meeting with her. I still have it on the table here in this hermitage / apartment. I could never forget her total vulnerability. She seemed so completely helpless, hopeless and alienated from everyone. I often send her the good energy from my prayer, when I look at her beautiful name. Her hair was dyed blonde and pink yesterday. She was with her father. She said, "I'm going to court today, so will you pray for me? Thanks for remembering me so much already. You are very good. I feel so good that someone remembered me. Thank you". She then hugged me and gave me a kiss on the cheek. I was honoured to meet Aggie.

Joseph said he never forgets Rosetta and I in prayer. He said, "Ye were there for me, when times were not good for me and ye are still there today, when I need ye. It is good for me to feel ye care about what happens to me. It helps me to live". Joseph lost some weight and he was delighted about that. He, too, has a radiant face. There is a clear glow in his expression, as if his pure spirit is shining directly through his skin. Today, his face seemed so transparent to me that I felt I could behold his soul and touch it. I could bow in reverence now before the God so totally alive in Joseph. His body is the tabernacle, which holds the treasure.

This is not an easy time for our homeless friends. It is wet, cold and dreary in the atmosphere outside these days. How could a lovely soul be asked to lie on the icy pavement today and tonight, when there is so much affluence in Cork city? As someone said recently, "Can you imagine Christmas without a home? Without a family near you? Without food? Security and friends? It must be so cold and harsh to feel the devastating and gnawing pain of loneliness, in a life that's on the edge".

What wonderful dreams these lovely young people must have had, as they grew up, only to be shattered for one reason or another, which condemned them to a life of such misery. Today, with the economic crisis, the situation for homeless people is much worse. There is very little chance of getting work for them. Even though they have said that they looked for work, it was found that there was not any available for them.

*Wednesday, 10 December*

We had our meditation in the Emergency Shelter.

John was doing a lovely mural on the wall, when we went in. "The theme is 'Tara'", he said, "The beauty I see is not out there. It is in me. I see beauty where there is beauty and I appreciate it. I need quiet, when I'm drawing, as I need to give it my best attention". I noticed John sat down at times, as if he needed to let space between him and the mural. I could hear that it was in that space he could really see his work and be inspired, so that he could allow the picture to unfold. He needed silence and stillness. I could see how well he lived out of his deep inner self, for so much of the time he was there. There was no room for ego here and that was so very beautiful. I felt deeply moved today, 'being with' John. Eckhart Tolle said, in his book, *The New Earth*, "The only thing that ultimately matters is this: can I sense my essential beingness, the I am, in the background of my life at all times?". I felt John was living out of this zone today. Awesome. He was totally present to what he was involved in, namely the creation of this lovely work of art. Of course, he himself is a magnificent work of art, handmade by the Designer and Maker of the whole of creation. So many of these lovely people are so talented in music, art, poetry, singing, writing and in so many other ways. These are peripheral gifts, but his essential gift to this is his own awesome presence, his gentleness, reverence, respect, sense of awe and wonder. I could see what a hard life John has had, but I was so aware, today, that his human spirit is stronger than everything that can happen to him. I was totally in awe, today, of how incredibly strong the sacred place within each person is, especially in John, as I beheld him being himself so exquisitely. The heart-beat of God rests in there. The Creator is alive in each one of us. That is how precious each one of us is. This is what Christmas is about – giving birth to one's true self through our very fragile, faltering and wounded humanity. This is incarnation.

## Sunday, 14 December

Today was the day of the street people's Christmas party. Rosetta and I felt very honoured to be invited by Robert to the get-together this afternoon. We were privileged to sit with some of our dear friends. There was a lovely atmosphere there today. I was moved by all or most of these street-people's capacity for enjoyment. They were very uninhibited, I must say. A drop of whiskey or some 'warmer-upper' helped matters, too, I felt! The music later was appreciated, too, I could see. The greatest joy for me, in being at the gathering, was that I felt totally one with these street-friends, those who felt rejected, abandoned, unwanted by so many people in their lives. It is almost a universal experience, I notice, for a human being to feel the hurt of rejection, being abandoned or unwanted. I share all these hurt feelings with my friends today. Yet, these 'obstacles' are the greatest gift that can be given, to help us come to a sense of 'who I truly am', when they are 'worked on'. There is always 'gold' hidden behind this hurt and pain – the discovery of one's true self deep within. No pain, no gain. There is no growth without pain. This is the good news! What is hidden in the heart of each street person today is that gold. This is what bonds and unites us all at the deepest level. This is pure gift. It was an awesome afternoon with these special friends.

## Tuesday, 16 December

I met Jennifer today. I said, "Jennifer, you are always good within you". I could see her lovely brown eyes shine, as she said, "Thank you, I know that". It was a moment of oneness for me with Jennifer. Awesome.

## *Wednesday, 17 December*

Rosetta and I did our meditation session today. As always, it is a special privilege to meditate silently in the 'home' of the street-people.

I noticed today that all the people Rosetta and I met were under 30 years of age. Society, they say, can put huge pressure on them to achieve and, as Gerald said himself, "Then I can't find out who I am. I need space to discover the real me". Aren't they brave, too, and very courageous to embark on this path? It is surely a way into the unknown, where there is very little security. It is only in embarking on this journey into the unknown, that we can truly KNOW THAT WHICH IS BEYOND ALL KNOWING. This is an awesome journey. I feel, as always, honoured to accompany and be accompanied by these great souls. The street-person is ME.

## *Saturday, 20 December*

Someone said, "Life is not measured by the number of breaths we take, but by the moments that take our breath away". I've been so privileged to experience those special moments today with these street-friends.

## *Wednesday, 24 December – Christmas Eve*

It was, as always, a sacred experience to meet so many of my special friends tonight. We had a ritual to celebrate the sacredness of each human being. We enjoyed some singing later of Christmas songs, then we had some refreshments to savour. It was a holy night.

I met a lady, who said she likes to take silent time out occasionally for herself. She finds the rush of life very stressful, so she needs lots of space for herself, she said. That is a great awareness for a young girl. I feel people see the impermanence of every form in this life, and feel their emptiness at times and then go deeper to find what endures and never ends. In an attitude of silence, the soul finds the path in a clearer light. It is this Creator / infinite / source of all life, that comes more alive for all of us in the silence.

I was privileged today to carve a piece of bog oak and this poem came to me on its completion.

### ME

*O oak of the bog,*
*You haunt me –*
*I loath your dropping jaw*

*And watchful eye*
*But, silhouetted against the evening sky,*
*I wait to hear your gentle voice, say 'Hi'.*

*You were unknown and strange to me,*
*Since first I saw your fearful stare,*
*But, through chip and saw,*
*I hear your call,*
*TO BE – once more – your name is AWE.*

*My creation is no mistake.*
*When you look at me face to face,*
*Deep in your caverns the prostitute dwells,*
*Where pain is measured by what*
*We call 'Hell'.*

*Why are you hidden, o beauty ever deep?*
*Could you not allow me even a peep,*
*To savour, to touch, your inner core,*
*But, you say to me, 'wait 'til I open that door'.*

*Your silence is deep, so deep,*
**I can be with you**
*In your majesty*
*Deeper than deep is your presence*
*This NOW*
*Gently to hear that, you invite me somehow.*

*Just for now, no word is enough,*
*If in silence you remain, I will*
*Whisper to you, much*
*In stillness just wait:*
*ATTENTIVE TO ME,*
*The your soul's LOVE bursts forth*
*Saying '**THIS IS ME**'.*

# 2009

## Tuesday, 6 January

I went to visit some friends in their 'home' for now. One person, Jack, invited me to see what was recorded on TV3 about homeless people, before Christmas. It was very well covered. I knew nearly all, if not all, of the street people interviewed.

One lady on the TV3 programme said her name was Jo. She was married and had five children. When her marriage broke up, she ended up drinking on the street. She had a very good job with a firm of solicitors. She lost all.

Pete was 'thrown out' of home, when he was 15. He then went on heroin. He robbed to feed his habit and often sat and begged on the street, he said, to make €25 to buy a packet. The interviewer asked him, "How did you feel when you sat down begging on the street?". He said, "Crap!"

Joseph was a tailor for 22 years. He is on the streets now for 12 years. He said, "I suppose I will die on the street".

Phil was in a good job in hotel management, but lost it, as he drank and ended up on the streets.

Larry said, "It was the last place I thought I'd end up. I was always very well-dressed, wore a good suit, white shirt and tie and now look at me now in the rags! I'm not used to this life at all".

It is an awful shock to anyone to find himself / herself living on the streets. It can be an opportunity for some to grow in a deeper awareness of who they really are at a deep level, while other people may drift and drift and sink deeper into despondency. Whatever each person's fate is, each one is a human being.

## Wednesday, 7 January

I met 11 friends, one lady and 10 men, sitting on the step near a hotel. I knew eight of them by name! It was nice to meet three new friends. They were all very friendly to me and seemed very pleased when I could remember their names. It was bitterly cold out today. Later, I visited the 'home' where Jenny (one of the 11) lived for now. She was able to cook a nice meal for herself, while I was there.

I feel all the people I met today were between 21 and 45 or so. Each person I met today was very good company, I must say. I was privileged to be in their awesome presence.

What a lovely surprise today to see Chelsea Calcott and her partner. She looked very well, happy and well-groomed. Her hair is now quite long and wavy. She lives in a flat now. She is pleased that she has settled down now. She sowed her wild oats very well, and is more contented within herself in recent times. I haven't seen Chelsea for many a long day. One can only accompany the street people so far and then let go and allow them accompany us in whatever way is appropriate. They may enable us to get in touch with our own feeling of failure and now it can be possible in time, to embrace it and even find joy in it. At a deeper level, we can hear that gratitude for the present moment and fullness of life now is true fulfilment. Surrender is surrender to the moment and not through a story by which I can interpret it and then try to resign myself to it. This is an egoic approach to any situation to try to make it work out, as I would wish it to be.

## Friday 9 January

It came to me recently, that my friend, who is wandering around the city and whom nobody wanted, is my best teacher. What is he saying to me today? "I do what I can, without expectation and within my God-given gifted limitations". I feel I've done all I could in a material way for him. He has a roof over his head now, I hear, and I can say that I feel richer in a deeper way, because I have met this man in my life. He is on the edge of his life, and accepts it as his lot. I'm often on the 'edge' of life, through experiences of rejection, but it has taken me years to accept 'being on the edge'. This man has awakened me to my own courage to stay with the 'edge' experience and treasure it now as a rare gift. I realise now that the more limited, the more narrowly egoic, my view of myself is, the more I will see, focus on and react to this man's egoic limitations, his utter unconsciousness. His 'faults', or what I perceive as his faults, become for me his identity. It means I see only the ego in him and thus strengthen the ego in myself. His call to me is to look at who I am deeply, my reverence, respect, etc., and from that zone to look at him with the eyes of love, seeing that he is not just his behaviour, but far far more, 'pure emanation of the glory of God / the Creator'. Words are too limited to describe another person's deep worth.

## Wednesday, 14 January

We are all called to be healed and to heal. The scars we carry can become a door for the sun to shine into our own lives firstly and then into the lives of others. It is because I have walked in darkness that I can say to others, "The sun will shine in you again, because it has shone for me in my life. I can share and have shared, many stories about my own journey that can prove that".

June joined me for meditation / relaxation this morning, for half an hour. She was so still. It was very moving to be with her in that sacred space. She had never done this before, but she loved it, she said.

I felt at meditation this morning that my being was my breath and that they are one and the same energy. There is a song that says, "Blow, blow, blow 'til I be but breath of the spirit blowing in me". I am that spirit already and so is every other human being. All we are called to is to be aware of it, as I was privileged to be today in a very deep and profound way. Awesome.

One person is of such infinite value, that if one person joins us for meditation, it is such a blessing on each one present. I meditate to BE. I do what I can, without expectations and within my God-given gifted limitations.

## Wednesday, 21 January

Recently, the garden hermitage had to be removed from the garden and given to a person, who will use it also for quiet, rest and relaxation. I feel sad on seeing it go, as it was lovely for people to sit there in that lovely haven immersed in nature, to relax, meditate and rest in the now. Some people, who brought in drugs there, didn't seem to appreciate that sacred space. The heroin scene seems to be getting more dangerous in Cork. Elderly people near the hermitage had been intimidated and were in danger. Out of the energy of silence, the guidance given was to let it go to someone who'd respect the sacredness of the space. It is sad to see that some few people, who are on drugs, can actually intimidate other people to such an extent that they can, in a subtle way, order them to let the drug victims take control. The young get a sense of 'aliveness' when they are on drugs. It is a temporary state, but can appear like the real thing. I can still send good energy to those poor young people, who are hooked on drugs, which are poisonous also.

I went into the Simon today. I greeted some friends there.

A student, who is doing a placement from college, joined Deane and I for meditation. It was an awesome experience. The silence and stillness there in the recreation room was so tangible, so inspiring, grounding and harmonious. I felt a deep oneness with Sonny and Deane.

## Wednesday, 28 January

I was privileged today to visit with some special friends. Sonny spent quality time today in meditation with me. His silence and stillness was awesome. We did 'What is meditation?'. It is a practice in awareness. 'What is awareness?' Awareness is consciousness being aware of itself. Meditation is an instrument that can help quiet our mind and enable us to discover who we truly are in the depths.

## Wednesday, 4 February

We had our meditation session. The silence was awesome. A staff member was happy to be still for half an hour. How much more effective a person's action is coming from this still space. He reminded me last week that there is no such thing as future; it is always now. I was very aware of that during the week, but at times, my egoic self wished to be gone ahead, so therefore, I felt dis-ease. I am aware that I'm a field of stillness at my core and that each person I meet on my journey at her / his core is also a field of stillness. Awesome. It was very special today to spend the full half hour in silence. Good energy always goes out from that environment to all in the building and beyond, when I'm conscious.

Séan Riendor said he found the meditation hard at the start, but he got into it and now spends time every day in meditation. Meditation is to the soul what breathing is to the body. He remembers all his friends every day. He still has a dream that he will get a flat and be happy there. He has a most radiant brightness in his lovely blue eyes, the windows of his lovely soul.

## Wednesday, 11 February

I can't forget the lovely compassionate face of Alexis Obaris. He has so much kindness in his eyes. He remembers people in his prayer. He spends time each day in prayer. He likes to say his beads and said, "I'm not forgetting 'Má – Rá – Ná – Thá', the meditation word, which by consciously repeating it, can quiet the mind and still the body". This is meditation with a mantra. Of course, there are many, many more types of formal meditation, e.g. breath meditation, meditation on sense perceptions, inner body meditation, etc. Each person can choose the one that best suits them.

## Friday, 13 February

Today, I observed Jo with his lovely sheepdog – black and white. The dog, Boxer, sat on the ground beside Jo, as Jo gazed at the river flowing along. The dog was so still sitting on the ground. He is the ever-faithful friend of Jo. I feel this is one way through which our street-friends can be awakened to their own stillness – by the loving presence of the dog.

## Wednesday, 18 February

Today, we meditated in Simon. Joni from France liked the meditation. She said, "It's about conscious breathing". I said, "If we can take even one conscious breath, anytime during the day, we notice how it can bring us to stillness".

The Simon Community are so kind to the many, who go in there to the shelter. I saw the beautiful dinner that was prepared for them today. I was invited to eat some dinner. I chose not to today, but to allow the food to be given to the people who needed good nourishment, especially those young women and men. The staff's care of these vulnerable young people is outstanding.

## Wednesday, 4 March

I sent love and peace-filled energy to all I saw, but did not meet, today in Simon. The street-women and men are such special people.

Gerald told me later, when we met again, that he loves to receive Holy Communion. Once, he said, when he had received Holy Communion, "That was the best meal I had today". What a beautiful reverence he has for the sacred. He was hearing, at a deeper level, the real nourishment for one's soul, which is receiving one's own one-ness within – our common union. He could, I felt, receive the bread, which is a symbol of life, in a relaxed alertness. It was how he received the gift, that made all the difference. A gift is not a gift, until I receive it. To really receive anything, I need to be very still, silent and at one. Gerald, without fully realising it, received the gift of his own life, as precious, sacred and fragile. There was a brightness in his eyes, as he shared with me his experience of receiving Holy Communion. He felt a sense of wholeness. He was nourished by being totally open to the moment. He was my teacher today.

I felt called to hear more deeply the sacredness of receiving in my daily life. Receiving from some people in the last few days even has inspired me, as it brought me to hearing my own sacred receptive space within me, which was awakened by so many 'receiving communion' experiences recently, and these were in meetings with very vulnerable great souls. We have more in common with one another than not in common at the level of being, because in fact we don't even differ by one fraction from another human being at the level of being, soul, Buddha nature, Tao, essence, source. That is our one uniting force – our holy communion; common – union – one-ness. When I can receive this / hear it deeply, no millionaire is as wealthy as me. I'm at home everywhere and with everyone. 'There is nothing I shall want', says the psalmist. 'Make your home in me, as I make my home in you', we hear in the *Scripture*. God lives in you, me, all; the bird, tree, too, has divine life. We are always in communion at the deepest level when we're aware. Each person I meet is me, at some level. Awesome.

## Wednesday, 11 March

I was honoured and privileged to meditate with Sonny Lerm and Mark Reems today. They are two lovely young men in their 20s. Their silence was deeply inspiring. Their stillness was tangible. We chatted then after the session.

It was awesome, timeless, sacred space, in the beautiful company of these friends today.

## Thursday, 12 March

I saw many friends today on the street. Men and women of infinite value. One man, as I passed him by asked me my name. I said, "I'm Catherine". He said, "I'm Joseph". He said, "I know I will go straight to heaven when I die. I'm a good person". He was radiant, as he uttered these words. I affirmed him.

## Wednesday, 18 March

It was my privilege to do the meditation session today in Simon. It is a special honour to do it, to send good energy all around to the most vulnerable people. I read somewhere recently that, if someone is happy, peaceful and relaxed, they can influence people for a mile all around them and 'up' these people's chances of contentment by 25 per cent! I feel the positive energy from one person can have even far more reaching consequences, depending on the purity and quality of the energy.

Arthur said, "I'm a sinner, so are you and so are we all. We're on the one road, where many paths lead". He has a sense of his own goodness, too. When I said, "Arthur, we are all total goodness inside in us and this NEVER EVER changes", he smiled a smile of agreement and comfort in that reality. He said, "Thank you, for your gift of presence with us here now". Later, I got the holy water for Arthur. I can take it to him, to have it, soon, if it would be of any comfort to him, as I'm sure it would be.

## Wednesday, 25 March

Personally, I have a new appreciation of water. Of course, all water is holy, because it is life. A blessing is a symbolic ritual, I feel, enabling people to be more aware of the power of water in its purity. Water itself is another reflection of divine life. A blessing adds nothing, I believe, to the blessed nature of this very powerful life force, which springs forth from the earth itself. Water was used in many rituals over the years in various religious sects and other gatherings of people, who use it as a means of signifying life. We can live only three days without water. I felt honoured, then, to hear more deeply of water's value, through the simple gesture of getting this 'holy water' for my friends.

## *Wednesday, 1 April*

I feel very honoured to be able to be enriched by these great people. I thanked Sean, Maura and Graham for their lovely presence, the gift of their best self. 'I am good because I am'. If we do nothing good, we are still good deep within. It is our non-conflictual zone, where God / spirit / source of life lives. 'The kingdom is with-in you'.

## *Wednesday, 8 April*

I had a very deeply moving chat with Ross. He is a very special human being. He believes everyone is good deep within. He sees the good in others. He finds life fascinating. He said, "I make the most of every day. I haven't tomorrow, only now. I take a drink and have a few friends. I'm not afraid to die. Some of my friends have died and I don't know when I'll die. When my day comes, that's the end of my life on the planet earth. I will continue doing what I'm doing, eating, resting etc., when I feel my end is near. We die as we live, don't we?".

I read today, 'The street-people tell me WHO I AM, the prophets let me know WHO I COULD BE, so what happens? I want to hide the street-person and I want to kill the prophet, when I'm not living consciously. The street-people are the creators, the very source of all that is of value in humanity, because they are my teachers who teach me how to be myself, how to love and how to see each one of us as equal'. It was treasured time, as always, with these special people.

## *Wednesday, 6 May*

Meditation is a great gift to myself and so many others, staff and street-people alike, over the years. As always, it was an awesome day with these special friends.

## *Wednesday, 17 June*

It is in remembering these stories that my time spent with these street-friends finds some meaning. Relationships are strengthened, new sparks are kindled and I come to realise that we all can have so much in common. Through our interaction with one another, we come, in time, to know who we, are more deeply. Unfortunately, some people never discover who they really are in this life.

# EPILOGUE

The journey continues daily in the present moment, as we continue silently to behold our own essence with a sense of awe and wonder. Can we allow another's essence to reflect our own back to us? When we can, we realise that, under the outward appearances, we are all one, the flower and the homeless person, the king and the child. However, there is in our wounded humanity a void, an emptiness and a lonely dark zone. We are like homeless children, lost to ourselves. There is a longing in us to come 'home'. No matter how well we satisfy our earthly dreams and wishes, even when we just land where we have longed to be, we will always be somewhat unhappy. This unease and unhappiness arises because we have not yet discovered who we are in our own true homeland with-in.

'God does not die on the day we cease to believe in a personal deity, but we die on the day when our lives cease to be illuminated by the steady radiance, renewed daily, of a wonder, the source of which is beyond all reason', said Dag Hammarskjöld.

May our homeless street-friends continue to inspire us, as we wait patiently behind the doors of our broken hearts for the wonder of our own humanity and being to be revealed to us through them.